DATA PROTECTION LAW IN IRELAND
Sources and Issues

DATA PROTECTION LAW IN IRELAND

Sources and Issues

Paul Lambert

BA, LL.B, LL.M, CTMA, Solicitor

Published by
Clarus Press Ltd,
Griffith Campus,
South Circular Road,
Dublin 8.

Typeset by
Marsha Swan

Printed by
MPG Books Ltd
Victoria Square, Bodmin, Cornwall.

ISBN
978-1-905536-53-5

Additional Materials
Additional materials for this book will be made
available on the Clarus Press website.
Visit www.claruspress.ie for further information.

Preface

In the not too distant past very few people would have heard of data protection. That is certainly no longer the case. While personal and informational privacy were always prized, the intricacies of this new area of law and rights were viewed by many organisations and practitioners as a niche issue outside of their day to day activities.

That day has gone. Data protection affects all organisations and all individuals every day.

Individuals and in particular users of technology are increasingly aware of the value of their personal informational privacy. However, recent events reiterate that there is still a lot to be done in terms of appraising and addressing the risks associated with certain electronic and online personal data.

Recent data loss and data breach incidents, and the escalating nature of hacking, sometimes involving tens of millions of users, truly bring focus to the importance of data protection and data security.

Just as the book is reaching publication, we can note that the EU in addition to the proposed Data Protection Regulation, is also proposing a new Directive dedicated to network and information security.

1995 was a very important year. Yet in the years following, no one could have predicted the level of uptake of the internet, and the increasing myriad of activities and websites accessible on the internet. The ever changing sophistication of online business models and of new opportunities for data collections and data processing activities bring new challenges to the data protection regime.

This, in part, is the reason for the EU proposals to overhaul the 1995 Data Protection Directive with a new, directly applicable, EU-wide Data Protection Regulation. The data protection regime will be wholly transformed – whether physical, wired or wireless.

The import and scope of data protection is vast indeed. Practically every organisation has data protection obligations. These will vary depending on what the organisation is doing, the sector, its size, whether it is commercial or non-profit, the types and categories of personal data being collected and processed, for what purposes, and contingent upon the nature of the risks of misuse, disclosure or loss of the data.

However, while expanded and new obligations arise via the new Regulation (etc.), certain rules remain at the core of data protection compliance, including the principles and legitimising processing conditions. Equally, how an organisation goes about compliance will differ depending upon whether the organisation is considering internal data protection issues, such as employees, or looking outwards at customers, users and prospects.

The range of issues and concerns which arise in data protection have also increased significantly since 1995. These can range from advertising/marketing/online behavioural marketing; online safety and online abuse; international transfers; new transfer solutions e.g. Binding Corporate Rules (BCR); the transfer of airline passenger personal data; internal access controls to personal data within organisations; increasing fines/penalties/damages; increased litigation; increasing emphasis in relation to children and their personal data; more emphasis on relationships between data controllers and (outsource) data processors acting on their behalf; social networking and related websites and the host of personal data issues they create; CCTV to smartphones; medical, biometric and genomic personal data; enhanced demands on national authorities; security; data loss; reporting of data loss and data breach incidents; preparing for prevention, minimisation, handling and learning from such incidents; increased operational and management responsibilities for dealing with data protection within the organisation; personal liability issues; Cloud computing; cookies; facial recognition; Spam; geolocation and location personal data; the growing importance of rights; access rights; deletion rights; enhanced right to be forgotten; the dual options of individual data subject complaints to the Data Protection Commissioner's Office *or* direct to the courts; the future of privacy and the growing risks to privacy; etc.

These are only some of the new and developing issues. While the book cannot hope to cover everything in the new modern data protection regime, it is hoped that it interests and assists those who need to cover the core basics and also get an overview of some of the new and developing issues facing organisations and individuals. Many of the new aspects of the data protection Regulation regime are also highlighted.

I would like to thank everyone at Clarus Press, the School of Law and the Law, Technology and Governance Masters students at NUI Galway for their stimulation and support. I would also like to thank Don and Bob for their longstanding interest in data protection in Ireland and how this has also influenced me.

Paul Lambert
March 2013

Contents

PART I: DATA PROTECTION

Contents

Table of Legislation

Table of Statutory Instruments

Table of European and International Legislation

Opinions (WP29)

Table of Cases

Table of Commission Decisions

PART I

Data Protection

CHAPTER I

Data Protection

Introduction

Everyone is concerned with the information relating to them which is in the hands of third-party organisations. This can often be legitimate. However, there are increasing instances where it is not legitimate and it has been collected without the individual knowing that it would be collected, nor what it would be used for. In addition, there are increasing instances of organisations legitimately collecting personal data relating to individuals, but which the organisation then seeks to use in an illegitimate manner, e.g. a charity selling its database of donors to a bank or marketing company without permission.

What is Personal Data?

What is personal information or personal data? The EU DP Directive 95[1] defines personal data as any information relating to an identified or identifiable natural person (known as a "data subject"). An identifiable person is a person who can be identified, whether directly or indirectly, in particular by reference to an identification number or factors specific to his or her physical, physiological, mental, economic, cultural or social identity.[2]

The Irish Data Protection Acts[3] expand on this with the following definition of personal data, namely, data relating to a living individual who is (or *can be* identified) either from the data directly or from the data in conjunction with other information or data that is in, or is likely to come into, the possession of the particular data controller.

1.　EU Data Protection Directive 1995 (Directive 95/46/EC of the European Parliament and of the Council of 24 October 1995 on the protection of individuals with regard to the processing of personal data and on the free movement of such data). Note also that the EU is now also called the Union.

2.　art 2(a) *ibid.*

3.　Data Protection Act 1988 and Data Protection (Amendment) Act 2003.

The Parties

Data protection involves a number of key parties, namely:

Individuals:	referred to as "data subjects". It is their personal information and personal data that is being protected;
Organisations:	referred to as "data controllers", who wish to collect, use and process individuals' personal data;
Outsourced organisation:	referred to as "data processors". The main data controller organisation has outsourced or delegated some of its processing activities to a third-party organisation, e.g. payroll processing regarding employees; marketing or market research regarding customers or prospective customers.

In addition, organisations also need to consider the following in relation to data protection compliance, and data protection issues which arise, namely,

Data Protection Officer:	the individual office holder in the organisation tasked with ensuring data protection compliance, education, etc.;
Board member:	organisations should ensure that data protection compliance is prioritised at organisational board level. The Data Protection Officer should regularly report to this board member;
IT Manager:	given the importance of security for personal data enshrined in the data protection regime, the IT Manager needs to be appraised and involved in assisting compliance.

Personal Data Use and Compliance

Appreciation and compliance with the data protection regime and in relation to personal data is important. First, every one of us has personal data relating to him or her. Second, every organisation and entity collects and processes personal data of individuals. Sometimes this is on a small scale. Sometimes it is on a massive scale. Data protection compliance obligations apply to all organisations, whether small, large, commercial enterprises, government organisations or even charities. Obligations also apply to the primary organisation involved (the "data controller" organisation) as well as to outsource entities such as agents, consultants, processors, etc.

Furthermore, the instances where personal data are used are ever increasing. Every reservation, booking, transaction, journey; every organisation that we deal with, whether governmental, enterprise, non-profit, etc., uses or creates data in relation to our person. The volume of such personal data collection and processing is now even more prevalent with the advent of digitisation, social networking and e-commerce. Commercial organisations realise the value in personal data. Increasingly, new business models are relying upon personal data.

The default position is that organisations must inform individuals that they intend to collect and use their personal data, for what purposes, and obtain consent to do so. Frequently, tensions arise when organisations do not do so, or seek to do so in a manner that does not fully or transparently respect the rights of individuals. While compliance is always possible, there are many instances of organisations getting it wrong and facing the consequences of penalty, prosecution or investigation.

What is Data Protection?

Data protection laws protect the privacy and personal information of individuals, i.e. the personal data of and in relation to individuals. They provide a regulatory protection regime around personal informational, privacy or personal data. Personal data is data or information that relates to or identifies, directly or indirectly, an individual. Data protection is in many respects wider than privacy and confidentiality. Personal data is defined in the EU DP Directive 95 and the Data Protection Acts in Ireland.

The data protection legal regime governs if, when and how organisations may collect and process personal data.

This applies to all sorts of personal information, from general to highly confidential and sensitive. Examples of the latter include sensitive health data, sexuality and details of criminal convictions.

The data protection regime is twofold in the sense of:

- providing obligations (which are *inward-facing* and *outward-facing*, see later) which organisations must comply with; and

- providing individuals or data subjects as they are known, with various data protection rights that they and or the Data Protection Commissioner's Office can invoke or enforce, as appropriate. Significantly, there are proposals to expand the ability to invoke the data protection rights, to privacy groups and collective non-governmental type organisations (see proposed DP Regulation[4] replacing the DP Directive 95). The DP

---

4.   EU draft Data Protection Regulation (Proposal for a Regulation of the European Parliament and of the Council on the protection of individuals with regard to the processing of personal

Regulation will bring "comprehensive reform"[5] to the EU and Irish data protection regime.

Organisations, as part of their compliance obligations, must register or notify the Data Protection Commissioner in relation to their data processing activities (unless exempted).

Certain specific sections of industry and certain specific activities (e.g. data transfers abroad, direct marketing, etc.), also have additional data protection compliance rules.

In terms of individuals, they can invoke their rights directly with organisations; with the Data Protection Commissioner; and also with the courts in legal proceedings. Damages/compensation can also be awarded. Injunction relief can also arise, such as in *Sunderland Housing*,[6] *Kordowski*[7] and *Microsoft v McDonald (t/a Bizards)*.[8] In addition, criminal offences can be prosecuted. Data protection compliance is therefore very important.

As regards implementing compliance frameworks, organisations must have defined structures, policies and teams in place to ensure that they know what personal data they have and for what purposes, and that it is held fairly, lawfully and in compliance with the data protection regime, and is safely secured against damage and loss. The cost of loss, and of security breach, can be significant financially, brand-wise and publicity-wise. Breaches can also give rise to criminal offences which can be prosecuted. In addition, personal liability can attach to organisational personnel separate and in addition to the organisation itself.

Why Data Protection?

Why do we have a data protection regime? We have a data protection regime because of the legal and political recognition that society respects the personal privacy and informational privacy of individuals. In the context of data protection, that means respect for, control of, and security in relation to informational personal data. The Data Protection Acts[9] protect personal data relating to individuals, which includes employees, contractors, customers and users.

---

data and on the free movement of such data (General Data Protection Regulation) COM(2012) 11 final).

5.   In Brief, *Communications Law* (2012)(17) p 3.
6.   *Sunderland Housing Company v Baines* [2006] EWHC 2359.
7.   *Law Society v Kordowski* [2011] EWHC 3185.
8.   *Microsoft Corp v McDonald (t/s Bizads)* [2006] EWHC 3410.
9.   Data Protection Act 1988 and Data Protection (Amendment) Act 2003.

Data protection exists in order to ensure:

- privacy in relation to personal information;
- consent of individuals is obtained to collect and process personal data;
- security in respect for the right to privacy and personal information;
- protection against privacy and informational privacy abuse;
- protection against privacy theft and identity theft;
- protection against unsolicited direct marketing (DM).

The threats to personal data and informational privacy have increased as the ease with which personal data can be collected and transferred electronically increases. This has increased further with digital technology, computer processing power, Web 2.0 (i.e. the second generation of internet websites and internet services), and social networking.[10]

History of Data Protection

The legal discussion in relation to privacy is frequently linked to the Warren and Brandeis's legal article in 1890 entitled "The Right to Privacy" published in the *Harvard Law Review*.[11] Arguably, data protection is (part of) the modern coalface of the debate in relation to privacy and privacy protection.[12] Indeed, data protection is in many respects wider than privacy rights. The EU data protection regime can be seen as setting standards in certain areas of informational privacy protection – which have come to be followed in other jurisdictions internationally, beyond the EU.[13] There have also been calls for international level data protection rules. Certainly, if this was to come to pass, it could add greater certainty for both organisations, industry and individual data subjects.

The growth of the processing of information relating to individuals in electronic computer data format from the 1970s onwards led to ever-increasing concerns regarding such processing. Existing laws were "insufficient to deal with concerns about the amount of information relating to individuals that was held by organisations in electronic form".[14] The main EU data protection instrument is the DP Directive 95.

---

10. Note generally, comments of the ICO in relation to Privacy by Design (PbD), and the report *Privacy by Design*, (2008), available at http://www.ico.gov.uk/for_organisations/data_ protection/topic_guides/privacy_by_design.aspx, last accessed 11 January 2013. The Regulation refers to Data Protection by Design (DPbD), Article 23.

11. Warren and Brandeis, "The Right to Privacy", *Harvard Law Review* (1890)(IV), p 193.

12. See Rule and Greenleaf, eds, *Global Privacy Protection – The First Generation* (Cheltenham: Elgar, 2008).

13. See Birnhack, "The EU Data Protection Directive: An Engine of a Global Regime", *Computer Law & Security Report* (2008)(2), p 508 at 512.

14. Carey, *Data Protection, A Practical Guide to UK and EU Law* (Oxford: OUP, 2009), p 1. Also,

This is implemented in Ireland by the Data Protection Acts (and secondary legislation). The purpose behind the Data Protection Acts is largely to promote openness and transparency of information held about individuals in filing systems, whether manual or computerised, and to protect the privacy and data protection interests and rights of such information.[15]

However, even prior to the DP Directive 95, concern for informational privacy in the computer environment was recognised in an early data protection regime. The Council of Europe proposed and enacted the Convention for the Protection of Individuals with Regard to Automatic Processing of Personal Data at Strasbourg on 28 January 1981.[16] Ultimately, the Data Protection Act 1988 was enacted following on from the Council of Europe Convention 1981 relating to data processing. Subsequently, this was updated and amended with the Data Protection (Amendment) Act in 2003 to implement the DP Directive 95.

The Convention for the Protection of Individuals with regard to the Automatic Processing of Personal Data sets out the following principles and requirements, namely, that personal data must be:

- obtained and processed fairly and lawfully;

- stored for specified and legitimate purposes and not used in a way incompatible with those purposes;

- adequate, relevant and not excessive in relation to the purposes for which the personal data are stored;

- accurate and, where necessary, kept up to date;

- preserved in a form that permits identification of the data subject for no longer than is required for the purpose for which those data are collected and stored.[17]

In addition, the Convention provides that

- personal data which reveals racial origin, political opinions or religious or other beliefs, as well as personal data relating to health or sexual life, or

---

Bainbridge, *Data Protection* (CLT, 2000), p 2.

15. MacDonald, *Data Protection: Legal Compliance and Good Practice for Employers* (London: Tottel, 2008), p 33.

16. Council of Europe Convention for the Protection of Individuals with Regard to Automatic Processing of Personal Data done at Strasbourg on the 28 January 1981, available at http://conventions.coe.int/Treaty/en/Treaties/Html/108.htm, last accessed 11 January 2013. Also, "Convention for the Protection of Individuals with Regard to Automatic Processing of Personal Data" (1981) 20 *International Legal Materials* at 317–325.

17. Convention arts 5–8.

criminal convictions may not be processed automatically unless Member State law provides appropriate safeguards;

- appropriate security measures must be taken to protect personal data stored in automated data files against accidental or unauthorised destruction, accidental loss and unauthorised access, alteration or dissemination;

- any data subject is entitled:

    - to establish the existence of an automated personal data file, its main purposes, as well as the identity, habitual residence or principal place of business of the data controller;

    - to obtain at reasonable intervals and without excessive delay or expense confirmation of whether personal data are stored in the automated data file as well as communication to the data subject of such data in an intelligible form;

    - to obtain rectification or erasure of such data if these have been processed contrary to the provisions of domestic law giving effect to the basic principles set out in Articles 5 and 6 of the Convention;

    - to have a remedy if a request for confirmation, communication, rectification or erasure is not complied with.[18]

Growing Importance of Data Protection

Data protection compliance is important for all organisations, large and small. One recent example of this importance is the Data Protection Commissioner's investigation of the multinational Facebook International in relation to certain specific data protection issues, and which investigation can have significance worldwide (Facebook International deals with Facebook activity outside of the US and Canada). This emphasises the significant and growing importance of Irish data protection.

The facial recognition feature of Facebook has also had to be turned off in Europe, also as a result of the Data Protection Commissioner audit.[19] It is also reported that Facebook introduced more transparent tools and preferences in relation to users' personal data,[20] again apparently on foot of the Irish audit.

---

18. *ibid.*

19. See DPC audit reports, available at http://www.dataprotection.ie/docs/Facebook_Ireland_ Audit_Report_December_2011/1187.htm (2011) and http://dataprotection.ie/viewdoc. asp?DocID=1232&m=f (2012), last accessed 11 January 2013.

20. "Facebook Releases Privacy Tool For New Users" (5 November 2012) IAPP, available at https:// www.privacyassociation.org/publications/2012_11_05_facebook_releases_privacy_tool_for_ new_users, last accessed 11 November 2012.

Recently, the Intel group has been approved under the EU Binding Corporate Rules (BCR) procedure to be exempted from the EU export ban in relation to personal data. This examination and approval process occurred under the auspices of the Irish Data Protection Commissioner.[21] The BCR procedure is one of the mechanisms by which an organisation can export or transfer personal data outside of the EEA. Without the BCR (or a similar exemption mechanism) the organisation would not be permitted to make such as transfer. These transfers are sometimes referred to as trans-border data flows. The default position is that trans-border data flows may not occur from the EEA to non-EEA countries, unless exempted.

An editorial in the *Computer Law & Security Review* notes that "[p]rivacy and data protection issues are never far from the horizon at the moment. There are waves of discussion in this area … and currently that wave is riding high".[22] The increasing "centralisation of information through the computerisation of various records has made the right of privacy a fundamental concern".[23] Data protection is important, increasingly topical and an issue of legally required compliance for all organisations. More importantly, it is part of management and organisational best practice. Individuals, employees and customers, expect that their personal data will be respected. They are increasingly aware of their rights, and increasingly enforce their rights.

Data protection is also increasing in coverage in mainstream media. This is due in part to the large number of recent data loss and data breach incidents. These have involved the personal data of millions of individuals being lost by commercial organisations, and also, more worryingly, by trusted government entities.

All organisations collect and process personal data. Whether they are big or new start-ups, they need to comply with the data protection regime. Many issues enhance the importance of getting the organisational data protection understanding and compliance model right from day one. These include investigations, fines, prosecutions, and being ordered to *delete* databases and adverse publicity on the front pages of the press media.

In addition, organisations often fail to realise that data protection compliance is frequently an issue of dual compliance. They need to be looking at both *inward* and *outward* data processing issues.

Internally, organisations have to be data protection compliant in relation to all of their employees' (and contractors') personal data. Traditionally this may have related

---

21. See DPC, available at http://www.dataprotection.ie/docs/20/1/12_Commissioner_approves_Intel_Corporation_Binding_Corp/1190.htm, last accessed 11 January 2013.
22. Editorial, Saxby, (2012) 28 *Computer Law & Security Review* 251–253 at 251.
23. "Personal Data Protection and Privacy", Counsel of Europe, available at http://hub.coe.int/web/coe-portal/what-we-do/rule-of-law/personal-data?dynLink=true&layoutId=35&dlgroupId=10226&fromArticleId=, last accessed 11 January 2013.

to HR files and employee contracts, but now includes issues of electronic communications, social networking, internet usage, filtering, monitoring, on-site activity, off-site activity, company devices, employee devices, etc.

Separately, organisations have to be concerned about personal data relating to persons outside of the organisation, e.g. customers, prospects, etc. Comprehensive data protection compliance is also required. The consequences are significant for non-compliance.

Substantial fines have been imposed in a number of recent cases. In some instances organisations have also been ordered to delete their databases. In a new technology start-up situation, this can be the company's most valuable asset.

Up until recently the issue of data loss was a small story. More recently, however, the loss of personal data files of millions of individuals – and from official governmental sources – made data loss a front page issue. There is increased scrutiny from the Data Protection Commissioner, and others, and new regulation is forthcoming.

In Ireland and elsewhere there are enhanced obligations to report all data breaches and data losses (unless exempted). There also proposals to have enhanced financial penalties. In some instances personal director responsibility for data loss arises. The need for compliance is now a boardroom issue and an issue of corporate compliance. Proactive and complete data protection compliance is also a matter of good corporate governance, brand loyalty and a means to ensuring user and customer goodwill.

The frequency and scale of recent breaches of security, e.g. Sony Playstation (70 million individuals' personal data[24] in one instance and 25 million in another[25]) make the topicality and importance of data security compliance for personal data ever more important. The largest UK data loss appears to be the Revenue and Customs loss of discs with the names, dates of birth, bank and address details for 25 million individuals.[26] There are many new UK cases involving substantial fines for data protection breaches. The Brighton and Sussex University Hospitals NHS Trust had a fine of £325,000 imposed by the ICO in relation to a data loss incident.[27] Zurich Insurance

---

24. See, for example, Martin, "Sony Data Loss Biggest Ever", *Boston Herald*, 27 April 2011, available at http://bostonherald.com/business/technology/general/view/2011_0427sony_data_loss_biggest_ever, last accessed 11 January 2013.
25. See, for example, Arthur, "Sony Suffers Second Data Breach With Theft of 25m More User Details", *Guardian*, 3 May 2011, available at http://www.guardian.co.uk/technology/blog/2011/may/03/sony-data-breach-online-entertainment, last accessed 11 January 2013.
26. See, for example, "Brown Apologises for Record Loss, Prime Minister Gordon Brown has said he 'Profoundly Regrets' the Loss of 25 Million Child Benefit Records", *BBC*, 21 November 2007, available at http://news.bbc.co.uk/2/hi/7104945.stm, last accessed 11 January 2013.
27. See, for example, "Largest Ever Fine for Data Loss Highlights Need for Audited Data Wiping", *ReturnOnIt*, available at http://www.returnonit.co.uk/largest-ever-fine-for-data-loss-highlights-need-for-audited-data-wiping.php, last accessed 11 January 2013.

was fined £2.3m for losing data in relation to 46,000 individual customers.[28] Most recently, text Spammers are being investigated and could face fines of £500,000[29] and a police authority has been fined £120,000 in relation to a data breach involving unencrypted personal data.[30] Sony was recently fined £250,000.

Separately, the UK ICO has also made a significant fine of £50,000 for a non-data loss incident. A financial organisation was fined for mixing up details of financial data relating to two separate individuals. This would have caused financial loss and damage for one of the individuals as they were not credited with all of their payments and contributions.[31] The account details were not kept accurate and up to date. This was despite complaint correspondence from one of the individuals over a period of time. The ICO commented:

> We hope this penalty sends a message to all organisations, but particularly those in the financial sector, that adequate checks must be in place to ensure people's records are accurate. Staff should also receive adequate training on how to manage and maintain them, with any concerns fully investigated in order to ensure problems are addressed at an early stage.[32]

The Data Protection Commissioner in Ireland also prosecuted Eircom and Meteor in relation to data breach incidents. They were fined €15,000 each in the District Court.[33] UPC, Vodafone and o2 were separately prosecuted and fined.[34] Certain fines in Ireland can now amount to €250,000, and will increase significantly under the DP Regulation.

---

28. See, for example, Oates, "UK Insurer Hit With Biggest Ever Data Loss Fine", *The Register*, 24 August 2010, available at http://www.theregister.co.uk/2010/08/24/data_loss_fine/, last accessed 11 January 2013. This was imposed by the Financial Services Authority (FSA).

29. Arthur, "Spam Text Senders Face Fines of Up To £500,000", *Guardian*, available at http://www.guardian.co.uk/technology/2012/oct/01/spam-text-senders-fines?INTCMP=SRCH, last accessed 11 January 2013.

30. "Police Force Fines £120,000 After Theft of Unencrypted Data", *Guardian*, available at http://www.guardian.co.uk/uk/2012/oct/16/police-force-fine-theft-memory-stick?INTCMP=SRCH, last accessed 11 January 2013.

31. See "Prudential Fined £50,000 for Customer Account Confusion", ICO, 6 November 2012, available at http://www.ico.gov.uk/news/latest_news/2012/prudential-fined-50000-for-customer-account-confusion-06112012.aspx, last accessed 11 January 2013.

32. See "Prudential Fined £50,000 for Customer Account Confusion", ICO, 6 November 2012, available at http://www.ico.gov.uk/news/latest_news/2012/prudential-fined-50000-for-customer-account-confusion-06112012.aspx, last accessed 11 January 2013.

33. Edwards, "Eircom, Meteor Charged Over Breach", *Irish Times*, 10 September 2012, available at http://www.irishtimes.com/newspaper/breaking/2012/0910/breaking27.html, last accessed 11 January 2013.

34. "Phone Firms Fined for Data Protection Breaches, UPC, Vodafone, o2 Have Pleaded Guilty to Breaches of the Data Protection Act at the Dublin District Court", RTÉ, 21 March 2011, available at http://www.rte.ie/news/2011/0321/telecommunication.html, last accessed 11 January 2013. The fines are reported as being €7,100, €3,850 and €2,000.

Member State data protection authorities are increasingly proactive and undertake audits of data protection compliance, as well as incidents of breaches. Facebook International has been audited by the Data Protection Commissioner,[35] as noted above. The DP Directive 95 and other Data Protection authorities are critical of Google over its privacy policy and practices.[36] The UK data protection authority (the ICO) is also involved in dealing with personal data issues relating to the recent press phone hacking scandal, which is also the separate subject of the Leveson Inquiry.[37]

The Data Protection Regime

Personal data protection is enshrined in the EU DP Directive 95 and the Data Protection Acts in Ireland. The Data Protection Acts[38] implements the DP Directive 95 in Ireland, as does respective national legislation in the other EU Member States. (The definitions, or building blocks, of data protection are referred to below.)

Outward-Facing Data Protection Compliance

The data protection regime, as implemented in the Data Protection Acts, creates legal obligations organisations must comply with when collecting and processing the personal data of individuals: "if someone can be distinguished from other people, data protection legislation is applicable".[39] This applies to customers and prospective customers. Hence these are *outward-facing* obligations. It can also apply to non-customers, who may be using a particular website but are not a registered customer, if their personal data is being collected.

Inward-Facing Data Protection Compliance

The data protection regime also applies to an organisation in its dealings regarding the personal data of its employees. Equally, where the organisation is engaging

---

35. The audit relates to Facebook internationally, outside of the US and Canada. See first stage of the audit report, of 21 December 2011 at http://dataprotection.ie/viewdoc.asp?m=&fn=/documents/Facebook%20Report/final%20report/report.pdf, last accessed 11 January 2013. It is entitled *Facebook Ireland Limited, Report of Audit*, and was conducted by the Irish Data Protection Commissioner's Office. Note also complaints and access requests referred to at Europe Against Facebook, available at http://europe-v-facebook.org/EN/en.html, last accessed 11 January 2013.

36. See letter from WP29 and the EU Data Protection Commissioners to Google, available at http://dataprotection.ie/docs/Home/4.htm, last accessed 11 January 2013.

37. Available at http://www.levesoninquiry.org.uk/. The ICO investigation is called Operation Motorman. For more details see "Operation Motorman – Steve Whittamore Notebooks", ICO website, available at http://www.ico.gov.uk/for_the_public/topic_specific_guides/operation_motorman.aspx, last accessed 11 January 2013.

38. *ibid*.

39. Costa and Poullet, "Privacy and the Regulation of 2012" (2012) 28 *Computer Law & Security Review* 254–262 at 256.

third-party independent contractors but is collecting, processing and using their personal data, the data protection regime will also apply. Hence, the data protection regime in relation to organisations is *inward-facing*.

A Rights-Based Regime

As well as creating legal compliance obligations for organisations, the data protection regime enshrines certain rights or data protection rights for individuals in terms of ensuring their ability to know what personal data is being collected, to consent – or not consent – to the collection of their personal data, and to control the uses to which their personal data may be put. There is also a mechanism through which individuals can complain to data controllers holding their personal data, the Data Protection Commissioner and to the courts directly.

Data Protection Commissioner

In order to ensure that the duties are complied with and the rights of individuals vindicated, there is an official authority established in Member States to monitor and act as appropriate in relation to the efficient operation of the data protection regime. In Ireland, this is the Data Protection Commissioner.

The importance of Member State data protection authorities, such as the Data Protection Commissioner in Ireland, is arguably enhanced in the forthcoming changes proposed in the DP Regulation.

Data Protection Rules Introduced

Data controllers (i.e. the organisation that collects and processes personal data, see definitions section below) must comply with a number of data protection issues, perhaps the foremost of which relate to:

- fairness;
- consent;
- accuracy;
- security; and
- proper and transparent purposes for processing.

The collecting, use and onward transfer of personal data must be fair, legitimate and transparent. There are particular definitions and provisions as regards the "processing" of personal data. There are also restrictions in relation to the ability of organisations to transfer personal data both to third-party organisations generally and also to third-party organisations outside of the EEA (the latter are sometimes referred to as trans border data flows).

The personal data must be correct and accurate. The reason is that damage or harm to the individual data subjects can be a consequence of inaccurately held personal data. For example, a credit rating could be adversely affected through incorrect or wrong personal data records being recorded regarding personal payment histories.

There is a general obligation in terms of safeguarding the personal data. Organisations must assess and implement security measures to protect personal data.

There is also an obligation on data controllers to register or notify the Data Protection Commissioner as regards their data processing activities (unless specifically exempted).

If personal data is permitted to be transferred to third countries, it must first qualify under a specific exemption, as well as the general security conditions. No such transfer is permitted from the EEA unless exempted.

Organisations have a duty of care to individuals as regards their personal data being processed by the organisation, particularly if loss or damage arises. Injunctive relief is also possible in appropriate circumstances, as well as other orders.

Data controllers and data processors have obligations in certain circumstances to have legal contracts in place between them. Data processors process and deal with personal data for and on behalf of a data controller in relation to specific, defined tasks, e.g. activities such as outsourced payroll, HR, marketing, market research, customer satisfaction surveys, etc.

General Criteria for Data Processing

Generally, in order to lawfully collect and process personal data, a data controller should be aware that:

- the individual data subject must consent to the collection and processing of their personal data;

- the data subject may object to processing or continued processing;

- legal data protection requirements are complied with;

- the prior information requirements, data protection principles, legitimate processing conditions, sensitive personal data legitimate processing conditions (in the case of sensitive personal data), and security obligations are required to be complied with (see below); and

- the rights and interests of the individual data subjects must be respected and complied with, e.g. access requests, deletion right, etc.

The interests of the data controller can sometimes be relevant in particular instances in deciding what data processing is necessary and permitted.

Date Protection Overview

The Data Protection Acts, on foot of the DP Directive 95, sets out a number of structures, obligations, rights and implementing criteria that are together the basis of the legal data protection regime in Ireland.

The main criteria and obligations to be followed, respected and complied with in order to be able to legally collect and process personal data include:

- the definitions of personal data and the data protection regime (the building blocks of data protection);

- the data protection principles, also known as the "data quality principles";

- the legitimate processing conditions;

- the requirement that processing of personal data be "legitimate" under at least one of the legitimate processing conditions;

- recognising the two categories of personal data covered by the data protection regime, namely, sensitive personal data and non-sensitive general personal data;

- in the case of sensitive personal data, complying with the additional sensitive personal data legitimate processing conditions;

- ensuring the fair obtaining of all personal data collected and processed;

- taking and ensuring appropriate security measures in relation to all processing activities;

- implementing formal legal contracts when engaging or dealing with third-party data processors (e.g. outsourcing data processing tasks or activities);

- complying with the separate criteria in relation to automated decision-making processes or automated decisions;

- complying with the legal criteria for direct marketing (DM);

- a duty of care exists in relation to the individual data subjects whose personal data the organisation is collecting and processing;

- the transfers of personal data outside of the EEA is strictly controlled. Personal data may not be transferred outside of the EEA unless specifically permitted under the data protection regime;

- access requests, or requests by individuals for copies of their personal data held by the organisation, must be complied with (unless excepted);

- registration obligations by organisations must be complied with;

- implementing internal privacy policies and terms;

- implementing outward-facing privacy policies for customers, etc.;

- implementing outward-facing website privacy statements (generally a data protection policy covers organisation-wide activities, whereas a website privacy statement governs only the online collection and processing of personal data);

- implementing mobile, computer and internet usage policies;

- implementing data loss, data breach, incident handling and incident reporting policies and associated reaction plans[40];

- data incidents, losses and breaches need to be reported to the Data Protection Commissioner (unless exempted);

- keeping abreast of the increasing trend towards sector/issue specific rules, e.g. Spam; direct marketing (DM); industry codes of conduct[41] in relation to personal data; and

- complying with new legal developments.

The EEA is wider than the EU Member States and includes Iceland, Liechtenstein and Norway. Switzerland has a similar type arrangement with the EU. EU data protection law frequently refers to the EEA, generally meaning the EU Member States plus the EEA countries.

Legitimate Processing

There is a prohibition on the collection and processing of personal data and sensitive personal data unless:

---

40. Note, for example, the ICO PECR security breach notifications – guidance for service providers, available at http://www.ico.gov.uk/for_organisations/guidance_index/data_protection_and_privacy_and_electronic_communications.aspx#privacy, last accessed 22 August 2012.
41. The Data Protection Acts 1988 and 2003 and the EU data protection regime provide for codes of conduct being agreed with national data protection authorities such as the DPC in relation to specific industry sectors.

- the processing complies with the data protection principles; and

- the processing comes with one of a limited number of specified conditions (the legitimate processing conditions or sensitive personal data legitimate processing conditions [as appropriate]);

- the processing must also comply with the security requirements.

Definitions

The Data Protection Acts contain a number of key definitions. These are central to understanding the data protection regime and complying with it. These are essentially the building blocks of the data protection regime. While these can be "complex concepts",[42] organisations need to fully understand them. Some examples of the matters defined include:

- data subject;
- data controller;
- data processor;
- personal data;
- processing;
- relevant filing system; and
- sensitive personal data.

The definitions are found in greater detail in Chapter 2.

What Are the Sources of Data Protection Law?

What are the various sources of data protection law? Organisations and individuals need to consider a number of sources of the law and policy underpinning the data protection regime. In addition, there are a growing number of sources of interpretation and understanding of data protection law. Reliance on the Data Protection Acts alone can, therefore, be insufficient. Data protection is, therefore, arguably quite different from many other areas of legal practice. In order to fully understand the data protection regime, one has to look beyond the text, or first principles, of the Data Protection Acts.

What are the sources of data protection law and policy? Some of these are referred to below.

---

42. Hallinan, Friedewald and McCarthy, "Citizens' Perceptions of Data Protection and Privacy in Europe" (2012) 28 *Computer Law & Security Review* 263–272 at 263.

Irish Data Protection Acts
Primarily, the data protection regime in Ireland is governed by the Data Protection Acts. In addition, it is also necessary to have regard to a number of other sources of law, policy and the interpretation of the data protection regime.

It is also necessary to look out for any amendments to these.

Irish Secondary Legislation
In addition to the Data Protection Acts, the following legal statutory instruments need to be considered:

- European Communities (Electronic Communications Networks and Services) (Privacy and Electronic Communications) Regulations 2011 (SI 336/2011);

- Data Protection (Fees) Regulations 2007 (SI 658/2007);

- Data Protection (Fees) Regulations 1988 (SI 347/1988);

- Data Protection Act 1988 (s 16(1)) Regulations 2007 (SI 657/2007);

- Data Protection (Registration) Regulations 1988 (SI 351/1988);

- Data Protection (Registration Period) Regulations 1988 (SI 350/1988);

- Data Protection (Access Modification)(Health) Regulations 1989 (SI 82/1989);

- Data Protection (Access Modification)(Social Work) Regulations 1989 (SI 83/1989);

- Data Protection Act 1988 (s 5(1)(d))(Specification) Regulations 1993 (SI 95/1993);

- Data Protection Act 1988 (Restriction of s 4) Regulations 1989 (SI 81/1989);

- Data Protection Act, 1988 (s 5(1)(d))(Specification) Regulations 2009 (SI 421/2009);

- Data Protection (Processing of Genetic Data) Regulations 2007 (SI 687/2007).

It is also necessary to look out for any amendments to these.

EU Data Protection Law

The main sources of EU data protection laws include:

- DP Directive 95;

- ePrivacy Directive (as amended by Directives 2006/24/EC and 2009/136/EC)[43];

- DP Regulation (once enacted); and

- Regulation (EC) No 45/2001 (re processing of personal data by the Community institutions and bodies).[44]

It is also necessary to look out for any amendments to these.

The EU review of the DP Directive 95 and the proposed update of the DP Directive 95 via the draft DP Regulation are arguably the most important developments in EU and Irish data protection since 1995 (see Part 4). There are significant implications for organisations and data protection practice.

Caselaw

Increasingly data protection cases (and cases that involve direct or indirect reference to personal data and information impacting the data protection regime), are coming to be litigated and determined before the courts.

One of the reasons is that individuals are increasingly aware of their rights under the data protection regime. A further reason is that technological developments have enhanced the potential abuse of personal data, from Spam, unsolicited direct marketing (DM), hacking, data loss, phishing, online abuse, email and internet scams, as well as litigation related access to personal data, etc. (The case of *Dublin Bus v Data Protection Commissioner*[45] confirmed that personal data access requests are permissible, even in the case of ongoing litigation.) Damages and compensation in relation to breach, loss and damage of a data subjects rights can also arise.

The caselaw that can be relevant to applying and interpreting the Irish data protection regime include:

---

43. Directive 2002/58/EC of the European Parliament and of the Council of 12 July 2002 concerning the processing of personal data and the protection of privacy in the electronic communications sector (Directive on privacy and electronic communications)(as amended by Directives 2006/24/EC and 2009/136/EC).

44. Regulation (EC) No 45/2001 of the European Parliament and of the Council of 18 December 2000 on the protection of individuals with regard to the processing of personal data by the Community institutions and bodies and on the free movement of such data, Regulation (EC) No 45/2001, OJ L 8, 12.1.2001, available at http://eur-lex.europa.eu/LexUriServ/LexUriServ.do?uri=OJ:L:2001:008:0001:0022:en:PDF, last accessed 11 January 2013.

45. *Dublin Bus v Data Protection Commissioner* [2012] IEHC 339 8/8/2012

- case studies and documentation from the Data Protection Commissioner;

- case complaints adjudicated by the Data Protection Commissioner;

- cases in England and Wales and Scotland;

- European Court of Justice (ECJ/CJEU[46]) cases;

- European Court of Human Rights (ECHR) cases; and

- relevant cases in other EU Member States and or Common Law jurisdictions.

Investigations

Increasingly investigations by the Data Protection Commissioner can have Irish and potentially worldwide significance. Examples include Facebook and Google (*Data Protection Commissioner/Facebook*, Audit by the Data Protection Commissioner [2011 and 2012]; and *EU Article 29 Working Party on Data Protection and Data Protection Authorities/Google*, Privacy Policy Change [2012]).

Investigations can occur as a result of complaints or via proactive Data Protection Commissioner investigations. The Data Protection Commissioner is also able to carry out investigation of his own volition without having to wait on the receipt of a complaint.

Data Protection Commissioner Guides

The Data Protection Commissioner provides a number of guides and interpretations in relation to specific data protection issues and industry sectors.[47] There are currently guides that include:

General Issues

- getting organised for data protection;

- key definitions;

- privacy statements;

- personal data;

- manual data and relevant filing system;

- age of consent;

- back-up systems;

---

46. Note the ECJ is also known as the Court of Justice of the European Union (CJEU).
47. See DPC, available at http://dataprotection.ie/ViewDoc.asp?fn=%2Fdocuments%2Fguidance %2Fdefault%2Ehtm&CatID=6&m=m, last accessed 11 January 2013.

- data security;
- data protection and CCTV;
- data protection and Cloud;
- guidance note for data controllers on purpose limitation and retention;
- guidance note for data controllers on the release of personal data to public representatives;
- guidance note for data controllers on purpose limitation and retention in relation to credit/debit/charge card transactions;
- guidance note for data controllers on keeping personal data obtained from the electoral register up-to-date;
- guidelines in relation to legal basis for private sector sharing of personal data;
- breach notification guidance;
- transfers abroad;
- guidance note on mobile telephone companies and local authority requests for customer data;
- guidance note for the charity and voluntary sector;
- guidance note on data protection in the electronic communications sector; and
- data sharing in the public sector.

Marketing
- direct marketing – a general guide;
- guidance note on data protection in the electronic communications sector;
- restrictions on the use of publicly available data for marketing purposes;
- data protection in the telecommunications sector;
- guide to the use of the national directory database for direct marketers;
- guidance note for electronic communications service providers on direct marketing telephone calls to their subscribers and former subscribers;
- guidance note for entities considering the use of Bluetooth technology, for direct marketing purposes;
- a consumer guide to dealing with unsolicited direct marketing; and
- subscriber FAQs on the national directory database (NDD).

Employment Related
- access requests and HR;
- staff monitoring;
- considerations when vetting prospective employees;
- biometrics in the workplace;
- whistleblower; and
- transfer of ownership of a business.

Medical Related
- the medical and health sector;
- access to medical records on a change of medical practitioner;
- referral of medical consultant's clinical notes for review without his or her or the patients' consent; and
- guidance note on research in the health sector.

Education
- biometrics in schools, colleges and other educational institutions.

It is recommended to regularly look at the Data Protection Commissioner website for guidance, amendments or new updates.

Data Protection Commissioner Determinations

In addition, there is a body of decided decisions in relation to complaints filed by individuals with the Data Protection Commissioner on various issues. These can assist in considering identical and similar situations regarding issues of data protection compliance[48] (see Chapter 24).

Legal Textbooks

There are an increasing number of data protection legal textbooks and guides. Frequently, IT legal textbooks will also have chapters or sections dedicated to data protection. Some examples of the former include:

- Clark, *Data Protection Law in Ireland* (Blackrock: Round Hall Press, 1990) (note: pre-Data Protection (Amendment) Act 2003);

---

48. In relation to the ICO and National Authorities generally regarding data protection; and also Greenleaf, "Independence of Data Privacy Authorities (Part 1): International Standards" (2012) 28 *Computer Law & Security Review* 3–13.

- Kelleher, *Privacy and Data Protection Law in Ireland* (West Sussex: Tottel, 2006);

- Carey, *Data Protection: A Practical Guide to Irish and EU Law* (Dublin: Thomson Round Hall, 2010);

- Goodbody, *A Practical Guide to Data Protection Law in Ireland* (Dublin: Thomson Round Hall, 2003); and

- Delany, *Carolan and Murphy, The Right to Privacy: A Doctrinal and Comparative Analysis* (Dublin: Thomson Round Hall, 2008).

Some related legal texts include:

- Lambert, *A Users Guide to Data Protection* (West Sussex: Bloomsbury, 2013);

- Jay, *Data Protection: Law and Practice* (London: Sweet and Maxwell, 2012);

- Jay and Clarke, *Data Protection Compliance in the UK: A Pocket Guide* (Ely: IT Governance Publishing, 2008);

- Jay and Hamilton, *Data Protection: Law and Practice* (London: Sweet and Maxwell, 2007);

- Bainbridge, *Data Protection Law* (St Albans: XPL, 2005);

- Carey, *Data Protection: A Practical Guide to UK and EU Law* (Oxford: Oxford University Press, 2008);

- Purtova, *Property Rights in Personal Data, A European Perspective* (Alphen aan Den Rijn: Kluwer, 2012);

- Macdonald, *Data Protection: Legal Compliance and Good Practice for Employers* (West Sussex: Tottel, 2008);

- Webster, *Data Protection in the Financial Services Industry* (Aldershot: Gower, 2006);

- Room, *Data Protection and Compliance in Context* (Swindon: British Computer Society, 2007);

- Kuner, *European Data Protection Law: Corporate Compliance and Regulation* (Oxford: Oxford University Press, 2007);

- Gough, ed, *Data Protection for Financial Firms: A Practical Guide to Managing Privacy and Information Risk* (London: Risk Books, 2009);

- Ticher, *Data Protection for Voluntary Organisations* (London: Directory of Social Change in association with Bates, Wells & Braithwaite, 2009);

- Buffington, *Data Protection for Virtual Data Centers* (Hoboken, NJ: Wiley, 2010);

- Webster, *Effective Data Protection: Managing Information in an Era of Change* (London: ICSA Information & Training, 2011);

- Kuschewsky, *Data Protection & Privacy: Jurisdictional Comparisons* (London: Thomson Reuters, 2012);

- Beyleveld et al, *Implementation of the Data Protection Directive in Relation to Medical Research in Europe* (Aldershot: Ashgate, 2005);

- Beyleveld, Townend and Wright, *Research Ethics Committees, Data Protection and Medical Research in European Countries* (Aldershot: Ashgate, 2005);

- Singleton, *Data Protection and Employment Practices* (Croydon: LexisNexis/Tolley, 2005);

- Engineering Employers' Federation, *Data Protection: A Practical for Employers* (London: Engineering Employers' Federation, 2005);

- Smith and Moseley, *The New Data Protection Liabilities & Risks for Direct Marketers: Handbook* (Hampton: Forum Business Media, 2005);

- Earle, *Data Protection in the NHS* (London: Informa, 2003);

- Morgan and Boardman, *Data Protection Strategy, Implementing Data Protection Compliance* (London: Sweet & Maxwell, 2012);

- Fawke & Townsend, *Data Protection & the Pensions Industry: Implications of the Data Protection Act* (London: Masons, 2002);

- Bygrave, *Data Protection Law: Approaching its Rationale, Logic and Limits* (The Hague/London: Kluwer, 2002);

- Asscher and Hoogcarspel, *Regulating Spam: A European Perspective after the Adoption of the E-Privacy Directive* (The Hague: TMC Asser; Cambridge: Cambridge University Press, 2006);

- Schachter, *Information and Decisional Privacy* (Durham, NC: Carolina Academic Press, 2003);

- Diffie and Landau, *Privacy on the Line, The Politics of Wiretapping and Encryption* (Cambridge, MA; London: MIT, 2007);

- Kuner, *European Data Protection Law: Corporate Regulation and Compliance* (Oxford: Oxford University Press, 2007);

- *First Report on the Implementation of the Data Protection Directive* (95/46/EC) (i.e. DP Directive 95);

- *Encyclopedia of Data Protection*;

- Butler, ed, *E-Commerce and Convergence: A Guide to the Law of Digital Media* (West Sussex: Tottel, 2012);

- Lloyd, *Information Technology Law* (Oxford: Oxford University Press, 2011);

- Murray, *Information Technology Law: The Law and Society* (Oxford: Oxford University Press, 2010) (chs 18, 19);

- Büllesbach et al, *Concise European IT Law* (Alphen aan den Rijn; London: Wolters Kluwer, 2010);

- Ryan, *The EU Regulatory Framework for Electronic Communications Handbook* (West Sussex: Bloomsbury, 2010);

- Edwards and Waelde, eds, *Law and the Internet* (Oxofrd: Hart, 2009) (chs 14–21);

- Bainbridge, *Introduction to Information Technology Law* (Harlow: Pearson Longman, 2008);

- Smith, *Internet Law and Regulation* (London: Sweet & Maxwell, 2007) (ch 7);

- Reed and Angel, eds, *Computer Law: The Law and Regulation of Information Technology* (Oxford: Oxford University Press, 2007) (chs 10, 11);

- Burnett, *Outsourcing – The Legal Contract* (London: Faculty of Information Technology of the Institute of Chartered Accountants, 2005);

- Burnett, *Outsourcing IT: The Legal Aspects: Planning, Contracting, Managing and the Law* (Farnham: Gower, 2009);

- Calder, *A Business Guide to Information Security: How to Protect Your Company's IT Assets, Reduce Risks and Understand the Law* (London: Kogan, 2005);

- Edwards, ed, *The New Legal Framework for E-Commerce in Europe* (Oxford: Hart, 2005);

- Conradi, ed, *Communications Law Handbook* (West Sussex: Bloomsbury, 2009); and

- Birkinshaw and Varney, *Government and Information: The Law Relating to Access, Disclosure and their Regulation* (West Sussex: Bloomsbury, 2012).

Legal Journals

There are also relevant learned journals and articles published in relation to data protection compliance and developing data protection issues. Some examples include:

- *Communications Law*;

- *Journal of Information Law and Technology* (JILT), available at http://elj:warick.ac.uk;

- *Computers and Law from the Society of Computers and Law*, available at www.scl.org;

- *Data Protection Law and Practice*;

- *Computer Law and Security Review*;

- SCRIPT-ed.

EU Article 29 Working Party on Data Protection

In terms of the interpretation and understanding of the data protection regime in the Ireland, the EU Article 29 Working Party, established under Article 29 of the DP Directive 95, is also required to be consulted. This is an influential body in relation to addressing and interpreting the data protection regime as well as problem areas in data protection practice. It is also influential as it is comprised of members from the respective data protection authorities in the EU, including the Irish Data Protection Commissioner.

The EU Article 29 Working Party on Data Protection issues working papers, opinions and related documentation. It is available at:

- http://ec.europa.eu/justice/policies/privacy/workinggroup/index_en.htm.

European Data Protection Supervisor

The European Data Protection Supervisor is also worth consulting and is arguably increasing in prominence and importance. Details are available at:

- http://www.edps.europa.eu/EDPSWEB/edps/EDPS).

Council of Europe

There are various important reference materials in relation to data protection and privacy emanating from the Council of Europe, such as:

- Council of Europe Convention on data protection, No 108 of 1981;

- Recommendation R(85) 20 on Direct Marketing;

- Recommendation R(86) 1 on Social Security;

- Recommendation R(97) 1 on the Media;

- Recommendation R(97) 5 on Health Data.

These and other documents are available at:

http://www.coe.int/t/dghl/standardsetting/dataprotection/Documents_TPD_en.asp.

The Council of Europe Convention on data protection[49] of 1981 predates the DP Directive 95 and is incorporated into the national law of many EU and other states (40 plus) prior to the DP Directive 95. This includes Ireland. The Council of Europe is reviewing and updating the Convention.[50]

Other Data Protection Authorities

Issues that may not yet be decided or formally reported on in Ireland can sometimes have been considered elsewhere. It can, therefore, be useful to consider the decisions and logic behind decisions, reports and opinions of the:

- data protection authorities of other EU Member States and EEA Member States;

- data protection authorities of other states, e.g. Canada.

The complaints and issues raised in *EU Article 29 Working Party on Data Protection and Data Protection Authorities/Google*, Privacy Policy Change [2012] also appear to have been endorsed and supported by the Asia Pacific Privacy Authorities.

The European Data Protection Supervisor provides links to the data protection authorities in the EU at:

- http://ec.europa.eu/justice/policies/privacy/nationalcomm/index_en.htm.

Other Official Sources

Related issues can sometimes arise under freedom of information legislation.[51]

Government or official reports can be beneficial and applicable on certain data protection topics. Industry codes that may be agreed with the Data Protection Commissioner can also be relevant to those industries, e.g. the insurance code of practice in relation to data protection[52]; and the Department of Education and Skills, which launched a Code of Practice.[53]

---

49. Convention for the Protection of Individuals with regard to Automatic Processing of Personal Data, Council of Europe (1982), available at http://conventions.coe.int/Treaty/en/Treaties/Html/108.htm, last accessed 11 January 2013. "Draft Convention for the Protection of Individuals with Regards to Automatic Processing of Personal Data" (1980) 19 *International Legal Materials* 284–298.
50. See Kierkegaard *et al*, "30 Years On – The Review of the Council of Europe Data Protection Convention 108" (2011) 27 *Computer Law & Security Review* 223–231.
51. See Freedom of Information Act 1997.
52. See DPC website. Available at http://www.dataprotection.ie/docs/20/08/08_-_Data_Protection_Commissioner_publishes_new_Data_P/840.htm, last accessed 11 January 2013.
53. See DPC website. Available at http://dataprotection.ie/viewdoc.asp?DocID=1134, last accessed 11 January 2013.

Industry bodies such as the *Irish Internet Association, Irish Computer Society* (ICS), the *Irish Direct Marketing Association* and the *Marketing Institute of Ireland* also publish recommendations and information regarding aspects of data protection. The ICS also host an Annual Data Protection Conference.

Tribunals can also be relevant, for example the Leveson Inquiry (albeit UK based), particularly in terms of protection for personal data, security, deliberate breaches, hacking, etc., and the related UK ICO Operation Motorman investigation. There is also a series of cases from hacking victims.

Key/Topical Cases and Legislation

Some of the key developments and issues that also influence the data protection regime and how it is interpreted include:

- security requirements for business;
- employee monitoring and consent;
- spam and direct marketing;
- the relationship between the data controller and the data processor, which relationship needs to be formalised in contract pursuant to the Data Protection Acts;
- disposal of computer hardware. Particular care is needed when considering the disposal of IT hardware, equipment and software. They may still contain personal data files. This can continue to be the case even when it appears that files have been wiped or deleted. There are many examples of accessible personal data still being available even after it is believed to have been deleted and the device handed over to a third party, or worse, sold on. The new recipient could be able to access the original personal data and records. This could quite easily be a breach of a number of principles of the data protection regime. It is always advised to take professional legal, IT and or forensic advice when considering disposing of computer devices; and
- websites and social networking compliance with the data protection regime.

Facebook has already altered various data protection related practices pursuant to the Data Protection Commissioner Audits, with certain issues ongoing.

Data Protection Websites and Blogs

There are a number of privacy and data protection websites and blogs, such as ICS (www.ics.ie), IIA (www.iia.ie), Datonomy (www.datonomy.eu/), the Data Protection Forum (www.dpforum.org.uk) and the Society of Computers and Law (www.scl.org).

Other Laws

Other laws can also be relevant in considering personal data and privacy.[54] Examples include:

- IT law;
- contract law;
- consumer law;
- eCommerce law;
- distance selling law;
- financial services law;
- health law; and
- child law.

This is by no means a complete list.

Conferences

There are a variety of conferences, annual events and training organisations related to data protection. Some are organised by professional conference firms, while others are non-profit technology, legal or related organisations. There are also other related conferences, for example, Irish Computer Society, ICS Annual Data Protection Conference, Irish Internet Association, eDiscovery Ireland Annual Conference, and the Copyright Association of Ireland.

---

54. See review of particular laws in Delfino, "European Union Legislation and Actions" (2011) 7 *European Review of Contract Law* 547–551, which includes reference to data protection law.

Reference

Useful reference material is available as set out below.

The Data Protection Commissioner is at:

> http://dataprotection.ie/docs/Home/4.htm.

The Data Protection Acts[55] are consolidated are at:

> http://dataprotection.ie/ViewDoc.asp?fn=%2Fdocuments%2Flegal%2FLaw
> OnDP%2Ehtm&CatID=7&m=l.

The EU Commission is at:

> http://ec.europa.eu/justice/data-protection/index_en.htm.

The EU Article 29 Working Party on Data Protection is at:

> http://ec.europa.eu/justice/policies/privacy/workinggroup/index_en.htm.

The ECJ/CJEU website is at:

> http://europa.eu/about-eu/institutions-bodies/court-justice/index_en.htm.

ECJ/CJEU cases[56] are at:

> http://curia.europa.eu/juris/recherche.jsf?language=en.

The ECHR website is at:

> http://www.echr.coe.int/ECHR/Homepage_En/.

---

55. Data Protection Act 1988 and Data Protection (Amendment) Act 2003.
56. Tzanou, "Balancing Fundamental Rights, United in Diversity? Some Reflections on the Recent Case Law of the European Court of Justice on Data Protection" (2010) 6 *CYELP* 53–74.

CHAPTER 2

What Are the Definitions of
Data Protection?

Introduction

What are the definitions central to data protection? It is critical to understanding the data protection regime to know and appreciate the definitions of the key terms that underpin the legal measures implementing the data protection regime. The definitions are the building blocks for the data protection regime. They are contained in the Data Protection Acts[1] and DP Directive 95.[2] There are also definitions in the new proposed DP Regulation[3] that should also be considered, as these will change the EU data protection legal regime. It will also become the main EU data protection legal measure for many years to come.

The various categories and definitions are referred to below.

Categories of Personal Data

Organisations need to be familiar with two separate categories of personal data in relation to their data protection actions and compliance obligations. It also affects what personal data they may collect in the first instance. The categories of personal data, are, namely, *general personal data* and *sensitive personal data*.

The first is *general personal data*. The second category is *sensitive personal data*. The importance of sensitive personal data is that it triggers additional and more onerous obligations of compliance and initial collection conditions. Unless it falls within the

---

1. Data Protection Act 1988 and Data Protection (Amendment) Act 2003.
2. EU Data Protection Directive 1995 (Directive 95/46/EC of the European Parliament and of the Council of 24 October 1995 on the protection of individuals with regard to the processing of personal data and on the free movement of such data).
3. EU draft Data Protection Regulation (Proposal for a Regulation of the European Parliament and of the Council on the protection of individuals with regard to the processing of personal data and on the free movement of such data (General Data Protection Regulation) COM(2012) 11 final).

definition of sensitive personal data, all personal data falls into the general personal data category.

Why is there a distinction? Certain types of personal data are more important and sensitive to individuals than other categories of personal data. This is recognised in the data protection regime. Additional rules are put in place. First, sensitive personal data is defined differently. Second, in order to collect and process sensitive personal data, an organisation must satisfy additional processing conditions, in addition to the *data protection principles* and the general *legitimate processing conditions*, namely complying with the *sensitive personal data legitimate processing conditions*.

General Personal Data

General personal data is referred to in Section 1 of the Data Protection Acts as follows, namely, data relating to a living individual who is (or can be) identified either from the data or from the data in conjunction with other information that is in, or is likely to come into, the possession of the data controller.

Sensitive Personal Data

Sensitive personal data contains higher compliance obligations and conditions. Section 1 of the Data Protection Acts refers to sensitive personal data being personal data relating to any of the following, namely the (a) racial or ethnic origin; (b) political opinions; (c) religious or philosophical beliefs; (d) trade union membership; (e) the physical or mental health or condition or sexual life; (f) the commission or alleged commission of any offence; or (g) any proceedings for an offence committed or alleged to have been committed, the disposal of such proceedings or the sentence of any court in such proceedings, relating to the data subject.

This can be summarised as personal data relating to:

- the racial or ethnic origin;
- political opinions;
- religious or philosophical beliefs;
- trade union membership;
- physical or mental health or condition or sexual life;
- commission or alleged commission of any offence; or
- any proceedings for an offence committed or alleged.

Article 8 of the DP Directive 95 refers to the processing of special categories of data. It states:

- Member States shall prohibit the processing of personal data revealing racial or ethnic origin, political opinions, religious or philosophical beliefs, trade union membership, and the processing of data concerning health or sex life;

- the above provision shall not apply where:

  - the data subject has given their explicit consent to the processing, except where the laws of the Member State provide that the prohibition[4] may not be lifted by giving consent; or

  - processing is necessary for the the obligations of the data controller in the field of employment law if authorised by Member State law with adequate safeguards; or

  - processing is necessary to protect the vital interests of the data subject or of another person if they are physically or legally incapable of giving their consent; or

  - processing is carried out in the course of its legitimate activities with appropriate guarantees by a foundation, association or any other non-profit-seeking body with a political, philosophical, religious or trade-union aim and on condition that the processing relates solely to the members of the body or to persons who have regular contact with it in connection with its purposes and the personal data are not disclosed to a third party without the consent of the data subjects; or

  - the processing relates to personal data which are manifestly made public by the data subject or is necessary for the establishment, exercise or defence of legal claims;

- There is a carveout from the restriction where processing of the data is required for the purposes of preventive medicine, medical diagnosis, the provision of care or treatment or the management of health-care services, and where those data are processed by a health professional subject under Member State law or rules established by national competent bodies to the obligation of professional secrecy or by a person subject to an equivalent obligation of secrecy;

- Subject to the provisions with suitable safeguards, Member States may, for reasons of substantial public interest, provide certain additional exemptions either by national law or by decision of the supervisory authority;

- Processing of data relating to offences, criminal convictions or security measures may be carried out only under the control of official authority, or national law safeguards, subject to derogations which may be granted by the Member State under national provisions providing suitable specific safeguards. A complete register of criminal convictions may be kept only under the control of official authority. Member States may provide that data relating to administrative sanctions or judgements in civil cases shall also be processed under the control of official authority;

---

4.   Referred to in para 1 *ibid.*

- Any such derogations must be notified to the Commission;

- Member States shall determine the conditions under which a national identification number or any other identifier of general application may be processed.

Article 9 of the DP Regulation relates to the processing of special categories of personal data. The processing of personal data, revealing race or ethnic origin, political opinions, religion or beliefs, trade-union membership, and the processing of genetic data or data concerning health or sex life or criminal convictions or related security measures shall be prohibited.[5]

Article 9(2) of the DP Regulation provides that Article 9(1)(above) shall not apply where:

- the data subject has given consent to the processing of those personal data, subject to the conditions laid down in Articles 7 and 8 of the DP Regulation, except where EU law or Member State law provide that the prohibition may not be lifted by the data subject; or

- processing is necessary for carrying out the obligations and exercising specific rights of the data controller in the field of employment law if authorised by EU law or Member State law which provides for adequate safeguards; or

- processing is necessary to protect the vital interests of the data subject or another person where the data subject is physically or legally incapable of giving consent; or

- processing is carried out in the course of its legitimate activities with appropriate safeguards by a foundation, association or any other non-profit seeking body with a political, philosophical, religious or trade-union aim, on condition that the processing relates solely to the members or to former members of the body or to persons who have regular contact with it in connection with its purposes and that the data are not disclosed outside that body without the consent of the data subjects; or

- the processing relates to personal data which are manifestly made public by the data subject; or

- processing is necessary for the establishment, exercise or defence of legal claims; or

- processing is necessary for the performance of a task carried out in the public interest, on the basis of EU law, or Member State law, which provides safeguards for the data subject's legitimate interests; or

---

5.   art 9(1) *ibid.*

- processing of personal data concerning health is necessary for health purposes and subject to the conditions and safeguards (referred to in Article 81); or

- processing is necessary for historical, statistical or scientific research purposes (subject to the conditions and safeguards in Article 83); or

- processing of data relating to criminal convictions or related security measures is carried out either under the control of official authority or is necessary for compliance with a legal obligation of the data controller, or to perform a task carried out for important public interest reasons, and if authorised by EU law or Member State law providing adequate safeguards. A complete register of criminal convictions must only be kept under the control of official authority.

The Commission has power to adopt delegated acts in accordance with Article 86 for the purpose of further specifying the criteria, conditions and appropriate safeguards for the processing of the special categories of personal data.[6]

Data Protection Definitions

There are various definitions in relation to personal data. These are the building blocks of the data protection regime and the respective obligations and rights as regards organisations and individuals.

Automated Data
Section 1 of the Data Protection Acts contains the following definition of "automated data". It means information that is (a) being processed by equipment operating automatically in response to instructions given for that purpose, or (b) recorded with the intention that it should be processed by means of such equipment.

Back Up Data
"Back-up data" means data kept only for the purpose of replacing other data in the event of it being lost, destroyed or damaged.[7]

Blocking
In relation to data, blocking means marking the data that it is not possible to process it for purposes in relation to which it is marked.[8]

---

6. art 9(3) and referred to in para 1 and the exemptions laid down in para 2 *ibid*.
7. s 1 *ibid*.
8. *ibid*.

Commissioner

The Data Protection Acts contains the following definition of "Commissioner". It has the meaning assigned to it by s 9 of the Data Protection Acts.[9]

Company

"Company" has the meaning assigned to it by the Companies Act 1963.[10]

Convention

Section 1 of the Data Protection Acts contains the following definition of "Convention". It means the Convention for the Protection of Individuals with regard to Automatic Processing of Personal Data done at Strasbourg on the 28 January 1981, the text of which is set out in the First Schedule to the Act.[11]

Court

Section 1 of the Data Protection Acts[12] contains the following definition of "Court": the Circuit Court.

Data

Section 1 of the Data Protection Acts[13] contains the following definition of "data": automated data and manual data.

Data Controller

"Data controller" means a person who, either alone or with others, controls the contents and use of personal data.

The DP Directive 95 provides the following definition of data "controller". It means the natural or legal person, public authority, agency or any other body that alone or jointly with others, decides the purposes and means of the processing of personal data. Where the purposes and means of processing are determined by Member State or EU laws, the data controller or the specific criteria for his or her nomination may be designated by Member State or EU law.

Article 4 of the draft DP Regulation contains the following definition of data "controller": the natural or legal person, public authority, agency or any other body that alone or jointly with others determines the purposes, conditions and means

---

9.   *ibid.*
10.   *ibid.*
11.   *ibid.*
12.   *ibid.*
13.   *ibid.*

of the processing of personal data; where the purposes, conditions and means of processing are determined by EU law or Member State law, the data controller or the specific criteria for their nomination may be designated by EU law or by Member State law.

Data Equipment

The Data Protection Acts contains the following definition of "data equipment": equipment for processing data.

Data Material

Section 1 of the Data Protection Acts contains the following definition of "data material": any document or other material used in connection with, or produced by, data equipment.[14]

Data Processor

"Data processor" means a person or organisation which processes personal data on behalf of a data controller but does not include an employee of a data controller who processes such data in the course of their employment.

The DP Directive 95[15] provides the following definition of "processor" as in data processor: a natural or legal person, public authority, agency or any other body that processes personal data on behalf of the data controller.

The draft DP Regulation[16] sets out the following definition of "processor": a natural or legal person, public authority, agency or any other body that processes personal data on behalf of the data controller.

Data Subject

Section 1 of the Data Protection Acts[17] contains the following definition of "data subject": an individual who is the subject of personal data.

The draft DP Regulation[18] sets out the following definition of "data subject": an identified natural person or a natural person who can be identified, directly or indirectly, by means reasonably likely to be used by the data controller or by any other natural or legal person, in particular by reference to an identification number, location data, online identifier or to one or more factors specific to the physical, physiological, genetic, mental, economic, cultural or social identity of the data subject.

---

14. *ibid.*
15. art 2 EU Data Protection Directive 1995 *supra.*
16. art 4 EU draft Data Protection Regulation *supra.*
17. Data Protection Act 1988 and Data Protection (Amendment) Act 2003.
18. art 4 EU draft Data Protection Regulation *supra.*

Directive
Section 1 of the Data Protection Acts contains the following definition of "Directive": Directive 95/46/EC of the European Parliament and of the Council of 24 October 1995 on the protection of individuals with regard to the processing of personal data and on the free movement of such data (DP Directive 95).

Direct Marketing
The Data Protection Acts[19] define "direct marketing" as including direct mailing other than direct mailing carried out in the course of political activities by a political party or its members, or a body established by or under statute or a candidate for election to, or a holder of, elective political office. The scope is therefore much wider.

Disclosure
"Disclosure", in relation to personal data, includes the disclosure of information extracted from such personal data and the transfer of such data but does not include a disclosure made directly or indirectly by a data controller or a data processor to an employee or agent for the purpose of enabling the employee or agent to carry out their duties; and where the identification of a data subject depends partly on the data and partly on other information in the possession of the data controller, the data shall not be regarded as disclosed unless the other information is also disclosed.[20]

EEA Agreement
Under the Data Protection Acts[21] "EEA Agreement" means the Agreement on the European Economic Area signed at Oporto on 2 May 1992 as adjusted by the Protocol signed at Brussels on 17 March 1993.

Enforcement Notice
Section 1 of the Data Protection Acts contains the following definition of "enforcement notice": a notice under s 10 of the Data Protection Acts.

Information Notice
Section 1 of the Data Protection Acts contains the following definition of "information notice": a notice under s 12 of the Data Protection Acts.

Manual Data
"Manual data" means information that is recorded as part of a relevant filing system or with the intention that it should form part of such a relevant filing system.[22]

---

19. s 1 *ibid.*
20. *ibid.*
21. *ibid.*
22. s 1 *ibid.*

Personal Data

"Personal data" means data relating to a living individual who is or can be identified either from the data or from the data in conjunction with other information that is in, or is likely to come into, the possession of the data controller.[23]

Article 2 of the DP Directive 95 provides the following definition of "personal data": namely, any information relating to an identified or identifiable natural person ("data subject"). An identifiable person is one who can be identified, directly or indirectly, in particular by reference to an identification number or to one or more factors specific to their physical, physiological, mental, economic, cultural or social identity.

Article 4 of the draft DP Regulation provides the following definition of "personal data": any information relating to a data subject.

Processing

The Data Protection Acts[24] contain the following definition: "processing" of or in relation to information or data, means performing any operation or set of operations on the information or data, whether or not by automatic means, including:

(a) obtaining, recording or keeping the information or data;

(b) collecting, organising, storing, altering or adapting the information or data;

(c) retrieving, consulting or using the information or data;

(d) disclosing the information or data by transmitting, disseminating or otherwise making it available; or

(e) aligning, combining, blocking, erasing or destroying the information or data.

Article 2 of the DP Directive 95 provides the following definition of "processing of personal data" ("processing"): any operation or set of operations which is performed upon personal data, whether or not by automatic means, such as collection, recording, organisation, storage, adaptation or alteration, retrieval, consultation, use, disclosure by transmission, dissemination or otherwise making available, alignment or combination, blocking, erasure or destruction of the personal data.

Article 4 of the draft DP Regulation sets out the following definition of "processing": any operation or set of operations performed upon personal data or sets of personal data, whether or not by automated means, such as collection, recording, organisation, structuring, storage, adaptation or alteration, retrieval, consultation, use, disclosure by transmission, dissemination or otherwise making available, alignment or combination, erasure or destruction of personal data.

---

23. *ibid.*
24. s 1 Data Protection Act 1988 and Data Protection (Amendment) Act 2003.

Prohibition Notice

Section 1 of the Data Protection Acts contains the following definition of "prohibition notice": a notice under s 11 of the Data Protection Acts.

Register

"Register" means the register established and maintained under s 16 of the Data Protection Acts.[25]

Relevant Filing System

"Relevant filing system" means any set of information relating to individuals to the extent that (although the information is not processed by means of equipment operating automatically in response to instructions given for that purpose), the set is structured, either by reference to individuals or criteria relating to individuals, in such a way that specific information relating to a particular individual is readily accessible.[26]

The DP Directive 95[27] and draft DP Regulation[28] provides the following definition of "personal data filing System"/"filing system": any structured set of personal data accessible according to specific criteria, whether centralised, decentralised or dispersed on a functional or geographical basis.

Sensitive Personal Data

Section 1 of the Data Protection Acts contains the following definition of "sensitive personal data" – personal data pertaining to the:

- racial or ethnic origin;

- political opinions;

- religious or philosophical beliefs;

- whether the data subject is a member of a trade union;

- physical or mental health or condition or sexual life;

- the commission or alleged commission of any offence; or

- any proceedings for an offence committed or alleged to have been committed, the disposal of such proceedings or the sentence of any court in such proceedings.

---

25. s 1 *ibid.*
26. *ibid.*
27. art 2 EU Data Protection Directive 1995.
28. art 4 EU draft Data Protection Regulation.

Additional Definitions
There are also additional definitions in the DP Directive 95[29] and draft DP Regulation.[30] These are set out below.

Third Party
Article 2 of the DP Directive 95 provides the following definition of "third party": any natural or legal person, public authority, agency or any other body other than the data subject, the data controller, the data processor and the persons who, under the direct authority of the data controller or the data processor, are authorised to process the data.

Recipient
Article 2 of the DP Directive 95 provides that "recipient" means a natural or legal person, public authority, agency or any other body to whom data are disclosed, whether a third party or not. However, authorities that may receive data in the framework of a particular inquiry shall not be regarded as recipients.

Consent
Article 2 of the DP Directive 95[31] provides that "the data subject's consent" means any freely given specific and informed indication of their wishes by which the data subject signifies their agreement to personal data relating to them being processed.

Article 4 of the draft DP Regulation provides that "the data subject's consent" means any freely given specific, informed and explicit indication of their wishes by which the data subject, either by a statement or by a clear affirmative action, signifies agreement to personal data relating to them being processed.

Recipient
Article 4 of the draft DP Regulation provides that "recipient" means a natural or legal person, public authority, agency or any other body to which the personal data are disclosed.

Personal Data Breach
Article 4 of the draft DP Regulation provides that "personal data breach" means a breach of security leading to the accidental or unlawful destruction, loss, alteration, unauthorised disclosure of, or access to, personal data transmitted, stored or otherwise processed.

---

29. art 2 EU Data Protection Directive 1995.
30. art 4.
31. *ibid.*

Genetic Data

Article 4 of the draft DP Regulation provides that "genetic data" means all data, of whatever type, concerning the characteristics of an individual that are inherited or acquired during early prenatal development.

Biometric Data

Article 4 of the draft DP Regulation provides that "biometric data" means any data relating to the physical, physiological or behavioural characteristics of an individual that allow their unique identification, such as facial images, or dactyloscopic data.

Data Concerning Health

Article 4 of the draft DP Regulation provides that "data concerning health" means any information that relates to the physical or mental health of an individual, or to the provision of health services to the individual.

Main Establishment

Article 4 of the draft DP Regulation provides that "main establishment" as regards the data controller means the place of its establishment in the EU where the main decisions as to the purposes, conditions and means of the processing of personal data are taken; if no decisions as to the purposes, conditions and means of the processing of personal data are taken in the EU, the main establishment is the place where the main processing activities in the context of the activities of an establishment of a data controller in the EU take place. As regards the data processor, "main establishment" means the place of its central administration in the EU.

Representative

Article 4 of the draft DP Regulation sets out the following definition of "representative": any natural or legal person established in the EU who, explicitly designated by the data controller, acts and may be addressed by any supervisory authority and other bodies in the EU instead of the data controller, with regard to the obligations of the data controller under the Regulation.

Enterprise

Article 4 of the draft DP Regulation sets out the following definition of "enterprise": any entity engaged in an economic activity, irrespective of its legal form, including in particular, natural and legal persons, partnerships or associations regularly engaged in an economic activity.

Group of Undertakings

Article 4 of the draft DP Regulation sets out the following definition of "group of undertakings": a controlling undertaking and its controlled undertakings.

Binding Corporate Rules

Article 4 of the draft DP Regulation sets out the following definition of "binding corporate rules": personal data protection policies of a data controller or data processor established on the territory of a Member State of the EU for transfers or a set of transfers of personal data to a data controller or data processor in third countries within a group of undertakings.

Child

Article 4 of the draft DP Regulation defines "child" as any person below the age of 18 years.

Supervisory Authority

Article 4 of the draft DP Regulation sets out the following definition of "supervisory authority": a public authority established by a Member State in accordance with Article 46 of the draft DP Regulation.

Misleading or Inaccurate Personal Data

Section 1(2) of the Data Protection Acts states that data are inaccurate if they are incorrect or misleading as to any matter of fact.

General

Section 1(3A) of the Data Protection Acts provides that a word or expression that is used in the Data Protection Acts and also in the DP Directive 95 has, unless the context otherwise requires, the same meaning in the Data Protection Acts as it has in the DP Directive 95.

Subject to any regulations under s 15(2) of the Acts, the Acts apply to data controllers processing of personal data if:

- the data controller is established in the State and the data are processed in the context of that establishment, or
- the data controller is not established in the State nor an EEA state but makes use of equipment in the State for processing the data otherwise than for the purpose of transit through the territory of the State.[32]

---

32. s 1(3B)(a) Data Protection Act 1988 and Data Protection (Amendment) Act 2003.

Each of the following shall be treated as established in the State:

- an individual normally resident in the State,

- a body incorporated under the law of the State,

- a partnership or unincorporated association formed under the law of the State, and

- a person who maintains in the State:

    - an office, branch or agency for any activity, or

    - a regular practice,

and the reference to establishment in EEA member state shall be construed accordingly.[33]

This may be even further expanded with the definitions of the draft Regulation.

A data controller[34] must, without prejudice to any legal proceedings that could be commenced against the data controller, designate a representative established in the State.[35]

Conclusion

It is important for organisations to distinguish, in advance of collecting personal data, whether the proposed data collection relates to general personal data or sensitive personal data. They also need to be able to confirm compliance procedures in advance of collecting and maintaining personal data, and particularly sensitive personal data. The organisation could be asked to demonstrate at a future date, that it obtained consent, and how it maintains general compliance. If it cannot, it may have to delete the data. It may have committed breaches and offences. It may potentially face prosecution, fines and/or being sued by the data subjects. Depending on the circumstances, personal liability can also arise.

---

33. *ibid.*
34. To whom para (a)(ii) of the subsection applies.
35. s 1(3B)(c) Data Protection Act 1988 and Data Protection (Amendment) Act 2003.

CHAPTER 3

Instruments of Data Protection

Introduction

What are the legal instruments of data protection? Primarily, they are the Data Protection Acts,[1] the EU DP Directive 95[2] and the proposed Regulation.[3]

Data Protection Acts

The Data Protection Acts implement the provisions of the EU DP Directive 95 on the protection of individuals with regard to the processing of personal data and on the free movement of such data. The DP Directive 95 ensures data protection and a common data protection regime across Member States in the EU. It is also extended to EEA Member States.

The Data Protection Acts have important implications for business and organisations which collect, process and deal in information relating to (living) individuals – in particular, customers and employees. It contains stringent data protection measures to safeguard personal and informational privacy and to ensure that personal data is not misused or used for purposes that are incompatible with data protection legislation.

Legal Instruments

The introduction or Recitals to the European legal instruments, while not legally binding compared to the main text of the Article provisions, are still influential in terms of interpreting the focus of the data protection regime, and also highlight

---

1. Data Protection Act 1988 and Data Protection (Amendment) Act 2003.
2. EU Data Protection Directive 1995 (Directive 95/46/EC of the European Parliament and of the Council of 24 October 1995 on the protection of individuals with regard to the processing of personal data and on the free movement of such data).
3. EU draft Data Protection Regulation (Proposal for a Regulation of the European Parliament and of the Council on the protection of individuals with regard to the processing of personal data and on the free movement of such data (General Data Protection Regulation) COM (2012) 11 final).

some of the history, purpose and policy behind particular data protections laws. It is, therefore, useful to consider the Recitals.

General Provisions in the DP Directive 95

The DP Directive 95 provides the overarching framework for data protection in the EU and EEA. The Directive provides the *data protection principles*, *legitimate processing conditions*, security requirements, individual data subject rights, fair collection processing rules, restrictions on trans-border data flows or transfers of personal data and sensitive personal data. The DP Directive 95 at a headline level also provides for

- privacy and data protection; and
- harmonisation of such measures throughout the EU.

Some of the pertinent Recitals to the DP Directive 95 include the following themes, which are also illustrative of the aims and intentions of the DP Directive 95: harmonisation[4]; privacy/data protection/fundamental rights/sectors[5]; technology/increased processing[6]; barriers[7]; automated processing[8]; Member States/jurisdiction[9]; third-party controllers and EU data subjects[10]; balance[11]; security and technical security[12]; access right to personal data[13]; right to object to processing[14]; security[15]; transmission[16]; specific processing risks[17]; court and judicial remedy[18]; trans-border data flows (TBDFs)[19]; and consent.[20]

Chapter I of DP Directive 95 contains the general provisions of the Directive. Article 1 refers to the object of the Directive. In particular Article 1(1) states that Member States shall protect the fundamental rights and freedoms of natural persons, and in particular their right to privacy with respect to the processing of personal data.

---

4. Recital 1 *ibid.*
5. Recitals 2, 3, 22, 23, 26, 27, 28, 30, 31, 33, 38, 39 and 68 *ibid.*
6. Recitals 4, 6 and 10 *ibid.*
7. Recitals 7, 8, 9 *ibid.*
8. Recital 11 *ibid.*
9. Recitals 18 and 19 *ibid.*
10. Recital 20 *ibid.*
11. Recital 25 *ibid.*
12. Recital 25 *ibid.*
13. Recital 41 *ibid.*
14. Recital 45 *ibid.*
15. Recital 46 *ibid.*
16. Recital 47 *ibid.*
17. Recital 53 *ibid.*
18. Recital 55 *ibid.*
19. Recitals 56, 57, 59, 60 and 66 *ibid.*
20. Recital 58 *ibid.*

Article 1(2) provides that Member States shall neither restrict nor prohibit the free flow of personal data between Member States for reasons connected with the protection afforded under Article 1(1).

General Provisions in the DP Regulation

Chapter I of the draft DP Regulation contains the general provisions. Article 1 refers to the subject matter and objectives. Particularly, Article 1(1) states that the DP Regulation lays down rules relating to the protection of individuals with regard to the processing of personal data and rules relating to the free movement of personal data.

Article 2(2) states that the DP Regulation protects the fundamental rights and freedoms of natural persons, and in particular their right to the protection of personal data. Article 3(3) provides that the free movement of personal data within the EU shall neither be restricted nor prohibited for reasons connected with the protection of individuals with regard to the processing of personal data.

Article 2 relates to material scope. The DP Regulation applies to the processing of personal data wholly or partly by automated means, and to the processing other than by automated means of personal data that form part of a filing system or are intended to form part of a filing system.[21]

However, Article 2(2) makes clear that the DP Regulation does not apply to the processing of personal data

- falling outside the scope of EU law, in particular national security;
- by the EU institutions, bodies, offices and agencies;
- by the Member States when carrying out activities within the scope of Chapter 2 of the Treaty on European Union (TEU);
- by a natural person (without any gainful interest) in the course of their own exclusively personal or household activity;
- by competent authorities for the prevention, investigation, detection or prosecution of criminal offences or the execution of criminal penalties.

In addition, Article 3(3) states that the DP Regulation shall be without prejudice to the application of Directive 2000/31/EC, i.e. the eCommerce Directive,[22] in particular

---

21. art 2(1) *ibid*.
22. Directive 2000/31/EC of the European Parliament and of the Council of 8 June 2000 on certain legal aspects of information society services, in particular electronic commerce, in the Internal Market (Directive on eCommerce). Note also UNCITRAL Model Law on Electronic Commerce; "UNCITRAL Model Law on Electronic Commerce" (1999) 7 *Tulane Journal of International and Comparative Law* 237–250.

of the three limited liability rules of certain activities of website intermediary service providers (ISPs) in Articles 12 to 15 of that Directive.[23]

Article 3 relates to territorial scope. Article 3(1) states that the DP Regulation applies to the processing relating to the activities of an establishment of a data controller or a data processor in the EU. Further, Article 2(2) states that the DP Regulation applies to the processing of personal data of data subjects residing in the EU by a data controller not established in the EU, where the processing activities are related to: (a) offering goods or services to data subjects in the EU; or (b) the monitoring of their behaviour.

Article 3(3) states that the DP Regulation applies to the processing of personal data by a data controller not established in the EU, but in a place where a Member State's law applies by virtue of public international law.

DP Directive 95: Scope

Article 3 relates to scope. The DP Directive 95 applies to the processing of personal data wholly or partly by automatic means, and to the processing otherwise than by automatic means of personal data that form part of a filing system or are intended to form part of a filing system.[24]

However, the processing of personal data in the course of an activity that falls outside the scope of Community law, such as those provided for by titles V and VI of the Treaty on European Union, and processing in relation to public security, defence, State security and the areas of criminal law.[25] It also does not apply to a natural person in the course of a purely personal or household activity.[26]

DP Directive 95: Member State Laws

Article 4 relates to the national law applicable. Each Member State shall apply the national provisions pursuant to the Directive to the processing of personal data where:

- the processing is carried out in the context of the activities of an establishment of the data controller on the territory of the Member State. When the data controller is established on the territory of several Member States, it must ensure that each establishment complies with the obligations laid down by the Member State law applicable;

---

23.   art 12 relates to mere conduit; art 13 relates to caching; and art 14 relates to hosting.
24.   art 3(1) *ibid.*
25.   art 3(2) *ibid.*
26.   art 3(2) *ibid.*

- the data controller is not established on the Member State's territory, but in a place where its national law applies by virtue of international public law;

- the data controller is not established on Community territory and, for purposes of processing personal data makes use of equipment, automated or otherwise, situated on the territory of the said Member State, unless such equipment is used only for purposes of transit through the territory of the Community.[27]

Article 4(2) provides that the data controller must designate a representative established in the territory of that Member State.

Data Protection Principles (Data Quality Principles)

The *data protection principles* are also known as the data quality principles, as referred to in the DP Directive 95. Section I of the Directive relates to principles relating to data quality. Article 6(1) provides that Member States must provide that personal data must be:

- processed fairly and lawfully;

- collected for specified, explicit and legitimate purposes and not further processed in a way incompatible with those purposes. (Further processing for historical, statistical or scientific purposes shall not be considered as incompatible provided that there are appropriate safeguards);

- adequate, relevant and not excessive in relation to the purposes for which they are collected and/or further processed;

- accurate and, where necessary, kept up to date. Every reasonable step must be taken to ensure that data that are inaccurate or incomplete, having regard to the purposes for which they were collected or for which they are further processed, erased or rectified;

- kept in a form that permits identification of data subjects for no longer than is necessary for the purposes for which the data were collected or for which they are further processed. Member States shall lay down appropriate safeguards for personal data stored for longer periods for historical, statistical or scientific use.

Article 6(2) provides that it shall be for the data controller to ensure that the first point above is complied with.

Chapter II of the draft DP Regulation refers to the *data protection principles*. Article 5 relates to principles relating to personal data processing. Personal data must be:

---

27.   art 4(1) *ibid.*

- processed lawfully, fairly and in a transparent manner in relation to the data subject;

- collected for specified, explicit and legitimate purposes and not further processed in a manner incompatible with those purposes;

- adequate, relevant, and limited to the minimum necessary in relation to the purposes for which they are processed. The personal data shall only be processed if, and as long as, the purposes could not be fulfilled by processing information that does not involve personal data;

- accurate and kept up to date. Every reasonable step must be taken to ensure that personal data that are inaccurate, having regard to the purposes for which they are processed, are erased or rectified without delay;

- kept in a form that permits identification of data subjects for no longer than is necessary for the purposes for which the personal data are processed. (Personal data may be stored for longer periods if processed solely for historical, statistical or scientific research purposes in accordance with the conditions of Article 83 and if a periodic reviews occur to assess the necessity of continued storage);

- processed under the responsibility and liability of the data controller, which shall ensure and demonstrate for each processing operation, compliance with the Regulation.

Legitimate Data Processing Conditions

Section II of the DP Directive 95 refers to the criteria for making data processing legitimate. Member States shall provide that personal data may be processed *only if* –

- the data subject has unambiguously given their consent; or

- processing is necessary for the performance of a contract to which the data subject is party or in order to take steps at the request of the data subject prior to entering into such a contract; or

- processing is necessary for compliance with a legal obligation ofthe data controller; or

- processing is necessary to protect the vital interests of the data subject; or

- processing is necessary for a task carried out in the public interest or in the exercise of official authority of the data controller or a third party to whom the data are disclosed; or

- processing is necessary for the legitimate interests pursued by the data controller or by the third party to whom the data are disclosed, except where such interests are overridden by the interests for fundamental rights and freedoms of the data subject that require protection under Article 1(1).[28]

Article 6 of the DP Regulation refers to the lawfulness of processing. Article 6(1) provides that processing of personal data shall only be lawful if at least *one* of the following applies:

(a) the data subject has given consent to the processing of their personal data for one or more specific purposes;

(b) the processing is necessary for the performance of a contract to which the data subject is party or in order to take steps at the request of the data subject prior to entering into such a contract;

(c) the processing is necessary for compliance with a legal obligation of the data controller;

(d) the processing is necessary to protect the vital interests of the data subject;

(e) the processing is necessary for a task carried out in the public interest or in the exercise of official authority vested in the data controller;

(f) the processing is necessary for the purposes of the legitimate interests pursued by a data controller, except where overridden by the interests or fundamental rights and freedoms of the data subject that require protection of personal data, in particular where the data subject is a child. This shall not apply to processing carried out by public authorities performing their tasks.

Under Article 6(2) processing of personal data that is necessary for the purposes of historical, statistical or scientific research shall be lawful subject to the conditions and safeguards referred to in Article 83.

Article 6(3) states that the basis of the processing referred to in Article 6(1)(c) and (e) (above) must be provided for in EU law; or the law of the Member State to which the data controller is subject.

The law of the Member State must meet an objective of public interest or must be necessary to protect the rights and freedoms of others, respect the essence of the right to the protection of personal data and be proportionate to the legitimate aim pursued.[29]

According to Article 6(4), where the purpose of further processing is not compatible with the one for which the personal data have been collected, the processing must have a legal basis. At least one of the grounds referred to in Article 6(1)(a) to (e) must

---

28. art 7 *ibid.*
29. art 6(3) *ibid.*

apply. This shall apply, in particular, to *any* change of terms and general conditions of a contract.[30] This would also include contracts and terms such as privacy statements and privacy policies.

The Commission shall be empowered to adopt *delegated acts* in accordance with Article 86. This is to permit the Commission to further specify the conditions[31] for various sectors and data processing situations. This includes in relation to the processing of personal data relating to a child.[32]

DP Regulation: Consent Conditions

Article 7 of the DP Regulation relates to the conditions for consent. The data controller bears the burden of proof for obtaining and demonstrating the data subject's consent to the processing of their personal data for specified purposes.[33]

Under Article 7(2), if the data subject's consent is to be given by a written declaration but which also concerns another matter, the requirement to give consent must be presented and distinguishable in its appearance from the other matter.

The data subject shall have the right to withdraw his or her consent at any time (Article 7(3)). The withdrawal of consent shall not affect the lawfulness of processing based on consent before its withdrawal.

Consent shall not provide a legal basis for processing where there is a significant imbalance between the position of the data subject and that of the data controller.[34]

Conclusion

Privacy and data protection are evolving as technology changes how personal data is collected, used and processed. The current data protection legal regime is viewed as requiring updating. The DP Directive 95 was enacted in 1995, prior to social networking, cloud computing, mass data storage, data mining, electronic profiling, Web 2.0 and the threats to the security surrounding personal data. Data protection needs to evolve to deal with with these issues. This is partly the reason for the proposed EU DP Regulation.

This is important for the issues it addresses as well as the current legal provisions it will enhance. As a regulation, as opposed to a directive, it means that it is directly

---

30. art 6(4) *ibid.*
31. Referred to in point (f) of para 1 *ibid.*
32. art 6(5) *ibid.*
33. art 7(1) *ibid.*
34. art 7(4) *ibid.*

applicable in Ireland without the need for a directive or Member State implementing legislation.[35] The law and practice of Irish data protection will be changed as will many of the obligations of organisations. This will also differ more for organisations in particular sectors.

Areas that are being highlighted include better awareness and more hands-on board management responsibility; planning and data protection assessment in advance of product or service launch via the Privacy by Design (PbD) concept; and explicit recognition of children under the data protection regime for the first time.

---

35.   Data Protection Act 1988 and Data Protection (Amendment) Act 2003.

CHAPTER 4

Data Protection Principles

Introduction

All organisations that collect and process personal data must comply with the obligations of the Irish data protection regime. It is, therefore, important to be familiar with the data protection regime. This is set out in the Data Protection Act and Data Protection (Amendment) Act of 1988 and 2003, respectively.

The Data Protection Acts[1] provide details as to what constitutes fair processing and identifies the information that must be given to data subjects not only where the personal data is obtained directly from the data subjects but also if it is obtained indirectly. They also refer to the times at which this information needs to be given. These can serve as preconditions to lawful data processing of personal data.

Organisations cannot collect and process personal data unless they:

- comply with the registration requirements;

- comply with the data protection principles (also known as the data quality principles);

- ensure the processing is carried out in accordance with the legitimate processing conditions (and the sensitive personal data legitimate processing conditions in the case of sensitive personal data);

- provide specific information to data subjects in advance of the collection and processing of personal data, known as the Prior Information Requirements;

- comply with the security requirements.

---

1. Data Protection Act and Data Protection (Amendment) Act of 1988 and 2003.

Data Protection Principles (also known as Data Quality Principles)

Section 2(1) of the Data Protection Acts sets out the *data protection principles* (also known as the data quality principles). Personal data must be processed fairly and lawfully. In particular, personal data shall not be processed unless at least one of the conditions in s 2A is met, and in the case of sensitive personal data, at least one of the conditions in s 2B is also met.

Section 2A contains the general personal data *legitimate processing conditions*.

Section 2B contains the *sensitive personal data legitimate processing conditions*.

All organisations with personal data must comply with the following *data protection principles*. The *data protection principles* state that, namely:

- the data or, as the case may be, the information constituting the personal data, shall have been obtained, and the personal data shall be processed, fairly;

- the personal data shall be accurate and complete and, where necessary, kept up to date;

- the personal data shall be obtained only for one or more specified, explicit and legitimate purposes;

- the personal data shall not be further processed in a manner incompatible with that purpose or those purposes;

- the personal data shall be adequate, relevant and not excessive in relation to the purpose or purposes for which they are collected or are further processed;

- the personal data shall not be kept for longer than is necessary for that purpose or those purposes;

- appropriate security measures shall be taken against unauthorised access to, unauthorised alteration, disclosure or destruction of the data, in particular where the processing involves the transmission of data over a network, and against all other unlawful forms of processing.

Data controllers must also give a copy of personal data to any individual, upon request (known as a data access request).

Section 2(1) of the Data Protection Acts states that a "data controller shall, as respects personal data kept ... comply with" the *data protection principles*.

Data Protection Principles

All organisations with personal data must comply with the following data protection principles, namely:

- the data or, as the case may be, the information constituting the data shall have been obtained, and the data shall be processed, fairly;

- the data shall be accurate and complete and, where necessary, kept up to date;

- the data shall be obtained only for one or more specified, explicit and legitimate purposes;

- the data shall not be further processed in a manner incompatible with that purpose or those purposes;

- the data shall be adequate, relevant and not excessive in relation to the purpose or purposes for which they are collected or are further processed;

- the data shall not be kept for longer than is necessary for that purpose or those purposes;

- appropriate security measures shall be taken against unauthorised access to, or unauthorised alteration, disclosure or destruction of, the data, in particular where the processing involves the transmission of data over a network, and against all other unlawful forms of processing.

Summary of Data Protection Principles

Personal data must be:

(1) obtained and processed fairly;

(2) accurate, complete and kept up to date;

(3) obtained only for one specified, explicit and legitimate purpose;

(4) not further processed in a manner incompatible with that purpose;

(5) adequate, relevant and not excessive in relation to the purpose;

(6) kept for longer than is necessary for that purpose;

(7) protected by appropriate security measures.

Data controllers must also give a copy of personal data to any individual, on request (i.e. an access request).

Data Processor

Section 2(2) of the Data Protection Acts states that a "data processor shall, as respects personal data processed … comply with paragraph (d) of subsection (1) of this section" – i.e. the security principle. Section 21(1) of the Data Protection Acts states that "Personal data processed by a data processor shall not be disclosed by [it] or by an employee or agent of [it], without the prior authority of the data controller on behalf of whom the data are processed." If the data processor contravenes this obligation an offence is committed.[2]

---

2.   s 21(2) *ibid.*

CHAPTER 5

Processing Pre-Conditions: What Are the Prior Information Requirements?

Introduction

Even prior to obtaining and processing personal data, organisations are obliged to provide certain information to individual data subjects. This is in order that data subjects can be properly informed and can decide whether or not to consent to the proposed data processing. An individual may consent to processing for a given transaction, but may be less willing to consent if they are informed that their details may then be sold on to unknown third parties.

Data Protection Acts and Fair Processing

The Data Protection Acts[1] refers to fair processing and provide that personal data shall not be treated, for the purposes of s 2(1)(a) of the Acts (directly obtained), as processed fairly unless:

- in the case of data obtained from the data subject, the data controller ensures, so far as practicable, that the data subject has, is provided with, or has made readily available to him or her, at least the information specified for directly obtained data (ss (2));

- in any other case (i.e. indirectly obtained personal data), the data controller ensures, so far as practicable, that the data subject has, is provided with, or has made readily available to him or her, at least the separate information specified as being required (ss (3)):

    - not later than the time when the data controller first processes the data; or

    - if disclosure of the data to a third party is envisaged, not later than the time of such disclosure.[2]

---

1. Data Protection Act 1988 and Data Protection (Amendment) Act 2003.
2. s 2D(1) *ibid.*

Prior Information Requirements for Directly Obtained Data

The prior information referred to in s 2D(1)(a)(for directly obtained personal data) are:

- the identity of the data controller;

- if he or she has nominated a representative for the purposes of the Data Protection Acts, the identity of the representative;

- the purpose or purposes for which the personal data are intended to be processed; and

- any other information which is necessary, having regard to the specific circumstances, to enable processing to be fair to the data subject such as information as to the recipients or categories of recipients of the data, whether replies to questions asked at the data collection are obligatory, the possible consequences of failure to give such replies and the existence of the right of access to and the right to rectify the data concerning them.[3]

Article 10 of the DP Directive 95 provides for information in cases of collection of personal data from the individual data subject. It states that Member States shall provide that the data controller or its representative, must provide a data subject from whom personal data are collected with at least the following information, except where he or she already have it, namely:

- the identity of the data controller and its representative, if any;

- the purposes of the processing;

- any further information such as:

  - the recipients or categories of recipients of the data;

  - whether replies to the questions are obligatory or voluntary, as well as the possible consequences of failure to reply;

  - the existence of the right of access to and the right to rectify the data concerning them:

in so far as such further information is necessary, having regard to the specific circumstances in which the data are collected, to guarantee fair processing in respect of the data subject.

This corresponds with Data Protection Acts s 2D(1)(a).

---

3.   Data Protection Acts s 2D(2)(a)–(d).

Prior Information Requirements for Indirectly Obtained Data

The information requirements referred to in s 2D(1)(b) are:

- the same information specified above;
- the categories of data concerned; and
- the name of the original data controller.[4]

However, subsection 2D(1)(b) does not apply

- where, in particular for processing for statistical, historical or scientific research purposes, the provision of the information proves impossible or would involve a disproportionate effort; or
- in any case where the processing is necessary for compliance with a legal obligation to which the data controller is subject other than an obligation imposed by contract,

if such conditions as may be specified in regulations made by the Minister after consultation with the Data Protection Commissioner are complied with.[5]

Article 11 of the DP Directive 95 provides and distinguishes information where the data have not been obtained from the individual data subject. In this case, where the personal data have not been obtained from the data subject, Member States shall provide that the data controller or his or her representative must at the time of obtaining personal data or if a disclosure to a third party is envisaged, no later than the time when the data are first disclosed, provide the data subject with at least the following information, except where he or she already have it, namely:

- the identity of the data controller and of his or her representative, if any;
- the purposes of the processing;
- any further information such as:
  - the categories of data concerned;
  - the recipients or categories of recipients;
  - the existence of the right of access to and the right to rectify the data concerning him or her.

in so far as such further information is necessary, having regard to the specific circumstances in which the data are processed, to guarantee fair processing in respect of the data subject (Article 11(1)).

---

4.   Data Protection Acts s 2D(3).
5.   Data Protection Acts s 2D(4).

Article 11(2) of DP Directive 95 provides that Article 11(2) shall not apply where, for processing for statistical, historical or scientific research purposes, the provision of such information proves impossible or would involve a disproportionate effort or if recording or disclosure is expressly laid down by law. In these cases Member States shall provide appropriate safeguards.

This corresponds with Data Protection Acts s 2D(1)(b).

DP Regulation

The draft DP Regulation also refers to these obligations.

Prior Information Requirements

Article 14(1) of the DP Regulation relates to the prior information requirements. It provides that, where personal data relating to a data subject are collected, the data controller shall provide the data subject with at least the following information:

- the identity and the contact details of the data controller and, if any, of the data controller's representative and of the data protection officer;

- the purposes of the intended processing for the personal data, including the contract terms and general conditions where the processing is based on Article 6(1)(b) and the legitimate interests pursued by the data controller where the processing is based on Article 6(1)(f);

- the period the personal data will be stored;

- the existence of the access right, the rectification or erasure right, concerning the personal data and the right to object to the processing of such personal data;

- the right to lodge a complaint to the national supervisory authority and the contact details of the national supervisory authority;

- the recipients, or categories of recipients, of the personal data;

- where applicable, if the data controller intends to transfer to a third country or international organisation and the level of protection afforded by that third country or international organisation by reference to an adequacy decision by the Commission;

- any further information necessary to guarantee fair processing in respect of the data subject, having regard to the specific circumstances in which the personal data are collected and processed.

Obligatory or Voluntary Information

Where the personal data are collected from the data subject, the data controller shall, in addition to the prior information referred to above, inform and advise the data subject whether the provision of the personal data is obligatory or voluntary.[6] The data controller shall also advice of the possible consequences of failure to provide such data.[7]

Indirectly Obtained

Where the personal data are not collected from the data subject, the data controller shall inform the data subject, in addition to the information referred to in paragraph 1, from which source the personal data originate.[8]

Timing of Information

Article 14(4) provides that the data controller shall provide the prior information[9]:

- at the time when the personal data are obtained from the data subject; or

- where the personal data are not collected from the data subject, at the time of the recording or within a reasonable period after the collection, having regard to the specific circumstances in which the data are collected or otherwise processed, or, if a disclosure to another recipient is envisaged, and at the latest when the data are first disclosed.

Exception

Article 14(5) provides that Article 14(1) to (4) shall not apply, where:

- the personal data subject has already the information referred to in Article 14(1), (2) and (3); or

- the personal data are not collected from the data subject and the provision of such information proves impossible or would involve a disproportionate effort; or

- the personal data are not collected from the data subject and recording or disclosure is expressly laid down by law; or

- the personal data are not collected from the data subject and the provision of such information will impair the rights and freedoms of others, as defined in EU law or Member State law in accordance with Article 21.

6.　art 14(2).
7.　*ibid.*
8.　art 14(3).
9.　Referred to in paras 1, 2 and 3 *ibid.*

Protection

Article 14(6) provides that in the case referred to in Article 14(5)(b), the data controller shall provide appropriate measures to protect the data subject's legitimate interests.

Commission Measures

The Commission shall be empowered to adopt *delegated acts* in accordance with Article 86 for the purpose of further specifying the criteria for categories of recipients, the requirements for the notice of potential access, the criteria for the further information necessary for specific sectors and situations, and the conditions and appropriate safeguards for the exceptions.[10] In doing so, the Commission shall take the appropriate measures for micro, small and medium-sized enterprises (SMEs).[11]

Furthermore, the Commission may lay down standard forms for providing the information, taking into account the specific characteristics and needs of various industry sectors and data processing situations where necessary.[12] Those implementing acts shall be adopted in accordance with the examination procedure referred to in Article 87(2).[13]

Conclusion

Unless the prior information conditions are complied with, there may remain a question as to the fairness and legality of the personal data collection and processing. These issues may not be able to be rectified retrospectively. Compliance from the date of initial collection, and even in advance of such collection, is required by organisations.

---

10. art 14(7) *ibid.*
11. *ibid.*
12. art 14(8) *ibid.*
13. *ibid.*

CHAPTER 6

Legitimate Processing Conditions

Introduction

Companies and organisations, in order to function, generally collect and maintain data on a variety of individual data subjects, be they employees, customers, prospective customers, etc. However, organisations must not mislead individual data subjects when obtaining and processing personal data and must also provide a number prior information requirements to the individual data subjects.[1] Without these, it could be deemed that there is unfair obtaining and processing. For example, an organisation may have obtained consent for processing and has informed individuals that their personal data will only be used in relation to activity A. However, if it really uses the personal data in relation to activities A, B, C and D, it will not be fair obtaining and processing in accordance with the *data protection principles*. The *data protection principles* will have been breached, in particular the first principle. The organisation has not fairly informed data subjects and has not obtained fair and informed consent.

In addition to the *data protection principles*, organisations must satisfy and meet one of the *legitimate processing conditions*.[2] These are divided into ordinary or general personal data and sensitive personal data.

General Legitimate Processing Conditions

The *legitimate processing conditions* are required to be complied with, *in addition* to the *data protection principles*. Section 2A of the Data Protection Acts contains the general or ordinary personal data *legitimate processing conditions*. In order to collect and process personal data, in addition to complying with the *data protection principles*, organisations must comply or fall within *one* of the following general or ordinary personal data *legitimate processing conditions*.

Section 2A of the Data Protection Acts contains conditions relevant for the purposes of the first data protection principle, in particular the processing of personal data. It states that personal data shall not be processed by a data controller unless s 2 of the

---

1.   See Section 2D, Data Protection Act 1988 and Data Protection (Amendment) Act 2003.
2.   See s 2A Data Protection Act 1988 and Data Protection (Amendment) Act 2003.

Act (as amended by the Act of 2003) is complied with by the data controller and at least *one* of the following conditions is met:

- the data subject has given his or her consent to the processing or, if the data subject, by reason of his or her physical or mental incapacity or age, is or is likely to be unable to appreciate the nature and effect of such consent, it is given by a parent or guardian or a grandparent, uncle, aunt, brother or sister of the data subject and the giving of such consent is not prohibited by law;

- the processing is necessary:

    - for the performance of a contract to which the data subject is a party;

    - in order to take steps at the request of the data subject prior to entering into a contract;

    - for compliance with a legal obligation to which the data controller is subject other than an obligation imposed by contract; or

    - to prevent:

        (I) injury or other damage to the health of the data subject; or

        (II) serious loss of or damage to property of the data subject, or otherwise to protect his or her vital interests where the seeking of the consent of the data subject or another person referred to in paragraph (a) of this subsection is likely to result in those interests being damaged.

- the processing is necessary:

    - for the administration of justice;

    - for the performance of a function conferred on a person by or under a legal enactment;

    - for the performance of a function of the Government or a Minister of Government; or

    - for the performance of any other function of a public nature performed in the public interest by a person;

- the processing is necessary for the purposes of the legitimate interests pursued by the data controller or by a third party or parties to whom the data are disclosed, except where the processing is unwarranted in any particular case by reason of prejudice to the fundamental rights and freedoms or legitimate interests of the data subject (2A(1)(d)).[3]

---

3.   s 2A (1) *ibid.*

The Minister may, after consultation with the Data Protection Commissioner, by legal regulations specify particular circumstances in which s 2A(1)(d) is, or is not, satisfied.[4]

These are the general personal data *legitimate processing conditions*. They might be summarised as follows:

- the data subject has given consent;

- the processing is necessary for the performance of a contract or in order to to take steps at the request of the data subject prior to entering into a contract;

- the processing meets compliance with a legal obligation;

- the processing is necessary to prevent injury or other damage to the health of a data subject; or serious loss of or damage to property of a data subject; or otherwise to protect his or her vital interests;

- the processing is necessary for the administration of justice;

- the processing is necessary under an enactment;

- the processing serves an official function; or

- the processing is necessary for the purposes of the legitimate interests pursued by the data controller or by a third party or parties to whom the data are disclosed, unless unwarranted by reason of prejudice to the fundamental rights and freedoms or legitimate interests of the data subject.

Sensitive Personal Data Legitimate Processing Conditions

In the case of sensitive personal data, an organisation must, *in addition* to complying with the *data protection principles*, be able to comply or fall within one of the *sensitive personal data legitimate processing conditions*.

The Data Protection Acts set out conditions relevant for the purposes of the processing of sensitive personal data. It states that sensitive personal data shall not be processed by a data controller unless:

- sections 2 (collection, processing, keeping, use and disclosure of personal data) and 2A (processing of personal data) are complied with; and

- in addition, at least one of the following conditions is met.

---

4.   *ibid.*

The conditions are:

- the consent (referred to in s 2A(1)(a) of the Data Protection Acts) is explicitly given;

- the processing is necessary for the purpose of exercising or performing any right or obligation which is conferred or imposed by law on the data controller in connection with employment;

- the processing is necessary to prevent injury or other damage to the health of the data subject or another person or serious loss in respect of, or damage to, property or to protect the vital interests of the data subject or another person where:

    - consent to the processing cannot be given by or on behalf of the data subject in accordance with s 2A(1)(a) of the Data Protection Acts; or

    - the data controller cannot reasonably be expected to obtain such consent,

or the processing is necessary to prevent injury to, or damage to the health of, another person, or serious loss in respect of, or damage to, the property of another person, in a case where such consent has been unreasonably withheld;

- the processing:

    - is carried out in the course of its legitimate activities by any body corporate, or any unincorporated body of persons, that:

        - (A) is not established, and whose activities are not carried on, for profit; and

        - (B) exists for political, philosophical, religious or trade union purposes;

    - is carried out with appropriate safeguards for the fundamental rights and freedoms of data subjects;

    - relates only to individuals who either are members of the body or have regular contact with it in connection with its purposes; and

    - does not involve disclosure of the data to a third party without the consent of the data subject;

- the information contained in the data has been made public as a result of steps deliberately taken by the data subject;

- the processing is necessary:

- for the administration of justice;
- for the performance of a function conferred on a person by or under an enactment; or
- for the performance of a function of the Government or a Minister of the Government;

- the processing:
  - is required for the purpose of obtaining legal advice or for the purposes of, or in connection with, legal proceedings or prospective legal proceedings; or
  - is otherwise necessary for the purposes of establishing, exercising or defending legal rights;

- the processing is necessary for medical purposes and is undertaken by:
  - a health professional; or
  - a person who in the circumstances owes a duty of confidentiality to the data subject that is equivalent to that which would exist if that person were a health professional;

- the processing is necessary in order to obtain information for use, subject to and in accordance with the Statistics Act 1993, only for statistical, compilation and analysis purposes;

- the processing is carried out by political parties, or candidates for election to, or holders of, elective political office, in the course of electoral activities for the purpose of compiling data on people's political opinions and complies with such requirements (if any) as may be prescribed for the purpose of safeguarding the fundamental rights and freedoms of data subjects;

- the processing is authorised by regulations that are made by the Minister and are made for reasons of substantial public interest;

- the processing is necessary for the purpose of the assessment, collection or payment of any tax, duty, levy or other moneys owed or payable to the State and the data has been provided by the data subject solely for that purpose;

- the processing is necessary for the purposes of determining entitlement to or control of, or any other purpose connected with the administration of any benefit, pension, assistance, allowance, supplement or payment under the Social Welfare (Consolidation) Act 1993, or any non-statutory scheme administered by the Minister for Social, Community and Family Affairs.[5]

---

5.   s 2B(1) *ibid.*

These *sensitive personal data legitimate processing conditions* may be summarised as follows:

- explicit consent is given;
- the processing is necessary for a legal obligation;
- the processing is necessary to protect the vital interests of the data subject;
- the processing is for a not for profit organisation, with appropriate safeguards;
- the information is made public by the data subject;
- the processing serves the administration of justice;
- the processing serves a legal function;
- the processing serves a government function;
- the processing is part of legal advice or establishing, exercising or defending legal rights;
- the processing serves medical purposes;
- the processing is in accordance with the Statistics Act 1993;
- the processing is for political parties or electoral activities;
- the processing is authorised by the Minister for substantial public interest;
- the processing serves tax purposes; or
- the processing is used to determine official benefits, pensions, and similar activities.

CHAPTER 7

Exemptions

Introduction

In considering compliance obligations it is also important to consider the exemptions that may apply.

Article 13 of the DP Directive 95,[1] under the heading of *Exemptions and Restrictions*, provides that Member States may adopt legislative measures to restrict the scope of the obligations and rights[2] when such a restriction constitutes necessary measures to safeguard:

(a) national security;

(b) defence;

(c) public security;

(d) the prevention, investigation, detection and prosecution of criminal offences, or of breaches of ethics for regulated professions;

(e) an important economic or financial interest of a Member State or of the EU, including monetary, budgetary and taxation matters;

(f) a monitoring, inspection or regulatory function connected with the exercise of official authority in cases referred to in (c), (d) and (e) above;

(g) the protection of the data subject or of the rights and freedoms of others.

In the context of the Data Protection Acts,[3] these include exemptions particular to the following:

- defence/security;
- offences, crime and taxation;

---

1. EU Data Protection Directive 1995 (Directive 95/46/EC of the European Parliament and of the Council of 24 October 1995 on the protection of individuals with regard to the processing of personal data and on the free movement of such data).
2. Provided for in arts 6(1), 10, 11(1), 12 and 21 *ibid.*
3. Data Protection Act 1988 and Data Protection (Amendment) Act 2003.

- back up data;
- statistics or research;
- legal obligation/legal requirements;
- prison, security and discipline;
- financial loss;
- international relations;
- quantum of claims;
- legal professional privilege;
- functions of the Data Protection Commissioner;
- injury, health or property damage;
- legal advice or proceedings;
- data subject request;
- health;
- social work;
- adoption register records;
- Ombudsman records;
- journalism, literature and art;
- historical research and archives.[4]

These are referred to in greater detail below.

Defence/Security

The Data Protection Acts do not apply to personal data that, in the opinion of the Minister or the Minister for Defence are, or at any time were, kept for the purpose of safeguarding the security of the State. This is set out in s 1(4). Essentially, this is limited to the Gardaí and the defence forces.

In addition, any restriction on processing in the Data Protection Acts does not apply if the disclosure is, in the opinion of a member of the Garda Síochána (not below chief superintendent) or an officer of the Permanent Defence Force (not below colonel), and is designated by the Minister for Defence, required for the purpose of safeguarding the security of the State. This is set out in s 8(a) the Data Protection Acts.[5]

---

4. *ibid.*
5. *ibid.*

Offences, Crime and Taxation

Any restrictions in the Data Protection Acts on the disclosure of personal data do not apply if the disclosure is required for the purpose of preventing, detecting or investigating offences, apprehending or prosecuting offenders or assessing or collecting any tax, duty or other moneys owed or payable to the State, a local authority or a health board, in any case in which the application of those restrictions would be likely to prejudice any of the matters above. This is set out in s 8(b) the Data Protection Acts.

Back Up Data

Section 4 of the Data Protection Acts, relating to right of access, does not apply to personal data "that are back up data". This is provided in s 5(1)(i). Back up data is defined in s 1 to mean data kept only for the purpose of replacing other data in the event of their being lost, destroyed or damaged.

Statistics or Research

Section 2(1)(c) subsections (ii) (data not processed further in a manner incompatible with purpose) and (iv) (data kept no longer than necessary) of the Data Protection Acts[6] do not apply to personal data kept for statistical or research or other scientific purposes. Such data and the keeping of such data must comply with such requirements (if any) as may be prescribed for the purpose of safeguarding the fundamental rights and freedoms of data subjects. The data or, as the case may be, the information constituting such data, shall not be regarded for the purposes of paragraph (a) of the said subsection as having been obtained unfairly by reason only that its use for any such purpose was not disclosed when it was obtained, if the data are not used in such a way that damage or distress is, or is likely to be, caused to any data subject. This exemption is contained in s 2(5) the Data Protection Acts.

Section 2D(1)(b) the Data Protection Acts relates to fair processing and provides that it shall not be fair processing unless the organisation ensures that the data subject is provided with the prior information requirements (s 2D(2)). However, this shall not apply where the processing of personal data is necessary for compliance with a legal obligation to which the organisation is subject other than an obligation imposed by contract.[7]

Section 4 of the Data Protection Acts relates to the right of access. However, it shall not apply to personal data kept only for the purpose of preparing statistics or carrying out research. The personal data must not be used or disclosed (other than to a person

---

6.   *ibid.*

7.   This is set out in s 2D(4)(a) Data Protection Act 1988 and Data Protection (Amendment) Act 2003.

to whom a disclosure of such personal data may be made in the circumstances specified in s 8) for any other purpose. Also, the resulting statistics or results must not be made available in a form which identifies the data subjects.[8]

Legal Obligation/Legal Requirements

The provision that there is no fair processing unless the organisation ensures that the data subject has the prior information specified in s 2D(1)(b) the Data Protection Acts does not apply:

- where, in particular for processing for statistical purposes or for the purposes of historical or scientific research, the provision of the information specified proves impossible or would involve a disproportionate effort, or

- in any case where the processing of the information contained or to be contained in the personal data by the data controller is necessary for compliance with a legal obligation of the data controller is subject, other than an obligation imposed by contract,

if such conditions as may be specified in regulations made by the Minister after consultation with the Data Protection Commissioner are complied with.[9]

Any restrictions in the Data Protection Acts on processing do not apply if the processing is required by or under any enactment or by a rule of law or order of a court.[10]

Prison Security and Discipline

Section 4 (the right of access) the Data Protection Acts shall not apply in any case in which the application of that section would be likely to prejudice the security of, or maintenance of good order and discipline in the following:

- a prison;

- a place of detention under s 2 of the Prisons Act 1970;

- a military prison under the Defence Act 1954; or

- Saint Patrick's Institution.[11]

---

8.   This is contained in s 5(1)(h) *ibid.*
9.   This is set out in s 2D(4)(b) *ibid.*
10. This is set out in s 8(e) *ibid.*
11. This is contained in s 5(c) *ibid.*

Financial Loss

If the Minister makes regulations to protect the public from financial loss in relation to banking, insurance, investment and financial services, there is an exemption from s 4 (the right of access) the Data Protection Acts.[12]

International Relations

Any restriction on processing in the Data Protection Acts does not apply if the processing is required in the interests of protecting the international relation of the State.[13]

Quantum of Claims

There is also an exemption from the s 4 right of access provisions in relation to estimating the amount of liability of the data controller under a claim.[14]

Legal Professional Privilege

The right of access in s 4 does not apply in respect of legal privilege in a legal case between a client and his or her legal advisers. This is set out in s 5(g) of the Data Protection Acts. It refers to "proceedings" and so may not extend to contemplated proceedings or legal privilege other than in relation to active proceedings. While it refers to "legal advisers", it would not be safe to assume that this automatically encompasses in-house legal advisers.

Functions of the Data Protection Commissioner

The right of access in s 4 does not apply in respect of the Data Protection Commissioner undertaking his or her functions.[15]

Injury, Health or Property Damage

Any restriction on processing in the Data Protection Acts does not apply if the processing is required urgently to prevent injury or other damage to the health of a person or serious loss of or damage to property.[16]

---

12. This is provided for in s 5(1)(d) *ibid.*
13. This is set out in s 8(c) *ibid.*
14. This is provided for in s 5(1)(f) *ibid.*
15. This is contained in s 5(gg) *ibid.*
16. This is set out in s 8(d) *ibid.*

Legal Advice or Proceedings

Any restriction on processing in the Data Protection Acts does not apply if the processing is required for the purposes of obtaining legal advice or for the purposes of, or in the course of, legal proceedings in which the person making the processing is a party or a witness.[17]

Data Subject Request

Any restriction on processing in the Data Protection Acts does not apply if the processing is made at the request or with the consent of the data subject or a person acting on his or her behalf.[18]

Health

The Data Protection (Access Modification)(Health) Regulations 1989[19] are introduced under the Data Protection Acts. An exemption is created whereby data access requests may not have to be complied with, at least partially, where personal data relates to the data subject's physical or mental state or condition but its release would likely cause serious harm to the data subject's physical or mental state or condition, or that of someone else.

The decision must be made by, or in consultation with, the "appropriate health professional", which is defined as:

- the registered medical practitioner, within the Medical Practitioners Act 1978,[20] or registered dentist, within the Dentists Act 1985,[21] currently or most recently responsible for the clinical care of the data subject in connection with the matters to which the data, the subject of the request, relates;

- where there is more than one such person, the person who is the most suitable to advise on those matters;

- a health professional who has the necessary experience and qualifications to advise on those matters.[22]

---

17. This is set out in s 8(f) *ibid.*
18. This is set out in s 8(h) *ibid.*
19. SI 82/1989.
20. SI 4/1978.
21. SI 9/1985.
22. Regulation 2, Data Protection (Access Modification)(Health) Regulations 1989 (SI 82/1989).

Social Work

The Data Protection (Access Modification)(Social Work) Regulations 1989[23] are made pursuant to the Data Protection Acts. They relate to personal data described as "social work data", meaning personal data kept or obtained in the course of carrying out social work by a Minister, local authority, health board, or voluntary organisation or other body that carries out social work and is funded by such minister, authority or board.[24]

Social work data shall not be supplied by a data controller to the data subject concerned in response to a data access request (s 4(1)(a) of the Data Protection Acts), if it would be likely to cause serious harm to the physical or mental health or emotional condition of the data subject.[25]

Section 4(4) of the Data Protection Acts shall not apply in relation to social work data other than the data controller or data subject if that individual is engaged in carrying out social work and the data relate to him or her in that capacity.[26]

The courts may also be called upon to intervene. Regulation 6 provides that the Regulation is without prejudice to the power of a court to withhold from a data subject, social work data kept by it and constituting information provided in a report supplied to it in any proceedings.[27]

Adoption Register Records

The Adoption Act 1952 prevents the disclosure of certain register details in relation to adoptions in Ireland.[28] The Data Protection (Restriction of s 4) Regulations 1989[29] also adopts this policy by amending or exempting from the access right provisions in the Data Protection Acts. Regulation 3 provides that the prohibition and restrictions on the disclosure, and the authorisations of the withholding, shall prevail in the interests of the data subjects concerned and any other individuals concerned.[30]

---

23. SI 83/1989.
24. Regulation 3, Data Protection (Access Modification)(Social Work) Regulations 1989 (SI 83/1989).
25. Regulation 4(1), *ibid.*
26. Regulation 5, *ibid.*
27. Regulation 6, *ibid.* Note also "surrogacy" case, High Court, Abbot J, January 2013.
28. s 22(5) of the Adoption Act 1952 provides as follows "An tArd-Chláraitheoir shall keep an index to make traceable the connexion between each entry and the corresponding entry in the register of births. That index shall not be open to public inspection; and no information from it shall be given to any person except by order of a Court or of the Board."
29. SI 81/1989.
30. Regulation 3, Data Protection (Restriction of Section 4) Regulations 1989 (SI 81/1989).

Ombudsman Records

The Ombudsman Act 1980 also provides restrictions on disclosures. Section 9(1) of that Act provides that information or documents obtained by the Ombudsman in the course of a preliminary examination, or investigation, under the Act shall not be disclosed except for:

- the examination or investigation of a statement, report or notification to be made under the Ombudsman Act, or

- any proceedings for an offence under the Official Secrets Act 1963, alleged to have been committed in respect of information or a document obtained by the Ombudsman by virtue of the Ombudsman Act,

and the Ombudsman shall not be called upon to give evidence in any proceedings (other than such proceedings as aforesaid) of matters coming to their knowledge in the course of a preliminary examination, or an investigation, under the Ombudsman Act.

Journalism, Literature and Art

Journalists and media organisations regularly collect and process personal data. This may also include *sensitive personal data*. As regards the data protection regime, there are exemptions for journalistic purposes processing. However, these are limited, and only provide exemptions from certain sections of the Data Protection Acts. In addition, specific criteria must be adhered to in order to come within the exemption. The exemption is also limited in relation to the organisations that may avail of the exemption.

Personal data that are processed only for journalistic, artistic or literary purposes shall be exempt from compliance with any provision of the Data Protection Acts specified in s 22A(2)[31] if:

- the processing is undertaken solely with a view to the publication of any journalistic, literary or artistic material;

- the data controller reasonably believes that, having regard in particular to the special importance of the public interest in freedom of expression, such publication would be in the public interest; and

- the data controller reasonably believes that, in all the circumstances, compliance with that provision would be incompatible with journalistic, artistic or literary purposes.[32]

---

31. Headed journalism, literature and art.
32. s 22A(1)(a)–(c), Data Protection Act 1988 and Data Protection (Amendment) Act 2003.

The Leveson Inquiry[33] report in the UK recommends that the equivalent provision in the UK is overbroad and should be amended accordingly.[34] It appears that this recommendation has been accepted at a political level. At the time of writing, the exact amendment wordings have not yet been made available.

The provisions of the Data Protection Acts from which compliance are exempted in relation to journalism are:

- s 2, other than s 2(1)(d);
- ss 2A, 2B and 2D;
- s 3;
- ss 4 and 6; and
- ss 6A and 6B.[35]

In considering for the purposes of s 22(1)(b) whether publication of the material concerned would be in the public interest, regard may be had to any code of practice approved under s 13(1) or (2) of the Data Protection Acts.

"Publication" in relation to journalistic, artistic or literary material is defined as the act of making the material available to the public, or any section of the public, in any form or by any means.[36]

The Data Protection Commissioner also provides guidance on this issue in *Case Study 6 of 2006*. This relates to complaints against the *News of the World* and *Sunday World* newspapers in relation to the taking of photographs and publishing a story using such images, which include images of children. It provides some guidance in relation to the limits of the media exemption. The Case Study states:

> Breaches of data protection rights of individuals by publication of material in the media … remain[s] an issue … I made two separate decisions … that newspapers had breached their obligations under the Data Protection Acts. One such case involved the *Sunday World*. The other, described below, involved the Irish edition of the *News of the World*. Both cases involved the publication of information about children of well-known individuals.
>
> I received a complaint on behalf of a data subject, a well-known individual, arising from material published in the *News of the World* (Irish edition) … The complaint related to the subject matter of the material published and the manner in which it was

---

33. Available at http://www.levesoninquiry.org.uk/.
34. Leveson Inquiry report, *An Inquiry into the Culture, Practices and Ethics of the Press: Report [Leveson] Volume 4*, Part H, available at http://www.official-documents.gov.uk/document/hc1213/hc07/0780/0780_iv.pdf.
35. s 22A(2) *ibid.*
36. s 22A(4) *ibid.*

obtained. The material published consisted of a photograph of the data subject and child while shopping, together with related text expressly identifying the data subject's child by name and age, and referring to a third party's perception as to how parent and child were getting along. The complainant alleged that consent was neither sought nor obtained prior to the taking of the photograph. The complainant further alleged that consent was not sought nor obtained prior to the publication of the material subsequently in the *News of the World* newspaper. In particular, the complainant alleged that the publication contravened Sections 2(1), 2A(1) and 22 of the Data Protection Acts. The complainant considered that their right to privacy outweighed any purported journalistic purpose or public interest in the publication of their photograph and accompanying text which was the subject of the complaint.

My Office commenced an investigation and wrote to the data controller, *News of the World* (Ireland). We sought its observations on the alleged contravention of the Acts, in particular in relation to the journalistic exemption contained in Section 22A. This Section provides a "public interest" exemption in respect of the processing of personal data for journalistic purposes. In response the newspaper highlighted that the data subject was a well-known personality who had been the subject of extensive media attention. It claimed that the data subject had, in the past, courted such attention. Given this background, it concluded that there was a public interest in revealing information about the data subject and the parent–child relationship, as illustrated by the photograph and accompanying text. It stated that the information revealed did not constitute sensitive personal data and that, therefore, the conclusion reached by the UK Courts in the case of *Naomi Campbell v MGN Limited* – cited as the only authority to date dealing with this particular issue – was not relevant to the present case. It concluded that, in the circumstances, 'the article amounted to a publication of journalistic material in the public interest ... that ... fall(s) squarely within the exemption provided by Section 22A of the 1988 and 2003 Acts.'[37]

The Data Protection Commissioner then commences the following analysis:

The primary issue to be decided in this case was whether the public interest exemption under section 22A of the Acts in respect of processing of personal data for journalistic etc. purposes applied in respect of the publication of the photograph and text relating to the data subject and child. If the public interest in publication exemption applied, then there would be no breach of the provisions of the Data Protection Acts in this case.

I am obliged by Section 3 of the European Convention on Human Rights Act, 2003, to perform my functions in a manner compatible with the State's obligations under the Convention's provisions. Accordingly, in arriving at my conclusion on the applicability of the Section 22A exemption to the facts of the case, I had regard to the provisions of Articles 8 and 10 of the European Convention on Human Rights and any

---

37. Case Study 6 of 2006, Data Protection Commissioner, available at http://www.dataprotection. ie/ViewDoc.asp?DocId=-1&CatID=81&m=c, last accessed 11 January 2013.

guidance that the European Court of Human Rights (ECtHR) had provided on how the rights to privacy and freedom of expression should be balanced – the same balance that was at issue in relation to the applicability of Section 22A of the Acts.

In this regard, I noted the Decision of the ECtHR in the case of *Von Hannover v Germany* (Application No 59320/00) – the Princess Caroline case. The Court held that the German courts, in refusing to grant Princess Caroline of Monaco injunctions against newspapers taking and publishing photographs of her, had infringed her rights under Article 8 of the Convention. The photographs in question had shown Princess Caroline engaged in various activities such as shopping, playing sport and at the beach. The Court, noting that the material related exclusively to details of the applicant's private life, considered that "the publication of the photos and articles in question, of which the sole purpose was to satisfy the curiosity of a particular readership regarding the details of the applicant's private life, cannot be deemed to contribute to any debate of general interest to society despite the applicant being known to the public". In that case, the Court considered that "anyone, even if they are known to the general public, must be able to enjoy a 'legitimate expectation' of protection and of respect for their private life".

While data protection law is not specifically dealt with in the *Von Hannover* Decision, this case was of assistance in helping me to come to a decision as to the appropriate balance between the public interest in freedom of expression and the individual's right to protection of their personal data, as required by Section 22A of the Acts.

Section 22A(3) of the Acts provides that, in evaluating whether a publication would be in the public interest, regard may be had to codes of practice approved by the Data Protection Commissioner pursuant to the Acts. While no such code has been approved, it seemed appropriate, in reaching a determination, to take note of the newspapers' own codes of practice. In making my assessment, I therefore took account of the National Newspapers of Ireland Code of Practice. In relation to children, the Code provides that they should not be identified unless there is a clear public interest in doing so. Relevant factors are identified as the age of the child, whether there is parental permission, and whether there are circumstances that make the story one of public interest, 'or, if the person is a public figure or child of a public figure, whether or how the matter relates to his [or] her public person or office.' I also noted that the UK Press Complaints Commission Code of Practice provides that editors must not use the fame of a parent as sole justification for publishing details of a child's private life and that "in cases involving children under 16, editors must demonstrate an exceptional public interest to over-ride the normally paramount interest of the child". I was of the view that these provisions represent a fair expression of how the principles of data protection legislation ought to be applied in relation to children and minors.

In coming to my decision, I also noted the allegation, which was not refuted by the data controller, that the photograph was taken without the consent of the data subject. I issued a Decision on this case under Section 10(1)(b)(ii) of the Acts. Among other things, I found that it did not appear to me that the public interest claimed by the data controller in publication of the material in question could be such as to justify setting aside the right to respect for a person's private and family life.

I was of the view that the publication of the photograph and text relating to the data subject and child, and the manner of their interaction, could not be justified in terms of the public interest under section 22A. I considered that the material published breached the entitlements of a child to interact with its parent in a normal way without their relationship being made the subject of public comment through publication in a newspaper.

Having therefore concluded that the journalistic exemptions under section 22A did not apply in this case, I considered whether the processing of personal data involved in the obtaining and publication of the material complied with the other provisions of the Acts, especially sections 2 and 2A thereof. On the basis of my examination, my decision was that the personal data relating to the data subject and child was not obtained or processed fairly, as required under section 2(1)(a) and 2A of the Acts.

This case demonstrates that data protection applies even in relation to the publication of material in the media. However, in such cases, the issue to be considered in the first instance is whether a general public interest could be deemed to apply to the publication of the material. If it does then the general requirements of data protection are set aside. However, if no public interest could legitimately be claimed, then the media must have due regard to their data protection obligations.[38]

In the UK, the case of *Douglas v Hello!* magazine also held that in that instance the journalistic exemption did not apply.[39] In addition, the author JK Rowling was able to obtain protection from intrusive photographers who were taking photographs of her with her children, who were not celebrities, in a public setting. The case involved newspapers and a news photography agency.[40]

Historical Research and Archives

Sections 2, 2A and 2B of the Data Protection Acts do not apply to:

- data kept solely for the purpose of historical research; or
- other data consisting of archives or departmental records (within the meaning, in each case, of the National Archives Act 1986),

---

38. Case Study 6 of 2006, Data Protection Commissioner, available at http://www.dataprotection. ie/ViewDoc.asp?DocId=-1&CatID=81&m=c, last accessed 11 January 2013.

39. *Douglas v Hello!* [2003] EMLR 31; [2003] 2 AER 996; [2003] EWHC 786 (Ch).

40. *Murray v Big Pictures (UK) Ltd* [2008] EWCA Civ 446 (7 May 2008), [2008] 2 FLR 599, [2008] 3 FCR 661, [2008] 3 WLR 1360, [2008] ECDR 12, [2008] EMLR 12, [2008] EWCA Civ 446, [2008] Fam Law 732, [2008] HRLR 33, [2008] UKHRR 736, [2009] Ch 481; from England and Wales Court of Appeal (Civil Division) Decisions.

and the keeping of which complies with such requirements (if any) as may be prescribed for the purpose of safeguarding the fundamental rights and freedoms of data subjects. This is provided for in s 1(3C) the Data Protection Acts.

Conclusion

The exemptions are important, when and where applicable. They will often be more relevant to particular sectors. Generally, the exemptions appear to be less litigated than other areas of data protection. The journalistic exemptions will come into focus once the specific amendments are published in the UK on foot of the Leveson report.

CHAPTER 8

Individual Data Subject Rights

Introduction

The data protection regime provides, or enshrines, a number of rights for individuals in relation to their informational privacy and data protection. These are important because organisations must respect these rights. They are also important because the individuals themselves can enforce their rights where, for example, they feel an organisation is abusing their rights and obligations. Some of these rights also apply regardless of any suspicion of a breach by an organisation.

Overview

Court and civil tortious remedies are available to data subjects; in addition to enforcing compliance with the prior information requirements, *data protection principles, legitimate processing conditions* and security requirements, the Data Protection Acts[1] contain a number of further important rights for individuals in respect of their personal data. The data protection rights enshrined in the data protection regime for individuals are set out in the *data protection principles* and, in particular, in ss 3–6B of the Data Protection Acts. Some of these rights are listed below.

Individuals have a right to be informed by an organisation as to its identity and details when it is collecting and processing the individual's personal data.

The organisation must disclose to the individual the purpose for which it is collecting and processing the individual's personal data.

If the organisation is forwarding or transferring the personal data to third-party recipients, it must disclose this to the individual as well as identify the third-party recipients. If it is permitted to transfer the personal data outside of the county, the organisation must then also identity which third-party country will be receiving the personal data.

---

1.   Data Protection Act 1988 and Data Protection (Amendment) Act 2003.

Possibly the most important right relates to the right of data subjects to access or obtain a copy of their personal data as held by organisations. Organisations must answer and reply to requests from the individual in relation to their data protection rights. This includes requests for access to a copy of the personal data held in relation to the individual. This is known as a *personal data access request*. Every individual about whom a data controller keeps personal information has a number of other rights under the Data Protection Acts, in addition to the right of access.[2] These include the right to have any inaccurate information rectified or erased, and to have personal data taken off a direct marketing or direct mailing list.[3]

The individual data subject has a right to prevent processing likely to cause damage or distress. A further right relates to automated decision taking. Importantly, individual data subjects have specific rights in relation to rectification, blocking, erasure and destruction. This is being further calibrated as encompassing the expanded right to oblivion/right to be forgotten in the DP Regulation.[4]

Individual data subjects are also entitled to compensation, as well as being entitled to complain to the Data Protection Commissioner and to file actions in the courts to obtain judicial remedies. The DP Directive 95[5] notes that data protection laws must not result in any lessening of the protection but must, on the contrary, seek to ensure a high level of protection in the EU.[6]

What Are the Data Subject Rights?

The main data subject rights are summarised opposite.

The first three refer to compliance-type rights. The others refer to proactive rights exercisable directly by individual data subjects. These categories can interact with each other depending on individual circumstances. Some of the rights are also exercisable regardless of any wrongdoing or breach by the data controller.

---

2. See DPC, available at http://www.dataprotection.ie/ViewDoc.asp?fn=/documents/guidance/Guide_Data_Contollers.htm&CatID=90&m=y, last accessed 11 January 2013.
3. See DPC, available at http://www.dataprotection.ie/ViewDoc.asp?fn=/documents/guidance/Guide_Data_Contollers.htm&CatID=90&m=y, last accessed 11 January 2013.
4. EU draft Data Protection Regulation (Proposal for a Regulation of the European Parliament and of the Council on the protection of individuals with regard to the processing of personal data and on the free movement of such data (General Data Protection Regulation) COM (2012) 11 final).
5. EU Data Protection Directive 1995 (Directive 95/46/EC of the European Parliament and of the Council of 24 October 1995 on the protection of individuals with regard to the processing of personal data and on the free movement of such data).
6. Recital (10) *ibid.*

Data Subject Rights

The rights of data subjects can be summarised as including:

- that the prior information requirements are satisfied (s 2D of the Data Protection Acts);

- that the data protection principles and legitimate processing conditions are complied with, including fair processing;

- that adequate security requirements are complied with;

- the right to establish the existence of personal data (s 3 Data Protection Acts);

- the right of access to personal data (s 4 Data Protection Acts);

- the right to object to processing likely to cause damage or distress (s 6A Data Protection Acts);

- the right to prevent processing for direct marketing (s 2(7) Data Protection Acts);

- the right to not be subjected to automated decision-taking processes (s 6B Data Protection Acts); and

- the right of rectification, blocking and erasure (s 6 Data Protection Acts).

Who Are the Recipients of the Rights?

The data protection rights apply generally in relation to any individuals whose personal data are being collected and processed. Specifically, they can include:

- employees;
- other workers such as contractors, temps, casual staff;
- agency staff;
- ex-employees and retired employees;
- job applicants, including unsuccessful applicants;
- volunteers;
- apprentices and trainees;
- customers and clients;
- prospective customers and clients; and
- suppliers.[7]

---

7.   MacDonald, *Data Protection: Legal Compliance and Good Practice for Employers* (London: Tottel, 2008) p 41.

It can also include:

- Related family members to the above.

Proactive Rights

The main proactive rights for data subjects are referred to below.

Right to Establish Existence of Personal Data: Data Protection Acts

Data subjects have a right to establish the existence of personal data. Section 3 of the Data Protection Acts[8] provides that an individual who believes that an organisation keeps personal data shall, when requested in writing, have a right to:

- be informed by the organisation whether it keeps any such data; and
- if it does, to be given by the organisation a description of the data and the purposes for which the data are kept.

This must be given as soon as may be and in any event not more than 21 days after the request has been given or sent to it.[9]

Right of Access

One of the rights that individual data subjects have is a *right of access* to personal data. Sections 3–6B of the Data Protection Acts[10] refers to the rights of data subjects and others. In particular, s 4 refers to the right of access to personal data. This applies to data subjects. It is an individual data subject's right. Certain fees may be charged for obtaining copies of personal data held by an organisation. These are minimal, however. There are also time limits to be complied with by data controllers in relation to replying to a data subject access request. It is also important to note that certain rights, including the access right, can be invoked by individuals at any time and for any reason. They do not have to wait for an apparent breach by an organisation.

Access Right Under the DP Directive 95

Article 12 of the DP Directive 95 also provides for the right of access. It provides that Member States shall guarantee every data subject the right to obtain from the data controller without constraint at reasonable intervals and without excessive delay or expense:

---

8. Data Protection Act 1988 and Data Protection (Amendment) Act 2003.
9. s 3 *ibid.*
10. Data Protection Act 1988 and Data Protection (Amendment) Act 2003.

- confirmation as to whether or not data relating to him or her are being processed and information at least as to the purposes of the processing, the categories of data concerned, and the recipients or categories of recipients to whom the data are disclosed;

- communication to him or her in an intelligible form of the data undergoing processing and of any available information as to their source;

- knowledge of the logic involved in any automatic processing of data concerning him or her at least in the case of the automated decisions referred to in Article 15(1);

- as appropriate the rectification, erasure or blocking of data the processing of which does not comply with the provisions of the Directive, in particular because of the incomplete or inaccurate nature of the data (12(b)); and

- notification to third parties to whom the data have been disclosed of any rectification, erasure or blocking carried out in compliance with (b), unless this proves impossible or involves a disproportionate effort.

Access Right Under the DP Regulation

The access right is also referred to and continued under Article 15 of the DP Regulation. It refers to the right of access for individual data subjects and provides that the data subject shall have the right to obtain from the data controller at any time, on request, confirmation as to whether or not personal data relating to the data subject are being processed. Where such personal data are being processed, the data controller shall provide the following information:

- the purposes of the processing;

- the categories of personal data concerned;

- the recipients or categories of recipients to whom the personal data are to be or have been disclosed, in particular to recipients in third countries;

- the period for which the personal data will be stored;

- the existence of the right to request from the data controller rectification or erasure of personal data concerning the data subject or to object to the processing of such personal data;

- the right to lodge a complaint to the supervisory authority and the contact details of the supervisory authority;

- communication of the personal data undergoing processing and of any available information as to their source;[11] and

---

11. See art 15(1)(g) *ibid.*

- the significance and envisaged consequences of such processing, at least in the case of measures referred to in Article 20.[12]

The data subject shall have the right to obtain from the data controller communication of the personal data undergoing processing.[13] Where the data subject makes the request in electronic form, the information shall be provided in electronic form, unless otherwise requested by the data subject.[14]

The Commission shall be empowered to adopt delegated Acts[15] to further specify the criteria and requirements for the communication to the data subject of the content of the personal data referred to in Article 15(1)(g)(i.e. communication of the personal data undergoing processing and of any available information as to their source).[16]

The Commission may specify standard forms and procedures for requesting and granting access to the information,[17] including for verification of the identity of the data subject and communicating the personal data to the data subject, taking into account the specific features and necessities of various sectors and data processing situations.[18] Those implementing acts shall be adopted in accordance with the examination procedure referred to in Article 87(2).[19]

What Must be Supplied?

Section 4 of the Data Protection Acts[20] provides that an individual shall, if they so requests a data controller by notice in writing, be informed by the data controller whether the data processed by or on behalf of the data controller include personal data relating to the individual.

If the data subject requests, they must be supplied by the data controller with a description of:

- the categories of data being processed by or on behalf of the data controller;
- the personal data constituting the data of which that individual is the data subject;
- the purpose or purposes of the processing; and

---

12. art 15 *ibid.*
13. *ibid.*
14. *ibid.*
15. In accordance with art 86.
16. art 15.
17. Referred to in para 1.
18. art 15 *ibid.*
19. *ibid.*
20. Data Protection Act 1988 and Data Protection (Amendment) Act 2003.

- the recipients or categories of recipients to whom the data are or may be disclosed.[21]

Time Limits

The data subject must have communicated to him or her in intelligible form:

- the information constituting any personal data of which that individual is the data subject;

- any information known or available to the data controller as to the source of those data unless the communication of that information is contrary to the public interest; and

- where the processing by automatic means of the data of which the individual is the data subject has constituted or is likely to constitute the sole basis for any decision significantly affecting him or her, be informed free of charge by the data controller of the logic involved in the processing.[22]

Possible Exceptions and Issues

This must be done as soon as may be and in any event not more than 40 days after compliance by the individual with the provisions and, where any of the information is expressed in terms that are not intelligible to the average person without explanation, the information shall be accompanied by an explanation of those terms.[23]

Where personal data relating to a data subject consist of an expression of opinion about the data subject by another person, the data may be disclosed to the data subject without obtaining the consent of that person to the disclosure.[24]

The obligations imposed to communicate to the data subject the personal data and details as to the source of the personal data[25] can be complied with by supplying the data subject with a copy of the information concerned in permanent form, unless:

- the supply of such a copy is not possible or would involve disproportionate effort; or

- the data subject agrees otherwise.[26]

---

21. s 4 *ibid.*
22. *ibid.*
23. *ibid.*
24. s 4(4A)(a) *ibid.* There are exemptions in the section, however.
25. s 4(1)(a)(iii) *ibid.*
26. s 4(9) *ibid.*

Where a data controller has previously complied with an access request,[27] the data controller is not obliged to comply with a subsequent identical or similar request under that subsection by the same individual unless, in the opinion of the data controller, a reasonable interval has elapsed between compliance with the previous request and the making of the current request.[28] In determining whether such reasonable interval has elapsed, regard shall be had to the nature of the data, the purpose for which the data are processed and the frequency with which the data are altered.[29]

The provision under s 4(1)(a)(iv) regarding automated data is not to be regarded as requiring the provision of information as to the logic involved in the taking of a decision if and to the extent only that such provision would adversely affect trade secrets or intellectual property (in particular any copyright protecting computer software).[30]

Making an Access Request

To make an access request the data subject must:

- apply in writing (which can include email);

- give any details that might be needed to help the organisation identify him or her and locate all the information the organisation may keep about him or her, e.g. previous addresses, customer account numbers;

- pay the organisation an access fee, if the organisation charges one. Such fee cannot exceed €6.35.[31]

Dealing with Access Requests

One commentary[32] refers to the advisability of having a process flow chart in place. The main components referred to include:

- data subject asks for personal data;

- data subject access request form issued;

- data subject access request form returned plus appropriate fee (if requested);

- personal data located, whether by legal department, data protection personnel, etc.;

- examining same in relation to any third-party information, health data, or exempt data;

---

27. Under s 4(1) *ibid.*
28. s 4(10) *ibid.*
29. s 4(11) *ibid.*
30. s 4(12) *ibid.*
31. See DPC, available at http://www.dataprotection.ie/ViewDoc.asp?fn=/documents/guidance/Guide_Data_Contollers.htm&CatID=90&m=y, last accessed 11 January 2013.
32. Morgan and Boardman, *Data Protection Strategy* (London: Sweet & Maxwell, 2003) p 252.

- data reviewed by legal department; and

- personal data copy issues to data subject.

The Data Protection Commissioner makes the following comments and suggestions for organisations in relation to access requests. On making an access request, any individual about whom personal data is kept is entitled to:

- a copy of the personal data being held about him or her;

- know the categories of their personal data and the purpose/s for processing it;

- know the identity of those to whom the data controller discloses the personal data;

- know the source of the personal data, unless it is contrary to public interest;

- know the logic involved in automated decisions;

- data held in the form of opinions, except where such opinions were given in confidence, and in such cases where the person's fundamental rights suggest that he or she should access the personal data in question.[33]

It is important that organisations have clear and *documented* procedures in place to ensure that all relevant manual files and computers are checked for personal data in respect of which the access request is being made.[34]

Response to Access Request

In response to an access request an organisation must:

- supply the information to the individual data subject promptly and within 40 days of receiving the request;

- provide the information in a form that will be clear to the ordinary person, e.g. any codes must be explained.[35]

If the organisation does not keep any information about the individual making the request, the organisation should inform the individual within 40 days.[36] An organisation is not obliged to refund any fee charged for dealing with the access request should it not, in fact, keep any personal data.[37] However, the fee must be refunded

---

33. See DPC, available at http://www.dataprotection.ie/ViewDoc.asp?fn=/documents/guidance/ Guide_Data_Contollers.htm&CatID=90&m=y, last accessed 11 January 2013.
34. *ibid.*
35. *ibid.*
36. *ibid.*
37. *ibid.*

if the organisation does not comply with the request, or if the organisation has to rectify, supplement or erase the personal data concerned.[38]

If the organisation restricts the individual's right of access in accordance with one of the very limited restrictions set down in the Data Protection Acts, the organisation must notify the data subject in writing within 40 days and it must include a statement of the reasons for refusal.[39] The organisation must also inform the individual of his or her entitlement to complain to the Data Protection Commissioner about the refusal.[40]

There are certain modifications to the basic right to access granted by the Data Protection Acts, which include the following:

- access to health and social work data[41];
- modifications to the right of access in the interest of the data subject or the public interest, designed to protect the individual from hearing anything about himself or herself that might cause serious harm to their physical or mental health or emotional well-being; and
- examinations data.[42]

In the case of examinations data, there is an increased time limit for responding to an access request from 40 to 60 days and an access request is deemed to be made at the date of the first publication of the results or at the date of the request, whichever is the later.[43]

The UK ICO also provides the following additional guidance or checklist[44]:

1. *Is this a subject access request?*

   No Handle the query as part of your normal course of business.

   Yes Go to 2.

---

38. *ibid.*
39. See DPC, available at http://www.dataprotection.ie/ViewDoc.asp?fn=/documents/guidance/ Guide_Data_Contollers.htm&CatID=90&m=y, last accessed 11 January 2013.
40. *ibid.*
41. See DPC, available at http://www.dataprotection.ie/ViewDoc.asp?fn=/documents/guidance/ Guide_Data_Contollers.htm&CatID=90&m=y, last accessed 11 January 2013.
42. *ibid.*
43. *ibid.*
44. *Data Protection Good Practice Note, Checklist for Handling Requests for Personal Information* (subject access requests), ICO, available at http://www.ico.gov.uk/for_organisations/data_ protection/subject_access_requests.aspx, last accessed 11 January 2013.

2. *Do you have enough information to be sure of the requester's identity?*

   No If you have good cause to doubt the requester's identity you can ask them to provide any evidence you reasonably need to confirm it. For example, you may ask for a piece of information held in your records that the person would be expected to know, such as membership details, or a witnessed copy of their signature. Once satisfied, go to 3.

   Yes Go to 3.

3. *Do you need any other information to find the records they want?*

   No Go to 4.

   Yes You will need to ask the individual promptly for any other information you reasonably need to find the records they want. You might want to ask them to narrow down their request. For example, if you keep all your customers' information on one computer system and your suppliers' information on another, you could ask what relationship they had with you. Or, you could ask when they had dealings with you. However, they do have the right to ask for everything you have about them and this could mean a very wide search. You have 40 calendar days to respond to a subject access request after receiving any further information you need and any fee you decide to charge. Go to 4.

4. *Are you going to charge a fee?*

   No Go to 5.

   Yes If you need a fee you must ask the individual promptly for one. The maximum you can charge is £10 unless medical or education records are involved (see guidance on our website). The 40 calendar days in which you must respond starts when you have received the fee and all necessary information to help you find the records. Go to 5.

5. *Do you hold any information about the person?*

   No If you hold no personal information at all about the individual you must tell them this.

   Yes Go to 6.

6. *Will the information be changed between receiving the request and sending the response?*

   No Go to 7.

   Yes You can still make routine amendments and deletions to personal information after receiving a request. However, you must not make any changes to the records as a result of receiving the request, even if you find inaccurate or embarrassing information on the record. Go to 7.

7. *Does it include any information about other people?*

> **No** Go to 8.

> **Yes** You will not have to supply the information unless the other people mentioned have given their consent, or it is reasonable to supply the information without their consent. Even when the other person's information should not be disclosed, you should still supply as much as possible by editing the references to other people. To help you on this point we have published more detailed guidance on dealing with subject access requests involving other people's information. Go to 8.

8. *Are you obliged to supply the information?*

> **No** If all the information you hold about the requester is exempt, then you can reply stating that you do not hold any of their personal information that you are required to reveal.

> **Yes** Go to 9.

9. *Does it include any complex terms or codes?*

> **No** Go to 10.

> **Yes** You must make sure that these are explained so the information can be understood. Go to 10.

10. Prepare the response.[45]

This is useful but one should always bear in mind that there can be differences between Irish and UK law and practice, nothwithstanding the common sources of Convention and EU law.

Right to Object to Processing

Data subjects have a right to object to the processing of data likely to cause damage or distress. It can be seen, therefore, that the concept of delete, oblivion or forgetting (as in the right to forget) is not a completely new concept.

Section 6A of the Data Protection Acts refers to the right to prevent processing likely to cause damage or distress. An individual is entitled *at any time*, by notice in writing served on a data controller, to request it to cease within a reasonable time, or not to begin, processing or processing for a specified purpose or in a specified manner any personal data in respect of which he or she is the data subject if the processing falls within s 6A(2) (see below) on the ground that, for specified reasons:

---

45.   *ibid.*

- the processing of those data, or their processing for that purpose or in that manner, is causing or likely to cause substantial damage or distress to him or her or to another person; and

- the damage or distress is or would be unwarranted.[46]

Section 6A(2) refers to processing that is necessary:

- for the performance of a task carried out in the public interest or in the exercise of official authority vested in the data controller or in a third party to whom the data are or are to be disclosed; or

- for the purposes of the legitimate interests pursued by the data controller to whom the data are or are to be disclosed, unless those interests are overridden by the interests of the data subject in relation to fundamental rights and freedoms and, in particular, his or her right to privacy with respect to the processing of personal data.

The right does not apply:

- in a case where the data subject has given his or her explicit consent to the processing;

- if the processing is necessary:

  - for the performance of a contract to which the data subject is a party;

  - in order to take steps at the request of the data subject prior to his or her entering into a contract;

  - for compliance with any legal obligation to which the data controller or data subject is subject other than one imposed by contract; or

  - to protect the vital interests of the data subject;

- to processing carried out by political parties or candidates for election to, or holders of elective political office, in the course of electoral activities; or

- in such other cases, if any, as may be specified in regulations made by the Minister after consultation with the Data Protection Commissioner.[47]

The data controller shall, not later than 20 days after the receipt of the notice, serve a notice on the data subject, stating that it has complied or intends to comply with the request or stating that it is of the opinion that the request is unjustified to any extent

---

46. s 6A(1) provides for same subject to s 6A(3) and unless otherwise provided by law, Data Protection Act 1988 and Data Protection (Amendment) Act 2003.

47. s 6A(3) *ibid.*

and the reasons for the opinion and the extent (if any) to which it has complied or intends to comply with it.[48]

If the Data Protection Commissioner is satisfied, on the application by an individual, that the data controller has failed to comply, the Commissioner may serve an enforcement notice ordering the organisation to take such steps to comply with the request.[49]

The DP Directive 95[50] refers to the data subject's right to object. Article 14 contains the data subject's right to object. It provides that Member States shall grant the data subject the right:

- to object at any time on compelling legitimate grounds relating to their particular situation to the processing of data relating to him, save where otherwise provided by Member State legislation. Where there is a justified objection, the processing instigated by the data controller may no longer involve those data;

- to object, on request and free of charge, to the processing of personal data relating to him that the data controller anticipates being processed for the purposes of direct marketing, or to be informed before personal data are disclosed for the first time to third parties or used on their behalf for the purposes of direct marketing, and to be expressly offered the right to object free of charge to such disclosures or uses.

It also provides that Member States shall take the necessary measures to ensure that data subjects are aware of the existence of the right.[51]

Right to Prevent Processing for Direct Marketing

Data subjects have a right to prevent processing for direct marketing. Section 2(7) of the Data Protection Acts[52] provides that, where personal data are kept for the purpose of direct marketing, the data subject concerned can request the data controller in writing:

- not to process the data for that purpose; or

- to cease processing the data for that purpose.

---

48. s 6A(4) *ibid.*
49. s 6A(5) *ibid.*
50. s VII, EU Data Protection Directive 1995.
51. art 14 *ibid.*
52. Data Protection Act 1988 and Data Protection (Amendment) Act 2003.

If requested not to process, the data controller:

- shall, where the data are kept only for the purpose aforesaid, as soon as may be and in any event not more than 40 days after the request has been given or sent to it, erase the data; and

- shall not, where the data are kept for that purpose and other purposes, process the data for that purpose after the expiration of the period aforesaid.[53]

If requested to cease processing, the data controller, not more than 40 days after the request, shall erase the data; and where the data are kept for that purpose and other purposes, cease processing the data for that purpose.[54] The data controller shall notify the data subject in writing and, where appropriate, inform them of those other purposes.[55]

Where a data controller anticipates that personal data, including personal data that is required by law to be made available to the public, will be processed for the purposes of direct marketing, the data controller shall inform the persons to whom the data relates that they may object, by means of a request in writing to the data controller and free of charge, to such processing.[56]

Right Against Automated Decisions

Data subjects have a right not to be subjected to automated decision-taking processes. This refers to decisions taken in relation to and affecting individuals but that are computer-based and automated, and that occur without human intervention. An example would be a financial institution making a credit application decision by automated computer without oversight by personnel of the institution. This is not the only such instance of automated decisions however. Indeed, such instances may be increasing.

It is referred to in s 6B of the Data Protection Acts. Section 6B(1) of the Data Protection Acts provides that a decision that produces legal effects concerning a data subject, or otherwise significantly affects a data subject, may not be based solely on processing by automatic means of personal data in respect of which they are the data subject and is intended to evaluate certain personal matters relating to them, such as, for example (but without prejudice to the generality of the foregoing), their performance at work, creditworthiness, reliability or conduct. The instances of and potential for such examples are increasing with technology advances.

53. s 2(7)(b)(I) *ibid.*
54. s 2(7)(b)(II) *ibid.*
55. s 2(7)(b)(III) *ibid.*
56. s 2(8) *ibid.*

This will not apply in a case in which a decision:

- is made in the course of steps taken:

  - for the purpose of considering whether or not to enter into a contract with the data subject;

  - with a view to entering into such a contract; or

  - in the course of performing such a contract; or

- is authorised or required by any enactment and the data subject has been informed of the proposal to make the decision; and

- either:

  - the effect of the decision is to grant a request of the data subject; or

  - adequate steps have been taken to safeguard the legitimate interests of the data subject by, for example (but without prejudice to the generality of the foregoing), the making of arrangements to enable him to make representations to the data controller in relation to the proposal.[57]

It also does not apply if the data subject consents to such processing.[58]

The DP Directive 95 also refers to automated individual decisions.[59] Article 15(1) provides that Member States shall grant the right to every person not to be subject to a decision that produces legal effects concerning him or significantly affects him or her and that is based solely on automated processing of data intended to evaluate certain personal aspects relating to him or her, such as their performance at work, creditworthiness, reliability, conduct, etc. Member States shall provide that a person may be subjected to such a decision if that decision:

- is taken in the course of the entering into or performance of a contract, provided the request for the entering into or the performance of the contract, lodged by the data subject, has been satisfied or that there are suitable measures to safeguard their legitimate interests, such as arrangements allowing him to put their point of view; or

- is authorised by a law that also lays down measures to safeguard the data subject's legitimate interests.[60]

---

57. s 6B(2)(a) *ibid.*
58. s 6B(2)(b) *ibid.*
59. art 15 EU Data Protection Directive 1995.
60. art 15(2) *ibid.*

Right of Rectification, Blocking or Erasure

Data subjects have a right of rectification, blocking and erasure. The Data Protection Acts provide user rights in relation to rectification, blocking, erasure *and destruction*. Section 6(1) provides that an individual shall, if he or she so requests in writing to a data controller who keeps personal data relating to him or her, be entitled to have rectified or, where appropriate, blocked or erased any such data in relation to which there has been a contravention by the data controller of the *data protection principles*; and the data controller shall comply with the request not more than 40 days after the request, provided that the data controller shall, as respects data that are inaccurate or not kept up to date, be deemed:

- to have complied with the request if it supplements the data with a statement (to the terms of which the individual has assented) relating to the matters dealt with by the data; and

- if it supplements the data as aforesaid, not to be in contravention of the data protection principles.[61]

Where a data controller complies, or is deemed to have complied, with a request, it shall, as soon as may be and in any event not more than 40 days after the request has been given or sent to it, notify:

- the individual making the request; and

- if such compliance materially modifies the data concerned, any person to whom the data were disclosed during the period of 12 months immediately before the giving or sending of the request unless such notification proves impossible or involves a disproportionate effort

of the rectification, blocking, erasure or statement concerned.[62]

The DP Directive 95 also provides for the right of rectification, erasure or blocking. Article 12 states that Member States shall guarantee every data subject the right to obtain from the data controller:

- as appropriate the rectification, erasure or blocking of data the processing of which does not comply with the provisions of the Directive, in particular because of the incomplete or inaccurate nature of the data;

- notification to third parties to whom the data have been disclosed of any rectification, erasure or blocking carried out in compliance, unless this proves impossible or involves a disproportionate effort.

---

61. s 6(1) *ibid.*
62. s 6(1) *ibid.*

Rectification Right: DP Regulation

The draft DP Regulation[63] refers to rectification and erasure. In particular, Article 16 provides that the data subject shall have the right to obtain from the data controller the rectification of personal data relating to them that are inaccurate. The data subject shall have the right to obtain completion of incomplete personal data, including by way of supplementing a corrective statement.

Erasure Right/Right to Be Forgotten: DP Regulation

Article 17(1) of the DP Regulation provides for the enhanced right to be forgotten and to erasure. It provides that the data subject shall have the right to obtain from the controller the erasure of personal data relating to them and the abstention from further dissemination of such data, especially in relation to personal data that are made available by the data subject while they were a child, where one of the following grounds applies:

- the data are no longer necessary in relation to the purposes for which they were collected or otherwise processed;

- the data subject withdraws consent on which the processing is based according to Article 6(1)(a), or when the storage period consented to has expired, and where there is no other legal ground for the processing of the data;

- the data subject objects to the processing of personal data[64];

- the processing of the data does not comply with the Regulation for other reasons.[65]

The DP Regulation provides that where the data controller[66] has made the personal data public, it shall take all reasonable steps, including technical measures, in relation to data for the publication of which the data controller is responsible, to inform third parties that are processing such data, that a data subject requests them to erase any links to, or copy or replication of that personal data.[67] Where the data controller has authorised a third-party publication of personal data, the data controller shall be considered responsible for that publication.[68]

Data controllers, in accordance with the DP Regulation, must carry out the erasure without delay, except to the extent that the retention of the personal data is necessary:

---

63. s 3.
64. Pursuant to art 19.
65. art 17(1) *ibid.*
66. Referred to in para 1.
67. art 17(2) *ibid.*
68. *ibid.*

- for exercising the right of freedom of expression in accordance with Article 80;

- for reasons of public interest in the area of public health;

- for historical, statistical and scientific research purposes;

- for compliance with a legal obligation to retain the personal data by EU or Member State law to which the data controller is subject; Member State laws shall meet an objective of public interest, respect the essence of the right to the protection of personal data and be proportionate to the legitimate aim pursued; or

- in the cases referred to in s 17(4) (see below).[69]

Article 17(4) of the DP Regulation[70] provides that instead of erasure, the data controller shall restrict processing of personal data where:

- their accuracy is contested by the data subject, for a period enabling the controller to verify the accuracy of the data;

- the data controller no longer needs the personal data for the accomplishment of its task but they have to be maintained for purposes of proof;

- the processing is unlawful and the data subject opposes their erasure and requests the restriction of their use instead; and

- the data subject requests to transmit the personal data into another automated processing system in accordance with Article 18(2).

Personal data referred to in Article 17(4) may, with the exception of storage, only be processed for purposes of proof, or with the data subject's consent, or for the protection of the rights of another natural or legal person or for an objective of public interest.[71]

Where processing of personal data is restricted pursuant to Article 17(4), the data controller shall inform the data subject before lifting the restriction on processing.[72]

The DP Regulation obliges data controllers to implement mechanisms to ensure that the time limits established for the erasure of personal data and/or for a periodic review of the need for the storage of the data are observed.[73]

Under the DP Regulation, once the erasure is carried out, the data controller shall not otherwise process such personal data.[74]

---

69. art 17(3) *ibid.*
70. *ibid.*
71. art 17(5) *ibid.*
72. art 17(6) *ibid.*
73. art 17(7) *ibid.*
74. art 17(8) *ibid.*

The Commission will also be empowered to adopt delegated acts[75] or measures for the purpose of further specifying:

- the criteria and requirements for the application of Article 17(1) for specific sectors and in specific data processing situations;

- the conditions for deleting links, copies or replications of personal data from publicly available communication services[76];

- the criteria and conditions for restricting the processing of personal data.[77]

Synodinou[78] refers to the "right to oblivion" and notes in relation to her research that media interests are not immune to the right to be forgotten. Examples are given where cases have been successful in preventing particular media stories dragging up past events long after they had occurred, including court cases.[79] Indeed, many countries already anonymise party names from decisions and judgements, such as Germany, Austria, Greece, Finland, Belgium, Hungary, the Netherlands, Poland and Portugal.[80] The right to be forgotten has also been recognised in France and Belgium.[81] It is also important to bear in mind that the draft Regulation introduces enhanced rights as regards deletion and being forgotten, not introducing such provisions *de nova*.

Right Against Enforced Subject Access

Individuals also have a right against being forced to make a data subject access request and to then disclose the details received pursuant to the access request to a third party. For example, an employer or prospective employer may feel entitled to ask employees to make a Garda access request or an insurance related access request, and to be able to obtain the results from the data subject. This is frequently misunderstood by certain organisations.

Section 4(13) of the Data Protection Acts provides that a person shall not, in connection with:

- the recruitment of another person as an employee;

- the continued employment of another person; or

---

75. See art 86 *ibid*.
76. As referred to in para 2.
77. Referred to in para 4, art 17(9), *ibid*.
78. Synodinou, "The Media Coverage of Court Proceedings in Europe: Striking a Balance Between Freedom of Expression and Fair Process" (2012) 28 *Computer Law & Security Review* 208–219 at 217.
79. *ibid* at 218.
80. *ibid* at 218 and fn 106.
81. Synodinou, *art cit* 217.

- a contract for the provision of services to it by another person, require that other person:

  - to make a request under s 4(1)(access request); or

  - to supply it with personal data relating to that other person obtained as a result of such a request.

A person who contravenes this provision shall be guilty of an offence.[82] Article 15 of the DP Directive 95 also refers to enforced subject access requests.

Court Remedies, Duty of Care, etc. to Data Subjects

Individuals are also entitled in enforcing their data protection rights, and in seeking remedies in relation to damage and loss suffered as a result of the misuse of their personal data, to seek court remedies. They are not confined to simply making complaints to the Data Protection Commissioner. It is important to note that certain remedies that an individual may wish to seek are not available from or via the Data Protection Commissioner.

This recognition of judicial, as well as official, routes to remedies, is also contained in the recent draft DP Regulation Recitals.[83] Data subjects also have the right to a judicial remedy against decisions of a supervisory authority concerning them. Proceedings against a supervisory authority should be brought before the courts of the Member State, where the supervisory authority is established.[84] Any damage a person may suffer as a result of unlawful processing should be compensated by the data controller or data processor.[85] The penalties should be imposed on any person, whether governed by private or public law, who fails to comply with the Regulation. Member States should ensure that the penalties are effective, proportionate and dissuasive and should take all measures to implement the penalties.[86]

Data controllers and data processors owe a duty of care to data subjects. Section 7 of the Data Protection Acts states that the purposes of the law of torts and to the extent that that law does not so provide, a person, being a data controller or a data processor, shall, so far as regards the collection by it of personal data or information intended for inclusion in such data or its dealing with such data, owe a duty of care to the data subject concerned.

---

82.   s 4(13)(b) *ibid*. A developing issue is usernames and passwords.
83.   EU draft Data Protection Regulation.
84.   Recital 113 *ibid*.
85.   Recital 118 *ibid*.
86.   Recital 119 *ibid*.

The DP Directive 95[87] also refers to judicial remedies, liability and sanctions. Article 22, referring to remedies, states that without prejudice to any administrative remedy for which provision may be made, *inter alia*, before the supervisory authority (i.e. Data Protection Commissioner), prior to referral to the judicial authority, Member States shall provide for the right of every person to a *judicial remedy* for any breach of the rights guaranteed him or her by the Member State law applicable to the processing in question.

Article 23 of the DP Directive 95 refers to liability and provides that:

- Member States shall provide that any person who has suffered damage as a result of an unlawful processing operation or of any act incompatible with the national provisions adopted pursuant to the Directive is entitled to receive compensation from the data controller for the damage suffered.

Conclusion

Organisations, in dealing with individuals and in considering the rights of data subjects, must be fully aware that the *data protection principles* must also be complied with as regards the data subject. The *data protection principles* ensure data must be:

- obtained and processed fairly;
- accurate, complete and kept up to date;
- obtained only for one specified, explicit and legitimate purpose;
- not further processed in a manner incompatible with that purpose;
- adequate, relevant and not excessive in relation to the purpose;
- kept for longer than is necessary for that purpose; and
- protected by appropriate security measures.

Data controllers must also give a copy of personal data to any individual, on request (i.e. an access request), as referred to above.

These rights are very important for organisations to recognise and protect. They need to be incorporated into the organisation from day one, as it may not be possible to retrospectively become compliant if the initial collection and processing was illegitimate. This is increasingly significant as data protection authorities become more proactive and as the levels of fines and penalties increase. The rights are expanding and becoming more explicit in the draft DP Regulation. It is important that organisations keep abreast of the expanding rights and obligations.

---

87. Chapter III, EU Data Protection Directive 1995.

CHAPTER 9

Notification and Registration

Introduction

Organisations are prohibited from undertaking data collection and processing without notification and registration (unless exempted[1]). Particular categories of information are required to be registered. The Data Protection Commissioner maintains the register. If the organisation makes any changes to the registered details, these must then be updated in the register.

Registration

Organisations can be obliged to register with the Data Protection Commissioner. Sections 19(1) and 16(1) of the Data Protection Acts[2] prohibit processing without registration. It provides that a data controller to whom s 16 of the Data Protection Acts applies shall not keep personal data unless there is a current entry on the register.

Details of Use Purposes in Registration

Section 17(1)(b) of the Data Protection Acts provides that if an organisation is processing in relation to two or more *related* purposes, such purposes should be made clear in the application for registration.

In the case of *unrelated* purposes, the organisation needs to provide separate registration applications (s 17(1)(c)).

Security Details for Sensitive Personal Data

The Data Protection Commissioner shall not accept a registration application in relation to sensitive personal data unless satisfied as regards the security measures in

---

1. See ss 19(1) and 16(1) of the Data Protection Act 1988 and Data Protection (Amendment) Act 2003.
2. Data Protection Act 1988 and Data Protection (Amendment) Act 2003.

place (s 17(3)). Organisations should pay particular attention to this issue, and ensure it is properly up to date.

Effect of Registration

Section 19(2) of the Data Protection Acts provides that once it registers, the organisation shall not:

- keep personal data of any description other than that specified in the entry;

- keep or use personal data for a purpose other than the purpose or purposes described in the entry;

- if the source from which such data, and any information intended for inclusion in such data, are obtained is required to be described in the entry, obtain such data or information from a source that is not so described;

- disclose such data to a person who is not described in the entry (other than a person to whom a disclosure of such data may be made in the circumstances specified in s 8 of the Data Protection Acts); or

- directly or indirectly transfer such data to a place outside the State other than one named or described in the entry.

Employees

Section 19(3) of the Data Protection Acts provides that an employee or agent referred to in s 19(2) above shall, as respects personal data kept or, as the case may be, to be kept by the data controller, be subject to the same restrictions in relation to the use, source, disclosure or transfer of the data as those to which the data controller is subject under that subsection.

Data Processors

Section 19(4) of the Data Protection Acts provides that a data processor[3] shall not process personal data unless there is for the time being an entry in the register.

Register of Notifications Exemptions

The Data Protection Act 1988 (Section 16(1)) Regulations 2007[4] specifies particular details in relation to registration. The Regulations provide that the following categories of data controller are exempt from the registration requirement, namely:

3. Covered by s 16 *ibid.*
4. SI 657/2007.

- data controllers who process data relating to personnel administration;

- candidates for and holders of elective political office who process personal data for electoral activities or for the purpose of providing advice or assistance;

- educational establishments;

- solicitors and barristers who process personal data for legal professional purposes;

- a wide exemption is proposed for normal commercial activity that by definition requires the processing of personal data, e.g. keeping details of customers and suppliers (with the exception of data controllers who process personal data relating to physical or mental health);

- companies that process personal data relating to shareholders, directors or other officers of the company with a view to compliance with the Companies Acts[5];

- data controllers who process personal data with a view to the publication of journalistic, literary or artistic material;

- categories of data controller or data processor to which a code of practice approved under s 13 of the Data Protection Acts applies; and

- data processors who process personal data on behalf of data controllers where the processing of the data would fall under one or more of the above categories.

The following categories of data controller are not exempt and are required to register:

- financial institutions;

- credit institutions;

- insurance undertakings;

- persons whose business consists wholly or mainly in direct marketing, providing credit references or collecting debts;

- internet access providers;

- electronic communications network or service providers;

- persons who process genetic data; and

- data processors who process personal data on behalf of data controllers who fall under one or more of the above categories.

---

5.   This might also be considered a legal obligation.

Separate regulations exist in relation to fees[6] and registration forms[7] and registration periods.[8]

How Does an Organisation Register?

Where an organisation is required to register and notify, it must notify the Data Protection Commissioner with details of the proposed registration. The online steps include:

Step 1: Organisation details

Step 2: Personal data details

Step 3: Sensitive personal data details

Step 4: Payment

The details requested in Step 2 include:

- details of purposes for which the personal data is to be collected and used;

- list and describe each application of personal data, relating to the purpose(s) listed above, together with the types of personal data (e.g. name, address, date of birth, email address, staff ID number, etc.) kept or used in connection with that application. Organisations must also give full details of any personal data kept in relation to the purpose(s) listed above, but not normally associated with any of the applications listed;

- application and discloses. For each application listed above list the persons or bodies (or categories of them) to whom the personal data may be disclosed. A disclosure of any personal data to a person specified above must not be made in any manner incompatible with the purpose(s) for which those data are kept. Otherwise, the disclosure will be in contravention of s 2(1)(c)(ii) of the DP Acts;

- details of transfers abroad. This includes identifying the country, a description of personal data and the purpose of the transfer.

The details are available at:

- https://www.dataprotection.ie/register/new/default.asp.

The notification and registration process requires specific detailed information on processing to be provided. One example is the description of the individual data subjects to whom the personal data relates and whose personal data is be used by the organisation.

---

6.   SI 658/2007.

7.   SI 351/1988.

8.   SI 350/1988.

The recipient details should also be included where the personal data is furnished to third parties. This is particularly so where it is proposed to make data transfers to locations outside of the EEA. The details and types of individual security measures must be described. (The UK ICO has also published a *Notification Handbook*.[9])

Duty to Notify Changes

There is also an obligation on data controllers to notify changes.

Offence

A person who contravenes s 19(1), (4) or (5), or knowingly contravenes any other provision of the section shall be guilty of an offence.[10]

Conclusion

The important thing for organisations is to be aware of what classes of personal data are being collected, for what purposes, and to notify these as part of the registration process. Any time that changes occur, including adding data collections or anticipating additional new purposes, updated registration details must be furnished to the Data Protection Commissioner so as to update the registration details. (New consents can also be required if there are new processing activities.)

---

9. *ICO Notification Handbook*, ICO, available at http://www.ico.gov.uk/upload/documents/ notifications_handbook_html/index.html, last 11 January 2012. It provides that in relation to the general description of the processing of personal information, each notification must include a general description of the processing of personal information being carried out, *ibid.*, section 3.1.5. On the register this description is structured by reference to the purposes for which data is being processed.
10. Data Protection Act 1988 and Data Protection (Amendment) Act 2003.

CHAPTER 10

Enforcement and Penalties
for Non-Compliance

Introduction

There are a series of offences set out in the Data Protection Acts.[1] These are designed to ensure compliance with the data protection regime, from registration to fair use of personal data. Organisations must fully comply with their obligations. Questions arise in relation to their continued use of personal data if it has not been collected fairly. Investigations, prosecutions and financial penalties can arise.

Enforcement

Section 10 of the Data Protection Acts relates to enforcement under the data protection regime. It provides that the Data Protection Commissioner may investigate, or cause to be investigated, whether any of the provisions of the Data Protection Acts have been, are being, or are likely to be contravened in relation to an individual either where the individual complains to him of a contravention of any of those provisions *or* he is otherwise of the opinion that there may be such a contravention.[2] It is clear that the Data Protection Commissioner need not wait for the receipt of an actual complaint.

Where a complaint is made, the Data Protection Commissioner shall investigate the complaint or cause it to be investigated, unless he is of opinion that it is frivolous or vexatious.[3] If the Commissioner is unable to arrange for amicable resolution, he shall then notify the individual of the decision.[4] The individual may, if aggrieved by the decision, appeal the decision to a court within 21 days of notification.[5]

---

1.   Data Protection Act 1988 and Data Protection (Amendment) Act 2003.
2.   s 10(1)(a), *ibid.*
3.   *ibid.*
4.   s 10(1)(b) *ibid.*
5.   *ibid.*

The Data Protection Commissioner may carry out or cause to be carried out such investigations as he considers appropriate in order to ensure compliance with the provisions of the Data Protection Acts and to identify any contravention thereof.[6] Again, the Data Protection Commissioner need not wait for an actual complaint.

Enforcement Notices

If the Data Protection Commissioner is of the opinion that a person has contravened or is contravening a provision of the Data Protection Acts (other than a provision the contravention of which is an offence), the Data Protection Commissioner may, by notice in writing (referred to in the Data Protection Acts as an enforcement notice) served on the person, require him to take such steps as are specified in the notice within such time as may be so specified to comply with the provision concerned.[7] Without prejudice to the generality of same, if the Data Protection Commissioner is of the opinion that a data controller has contravened the *data protection principles*, the enforcement notice may require the data controller:

- to block, rectify, erase or destroy any of the data concerned; or

- to supplement the data with such statements relating to the matters dealt with by them as the Data Protection Commissioner may approve of; and as respects data that are inaccurate or not kept up to date, if he supplements them as aforesaid, he shall be deemed not to be in contravention.[8]

Contents and Time of Enforcement Notice

Section 10 of the Data Protection Acts also provides for Data Protection Commissioner enforcement notices, as follows. An enforcement notice shall:

(a) specify any provision of the Data Protection Acts that, in the opinion of the Data Protection Commissioner, has been or is being contravened and the reasons for his or her having formed that opinion; and

(b) state that the person concerned may appeal to the Court against the require-ment specified in the notice within 21 days from the service of the notice.[9]

The time specified in an enforcement notice for compliance shall not be expressed to expire before the end of the period of 21 days, or pending the determination of an appeal.[10]

---

6. *ibid.*
7. s 10(2) *ibid.*
8. s 10(3) *ibid.*
9. s 10(4) *ibid.*
10. s 10(5) *ibid.*

Urgent Enforcement

If the Data Protection Commissioner:

- by reason of special circumstances, is of opinion that a requirement specified in an enforcement notice should be complied with urgently; and

- includes a statement to that effect in the enforcement notice, ss 10(4)(b) and (5) shall not apply in relation to the notice. The notice shall contain a statement of the effect of the provisions of s 26 (other than subsection (3)) of the Data Protection Acts and shall not require compliance with the requirement before the end of the period of seven days beginning on the date on which the notice is served.[11]

Compliance with Enforcement Notice

On compliance by a data controller, it shall, as soon as may be and in any event not more than 40 days after such compliance, notify:

- the data subject concerned; and

- if such compliance materially modifies the data concerned, any person to whom the data were disclosed during the period beginning 12 months before the date of the service of the enforcement notice concerned and ending immediately before such compliance unless such notification proves impossible or involves a disproportionate effort, of the blocking, rectification, erasure, destruction or statement concerned.[12]

The Data Protection Commissioner may cancel an enforcement notice. If so, the Data Protection Commissioner shall notify the person accordingly on whom it was served in writing.[13]

A person who, without reasonable excuse, fails or refuses to comply with a requirement specified in an enforcement notice shall be guilty of an offence.[14]

Prohibition Notices

Organisations also need to be aware of prohibition notices. Section 11(10) of the Data Protection Acts refers to prohibition notices that can be issued by the Data Protection Commissioner. A prohibition notice shall:

---

11. s 10(6) *ibid.*
12. s 10(7) *ibid.*
13. s 10(8) *ibid.*
14. s 10(9) *ibid.*

- prohibit the transfer concerned either absolutely or until the person afore-said has taken such steps as are specified in the notice for protecting the interests of the data subjects concerned;

- specify the time when it is to take effect;

- specify the grounds for the prohibition; and

- state that the person concerned may appeal to the Court against the prohibition specified in the notice within 21 days from the service of the notice.[15]

The time specified in a prohibition notice for compliance with the prohibition specified therein shall not be expressed to expire before the end of the period of 21 days and, if an appeal is brought against the prohibition, the prohibition need not be complied pending the determination or withdrawal of the appeal.[16]

In addition, if the Data Protection Commissioner, by reason of special circumstances, is of opinion that a prohibition specified in a prohibition notice should be complied with urgently, and includes a statement to that effect in the notice, s 11(10)(d)(appeal to Court within 21 days) and s 11(11)(21 days for compliance) shall not apply to the notice but the notice shall contain a statement of the effect of the provisions of s 26 (other than subsection (3)) of the Data Protection Acts and shall not require compliance with the prohibition before the end of the period of seven days beginning on the date on which the notice is served.[17]

The Data Protection Commissioner may cancel a prohibition notice. If it is cancelled, the Commissioner shall notify the organisation on whom it was served in writing.[18]

Information Notices/Power to Require Information

Organisations also need to be aware of information notices. The Data Protection Commissioner can issue information notices requiring data controllers and data processors to supply information. Section 12 of the Data Protection Acts states that the Data Protection Commissioner may, by notice in writing (an information notice) served on an organisation, require the organisation to furnish in writing, within such time as may be specified in the notice, such information in relation to matters specified in the notice.[19]

An information notice shall state that the person concerned may appeal to Court against the requirement specified in the notice within 21 days from the service of the notice; and the time specified in the notice for compliance with a requirement

---

15. s 11(10) *ibid.*
16. s 11(11) *ibid.*
17. s 11(12) *ibid.*
18. s 11(13) *ibid.*
19. s 12(1) *ibid.*

specified therein shall not be expressed to expire before the end of the period of 21 days and, if an appeal is brought, the requirement need not be complied with pending the determination or withdrawal of the appeal.[20]

Urgent Information Notice

If the Data Protection Commissioner, by reason of special circumstances, is of the opinion that a requirement specified in an information notice should be complied with urgently, and includes a statement to that effect in the notice, s 12(2) shall not apply in relation to the notice. The notice shall contain a statement of the effect of the provisions of s 26 (other than s 12(3)) of the Data Protection Acts and shall not require compliance with the requirement before the end of the period of seven days beginning on the date on which the notice is served.[21]

No enactment or rule of law prohibiting or restricting the disclosure of information shall preclude a person from furnishing to the Data Protection Commissioner any information that is necessary or expedient for the performance by the Data Protection Commissioner of his or her functions.[22] This does not apply to information that in the opinion of the Minister or the Minister for Defence is, or at any time was, kept for the purpose of safeguarding the security of the State or information that is privileged from disclosure in proceedings in any court.[23]

Offence

An organisation which, without reasonable excuse, fails or refuses to comply with a requirement specified in an information notice or who in purported compliance with such a requirement furnishes information to the Data Protection Commissioner that the person knows to be false or misleading in a material respect shall be guilty of an offence.[24]

Forfeiture and Erasure

Where a court convicts a person of an offence under the Data Protection Acts, the Data Protection Acts provide that the Court has discretion to order any *data material* to be forfeited or destroyed.[25] Data material refers any document or other material used in connection with, or produced by, data equipment connected with the commission of the offence.[26] The Court may also order any relevant *data* to be erased.[27]

---

20. s 12(2) *ibid.*
21. s 12(3) *ibid.*
22. s 12(4)(a) *ibid.*
23. s 12(4)(b) *ibid.*
24. s 12(5) *ibid.*
25. s 31(2) *ibid.*
26. s 1 *ibid.* This is the definitions section.
27. s 31(2) *ibid.*

A Court would use this power to prevent any further damage being done by the use of the material or of the data.[28]

When exercising this power, the Court must give the owner of the data concerned or anyone who is otherwise interested in them (other than the person convicted), an opportunity to show cause why a forfeiture or erasure order should not be made.[29]

Prior Checking by Data Protection Commissioner

There is also provision made in relation to prior checking by the Data Protection Commissioner. This is referred to in s 12A of the Data Protection Acts. It provides that it applies to any processing that is of a prescribed description, being processing that appears to the Data Protection Commissioner to be particularly likely:

- to cause substantial damage or substantial distress to data subjects; or

- otherwise significantly to prejudice the rights and freedoms of data subjects.[30]

The Data Protection Commissioner, on receiving an application for registration[31] by a person to whom s 16 of the Data Protection Acts applies, in the register and any prescribed information and any other information that the Commssioner may require, or a request from a data controller on that behalf, shall consider and determine:

- whether any of the processing to which the application or request relates is processing to which this section applies; and

- if it does, whether the processing to which this section applies is likely to comply with the provisions of the Data Protection Acts.[32]

The Data Protection Commissioner shall, within the period of 90 days from receipt of an application, serve a notice on the data controller concerned stating the extent to which, in the opinion of the Data Protection Commissioner, the proposed processing is likely or unlikely to comply with the provisions of the Data Protection Acts.[33]

Before the end of such period, the Data Protection Commissioner may by reason of special circumstances extend the period once for a period not exceeding 90 days.[34]

---

28. See DPC, available at https://www.dataprotection.ie/viewdoc.asp?DocID=97, last accessed 11 January 2013.
29. s 31(3), Data Protection Act 1988 and Data Protection (Amendment) Act 2003.
30. s 12A(1) *ibid*.
31. s 17 *ibid*.
32. s 12A(2)(b) *ibid*.
33. s 12A(3) *ibid*.
34. s 12A(4) *ibid*.

If the Data Protection Commissioner serves an information notice on the data controller concerned before the end of the period or that period as extended, the period from the date of service of the notice to the date of compliance with the requirement in the notice; or if the requirement is set aside under s 26 of the Data Protection Acts, the period from the date of such service to the date of such setting aside shall be added to the period or that period as so extended.[35] This in effect provides an extension.

Data processing to which this section applies shall not be carried on unless:

- the data controller has previously made an application under s 17 of the Data Protection Acts and furnished the information specified in that section to the Data Protection Commissioner; or made a request under subsection (2) of this section; and

- the data controller has complied with any information notice served on it in relation to the matter; and

- the period of 90 days from the date of the receipt of the application or request referred to in subsection (3) of this section (or that period as extended under subsections (4) and (5) of this section or either of them) has elapsed without the receipt by the data controller of a notice under subsection (3); or

- the data controller has received a notice under subsection (3) stating that the particular processing proposed to be carried on is likely to comply with the provisions of the Data Protection Acts; or

- the data controller:

    - has received a notice under subsection (3) stating that, if the requirements specified by the Data Protection Commissioner and appended to the notice are complied with by the data controller, the processing proposed to be carried on is likely to comply with the provisions of the Data Protection Acts[36]; and

    - has complied with those requirements.[37]

A person who contravenes the section shall be guilty of an offence.[38]

An appeal against such a notice or a requirement appended to the notice may be made to the Court.[39]

---

35. s 12A(5) *ibid.*
36. *ibid.*
37. s 12A(6) *ibid.*
38. s 12A(7) *ibid.*
39. s 12A(8) *ibid.*

The Minister, after consultation with the Data Protection Commissioner, may by regulation substitute the number of days specified.[40]

A data controller shall pay to the Data Protection Commissioner such fee (if any) as may be prescribed. Different fees may be prescribed in relation to different categories of processing.[41]

References in this section to a data controller includes a reference to a data processor.[42] Both are therefore encompassed.

Breaches and Offences

The Data Protection Acts and the data protection regime set out the rules data controllers must obey. Breaches of these rules sometimes involve offences that are punishable by fines and prosecutions. It is, therefore, important for organisations, and officers within the organisations, to be aware of the potential for breaches and the consequences, so that these can be eliminated or at least reduced.

An organisation can commit criminal offences in relation to its data processing activities, such as:

- enforced data subject access (s 4(13));
- breach of prohibition notice (s 11(15));
- breach of an enforcement notice (s 10(9));
- breach of information notice (s 12(5));
- processing subject to prior checking (s 12A(7));
- breach of registration requirement (s 19(6));
- breach of correct details on register (s 20(2));
- breach of disclosure by data processor (s 21(2));
- breach by access and disclosure without authority (s 22(1));
- breach by obstructing an authorised officer (s 24(6));
- breach by disclosing confidential information from Data Protection Commissioner (s 10(2)).

Breaches can also apply to directors, employees, etc., as well as the organisation itself.

---

40. s 12A(9) *ibid.*
41. s 12A(10) *ibid.*
42. s 12A(11) *ibid.*

Offences by Data Processors

Non-compliance with the data protection regime by processors can also result in offences being committed. Data processors can commit the following offences:

- failure to comply with an enforcement notice;
- failure to comply with an information notice;
- failure to comply with a prohibition notice;
- disclosure of personal data without authorisation of the data controller.

Section 21 of the Data Protection Acts states that personal data processed by a data processor shall not be disclosed by it, or by an employee or agent of it, without the prior authority of the data controller on behalf of whom the data are processed. A person who knowingly contravenes this shall be guilty of an offence.[43]

Offences by Persons

A person who (a) obtains access to personal data, or obtains any information constituting such data, without the prior authority of the data controller or data processor by whom the data are kept, and (b) discloses the data or information to another person, shall be guilty of an offence. This does not apply to a person who is an employee or agent of the data controller or data processor concerned.[44]

Offences by Directors, etc.

Organisations also need to be careful in that their directors and staff can be guilty of offences as well as the organisation. Section 29 of the Data Protection Acts provides that where an offence under the Data Protection Acts has been committed by a body corporate and is proved to have been committed with the consent or connivance of or to be attributable to any neglect on the part of a person, being a director, manager, secretary or other officer of that body corporate, or a person who was purporting to act in any such capacity, that person, as well as the body corporate, shall be guilty of that offence and be liable to be proceeded against and punished accordingly. Where the affairs of a body corporate are managed by its members, the offence section shall apply in relation to the acts and defaults of a member in connection with their functions of management as if he or she were a director or manager of the body corporate.

This emphasises the importance of organisations and their personnel ensuring that data protection is respected and complied with.

---

43. s 21 *ibid.*
44. s 22 *ibid.*

Offences by Direct Marketers

Organisations also need to be aware of additional offences as regards direct marketing, on foot of the Regulations implementing the ePrivacy Directive. These offences are incorporated in the European Communities (Electronic Communications Networks and Services)(Privacy and Electronic Communications) Regulations 2011.[45]

The offenses are set out below, namely:

- sending unsolicited marketing messages to individuals by fax, SMS, email or automated dialling machine;

- sending unsolicited marketing by fax, SMS, email or automated dialling machine to a business if it has objected to the receipt of such messages;

- marketing by telephone where the subscriber has objected to the receipt of such calls;

- failing to identify the caller or sender or failing to provide a physical address or a return email address;

- failing to give customers the possibility of objecting to future email and SMS marketing messages with each message sent;

- concealing the identity of the sender on whose behalf the marketing communication was made;

- making marketing phone calls to mobile telephones without consent; and

- sending SMS information messages with "tagged on" marketing content.[46]

There are also provisions in relation to offences by officers of the organisations.[47]

Offences by Electronic Communications Companies under SI 336/2011

Organisations also need to consider additional offences under the European Communities (Electronic Communications Networks and Services)(Privacy and

---

45. SI 336/2011. The Regulations give effect to Directive 2002/58/EC of the European Parliament and of the Council of 12 July 2002 concerning the processing of personal data and the protection of privacy in the electronic communications sector (ePrivacy Directive), and the amendments to that Directive as introduced by Directive 2009/136/EC of the European Parliament and of the Council of 25 November 2009.
46. European Communities (Electronic Communications Networks and Services)(Privacy and Electronic Communications) Regulations 2011 (SI 336/2011).
47. Regulation 25, European Communities (Electronic Communications Networks and Services)(Privacy and Electronic Communications) Regulations 2011 (SI 336/2011).

Electronic Communications) Regulations 2011 (SI 336/2011).[48] These are set out below:

- failure to take appropriate technical and organisational measures to safe-guard the security of services;

- failure to notify subscribers without delay of a particular risk of a breach of the security of the public communications network;

- failure to notify the Data Protection Commissioner where there has been a personal data breach;

- failure to notify the subscriber or individual concerned where there has been a personal data breach that is likely to adversely affect the personal data or privacy of the subscriber or individual concerned;

- failure to maintain an inventory of personal data breaches;

- refusal to co-operate with an audit carried out by the Data Protection Commissioner.[49]

Fines, Penalties and Damages

Organisations need to consider that where they fail to comply with the data protection regime, fines and penalties can be imposed. Damages and compensation can also arise.

Criminal

Summary proceedings for an offence under the Data Protection Acts may be brought and prosecuted by the Data Protection Commissioner. Under s 31 of the Data Protection Acts, the maximum fine on summary conviction of such an offence is set at €3,000. On conviction on indictment, the maximum penalty is a fine of €100,000.[50]

If the commission of an offence under the Data Protection Acts also involves violence – for example, if an "authorised officer" is assaulted in trying to gain access to a premises under s 24 – then the offender can be proceeded against for assault and be liable to imprisonment.[51]

---

48. The Regulations give effect to Directive 2002/58/EC of the European Parliament and of the Council of 12 July 2002 concerning the processing of personal data and the protection of privacy in the electronic communications sector (ePrivacy Directive), and the amendments to that Directive as introduced by Directive 2009/136/EC of the European Parliament and of the Council of 25 November 2009.

49. European Communities (Electronic Communications Networks and Services)(Privacy and Electronic Communications) Regulations 2011 (SI 336/2011).

50. See DPC, available at https://www.dataprotection.ie/viewdoc.asp?DocID=97, last accessed 11 January 2013.

51. *ibid.*

A person guilty of an offence under the Data Protection Acts shall be liable:

- on summary conviction, to a fine not exceeding €3,000; or

- on conviction on indictment, to a fine not exceeding €100,000.[52]

Where a person is convicted of an offence under the Data Protection Acts, the court may order any data material that appears to the court to be connected with the commission of the offence to be forfeited or destroyed and any relevant data to be erased.[53]

The court shall not make an order under s 31(2) of this section in relation to data material or data where it considers that some person other than the person convicted of the offence concerned may be the owner of, or otherwise interested in, the data unless such steps as are reasonably practicable have been taken for notifying that person and giving him an opportunity to show cause why the order should not be made.[54]

Section 13 of the Criminal Procedure Act 1967 applies in relation to an offence under the Data Protection Acts that is not being prosecuted summarily as if, in lieu of the penalties provided for in s 13(3)(a) of that section, there were specified therein the fine provided for in s 13(1)(a) of this section and the reference in s 13(2)(a) of the said s 13 to the penalties provided for by s 13(3) shall be construed and have effect accordingly.

Civil

Civil sanctions can also arise. Where a person suffers damage as a result of a failure by a data controller or data processor to meet their data protection obligations, then the data controller or data processor may be subject to civil sanctions by the person affected. The injury and damage suffered by a data subject will be damage to their reputation, possible financial loss and mental distress. The data subject may also have remedies under the existing law (defamation where appropriate, breach of confidentiality, negligence because in some cases a data controller or a data processor would owe a duty of care to data subjects about whom data are being kept or processed – a duty to see that damage is not caused to them by negligent handling of the data in question). In case a data controller or data processor may not be subject to this duty of care, s 7 of the Data Protection Acts remedies this by ensuring that such a duty will be implied in all cases where personal data are kept or processed.[55]

In the UK, the ICO recently fined a financial organisation for incorrectly storing and

---

52. s 31 Data Protection Act 1988 and Data Protection (Amendment) Act 2003.
53. *ibid.*
54. *ibid.*
55. See DPC, available at https://www.dataprotection.ie/viewdoc.asp?DocID=97, last accessed 11 January 2013.

mingling financial data relating to individuals.[56] The fine was £50,000 and is reported as the first such fine for incorrectly storing personal data other than in a data loss incident. The individual could have suffered financial loss and damage as a result of not having financial details correctly stored. Sony was also fined £250,000 for data breach by hacking.

Direct Marketing

In relation to direct marketing, s 2(7) of the Data Protection Acts provides that where personal data are kept for the purpose of direct marketing, and the data subject concerned requests the data controller in writing:

- not to process the data for that purpose; or
- to cease processing the data for that purpose;
- the data controller:
    - shall, where the data are kept only for the purpose aforesaid, as soon as may be and in any event not more than 40 days after the request has been given or sent to him or her, erase the data; and
    - shall not, where the data are kept for that purpose and other purposes, process the data for that purpose after the expiration of the period aforesaid;
- as soon as may be and in any event not more than 40 days after the request has been given or sent to the data controller, it:
    - shall, where the data are kept only for the purpose aforesaid, erase the data; and
    - shall, where the data are kept for that purpose and other purposes, cease processing the data for that purpose; and
- the data controller shall notify the data subject in writing accordingly and, where appropriate, inform them of those other purposes.[57]

Where a data controller anticipates that personal data, including personal data that is required by law to be made available to the public, kept by it will be processed for the purposes of direct marketing, the data controller shall inform the persons to whom the data relates that they may object, by means of a request in writing to the data controller and free of charge, to such processing.[58]

---

56. See "Prudential Fined £50,000 for Customer Account Confusion", ICO, 6 November 2012, available at http://www.ico.gov.uk/news/latest_news/2012/prudential-fined-50000-for-customer-account-confusion-06112012.aspx, last accessed 11 January 2013.
57. s 2(7)(b) *ibid.*
58. s 2(8) *ibid.*

Penalties for Offences

Summary proceedings for an offence under SI 336/2011[59] may be brought and prosecuted by the Data Protection Commissioner. Each unsolicited call or message can attract a fine of up to €5,000 on summary conviction. If convicted on indictment, the fines range from €50,000 for a natural person to €250,000 if the offender is a body corporate.[60]

Courts may also order the destruction of data that is connected with the commission of an offence.

In the UK organisations can now be fined up to £500,000 by the UK ICO for unwanted marketing phone calls and emails in accordance with the updated and amended UK PECR Regulations implementing the ePrivacy Directive.[61]

Prohibition of Transfers

Section 11 of the Data Protection Acts relates to trans-border data flows. There is a default ban on transfers of personal data outside of the EEA (unless exempted). The section provides that the transfer of personal data to a country or territory outside the EEA may not take place unless that country or territory ensures an adequate level of protection for the privacy and the fundamental rights and freedoms of data subjects in relation to the processing of personal data having regard to all the circumstances surrounding the transfer and, in particular, but without prejudice to the generality of the foregoing, to:

- the nature of the data;
- the purposes for which and the period during which the data are intended to be processed;
- the country or territory of origin of the information contained in the data;
- the country or territory of final destination of that information;
- the law in force in the country or territory[62];
- any relevant codes of conduct or other rules that are enforceable in that country or territory;

---

59. European Communities (Electronic Communications Networks and Services)(Privacy and Electronic Communications) Regulations 2011.
60. See DPC, available at https://www.dataprotection.ie/viewdoc.asp?DocID=97, last accessed 11 January 2013.
61. See UK ICO, available at http://www.ico.gov.uk/for_organisations/privacy_and_electronic_communications.aspx, last accessed 11 January 2013.
62. Referred to in para (d) *ibid.*

- any security measures taken in respect of the data in that country or territory; and

- the international obligations of that country or territory.[63]

Where in any proceedings under the Data Protection Acts a question arises:

- whether the adequate level of protection[64] is ensured by a country or territory outside the EEA to which personal data are to be transferred; and

- a Community finding has been made in relation to transfers of the kind in question;

the question shall be determined in accordance with that finding.[65]

A "Community finding" means a finding of the European Commission in relation to whether an adequate level of protection specified is ensured by a specific country or territory outside the EEA.[66] The Commission has made such findings in relation to particular jurisdictions as have an adequate level of protection.[67]

The restriction in the section shall not apply to a transfer of data if:

- the transfer of the data or the information constituting the data is required or authorised by or under any enactment, or any convention or other instrument imposing an international obligation on the State;

- the data subject has given their consent to the transfer;

- the transfer is necessary for the performance of a contract between the data subject and the data controller or to take steps at the request of the data subject with a view to there entering into a contract with the data controller;

- the transfer is necessary for the conclusion of a contract between the data controller and a person other than the data subject that is entered into at the request of the data subject, and is in the interests of the data subject, or for the performance of such a contract;

- the transfer is necessary for reasons of substantial public interest;

---

63. s 11(1) Data Protection Act 1988 and Data Protection (Amendment) Act 2003.
64. Specified in subsection (1) of the section.
65. s 11(2) Data Protection Act 1988 and Data Protection (Amendment) Act 2003.
66. s 11(2)(b) *ibid.*
67. Community findings have been made in relation to the following jurisdictions, namely, Andorra, Argentina, Australia, Canada, Switzerland, Faeroe Islands, Guernsey, Israel, Isle of Man and Jersey. There are also community finding as regards US Safe Harbors and the transfer of passenger data to the US. See EU Commission, available at http://ec.europa.eu/justice/data-protection/document/international-transfers/adequacy/index_en.htm, last accessed 20 November 2012.

- the transfer is necessary for the purpose of obtaining legal advice or for the purpose of or in connection with legal proceedings or prospective legal proceedings or is otherwise necessary for the purposes of establishing or defending legal rights;

- the transfer is necessary in order to prevent injury or other damage to the health of the data subject or serious loss of or damage to property of the data subject or otherwise to protect their vital interests, and informing the data subject of, or seeking their consent to, the transfer is likely to damage their vital interests;

- the transfer is of part only of the personal data on a register established by or under an enactment, being a register intended for consultation by the public; or a register intended for consultation by persons having a legitimate interest in its subject matter, and, in the case of a register intended for consultation by persons having a legitimate interest in its subject matter, the transfer is made, at the request of, or to, a person referred to in that clause and any conditions to which such consultation is subject are complied with by any person to whom the data are or are to be transferred; or

- the transfer has been authorised by the Data Protection Commissioner where the data controller adduces adequate safeguards with respect to the privacy and fundamental rights and freedoms of individuals and for the exercise by individuals of their relevant rights under the Data Protection Acts or the transfer is made on terms of a kind approved by the Data Protection Commissioner as ensuring such safeguards;

- The Data Protection Commissioner shall inform the Commission and the supervisory authorities of the other states in the EEA of any such authorisation or approval (above);

- The Data Protection Commissioner shall comply with any decision of the European Commission under the procedure laid down in Article 31(2) of the DP Directive 95 made for the purposes of Article 26(3) or (4) of the DP Directive 95.[68]

The Minister may, after consultation with the Data Protection Commissioner, by regulations specify the circumstances in which a transfer of data is to be taken for the purposes of subsection (4)(a)(v) of this section to be necessary for reasons of substantial public interest; and the circumstances in which such a transfer that is not required by or under an enactment is not to be so taken.[69]

Where, in relation to a transfer of data to a country or territory outside the EEA, a data controller adduces the safeguards for the data subject concerned referred to in subsection (4)(a)(ix) of this section by means of a contract embodying the contractual

68. s 11(4) Data Protection Act 1988 and Data Protection (Amendment) Act 2003.
69. s 11(5) *ibid.*

clauses referred to in Article 26(2) or (4) of the DP Directive 95, the data subject shall have the same right:

- to enforce a clause of the contract conferring rights on them or relating to such rights; and

- to compensation or damages for breach of such a clause that they would have if they were a party to the contract.[70]

The Data Protection Commissioner may, subject to the provisions of this section, prohibit the transfer of personal data from the State to a place outside the State unless such transfer is required or authorised by or under any enactment or required by any convention or other instrument imposing an international obligation on the State.[71] In determining whether or not to prohibit a transfer of personal data under this section, the Data Protection Commissioner shall also consider whether or not the transfer would be likely to cause damage or distress to any person and have regard to the desirability of facilitating international transfers of data.[72] A prohibition shall be effected by the service of a notice (referred to in the Data Protection Acts as a prohibition notice) on the person proposing to transfer the data concerned.[73]

Prosecution of Offenses

Summary proceedings for an offence under the Data Protection Act may be brought and prosecuted by the Data Protection Commissioner. Section 10(4) of the Petty Sessions (Ireland) Act 1851, summary proceedings for an offence under the Data Protection Act, may be instituted within one year from the date of the offence.[74]

Civil Sanctions

Certain types of data will convey inherent additional risks over others, such as loss of financial personal data. This can be argued to require higher obligations for the organisation.

One interesting area to consider going forward is online abuse and damage, such as viral publication, defamation, bulletin boards, discussion forums and websites (or sections of websites), and social networking and related websites. Where damage occurs as a result of use, misuse or loss of personal data or results in abuse, threats, defamation, liability could, depending on the circumstances, arise for the individual tortfeasors as well as the website. The variety of damage is increasing.

---

70. s 11(6) *ibid.*
71. s 11(7) *ibid.*
72. s 11(8) *ibid.*
73. s 11(9) *ibid.*
74. s 30 *ibid.*

While there are certain limited defences in the eCommerce Directive,[75] one should recall that the data protection regime (and its duty of care and liability provisions) are separate and stand alone from the eCommerce Directive legal regime. Indeed, even in terms of the eCommerce defences one should also recall that (a) an organisation must first fall within an eCommerce defence, and not lose that defence, in order to avail of it; and (b) there is no automatic entitlement by an internet service provider (ISP) or website to a global eCommerce defence. In fact there is not one eCommerce defence but three very specific defences relating to specific and technical activities. Not all or every ISP activity will fall into one of these defences. Neither will one activity fall into all three defences.

It is also possible to conceive of a website that has no take-down procedures, inadequate take-down procedures (assuming there are such procedures), or non-expeditious procedures, and whom will face potential liability under privacy and data protection as well as eCommerce liability. For example, an imposter social networking profile that contains personal data and defamatory material could attract liability for the website operator under data protection, and under normal liability if none of the eCommerce defences were unavailable or were lost. The latter could occur if, for example, the false impersonating profile was notified to the website (or it was otherwise aware) but it did not do anything.[76]

The Australian case of *Milorad Trkulja v Google* held that Google was guilty of defamation and *inter alia* did not operate adequate take downs.[77] Damages of AU$200,000 were awarded. Yahoo! was also held to be a liable publisher in the amount of AU$225,000.[78] In New Zealand a court has also indicated that online website service providers, in this instance Google, can be a publisher, as has *Tamiz* (UK CA).[79]

DP Directive 95

The DP Directive 95[80] refers to these various issues.

---

75. Directive 2000/31/EC of the European Parliament and of the Council of 8 June 2000 on certain legal aspects of information society services, in particular electronic commerce, in the Internal Market (Directive on electronic commerce). Available at http://eur-lex.europa.eu/LexUriServ/LexUriServ.do?uri=CELEX:32000L0031:en:NOT. Last accessed 11 January 2013.

76. This is a complex and developing area of law, common law, civil law, Directive, forthcoming DP Regulation and caselaw, both in the UK and internationally. A full and detailed analysis is beyond the scope of this work.

77. *Milorad Trkulja v Google*, Supreme Court of Victoria, Melbourne, [2012] VSC 533, 12 November 2012.

78. *Trkulja v Yahoo! Inc & Anor* [2012] VSC 88.

79. *A v Google*, HC AK CIV: 2011-404-002780, 5 March 2012.

80. EU Data Protection Directive 1995 (Directive 95/46/EC of the European Parliament and of the Council of 24 October 1995 on the protection of individuals with regard to the processing of personal data and on the free movement of such data).

Courts

Chapter III of the DP Directive 95 refers to judicial remedies, liability and sanctions. Article 22 refers to remedies. It provides that without prejudice to any administrative remedy for which provision may be made, *inter alia*, before the supervisory authority referred to in Article 28, prior to referral to the judicial authority, Member States shall provide for the right of every person to a judicial remedy for any breach of the rights guaranteed him or her by the Member State law applicable to the processing in question.

Damages and Compensation

Article 23 of DP Directive 95 refers to liability. Article 23(1) provides that Member States shall provide that any person who has suffered damage as a result of an unlawful processing operation or of any act incompatible with the national provisions adopted pursuant to the Directive is entitled to receive compensation from the data controller for the damage suffered. Article 23(2) provides that the data controller may be exempted from this liability, in whole or in part, if he or she proves that he or she is not responsible for the event giving rise to the damage.

Sanctions

Article 24 of DP Directive 95[81] refers to sanctions. It provides that the Member States shall adopt suitable measures to ensure the full implementation of the provisions of the Directive and shall in particular lay down the sanctions to be imposed in case of infringement of the provisions adopted pursuant to the Directive.

DP Regulation

The draft DP Regulation[82] further expands on these matters.

Remedies

Chapter VIII of the DP Regulation refers to remedies, liability and sanctions. Article 73 refers to the right to lodge a complaint with a supervisory authority. Without prejudice to any other administrative or judicial remedy, every data subject shall have the right to lodge a complaint with a supervisory authority in any Member State if they consider that the processing of personal data relating to them does not comply with the Regulation.[83]

---

81. *ibid.*

82. EU draft Data Protection Regulation (Proposal for a Regulation of the European Parliament and of the Council on the protection of individuals with regard to the processing of personal data and on the free movement of such data (General Data Protection Regulation) COM (2012) 11 final).

83. art 73(1) *ibid.*

Any body, organisation or association that aims to protect data subjects' rights and interests concerning the protection of their personal data and has been properly constituted according to the law of a Member State shall have the right to lodge a complaint with a supervisory authority in any Member State on behalf of one or more data subjects if it considers that a data subject's rights under the Regulation have been infringed as a result of the processing of personal data.[84]

Independently of a data subject's complaint, any body, organisation or association referred to above in the preceding paragraph shall have the right to lodge a complaint with a national supervisory authority in any Member State, if it considers that a personal data breach has occurred.[85]

Article 74 refers to the right to a judicial remedy against a supervisory authority. Article 74(1) refers to and provides that each natural or legal person shall have the right to a judicial remedy against decisions of a supervisory authority concerning them.

Article 74(2) provides that each data subject shall have the right to a judicial remedy obliging the supervisory authority to act on a complaint in the absence of a decision necessary to protect their rights, or where the supervisory authority does not inform the data subject within three months on the progress or outcome of the complaint pursuant to point (b) of Article 52(1).

Proceedings against a supervisory authority shall be brought before the courts of the Member State where the supervisory authority is established.[86]

A data subject that is concerned by a decision of a supervisory authority in another Member State than where the data subject has its habitual residence may request the supervisory authority of the Member State where it has its habitual residence to bring proceedings on its behalf against the competent supervisory authority in the other Member State.[87]

Member States shall enforce final decisions by the courts referred to in this Article.[88]

Article 75 refers to the right to a judicial remedy against a data controller or data processor. Without prejudice to any available administrative remedy, including the right to lodge a complaint with a supervisory authority as referred to in Article 73, every natural person shall have the right to a judicial remedy if they consider that their rights under the Regulation have been infringed as a result of the processing of their personal data in non-compliance with the Regulation.[89]

---

84. art 73(2) *ibid.*
85. art 73(3) *ibid.*
86. art 74(3) *ibid.*
87. art 74(4) *ibid.*
88. art 74(5) *ibid.*
89. art 75(1) *ibid.*

Proceedings against a data controller or a data processor shall be brought before the courts of the Member State where the data controller or data processor has an establishment.[90]

Alternatively, such proceedings may be brought before the courts of the Member State where the data subject has its habitual residence, unless the data controller is a public authority acting in the exercise of its public powers.

Where proceedings are pending in the consistency mechanism referred to in Article 58, which concern the same measure, decision or practice, a court may suspend the proceedings brought before it, except where the urgency of the matter for the protection of the data subject's rights does not allow to wait for the outcome of the procedure in the consistency mechanism.[91]

Member States shall enforce final decisions by the courts referred to in this.[92]

Article 76 refers to common rules for court proceedings. Under Article 76(1) any body, organisation or association referred to in Article 73(2) shall have the right to exercise the rights referred to in Articles 74 and 75 on behalf of one or more data subjects. Each supervisory authority shall have the right to engage in legal proceedings and bring an action to court, in order to enforce the provisions of the Regulation or to ensure consistency of the protection of personal data within the EU.[93]

Where a competent court of a Member State has reasonable grounds to believe that parallel proceedings are being conducted in another Member State, it shall contact the competent court in the other Member State to confirm the existence of such parallel proceedings.[94]

Article 76(4) provides that should such parallel proceedings in another Member State concern the same measure, decision or practice, the court may suspend the proceedings.

Member States shall ensure that court actions available under Member State law allow for the rapid adoption of measures, including interim measures, designed to terminate any alleged infringement and to prevent any further impairment of the interests involved.[95]

Article 77 refers to the right to compensation and liability. Under Article 77(1) any person who has suffered damage as a result of an unlawful processing operation or of

---

90. art 75(2) *ibid.*
91. art 75(3) *ibid.*
92. art 75(4) *ibid.*
93. art 7(2) *ibid.*
94. art 76(3) *ibid.*
95. art 76(5) *ibid.*

an action incompatible with the Regulation shall have the right to receive compensation from the data controller or the data processor for the damage suffered.

Where more than one data controller or processor is involved in the processing, each data controller or data processor shall be jointly and severally liable for the entire amount of the damage.[96]

Article 77(3) states that the data controller or the data processor may be exempted from this liability, in whole or in part, if the data controller or the data processor proves that they are not responsible for the event giving rise to the damage.

Article 78 refers to penalties. Article 78(1) provides that Member States shall lay down the rules on penalties, applicable to infringements of the provisions of the Regulation and shall take all measures necessary to ensure that they are implemented, including where the data controller did not comply with the obligation to designate a representative. The penalties provided for must be effective, proportionate and dissuasive.

Article 78(2) states that where the data controller has established a representative, any penalties shall be applied to the representative, without prejudice to any penalties that could be initiated against the data controller.

Article 78(3) provides that each Member State shall notify to the Commission those provisions of its law that it adopts pursuant to paragraph 1, by the date specified in Article 91(2) at the latest and, without delay, any subsequent amendment affecting them.

Article 79 relates to administrative sanctions. Article 79(1) provides that each supervisory authority shall be empowered to impose administrative sanctions in accordance with this Article.

Article 79(2) provides that the administrative sanction shall be in each individual case effective, proportionate and dissuasive. The amount of the administrative fine shall be fixed with due regard to the nature, gravity and duration of the breach, the intentional or negligent character of the infringement, the degree of responsibility of the natural or legal person and of previous breaches by this person, the technical and organisational measures and procedures implemented pursuant to Article 23 and the degree of co-operation with the supervisory authority in order to remedy the breach.

Article 79(3) provides that in case of a first and non-intentional non-compliance with the Regulation, a warning in writing may be given and no sanction imposed, where:

- a natural person is processing personal data without a commercial interest; or

---

96. art 77(2) *ibid.*

- an enterprise or an organisation employing fewer than 250 persons is processing personal data only as an activity ancillary to its main activities.

The supervisory authority shall impose a fine up to €250,000, or in case of an enterprise up to 0.5 per cent of its annual worldwide turnover, to anyone who, intentionally or negligently:

- does not provide the mechanisms for requests by data subjects or does not respond promptly or not in the required format to data subjects pursuant to Articles 12(1) and (2);

- charges a fee for the information or for responses to the requests of data subjects in violation of Article 12(4).[97]

The supervisory authority shall impose a fine up to €500,000, or in case of an enterprise up to 1 per cent of its annual worldwide turnover, to anyone who, intentionally or negligently:

- does not provide the information, or does provide incomplete information, or does not provide the information in a sufficiently transparent manner, to the data subject pursuant to Articles 11, 12(3) and 14;

- does not provide access for the data subject or does not rectify personal data pursuant to Articles 15 and 16 or does not communicate the relevant information to a recipient pursuant to Article 13;

- does not comply with the expanded right to be forgotten or to erasure, or fails to put mechanisms in place to ensure that the time limits are observed or does not take all necessary steps to inform third parties that a data subject's requests to erase any links to, or copy or replication of the personal data pursuant Article 17;

- does not provide a copy of the personal data in electronic format or hinders the data subject to transmit the personal data to another application in violation of Article 18;

- does not or not sufficiently determine the respective responsibilities with data controllers pursuant to Article 24;

- does not or not sufficiently maintain the documentation pursuant to Articles 28, 31(4) and 44(3);

- does not comply, in cases where special categories of data are not involved pursuant to Articles 80, 82 and 83, with rules in relation to freedom of expression or with rules on processing in the employment context or with the conditions for processing for historical, statistical and scientific research purposes.[98]

---

97.   art 79(4) *ibid.*
98.   art 79(1) *ibid.*

Also, the supervisory authority shall impose a fine up to €1,000,000 or, in case of an enterprise up to 2 per cent of its annual worldwide turnover, to anyone who, intentionally or negligently:

- processes personal data without any or sufficient legal basis for the processing or does not comply with the conditions for consent pursuant to Articles 6, 7 and 8;

- processes special categories of data in violation of Articles 9 and 81;

- does not comply with an objection or the requirement pursuant to Article 19;

- does not comply with the conditions in relation to measures based on profiling pursuant to Article 20;

- does not adopt internal policies or does not implement appropriate measures for ensuring and demonstrating compliance pursuant to Articles 22, 23 and 30;

- does not designate a representative pursuant to Article 25;

- processes or instructs the processing of personal data in violation of the obligations in relation to processing on behalf of a data controller pursuant to Articles 26 and 27;

- does not alert on or notify a personal data breach or does not timely or completely notify the data breach to the supervisory authority or to the data subject pursuant to Articles 31 and 32;

- does not carry out a data protection impact assessment or processes personal data without prior authorisation or prior consultation of the supervisory authority pursuant to Articles 33 and 34;

- does not designate a data protection officer or does not ensure the conditions for fulfilling the tasks pursuant to Articles 35, 36 and 37;

- misuses a data protection seal or mark in the meaning of Article 39;

- carries out or instructs a data transfer to a third country or an international organisation that is not allowed by an adequacy decision or by appropriate safeguards or by a derogation pursuant to Articles 40 to 44;

- does not comply with an order or a temporary or definite ban on processing or the suspension of data flows by the supervisory authority pursuant to Article 53(1);

- does not comply with the obligations to assist or respond or provide relevant information to, or access to premises by, the supervisory authority pursuant to Articles 28(3), 29, 34(6) and 53(2);

• does not comply with the rules for safeguarding professional secrecy pursuant to Article 84.[99]

The Commission shall be empowered to adopt delegated acts (in accordance with Article 86) for the purpose of updating the amounts of the administrative fines referred to in Article 79(4), (5) and (6), taking into account the criteria referred to in Article graph 79(2).[100]

Conclusion

Increasingly, data protection breaches and other non-complaince will result in civil remedies and monetary awards and compensation to data subject. If a request for information or other notice is received from the Data Protection Commissioner it may be appropriate to seek immediate legal advice. The Data Protection Commissioner can also issue enforcement notices. In addition, the Data Protection Commissioner may also pursue monetary penalties. Organisations should ensure proper policies, awareness of data protection issues and ongoing training across all personnel who have an impact on and responsibility regarding data protection operations.

---

99.   art 79(16) *ibid.*
100. art 79(1) *ibid.*

CHAPTER 11

Security of Personal Data

Introduction

Personal data or "[p]ersonally identifiable information (PII) data has become the prime target of hackers and cyber-criminals. It can be exploited in many ways, from identity theft, spamming and phishing right through to cyber-espionage".[1] The data protection regime sets information and data security obligations on all data controllers, as well as data processors. These IT and personal data security requirements must be complied with. While security risks have increased with the internet,[2] security issues are not just limited to the organisation's internet. A security breach has cost Sony £250,000 in fines in the UK.

Appropriate Security Measures

There are specific requirements with regard to the security measures that need to be implemented under the Data Protection Acts.[3]

Organisations and data controllers must take appropriate security measures against unauthorised access to, or unauthorised alteration, disclosure or destruction of, the data, in particular where the processing involves the transmission of data over a network, and against all other unlawful forms of processing. As these risks grow,[4] so too must the effort of organisations. However, it is not the case that one solution will be sufficient in all instances. Today's solution may not work tomorrow.

The requirements regarding security of processing are contained in the *data protection principles*.[5] The data controller must take appropriate technical and organisational measures against unauthorised or unlawful processing of personal data and against accidental loss or destruction of, or damage to, personal data.

---

1. Rozenberg, "Challenges in PII Data Protection" (2012) *Computer Fraud & Security* 5–9 at 5.
2. "Security of the Internet and the Known Unknowns" (2012)(55) *Communications of the ACM* 35–37.
3. Data Protection Act 1988 and Data Protection (Amendment) Act 2003.
4. See, for example, "The Cybersecurity Risk" (2012)(55) *Communications of the ACM* 29–32.
5. Data Protection Acts s 2(1)(d).

The data controller must ensure the following:

Appropriate security measures shall be taken against unauthorised access to, or unauthorised alteration, disclosure or destruction of, the data, in particular where the processing involves the transmission of data over a network, and against all other unlawful forms of processing.

The different elements and requirements, therefore, include:

- not just security measures, but security measures that are appropriate. This means that the security measures will vary from organisation to organisation, and sector to sector, as well as depending upon the history of risk in the individual organisation;

- preventing unauthorised access;

- preventing unauthorised alteration;

- preventing unauthorised disclosure; or

- preventing unauthorised destruction; and

- especially where there is a network involved, preventing all other unlawful forms of processing.

The security obligations are therefore serious and demanding.

Ensuring Appropriate Security Measures

Data controllers must have an adequate level of protection and security as regards their storage, etc., of personal data. What are security and "appropriate security measures"? What must the organisation do? The *data protection principles* contained in s 2 of the Data Protection Acts refer to security obligations.[6] In determining appropriate technical and organisational measures, a data controller may have regard to a number of factors.

The Data Protection Acts s 2C provides that, in determining appropriate security measures for the purposes of s 2(1)(d) of the Acts, in particular (but without prejudice to the generality of that provision) where the processing involves the transmission of data over a network, a data controller:

- may have regard to the state of technological development and the cost of implementing the measures; and

- shall ensure that the measures provide a level of security appropriate to:

---

6.   s 2(1)(d) *ibid.*

- the harm that might result from unauthorised or unlawful processing, accidental or unlawful destruction or accidental loss of, or damage to, the data concerned; and

- the nature of the data concerned;

- may have regard to the state of technological development and the cost of implementing the measures.[7]

A data controller or data processor shall take all reasonable steps to ensure that:

- persons employed by it and

- other persons at the place of work concerned

are aware of and comply with the relevant security measures aforesaid.[8]

Where processing of personal data is carried out by a data processor on behalf of a data controller, the data controller shall:

- ensure that the processing is carried out in pursuance of a contract in writing or in another equivalent form between the data controller and the data processor and that the contract provides that the data processor carries out the processing only on and subject to the instructions of the data controller and that the data processor complies with obligations equivalent to those imposed on the data controller by s 2(1)(d) of the Data Protection Acts;

- ensure that the data processor provides sufficient guarantees in respect of the technical security measures, and organisational measures, governing the processing; and

- take reasonable steps to ensure compliance with those measures.[9]

Employees and Security

Organisations need to appraise and involve employees in addressing security concerns. Employees need to be made aware of the overall need for security and also of the security obligations and protocols with which they are required to comply.

---

7.   s 2C(1) *ibid.*
8.   s 2C(2) *ibid.*
9.   s 2C(3) *ibid.*

Data Protection Acts: Engaging Data Processors

Data processors[10] also have obligations in relation to processing personal data and security.

The Data Protection Acts at s 2C(3) provide that where processing of personal data is carried out by a data processor on behalf of a data controller, the data controller must, in order to comply with the seventh principle:

- ensure that the processing is carried out in pursuance of a contract in writing or in another equivalent form between the data controller and the data processor and that the contract provides that the data processor carries out the processing only on and subject to the instructions of the data controller and that the data processor complies with obligations equivalent to those imposed on the data controller by s 2(1)(d) of the Data Protection Acts;

- ensure that the data processor provides sufficient guarantees in respect of the technical security measures, and organisational measures, governing the processing; and

- take reasonable steps to ensure compliance with those measures.

Where processing of personal data is carried out by a data processor on behalf of a data controller, then the data controller must have a contract in writing with the data processor containing certain clauses and obligations. Contracts with data processors must address the following:

- that processing must be carried out in pursuance of a contract in writing;

- that the data processor carries out the processing only on and subject to the instructions of the data controller;

- that the data processor must comply with the above security requirements.

There are specific requirements where data processors are engaged and relied upon. Where data controllers engage data processors then the data controller must:

- have a contract in writing or other equivalent form that provides that the data processor will act only on instructions of the data controller and that will comply with the data security measures to which the data controller is subject;

- ensure the data processor provides sufficient guarantees in respect of the technical security measures and organisational measures it implements;

- takes reasonable steps to ensure compliance with such matters.

---

10. Note generally, for example, Morgan, "Data Controllers, Data Processors and Data Sharers" (4 March 2011) SCL *Computers and Law*.

What actions should an organisation take if third parties process their organisation's data? The following may assist:

- Ideally an organisation should have advance procedures and policies in place to cater for such an eventuality, for example ensuring that an appropriate senior manager/board member has an assigned role and takes responsibility for date protection compliance, including dealing with breaches, and also having a documented IT security incident handing procedure policy in place. Needless to say, it must be properly policed, implemented, reviewed and updated appropriately;

- Once a breach does occur, a proper procedure can assist in containing the breach and recovering from same, assessing the ongoing risk, notifying the breach as appropriate, evaluating and reacting to the breach and the risk;

- All of the appropriate personnel within the organisation should be aware of the procedures and consulted as appropriate, including, for example, the managing director, data protections legal, IT, and media/press officer;

- A part of the procedure will have a designated list of external contact points, some or all of whom may need to be notified and contacted, as appropriate;

- Obviously the nature of organisations, and of breaches themselves, differ and the IT security incident handing procedure policy will need to be tailored. After all, the cause of a data security breach can be any of a number of reasons;

- Also, such a policy, while covering breaches of data protection and privacy, may well encompass wider issues, such as outsourcing, backups, disaster recovery, business continuity, etc.;

- Business in other jurisdictions may require additional measures. For example, if a business owns or has access to personal information of Californian residents then it may have a legal duty to notify those individuals if that information (such as names and credit card details) has been accessed illegally.

Security and EU Article 29 Working Party on Data Protection

The influential EU Article 29 Working Party on Data Protection has published a document relating to personal data and information security.[11] This is an EU organisation made up of representatives of all EU data protection authorities. The opinion was published on 29 May 2002.[12] It refers to the surveillance of employees' electronic communications.

---

11. See http://ec.europa.eu/justice/data-protection/article-29/index_en.htm, last accessed 14 January 2013.

12. Article 29 Working Party, Working document on the surveillance of electronic communications in the workplace (WP 55), available at http://ec.europa.eu/justice/policies/privacy/docs/wpdocs/2002/wp55_en.pdf, last accessed 14 January 2013.

In terms of compliance it raises a number of concerns for organisations to consider when dealing with their policies and activities regarding such personal data. It suggests that organisations ask if the proposed processing of the employees' personal data is:

- transparent?
- necessary?
- fair?
- proportionate?
- and to be used for what purpose?[13]

It also suggests that organisations should consider if each proposed processing activity can be achieved through some other, less obtrusive means.[14]

It refers to the organisation informing those outside of the organisation as appropriate in relation to the proposed processing.[15]

It also refers to issues of proportionality in suggesting that an organisation, in processing personal data, should adopt the minimum processing necessary, and pursue a strategy of prevention versus detection. Detection leans more towards blanket monitoring of employees, whereas prevention is viewed as more appropriate and employee-privacy friendly. Of course, where an issue comes to the organisation's attention, it could then investigate that issue, as opposed to actively monitoring all employees continuously. An example would be using IT filtering systems, which alert the IT manager that there may be an issue to look at further, rather than the IT manager actively looking at and monitoring all employee communications.[16]

DP Directive 95 and Confidentiality

Section VIII of the DP Directive 95[17] refers to confidentiality and security of processing. Article 16 refers to the confidentiality of processing. It provides that any person acting under the authority of the data controller or of the data processor, including the data processor, who has access to personal data must not process it except on instructions from the data controller, unless required to do so by law.

---

13. *ibid.*
14. *ibid.*
15. *ibid.*
16. *ibid.*
17. EU Data Protection Directive 1995 (Directive 95/46/EC of the European Parliament and of the Council of 24 October 1995 on the protection of individuals with regard to the processing of personal data and on the free movement of such data).

DP Directive 95 and Security

Article 17 of the DP Directive 95 refers to security of processing. Article 17(1) provides that Member States shall provide that the data controller must implement appropriate technical and organisational measures to protect personal data against accidental or unlawful destruction or accidental loss, alteration, unauthorised disclosure or access, in particular where the processing involves the transmission of data over a network, and against all other unlawful forms of processing. It also provides that, having regard to the technology available and the cost of its implementation, such measures shall ensure a level of security appropriate to the risks represented by the processing and the nature of the data to be protected.

Member States shall provide that the data controller must, where processing is carried out on its behalf, choose a data processor providing sufficient guarantees in respect of the technical security measures and organisational measures governing the processing to be carried out, and must ensure compliance with those measures.[18]

The carrying out of processing by way of a data processor must be governed by a contract or legal act binding the data processor to the data controller and stipulating in particular that:

- the data processor shall act only on instructions from the data controller;
- the obligations set out in paragraph 1, as defined by the law of the Member State in which the data processor is established, shall also be incumbent on the data processor.[19]

For the purposes of keeping proof, the parts of the contract or the legal act relating to data protection and the requirements relating to the measures referred to above shall be in writing or in another equivalent form.[20]

DP Regulation and Security

Section 2 of the DP Regulation[21] relates to data security. Article 30 specifically refers to security of processing. The data controller and the data processor shall implement appropriate technical and organisational measures to ensure a level of security appropriate to the risks represented by the processing and the nature of the personal

---

18. art 17(2) *ibid.*
19. art 17(3) *ibid.*
20. art 17(4) *ibid.*
21. EU draft Data Protection Regulation (Proposal for a Regulation of the European Parliament and of the Council on the protection of individuals with regard to the processing of personal data and on the free movement of such data (General Data Protection Regulation) COM (2012) 11 final).

data to be protected, having regard to the technology available and the cost of its implementation.[22]

The data controller and the data processor shall, following an evaluation of the risks, take the measures referred to in Article 30 above to protect personal data against accidental or unlawful destruction or accidental loss and to prevent any unlawful forms of processing, in particular any unauthorised disclosure, dissemination or access, or alteration of personal data.[23]

Article 30(3) provides that the Commission shall be empowered to adopt delegated acts (in accordance with Article 86) for the purpose of further specifying the criteria and conditions for the technical and organisational measures referred to in paragraphs Article 30(1) and (2) above, including the determinations of what constitutes the state of the art, for specific sectors and in specific data processing situations, in particular taking account of developments in technology and solutions for privacy by design and data protection by default, unless Article 30(4) below applies.

The Commission may adopt, where necessary, implementing acts for specifying the requirements laid down in Article 30(1) and (2) to various situations, in particular to:

- prevent any unauthorised access to personal data;

- prevent any unauthorised disclosure, reading, copying, modification, erasure or removal of personal data; and

- ensure the verification of the lawfulness of processing operations.[24]

In addition, those implementing acts shall be adopted in accordance with the examination procedure referred to in Article 87(2).

DP Regulation: Notification of Security Breaches

Article 31 of the DP Regulation refers to notification of a personal data breach[25] to the supervisory authority, i.e. the Data Protection Commissioner.

In the case of a personal data breach, the data controller shall without undue delay and, where feasible, not later than 24 hours after having become aware of it, notify the personal data breach to the supervisory authority.[26] The notification to the

---

22. s 2(1) *ibid.*
23. s 2(2) *ibid.*
24. s 2(4) *ibid.*
25. Note, for example, Wainman, "Data Protection Breaches: Today and Tomorrow" (30 June 2012) SCL *Computers and Law.* Also see Dekker, Karsberg and Daskala, *Cyber Incident Reporting in the EU* (2012).
26. art 31(1) EU draft Data Protection Regulation.

supervisory authority shall be accompanied by a reasoned justification in cases where it is not made within 24 hours.[27]

Article 31(2) provides that pursuant to Article 26(2)(f), the data processor shall alert and inform the data controller immediately after the establishment of a personal data breach.

The notification referred to above must at least:

- describe the nature of the personal data breach, including the categories and number of data subjects concerned and the categories and number of data records concerned;

- communicate the identity and contact details of the data protection officer or other contact point where more information can be obtained;

- recommend measures to mitigate the possible adverse effects of the personal data breach;

- describe the consequences of the personal data breach; and

- describe the measures proposed or taken by the data controller to address the personal data breach.[28]

Data controllers shall document any personal data breaches, comprising the facts surrounding the breach, its effects and the remedial action taken.[29] This documentation must enable the supervisory authority to verify compliance with this Article. The documentation shall only include the information necessary for that purpose.

The Commission shall be empowered to adopt delegated Acts (in accordance with Article 86) for the purpose of further specifying the criteria and requirements for establishing the data breach referred to above and for the particular circumstances in which a data controller and a data processor is required to notify the personal data breach.[30]

The Commission may lay down the standard format of such notification to the supervisory authority, the procedures applicable to the notification requirement and the form and the modalities for the documentation referred to in Article 31(4), including the time limits for erasure of the information contained therein. Those implementing acts shall be adopted in accordance with the examination procedure referred to in Article 87(2).[31]

---

27. *ibid.*
28. art 31(3) *ibid.*
29. art 31(4) *ibid.*
30. art 31(5) *ibid.*
31. art 31(6) *ibid.*

DP Regulation: Notification of Personal Data Breach to Data Subject

Article 32 of the DP Regulation refers to communication of a personal data breach[32] to the data subject. When the personal data breach is likely to adversely affect the protection of the personal data or privacy of the data subject, the data controller shall, after the notification referred to in Article 31, communicate the personal data breach to the data subject without undue delay.[33]

The communication to the data subject referred to in paragraph Article 32(1) above shall describe the nature of the personal data breach and contain at least the information and the recommendations provided for in Article 31(3)(b) and (c).[34]

The communication of a personal data breach to the data subject shall not be required if the data controller demonstrates to the satisfaction of the supervisory authority that it has implemented appropriate technological protection measures, and that those measures were applied to the data concerned by the personal data breach.[35] Such technological protection measures shall render the data unintelligible to any person who is not authorised to access it.

Without prejudice to the data controller's obligation to communicate the personal data breach to the data subject, if the data controller has not already communicated the personal data breach to the data subject of the personal data breach, the supervisory authority, having considered the likely adverse effects of the breach, may require it to do so.[36]

The Commission is empowered to adopt delegated acts for the purpose of further specifying the criteria and requirements as to the circumstances in which a personal data breach is likely to adversely affect the personal data referred to in Article 32(1).[37] Also, the Commission may lay down the format of the communication to the data subject and the procedures applicable to that communication.[38]

Organisational Security Awareness

There is an issue of ensuring security awareness within the organisation. Data controllers and data processors must take all reasonable steps to ensure that persons employed by them and other persons at the place of work are aware of and comply with the relevant security measures.

---

32. Note, for example, Wainman, "Data Protection Breaches", *art cit*. Also see Dekker, *Cyber Incident Reporting, op cit.*
33. art 32(1) EU draft Data Protection Regulation.
34. art 32(2) *ibid.*
35. art 32(3) *ibid.*
36. art 32(4) *ibid.*
37. art 32(5) *ibid.*
38. art 32(6) *ibid.*

Identifying and Controlling Organisational IT Security

Who needs to be in charge of IT and data security in an organisation? What organisational security measures should be in place?

The Data Protection Acts do not require that a named individual be appointed with responsibility for security compliance. However, there are specific organisational responsibilities regarding security set out in the Data Protection Acts and these include a specific requirement that all staff are aware of and comply with the security standards set out in the data protection regime.

These security requirements apply where an organisation collects and processes any personal data. Typically personal data would include information that identifies (living) individuals such as employees or customers. Accordingly, for most organisations, data protection compliance is likely to be an issue that crosses various aspects of the business such as human resources, IT and customer support. It is not necessarily just an IT function. An organisation's decision as to who should be responsible for IT and data security should be made with this in mind.

The security standards set out in the Data Protection Acts can be summarised as obliging the organisation to take "appropriate" security measures to guard against unauthorised access, alteration, disclosure or destruction of any personal data.

In determining what is "appropriate", the organisation can take into account the state of technological development and the cost of implementing the security measures. However, the organisation is obliged to ensure that the measures it decides to adopt provide a level of security appropriate to the harm that might result from a security compromise given the nature of the data concerned. For example, a hospital processing sensitive health data would be expected to adopt a particularly high security standard while a corner shop processing personal data for a paper round might be subject to a less onerous standard.

In light of some high-profile cases of personal data theft or personal data loss, it should also be noted that the Data Protection Commissioner's office may take the view that an appropriate level of security for laptop computers used in the financial services and health industries required the use of encryption in respect of the data stored on the hard drive (over and above the use of user name and password log-in requirements).

In adopting security measures within an organisation, it should be noted that the legal standard governing personal data is over and above any other legal obligations of confidentiality that could be owed to third parties at common law or under a contract that contains confidentiality provisions.

Appraising Employees

What guidance should be given to an organisation's employees regarding IT and data security? An organisation might consider these issues.

The overriding principle here is that, for it to be effective, an employee must have clear notice of all aspects of the organisation's IT and data security policy. The following refers to same in greater detail.

General Policy
Organisations should reserve the right "to monitor" use of the computer and tele-phone system, including email. Disclosure of sensitive or confidential information about the company or personal data about any individual should without authorisa-tion should be forbidden (constant general monitoring may be difficult).

Email
Employees should be made aware that email is an essential business tool but not without its risks. Business communications should be suitable and not too informal or contain inappropriate material. Personal use of email must be reasonable.

Internet Access
Downloading of any software without approval should be forbidden. No improper or illegal activities (abuse, hacking, etc.) should be tolerated. Access to certain types of websites (adult, criminal, hate, violent, etc.) should be expressly restricted. Origination or dissemination of inappropriate or abusive material should be forbidden.

Mobile Telephones and Devices
Downloading of any software, and content, without approval should be forbidden. No improper or illegal activities (abuse, hacking, etc.) should be tolerated. Access to certain types of websites (adult, criminal, hate, violent, etc.) should be expressly restricted. Origination or dissemination of inappropriate or abusive material should be forbidden.

Vehicles
Increasingly tracking and other data from vehicles can be related to identified employees. It is important for organisations to consider these personal data issues.

Internet Social Networking
Social networking without approval should be forbidden. No improper or illegal activities (online abuse, etc.) should be tolerated. Access to certain types of websites

may have to be expressly restricted. Origination, promotion, endorsement or dissemination of inappropriate, illegal, abusive, threatening, defamatory, etc., material should be forbidden.

Software Installation & Management

Purchase and/or installation of software, and or content, not approved should be forbidden. All software must be required to be tested before installation on the system to ensure that it is free from viruses, malware, etc.

Password Security

Clear guidelines as to the use of passwords should be given including the strength of password required, the importance of keeping one's password(s) confidential, the changing of passwords at regular intervals and (in the light of recent events) the application of password security (at least) to laptops, mobile phones and PDAs. In some businesses, stronger encryption will be appropriate and employees should be required to comply with procedures in this regard. Carrying organisational data on vulnerable media such as memory sticks should be discouraged.

Connecting Hardware

Employees should be required not to connect any hardware (memory sticks, hard drives, etc.) without following specified procedures and obtaining appropriate authorisation.

Remote Access

For many businesses, remote access, including web-based remote access, is a vital tool. However, policies should deal with such matters as accessing remotely from insecure locations as internet cafés, etc., and emphasise the importance of logging off effectively.

Bring Your Own Devive (BYOD)

Increasingly organisations are faced with the dilemma of permitting employees to bring their own electronic devices into the work environment, which may interact with the organisation's network systems and data. This creates inevitable risks and complications for organisations if permitted.

Organisational Security Measures

What measures should an organisation take? Some suggestions may include:

- Ensure that the organisation has the appropriate security equipment and software to protect the organisation's systems if granting third-party access.

If providing access to a third party involves opening business systems up to a public network such as the internet, it is essential that suitable security measures are taken;

- Obtain a complete listing of the IT provider personnel who have access to organisational systems and detail their level, status (full time/contractor) and ensure that their employment contracts incorporate terms similar to the above;

- Third parties should be granted access to the organisation's systems only when the relevant individuals in the organisation (e.g. a business manager, in conjunction with IT staff) have agreed that there is a business need for such access to be granted. Access should only be for a temporary period and renewed at regular intervals;

- Third-party computer accounts should be monitored (subject to legal agreements between the organisation and the third party and in accordance with legal requirements) and disabled as soon as access is no longer required;

- Ensure that sensitive files are segregated in secure areas/computer systems and available only to qualified persons;

- Ensure that the organisation has inventoried the various types of data being stored and classified according to how important it is and how costly it would be for the organisation if it were lost or stolen;

- Scan computers (especially servers) for unauthorised programs that transmit information to third parties such as hackers;

- Programs that have a hidden purpose are known as Trojans. Individuals may have inadvertently or deliberately downloaded free programs from the internet that send back information such as passwords to hackers or internet usage information to marketers to, for example, build up trends of one's profile;

- Ensure that third parties only have access to information and computer settings on a need-to-know basis;

- The System Administrator for the organisation's computer systems should set up computer accounts for third parties so that these third parties do not have access to all information on the organisation's systems or have the permission to install non-standard software and change computer settings;

- When engaging an external business to destroy records or electronic media, ensure references are checked. Draft a contract setting out the terms of the relationship. Ensure that destruction is done on-site and require that a certificate of destruction be issued upon completion.

Particular attention also needs to be given to the deletion of data, and the decommissioning or transfer of devices so that all personal data are deleted. This requires expert advice. Just because certain data may be deleted does not mean that it is not retrievable or that it is deleted from all locations.

Breach Laws to Consider

What laws might affect an organisation if an organisation has an IT or data security breach? Suggested legal issues and laws to consider include:

- Data Protection Acts;
- DP Directive 95[39];
- ePrivacy Directive[40];
- Electronic Commerce Act 2000;
- European Communities (Directive 2000/31/EC) Regulations 2003;
- European Communities (Protection of Consumers in Respect of Contracts made by Means of Distance Communication) Regulations 2001;
- European Communities (Unfair Terms in Consumer Contracts) Regulations 2000[41];
- European Communities (Unfair Terms in Consumer Contracts) Regulations (SI 27/1995);
- Child Pornography Prevention Act 1996;
- Child Trafficking and Pornography Acts 1998 and 2004;
- Child Trafficking and Pornography (Amendment) Act 2004;
- Childrens Act 2001 and Constitutional Amendment re Children;
- Consumer Credit Act 1995;
- Consumer Information Act 1978;
- Copyright and Related Rights Act 2000 (as amended);
- Criminal Damage Act 1991;
- Criminal Evidence Act 1992;
- Criminal Justice Acts 1993, 1994, 2006;
- Criminal Justice (Theft and Fraud Offences) Act 1991 and 2001;
- Employment Equality Acts 1998 (as amended);
- European Convention on Human Rights Act 2003;

---

39. EU Data Protection Directive 1995.
40. Directive 2002/58/EC of the European Parliament and of the Council of 12 July 2002 concerning the processing of personal data and the protection of privacy in the electronic communications sector (Directive on privacy and electronic communications)(as amended by Directives 2006/24/EC and 2009/136/EC).
41. SI 307/2000.

- Evidence;

- Freedom of Information Acts 1997 and 2003;

- Human Rights Act 1998;

- Interception of Postal Packets and Telecommunications Messages (Regulation) Act 1993;

- Minimum Notice and Terms of Employment Acts 1973 and 2001;

- Civil Liability Act 1961;

- Prohibition of Incitement to Hatred Act 1989;

- Safety, Health and Welfare at Work Act 2005;

- Sale of Goods and Supply of Services Act 1980;

- European Convention on Human Rights; and

- ePrivacy Regulations/PECR.

Other issues to consider include:

- official guidance and current stated positions of regulators and guidance bodies; and

- international standards for organisations, e.g. technical security standards, etc.

Third-Party Security Providers

What actions should an organisation take if a third party is responsible for IT security or has access to its IT system? This is becoming increasingly popular in practice through outsourcing, cloud, vendor, etc., agreements. Some issues to consider include:

- understand the security framework and document security, the various risks, exposures, etc.;

- evaluate what measures to take with the organisation's IT provider;

- take legal advice on drafting appropriate contracts that secure what your IT provider is securing;

- ensure that confidentiality clauses are included to protect all of the organisation's intellectual property assets;

- have the organisation's IT provider supply a complete security document outlining the hardware, topology, software and methodologies deployed;

- ensure that the organisation's IT provider has staff participate in regular training programs to keep abreast of technical and legal issues;

- ensure that the organisation's IT provider develops a security breach response plan in the event that the company experiences a data breach;

- develop security guidelines for laptops and other portable devices if and when transported off-site;

- have the organisation's IT provider ensure that all employees follow strict encryption, password and virus-protection procedures and develop a mechanism where employees are required to change passwords often, using foolproof methods especially for terminating employees;

- Ensure that the organisation's IT provider has a records retention/disposal schedule for personal data, whether stored in paper, electronic or computer media.

Security Awareness

EU Council Resolution 2002/C43/02 of 28 January 2002 indicates the recognition and official concern in relation to the loss of personal data, and the fact that technology has changed significantly since the DP Directive 95.

It refers to the dangers of information loss, attacks on organisations, and issues of network and information security for organisations and individuals. It indicates that EU Member States should engage in information campaigns addressing the issues of security and personal data. There is a need to promote best practice, such as the internationally recognised standards for IT, e.g. ISO 15408.

There is also an increase in eGovernment and an associated need to promote secure eGovernment.

It notes the increase of attacks of the security of personal data though technology, but some of the solutions may also come from new technologies. Some of these are referred to as privacy-enhancing technologies, or PETs.[42]

In addition, it also refers to the increase of mobile and wireless communications technologies and the need for introducing and enhancing wireless security.

Keeping on top of the increasing threats to information security is an ongoing task. The threats are ever changing, and so equally should be the effort to prevent breaches, and to deal with them if and when they occur. Some of the most current information security threats are highlighted annually by various IT security vendors as well as police and investigative officials.

---

42. See, for example, Beric and Carlisle, "Investigating the Legal Protection of Data, Information and Knowledge Under the EU Data Protection Regime" (2009)(23) *International Review of Law, Computers & Technology* 189–201.

Data Protection Commissioner Security Guidance

The Data Protection Commissioner advises that that appropriate security measures be put in place that take account of the harm that would result from unauthorised access to the information. This should take account of available technology and the cost of installation. In addition to technical security measures, due regard should be had for physical security measures such as access control for central IT servers and local PCs.[43] Furthermore, detailed guidance entitled *Data Security Guidance* is provided by the Data Protection Commissioner at http://www.dataprotection.ie/viewdoc.asp?DocID=1091.

According to the Data Protection Commissioner, physical security safeguards should include the following considerations:

- perimeter security (monitoring of access, office locked and alarmed when not in use);

- restrictions on access to sensitive areas within the building (such as server rooms);

- computer location (so that the screen may not be viewed by members of the public);

- storage of files (files not stored in public areas with access restricted to staff with a need to access particular files); and

- secure disposal of records (effective "wiping" of data stored electronically; secure disposal of paper records).[44]

The UK ICO has also issued a guide entitled *A Practical Guide to IT Security, Ideal for Small Businesses*.[45] The ICO has commented in relation to encryption issues,[46] (as has the Data Protection Commissioner) and provides the following tips and suggestions for maintaining and implementing IT security for personal data[47]:

For Computer Security
- install a firewall and virus-checking on the organisation's computers;

- make sure that the organisation's operating system is set up to receive automatic updates;

---

43. See DPC, available at https://www.dataprotection.ie/viewdoc.asp?DocID=650, last accessed 11 January 2013.
44. See DPC, available at https://www.dataprotection.ie/viewdoc.asp?DocID=1091, last accessed 11 January 2013.
45. Available at http://www.ico.gov.uk/, last accessed 11 January 2013.
46. Available at http://www.ico.gov.uk/news/current_topics/Our_approach_to_encryption.aspx, last accessed 11 January 2013.
47. Available at http://www.ico.gov.uk/for_organisations/data_protection/security_measures.aspx, last accessed 11 January 2013.

- protect the organisation's computer by downloading the latest patches or security updates;

- only allow the organisation's staff access to the information they need to do their job and do not let them share passwords;

- encrypt any personal information held electronically that would cause damage or distress if it were lost or stolen;

- take regular back-ups of the information on the organisation's computer system and keep them in a separate place so that if computers are lost, the information is not;

- securely remove all personal information before disposing of old computers (by using technology or destroying the hard disk); and

- consider installing anti-spyware tools. Spyware is the generic name given to programs that are designed to secretly monitor your activities on the organisation's computer. Spyware can be unwittingly installed within other file and program downloads, and its use is often malicious. It can capture passwords, banking credentials and credit card details, then relay them back to fraudsters. Anti-spyware helps to monitor and protect the organisation's computer from spyware threats, and it is often free to use and update.[48]

For Using Emails Securely

- Consider whether the content of the email should be encrypted or password protected. The organisation's IT or security team should be able to assist with encryption;

- When typing in the name of the recipient, some email software will suggest similar addresses to those emails used before. If the organisation has previously emailed several people whose name or address starts the same way – e.g. Dave – the auto-complete or auto-suggest function may bring up several Daves. Make sure employees choose the right address;

- If the organisation wants to send an email to a recipient without revealing their address to other recipients, make sure the organisation uses blind carbon copy (bcc), not carbon copy (cc). With "cc" every recipient of the message will be able to see the other address(es) it was sent to;

- Be careful when using a group email address. Check who is in the group and make sure the organisation really want to send the message to everyone;

- If the employee sends a sensitive email from a secure server to an insecure recipient, security will be threatened. The employee may need to check that the recipient's arrangements are secure enough before sending the message.[49]

---

48. *ibid.*
49. *ibid.*

For Using Faxes Securely

- Consider whether sending the information by a means other than fax is more appropriate, such as using a courier service or secure email. Make sure the organisation only sends the information that is required. For example, if a solicitor asks the organisation to forward a statement, send only the statement specifically asked for, not all statements available on the file;

- Employees should double check the fax number being used. It is best to dial from a directory of previously verified numbers;

- Check that the fax recipient has adequate security measures in place. For example, the organisation's fax should not be left uncollected in an open plan office;

- If the fax is sensitive, ask the recipient to confirm that they are at the fax machine, they are ready to receive the document, and that there is sufficient paper in the machine;

- Ring up or email to make sure the whole document has been received safely;

- Use a cover sheet. This will let anyone know who the information is for and whether it is confidential or sensitive.[50]

For Other Security

- Shred all confidential paper waste;

- Check the physical security of the organisation's premises;

- Train the organisation's staff:

  - so they know what is expected of them;

  - to be wary of people who may try to trick them into giving out personal details;

  - so that they can be prosecuted if they deliberately give out personal details without permission;

  - to use a strong password – these are long (at least seven characters) and have a combination of upper and lower case letters, numbers and the special keyboard characters like the asterisk or currency symbols;

  - not to send emails about other people which are offensive, or refers to their private lives or refers to anything else that could bring the organisation into disrepute;

  - not to believe emails that appear to come from the bank that ask for the organisation's account, credit card details or the organisation's password (a bank would never ask for this information in this way);

---

50. *ibid.*

– not to open spam – not even to unsubscribe or ask for no more
mailings. Tell them to delete the email and either get spam filters
on the organisation's computers or use an email provider that offers
this service.[51]

Data Protection Commissioner: Security Breaches

The Data Protection Commissioner has issued a Personal "Data Security Breach
Code of Practice" to help organisations to react appropriately when they become
aware of breaches of security involving customer or employee personal information.

However, it does not include the public sector. Separate guidance from the
Department of Finance on data security, however, advises departments and agencies
to report data breaches immediately to the Commissioner.

The Code of Practice does not apply to providers of publicly available electronic
communications networks or services. The European Communities (Electronic
Communications Networks and Services)(Privacy and Electronic Communications)
Regulations 2011[52] places specific obligations on providers of publicly available
electronic communications networks or services to safeguard the security of their
services. These obligations are dealt with separately.

The Data Protection Commissioner issued the Code on 29 July 2011, entitled
Personal Data Security Breach Code of Practice. It was approved by the Data Protection
Commissioner under s 13(2)(b) of the Data Protection Acts. It provides as follows:

- The Data Protection Acts impose obligations on data controllers to process
  personal data entrusted to them in a manner that respects the rights of data
  subjects to have their data processed fairly.[53] Data controllers are under a
  specific obligation to take appropriate measures to protect the security of
  such data.[54] The Code of Practice does not apply to providers of publicly
  available electronic communications networks or services;

- The Code of Practice addresses situations where personal data has been put
  at risk of unauthorised disclosure, loss, destruction or alteration. The focus
  of the Data Protection Commissioner in such cases is on the rights of the
  affected data subjects in relation to the processing of their personal data;

- Where an incident gives rise to a risk of unauthorised disclosure, loss,
  destruction or alteration of personal data, in manual or electronic form,
  the data controller must give immediate consideration to informing those

---

51. *ibid.*
52. SI 336/2011.
53. s 2(1) *ibid.*
54. s 2(1)(d) *ibid.*

affected. Such information permits data subjects to consider the consequences for each of them individually and to take appropriate measures. In appropriate cases, data controllers should also notify organisations that may be in a position to assist in protecting data subjects, including, where relevant, An Garda Síochána, financial institutions, etc.;

- If the data concerned is protected by technological measures such as to make it unintelligible to any person who is not authorised to access it, the data controller may conclude that there is no risk to the data and therefore no need to inform data subjects. Such a conclusion would only be justified where the technological measures (such as encryption) were of a high standard;

- All incidents of loss of control of personal data in manual or electronic form by a data processor must be reported to the relevant data controller as soon as the data processor becomes aware of the incident;

- All incidents in which personal data has been put at risk should be reported to the Data Protection Commissioner when the full extent and consequences of the incident has been reported without delay directly to the affected data subject(s) and it affects no more than 100 data subjects and it does not include sensitive personal data or personal data of a financial nature. In case of doubt – in particular *any* doubt related to the adequacy of technological risk-mitigation measures – the data controller should report the incident to the Data Protection Commissioner;

- Data controllers reporting to the Office of the Data Protection Commissioner in accordance with the Code should make initial contact with the Office within two working days of becoming aware of the incident, outlining the circumstances surrounding the incident. This initial contact may be by email (preferably), telephone or fax, and must not involve the communication of personal data. The Data Protection Commissioner will make a determination regarding the need for a detailed report and/or subsequent investigation based on the nature of the incident and the presence or otherwise of appropriate physical or technological security measures to protect the data;

- Should the Data Protection Commissioner request a data controller to provide a detailed written report of the incident, the office will specify a timeframe for the delivery of the report based on the nature of the incident and the information required. Such a report should reflect careful consideration of the following elements:

  - the amount and nature of the personal data that has been compromised;

  - the action being taken to secure and/or recover the personal data that has been compromised;

- the action being taken to inform those affected by the incident or reasons for the decision not to do so;

- the action being taken to limit damage or distress to those affected by the incident;

- a chronology of the events leading up to the loss of control of the personal data; and

- the measures being taken to prevent repetition of the incident;

- Depending on the nature of the incident, the Data Protection Commissioner may investigate the circumstances surrounding the personal data security breach. Investigations may include on-site examination of systems and procedures and could lead to a recommendation to inform data subjects about a security breach incident where a data controller has not already done so. If necessary, the Data Protection Commissioner may use his or her enforcement powers to compel appropriate action to protect the interests of data subjects;

- Even where there is no notification of the Data Protection Commissioner, the data controller should keep a summary record of each incident that has given rise to a risk of unauthorised disclosure, loss, destruction or alteration of personal data. The record should include a brief description of the nature of the incident and an explanation of why the data controller did not consider it necessary to inform the Data Protection Commissioner. Such records should be provided to the Data Protection Commissioner upon request;

- The Code of Practice applies to all categories of data controllers and data processors to which the Data Protection Acts apply.[55]

Commenting on the new Code, the Data Protection Commissioner notes[56] the following:

> *Obligations on Providers of Publicly Available Electronic Communications Networks or Services*
> … the European Communities (Electronic Communications Networks and Services) (Privacy and Electronic Communications) Regulations 2011[57] place specific obligations on providers of publicly available electronic communications networks or services to safeguard the security of their services. At a general level, such undertakings are required to have in place appropriate *technical* and *organisational* measures to keep personal data safe and secure. More specifically, providers of publicly available electronic communications networks or services are required to:

---

55. *Personal Data Security Breach Code of Practice*, Data Protection Commissioner, 2011.
56. See DPC, available at http://www.dataprotection.ie/docs/Breach_Notification_Guidance/901. htm, last accessed 11 January 2013.
57. SI 336/2011.

- have a security policy in place (and be in a position to demonstrate that the security policy has been implemented and kept relevant);

- ensure that personal data can only be used by authorised personnel for authorised purposes; and

- protect personal data against unlawful use or access.

In case of any particular risk to the security of the network, providers of publicly available electronic communications networks or services must provide information to subscribers *without delay* about the risks and any possible remedies (including the likely costs involved) even where the proposed measures are outside the direct control of the undertaking.

In case of a personal data security breach affecting even one individual, providers of publicly available electronic communications networks or services must *without undue delay*:

- notify the Office of the Data Protection Commissioner of the breach (even in circumstances where it considers the data would be unintelligible to third parties), including a description of the measures to be taken to address the breach; and

- notify any individual that may be adversely affected by the breach.

It is not necessary to notify individuals if the Data Protection Commissioner is satisfied that the data would be unintelligible to third parties. The Data Protection Commissioner can require an undertaking to notify individuals if the undertaking does not consider it necessary. Any notification to individuals affected by a personal data security breach must contain:

- an outline of the breach;

- a contact point for obtaining more information; and

- recommended measures to mitigate any possible adverse effects from the breach.

Additionally providers of publicly available electronic communications networks or services must maintain an inventory of personal data breaches which can be checked by the Data Protection Commissioner.

Failure to comply with these obligations can result in a criminal prosecution with fines of up to €5,000 and on indictment €250,000 per offence.

Prevention is better than Cure
Following the steps outlined in the Code of Practice following a data security breach is no substitute for the proper design of systems to secure personal data from accidental or

deliberate disclosure … As part of a data security policy, an organisation should antici-
pate what it would do if there were a data breach. Some questions [to consider are]:

- What would [the] organisation do if it had a data breach incident?

- [Has the organisation got] a policy in place that specifies what a data breach
  is? (It is not just lost USB keys/disks/laptops. It may include any loss of
  control over personal data entrusted to organisations, including inappropriate
  access to personal data on [the IT] systems or the sending of personal data to
  the wrong individuals.)

- How would [the organisation] know that [the] organisation had suffered
  a data breach? Does staff at all levels understand the implications of losing
  personal data?

- Has [the] organisation specified whom staff tell if they have lost control of
  personal data?

- Does [the] policy make clear who is responsible for dealing with an incident?

- Does [the] policy meet the requirements of the Data Protection Commissioner's
  approved Personal Data Security Breach Code of Practice?[58]

UK Breaches

The UK ICO advises[59] that the following must be complied with:

Keep a Log of Personal Data Breaches
[The organisation] must keep a record of all personal data breaches in an inventory or
log. It must contain:

- the facts surrounding the breach;

- the effects of that breach; and

- remedial action taken.

[The ICO has] produced a *template log* to help [organisations] record the information
[it] need[s].

Notify Breaches to the ICO
[The organisation] must notify the ICO of any personal data breaches. This notification must include at least a description of:

---

58. See DPC, available at http://www.dataprotection.ie/docs/Breach_Notification_Guidance/901.
    htm, last accessed 11 January 2013.
59. Available at http://www.ico.gov.uk/for_organisations/privacy_and_electronic_communications/
    the_guide/security_breaches.aspx, last accessed 11 January 2013.

- the nature of the breach;

- the consequences of the breach; and

- the measures taken or proposed to be taken by the provider to address the breach.

... if the breach is of a particularly serious nature [organisations] need to notify ... the breach as soon as possible...

When thinking about whether a breach is of a serious nature, ... consider:

- the type and sensitivity of the data involved;

- the impact it could have on the individual, such as distress or embarrassment; and

- the potential harm, such as financial loss, fraud, or theft of identity.

...

Notify Breaches to Subscribers
[The organisation] may also need to tell [its] subscribers. If the breach is likely to adversely affect their personal data or privacy [the organisation] need[s] to, without unnecessary delay, notify them of the breach. [The organisation] needs to tell [subscribers of]:

- the nature of the breach;

- contact details for [the] organisation where they can get more information; and

- how they can mitigate any possible adverse impact of the breach.

[Consider if there are] measures in place which would render the data unintelligible and that those measures were applied to the data concerned in the breach.

If [the organisation does not] tell subscribers, the ICO can require [the organisation to] do so, if it considers the breach is likely to have an adverse effect on them.[60]

Disposal of Computer Hardware

Particular care is needed when considering the disposal of IT hardware, equipment and software, as they may still contain personal data files. This can continue to be the case even when it appears that files have been wiped or deleted. It is always advised to take professional legal, IT and/or forensic advice.

---

60. *ibid.*

EU Security Directive Proposed

The EU Commission announced a new strategy to address cyber security, responses and tackling security breaches on 7 February 2013. This includes a new proposed Directive concerning measures to ensure a high common level of network and information security across the EU. Organisations will have to watch how this develops.

Conclusion

Security is a legal data protection compliance requirement, as well as best business practice. This is one of the more prominent areas of compliance where time never stands still. The security risks and needs must constantly be appraised and updated. It is also essential to ensure that outsourced data processing activities are also undertaken in an appropriately secure manner. Increasingly the area of appraisals and procedures surrounding security breaches and data loss instances are regulated. If such an event arises, the Data Protection Commissioner as well as individual data subjects may have to be informed. Liability issues should also be a constant concern for organisations as regards security and risk. The fine of £250,000 imposed on Sony by the UK ICO in relation to a hacking security breach affecting millions of users is a timely reminder of the importance of constant security vigilance. Twitter also recently had to announce a significant security breach of 250m users.

CHAPTER 12

Outsourcing and Data Processors

Introduction

While many organisations may feel they do not engage third parties to deal with their personal data and databases, closer inspection often indicates that this assumption is not correct. Many organisations, across all sectors of activity, engage third parties or outsource certain of their internal activities.[1]

One example is where an organisation may find it more convenient to outsource its payroll functions to another organisation specialising in such activities. It is necessary, therefore, that the employee personal data, or certain of it, is transferred to the third party organisation for processing. This third party is a data processor acting for the organisation. A contract must be in place and appropriate security standards implemented.

Sometimes organisations outsource other activities, such as marketing, recruitment, employment of consultants or agents or part-time employees. Organisations increasingly outsource market research and customer satisfaction surveys to third parties. These are all data processors where personal data is involved.

If an organisation must transfer or export personal data outside of the EEA and lawfully permit transfers outside of the restriction ban, it must satisfy the following, as appropriate:

- an export to one of the safe permitted countries; or

- an export to the US under the Safe Harbour program; or

- an export pursuant to the accepted standard contractual clauses; or

- an export pursuant to the accepted binding corporate rules (BCR).

---

1. See generally Van Alsenoy, "Allocating Responsibility Among Controllers, Processors, and 'Everything In Between': The Definition of Actors and Roles in Directive 95/46/EC" (2012) (28) *Computer Law & Security Review* 25–43; Morgan, "Data Controllers, Data Processors and Data Sharers" (4 March 2011) SCL *Computers and Law*.

Data Processors and Security

Data processors also have obligations in relation to processing personal data and security. Where processing of personal data is carried out by a data processor on behalf of a data controller, then the data controller must have a contract in writing in place with the data processor, containing certain clauses and obligations. The contracts with data processors must address the following:

- processing must be carried out in pursuance of a contract in writing or another equivalent form;
- the contract must provide that the data processor carries out the processing only on, and subject to, the instructions of the data controller;
- the data processor must comply with the "security" requirements.

There are also certain other requirements. The data controller:

- must ensure the data processor provides sufficient guarantees in respect of the technical security measures and organisational measures governing the processing; and
- must take reasonable steps to ensure compliance with these measures.

Data Protection Acts: Engaging Data Processors

The Data Protection Acts[2] s 2C(3) provides that where processing of personal data is carried out by a data processor on behalf of a data controller, the data controller must, in order to comply with the seventh principle:

- ensure that the processing is carried out in pursuance of a contract in writing or in another equivalent form between the data controller and the data processor and that the contract provides that the data processor carries out the processing only on, and subject to, the instructions of the data controller and that the data processor complies with obligations equivalent to those imposed on the data controller by s 2(1)(d) of the DP Directive 95[3];
- ensure that the data processor provides sufficient guarantees in respect of the technical security measures, and organisational measures, governing the processing; and
- take reasonable steps to ensure compliance with those measures.

---

2. Data Protection Act 1988 and Data Protection (Amendment) Act 2003.
3. EU Data Protection Directive 1995 (Directive 95/46/EC of the European Parliament and of the Council of 24 October 1995 on the protection of individuals with regard to the processing of personal data and on the free movement of such data).

There are specific requirements where data processors are engaged. Where data controllers engage data processors then the data controller must:

- have a contract in writing or other equipment form that provides that the data processor will act only on instructions of the data controller and will comply with the data security measures to which the data controller is subject;

- ensure the data processor provide sufficient guarantees in respect of the technical security measures and organisational measures it implements; and

- take reasonable steps to ensure compliance with such matters.

What actions should an organisation take if third parties process their organisation's data? Organisations should consider the following:

- Ideally an organisation should have advance procedures and policies in place to cater for such an eventuality, for example ensuring that an appropriate senior manager/board member has an assigned role and takes responsibility for data protection compliance, including dealing with breaches, and also having a documented IT security incident handing procedure policy in place. Needless to say, it must be properly policed, implemented, reviewed and updated;

- Once a breach does occur, a proper procedure can assist in containing the breach and recovering from same, and assessing the ongoing risk;

- Notify the breach as appropriate, evaluating and reacting to the breach and the risk;

- All of the appropriate personnel within the organisation should be aware of the procedures and consulted as appropriate, including, for example, the managing director, legal, IT, and media/press officer;

- A part of the procedure will have a designated list of external contact points, some or all of whom may need to be notified and contacted, as appropriate;

- Obviously the nature of organisations, and of the breaches themselves, differ and the IT security incident handing procedure policy will need to be tailored. After all, the cause of a data security breach can be any of a number of reasons;

- Such a policy, while covering breaches of data protection and privacy, may well encompass wider issues, such as outsourcing, backups, disaster recovery, business continuity, etc.;

- If doing business in other jurisdictions the organisation may need to take additional measures. For example, if the organisation own or have access to personal information of certain jurisdictions then the organisation may have a legal local duty to notify those individuals if that information (such as names and credit card details) has been accessed illegally.

Conclusion

It is also important that the organisation undertake ongoing assessments and checks regarding the operation of the data processing undertaken by the data processor. This should also include the security and compliance measures. This will be an increasing issue as personal data continues to expand in the online environment.

How to Comply with the Data Protection Regime

How does an organisation comply with the data protection regime? What are the different components of compliance? The tables below set out the headline details of how to comply with the data protection regime.

Complying with Data Protection

All organisations collect and process at least some personal data as defined under the Data Protection Acts and the data protection regime. Therefore, an organisation must ensure it only collects and processes personal data if complying with:

- the obligation to only collect and process personal data if in compliance with the Data Protection Acts;

- the *data protection principles*;

- the *legitimate processing conditions*;

- the *sensitive personal data legitimate processing conditions*;

- the security conditions;

- the notification and registration conditions;

- the data breach notification conditions;

- the personal data outsourcing and data processor conditions;

- the personal data transfer ban or trans-border data flow restrictions;

- the individual data subject rights, including access, deletion, etc.;

- queries, audits and investigation orders from the Data Protection Commissioner; and

- the time limits for undertaking various tasks and obligations.

Data Protection Principles

All organisations with personal data must comply with the following *data protection principles*, namely:

- The data or, as the case may be, the information constituting the data shall have been obtained, and the data shall be processed, fairly;

- The data shall be accurate and complete and, where necessary, kept up to date;

- The data shall be obtained only for one or more specified, explicit and legitimate purpose(s);

- The data shall not be further processed in a manner incompatible with that purpose or those purposes;

- The data shall be adequate, relevant and not excessive in relation to the purpose or purposes for which they are collected or are further processed;

- The data shall not be kept for longer than is necessary for that purpose or those purposes;

- Appropriate security measures shall be taken against unauthorised access to, or unauthorised alteration, disclosure or destruction of, the data, in particular where the processing involves the transmission of data over a network, and against all other unlawful forms of processing.

Summary of Data Protection Principles

Personal data must be:

(1) obtained and processed, fairly;

(2) accurate, complete and kept up to date;

(3) obtained only for one specified, explicit and legitimate purpose;

(4) not further processed in a manner incompatible with that purpose;

(5) adequate, relevant and not excessive in relation to the purpose;

(6) kept for longer than is necessary for that purpose;

(7) protected by appropriate security measures.

Data controllers must also give a copy of personal data to any individual on request (i.e. an access request).

Sensitive Personal Data

Sensitive personal data (s 1 Data Protection Acts) can be summarised as personal data relating to:

- racial or ethnic origin, political opinions or religious or philosophical beliefs;
- trade union membership;
- physical or mental health or condition or sexual life;
- commission or alleged commission of any offence by the data subject; or
- any proceedings for offence committed or alleged.

Legitimate Processing Conditions

The *legitimate processing conditions* can be summarised as follows:

- the data subject has given consent;
- the processing is necessary for the performance of a contract, to take steps at the request of the data subject prior to entering into a contract;
- compliance with a legal processing obligation;
- processing to prevent injury or other damage to health of data subject; or serious loss of or damage to property of data subject; or otherwise to protect his or her vital interests;
- processing necessary for the administration of justice;
- processing necessary under an enactment;
- official processing function;
- processing necessary for the purposes of the legitimate interests pursued by the data controller or by a third party or parties to whom the data are disclosed, unless unwarranted by reason of prejudice to the fundamental rights and freedoms or legitimate interests of the data subject.

Sensitive Personal Data Legitimate Processing Conditions

The *sensitive personal data legitimate processing conditions* may be summarised as follows:

- consent is given explicitly;
- necessary for a legal obligation;
- necessary to protect the vital interests of the data subject;
- not for profit organisation, with appropriate safeguards;
- information made public by the data subject;
- administration of justice;
- legal function;
- government function;
- legal advice or establishing, exercising or defending legal rights;
- medical purposes;
- in accordance with the Statistics Act 1993;
- political parties or electoral activities;
- authorised by Minister for substantial public interest;
- tax purposes;
- determining official benefits, pensions, etc.

PART 2

Organisations and Inward-Facing Obligations

CHAPTER 13

Processing Employee Personal Data

Introduction

Organisations sometimes focus on their customer-relations data compliance issues. However, it is important for new and existing organisations to look inwards. There are important inward-facing data protection obligations. Personal data includes the personal data of employees also. In addition, the employees of the organisation also have data subject rights that must be respected.

Inward-Facing Considerations

Organisations must comply with the data protection regime as regards their inward-facing personal data. This primarily relates to the employees of the organisation. This raises a number of issues both in terms of who the employees are, what personal data is being collected and processed, for what purpose or purposes, where is it located, whether or not anyone else obtains the data, etc., and how the organisation ensures that it is data protection compliant in relation to same.

In relation to employee personal data, organisations must ensure compliance with the:

- data protection principles;
- legitimate processing conditions;
- sensitive personal data legitimate processing conditions; and
- security requirements.

Who Is Covered?

Who is covered by the inward-facing organisational data protection obligations? While full-time employees are the most obvious example, they are not the only ones. Organisations must consider the inward-facing personal data of:

- full-time employees;
- part-time employees;
- other workers such as temps and casual staff;
- agency staff;
- contractors;
- ex-employees;
- retired employees;
- job applicants, including unsuccessful applicants;
- volunteers;
- apprentices and trainees;
- work experience staff;
- suppliers.[1]

It can also include:

- Related family members to the above.

Where an organisation engages with any of the above, it will have to ensure that the data protection regime is complied with.

Compliance with the Data Protection Principles

In dealing with employee personal data, as well as potential employees and any of the categories outlined above, it is necessary for the organisation to comply with the *data protection principles*.

The *data protection principles* apply in the work environment as well as elsewhere. Employee personal data must be:

(1) obtained and processed, fairly;

(2) accurate, complete and kept up to date;

(3) obtained only for one specified, explicit and legitimate purpose;

(4) not further processed in a manner incompatible with that purpose;

(5) adequate, relevant and not excessive in relation to the purpose;

(6) kept for longer than is necessary for that purpose;

(7) protected by appropriate security measures.

---

1. MacDonald, *Data Protection: Legal Compliance and Good Practice for Employers* (London: Tottel, 2008) p 41.

Data controllers must also give a copy of personal data to any individual employee, on request (i.e. an access request).[2]

All of the principles must be complied with. Compliance with the *data protection principles* applies to all employee and inward-facing personal data collected and/or processed by an organisation. It also applies regardless of registration requirements.

Ordinary Personal Data Legitimate Processing Conditions

When dealing with the above inward-facing categories of employees, agents, contractors, etc., the *legitimate processing conditions* are required to be complied with in addition to the *data protection principles*.

Schedule 2A of the Data Protection Acts[3] contains the general *legitimate processing conditions*, e.g. employee non-sensitive personal data. In order to comply with the general personal data *legitimate processing conditions*, the organisation must fall within *one* of the following conditions, namely:

(a) the data subject has given his or her consent to the processing or, if the data subject, by reason of his or her physical or mental incapacity or age, is or is likely to be unable to appreciate the nature and effect of such consent, it is given by a parent or guardian or a grandparent, uncle, aunt, brother or sister of the data subject and the giving of such consent is not prohibited by law;

(b) the processing is necessary:

    (i)   for the performance of a contract to which the data subject is a party;

    (ii) in order to take steps at the request of the data subject prior to entering into a contract;

    (iii) for compliance with a legal obligation to which the data controller is subject other than an obligation imposed by contract; or

    (iv) to prevent:

        (I) injury or other damage to the health of the data subject; or

        (II) serious loss of or damage to property of the data subject;

or otherwise to protect his or her vital interests where the seeking of the consent of the data subject or another person referred to in paragraph (a) of this subsection is likely to result in those interests being damaged;

---

2.   See s 2 of the Data Protection Acts.
3.   Data Protection Act 1988 and Data Protection (Amendment) Act 2003.

(c) the processing is necessary:

  (i) for the administration of justice;

  (ii) for the performance of a function conferred on a person by or under an enactment;

  (iii) for the performance of a function of the government or a minister of the government; or

  (iv) for the performance of any other function of a public nature performed in the public interest by a person;

(d) the processing is necessary for the purposes of the legitimate interests pursued by the data controller or by a third party or parties to whom the data are disclosed, except where the processing is unwarranted in any particular case by reason of prejudice to the fundamental rights and freedoms or legitimate interests of the data subject.

The Minister may, after consultation with the Data Protection Commissioner, by regulations specify particular circumstances in which s 2A(1)(d) is, or is not, to be taken as satisfied.

Frequently, an organisation would seek to fall within the legitimate interests condition above. These obligations might be summarised as follows:

- the data subject has given consent;
- the processing is necessary for the performance of a contract to take steps at the request of the data subject prior to entering into a contract;
- compliance with a legal obligation;
- to prevent injury or other damage to health of data subject or serious loss of or damage to property of data subject, or otherwise to protect his or her vital interests;
- necessary for the administration of justice;
- necessary under an enactment;
- official function;
- necessary for the purposes of the legitimate interests pursued by the data controller or by a third party or parties to whom the data are disclosed, unless unwarranted by reason of prejudice to the fundamental rights and freedoms or legitimate interests of the data subject.

Legitimate Processing and an Organisation's Employees

Unlike certain other areas, the legitimate processing of employee personal data does not require employee consent. However, many organisations would have originally expected and proceeded on the basis that consent was so required. They would have incorporated (deemed) consent clauses into employment contracts, etc.

As indicated above, s 2A(1)(d) of the Data Protection Acts enables organisations to rely upon the legitimate processing condition that processing is necessary for the purposes of *legitimate interests* pursued by the data controller or by the third party or parties to whom the data are disclosed, except where the processing is unwarranted in any particular case by reason of prejudice to the rights and freedoms or legitimate interests of the data subject.

An alternative may be to say that the processing is necessary as part of a contract to which the employee is a party, in particular the employment contract.[4]

Both the legitimate interest ground and the contract ground might be looked at in situations where the organisation may not be able to rely on the consent ground.

Sensitive Personal Data Legitimate Processing Conditions

An organisation may also feel the need on occasion to store and use sensitive personal data in relation to employees, such as medical and health data. In the case of sensitive personal data, an organisation must, in addition to satisfying all of the *data protection principles*, be able to comply or fall within *one* of the *sensitive personal data legitimate processing conditions*, i.e.:

    (a) sections 2 and 2A (as amended and inserted, respectively, by the Act of 2003) are complied with; and

    (b) in addition, at least one of the following conditions is met:

        (i) the consent referred to in paragraph (a) of subsection (1) of section 2A (as inserted by the Act of 2003) of this Act is explicitly given;

        (ii) the processing is necessary for the purpose of exercising or performing any right or obligation which is conferred or imposed by law on the data controller in connection with employment;

        (iii) the processing is necessary to prevent injury or other damage to the health of the data subject or another person or serious loss in respect of, or damage to, property or otherwise to protect the vital interests of the data subject or of another person in a case where:

---

4.   s 2A(1)(b)(i) *ibid.*

(I) consent to the processing cannot be given by or on behalf of the data subject in accordance with s 2A(1)(a)(inserted by the Act of 2003) of this Act; or

(II) the data controller cannot reasonably be expected to obtain such consent, or the processing is necessary to prevent injury to, or damage to the health of, another person, or serious loss in respect of, or damage to, the property of another person, in a case where such consent has been unreasonably withheld;

(iv) the processing:

(I) is carried out in the course of its legitimate activities by any body corporate, or any unincorporated body of persons, that:

(A) is not established, and whose activities are not carried on, for profit; and

(B) exists for political, philosophical, religious or trade union purposes;

(II) is carried out with appropriate safeguards for the fundamental rights and freedoms of data subjects;

(III) relates only to individuals who either are members of the body or have regular contact with it in connection with its purposes; and

(IV) does not involve disclosure of the data to a third party without the consent of the data subject;

(v) the information contained in the data has been made public as a result of steps deliberately taken by the data subject;

(vi) the processing is necessary:

(I) for the administration of justice;

(II) for the performance of a function conferred on a person by or under an enactment; or

(III) for the performance of a function of the government or a minister of the government;

(vii) the processing:

(I) is required for the purpose of obtaining legal advice or for the purposes of, or in connection with, legal proceedings or prospective legal proceedings; or

(II) is otherwise necessary for the purposes of establishing, exercising or defending legal rights;

(viii) the processing is necessary for medical purposes and is undertaken by:

(I) a health professional; or

(II) a person who in the circumstances owes a duty of confidentiality to the data subject that is equivalent to that which would exist if that person were a health professional;

(ix) the processing is necessary in order to obtain information for use, subject to and in accordance with the Statistics Act 1993, only for statistical, compilation and analysis purposes;

(x) the processing is carried out by political parties, or candidates for election to, or holders of, elective political office, in the course of electoral activities for the purpose of compiling data on people's political opinions and complies with such requirements (if any) as may be prescribed for the purpose of safeguarding the fundamental rights and freedoms of data subjects;

(xi) the processing is authorised by regulations that are made by the Minister and are made for reasons of substantial public interest;

(xii) the processing is necessary for the purpose of the assessment, collection or payment of any tax, duty, levy or other moneys owed or payable to the State and the data has been provided by the data subject solely for that purpose;

(xiii) the processing is necessary for the purposes of determining entitlement to or control of, or any other purpose connected with, the administration of any benefit, pension, assistance, allowance, supplement or payment under the Social Welfare (Consolidation) Act 1993, or any non-statutory scheme administered by the Minister for Social, Community and Family Affairs.

These *sensitive personal data legitimate processing conditions* may be summarised as follows:

- explicit consent is given;
- necessary for a legal obligation;
- necessary to prevent injury or other damage to health or serious loss or damage to property or protect the vital interests of the data subject,

  (I) consent to the processing cannot be given by or on behalf of the data subject in accordance with s 2A(1)(a) of this Act; or

>   (II) the data controller cannot reasonably be expected to obtain such
>   consent, or the processing is necessary to prevent injury to, or damage
>   to the health of, another person, or serious loss in respect of, or damage
>   to, the property of another person, in a case where such consent has
>   been unreasonably withheld;

- not for profit organisation for political, philosophical, religious or trade union purposes with appropriate safeguards;

- the information contained in the data has been made public as a result of steps deliberately taken by the data subject;

- administration of justice;

- legal function; or

- Government function;

- obtaining legal advice or in connection with legal proceedings; or establishing, exercising or defending legal rights;

- medical purposes and is undertaken by a health professional; or

- in accordance with the Statistics Act 1993;

- political parties or electoral activities;

- authorised by Ministerial regulations for substantial public interest;

- tax purposes;

- determining official benefits, pensions, etc.

Furthermore, regulations can also set out further obligations in relation to the processing of sensitive personal data.

Sensitive Data Legitimate Processing and an Organisation's Employees

However, where sensitive personal data is involved, the organisation may have to obtain consent, unless otherwise specifically permitted in relation to one of the other particular purpose conditions set out above.

Consent

If it is the case that none of the condition criteria apply or permit a specific data processing use, then the organisation must obtain appropriate consent.

In considering the legitimising criteria the organisation should pay particular attention to the conditional word "necessary". If not strictly necessary, and demonstrably so in the event that it is ever necessary to justify it when subsequently queried, it means that it may be necessary to fall back to the consent criteria.

Explicit consent, for example, with sensitive personal data usage, can mean having to obtain written consent. There is also a reference to freely given consent. Where employee consent is utilised or required, an issue can sometimes arise as to whether it is voluntarily and freely given. If the employee feels forced into giving consent they, or the Data Protection Commissioner, might subsequently say that the consent is invalid, thus compromising the legitimacy of the particular processing.

Compliance and Policies

It is essential for all organisations to implement appropriate written policies. These will vary, as there are different types of policy, albeit all related. In addition, each policy will be specifically tailored to meet the needs and circumstances of the particular organisation.

Once finalised, the policy or policies should be properly and effectively communicated to all employees. It may also have to be made available to others who work in or for the organisation, e.g. contractors.

Those in the organisation with responsibility for dealing with personal data also need to be particularly familiarised with the policies, security measures, and data protection processes, as well as effectively trained in relation to all aspects of data protection compliance.

As with all legal, business and organisational policies relating to regulatory compliance, data protection policies need to be regularly monitored and updated as requirement dictates. This can be because of legal changes, DPC *guideline changes*, business and activity changes, changing security and risk requirements, etc.

Data Protection Commissioner – Vetting

The Data Protection Commissioner has provided guidance on the issue of vetting employees.[5] It states as follows:

> *Guidance Note: data protection considerations when vetting prospective employees*
>
> 1. Purpose of the Guidance Note
>
> This guidance note focuses on data protection considerations that must be taken into account before vetting prospective employees/volunteers/students in certain specified sectors. It provides guidance for organisations on how to treat information that is

---

5. See DPC, available at http://www.dataprotection.ie/viewdoc.asp?DocID=1095, last accessed 11 January 2013.

provided to them on foot of a vetting procedure. This note also provides background information about how vetting procedures currently operate in this jurisdiction.

Under the Data Protection Acts information about the commission or the alleged commission of an offence by a person falls within the definition of sensitive personal data. Currently, there is no comprehensive statutory basis which underpins the vetting process. The Office of the Data Protection Commissioner supports the current procedure for managing requests for vetting in this jurisdiction. The procedure is based on the consent of the person to the release of certain types of information held by An Garda Síochána in respect of that person.

2. How the vetting process works

a) Who can be requested to undergo vetting?
The Central Vetting Unit within An Garda Síochána conducts vetting for organisations that are registered with the Unit for this purpose. At present, employees/volunteers/students are requested to consent to a vetting procedure before working in the following roles:

- Prospective employees of the Health Service Executive and agencies funded by the Health Service Executive where the work involves access to children and vulnerable adults;

- New teachers in the primary and post-primary sector;

- New employees and volunteers in the youth work sector and certain sports organisations;

- Staff, students and volunteers in the childcare sector;

- Staff working in care homes for older people.

Vetting also takes place in relation to:

- State employees;

- Employees covered by the Private Security Services Act 2004.

Standard procedures are in place for organisations registered with An Garda Síochána for vetting purposes. For vetting to occur, vetting subjects must complete a formal Garda Vetting Application Form. Vetting subjects must give written authorisation for An Garda Síochána to disclose to the registered organisation details of all prosecutions, successful or not, pending or completed and/or details of all convictions, recorded in the State or elsewhere in respect of them held on record by An Garda Síochána. Only specific people recognised as authorised signatories in the approved organisations can submit signed authorisation forms to the Garda Vetting Unit for processing. Once processed, vetting results are transmitted from the Garda Central Vetting Unit directly to the authorised signatory that submitted the application in respect of the individual for further consideration by the organisation.

b) Information that may be released as part of the vetting process

When a vetting subject gives their written permission for An Garda Síochána to disclose details of all prosecutions, successful or not, pending or completed and/or details of all convictions, recorded in the state or elsewhere in respect of them to a registered organisation, all such details as held on record by An Garda Síochána in respect of the vetting subject are disclosed. In the case where vetting subjects have been prosecuted, notwithstanding the court outcome in respect of the prosecution, the factual details contained in the resultant court outcome are disclosed to the authorised signatory.

c) Dispute Resolution

All organisations registered for Garda Vetting participate in a dispute resolution procedure designed to address any instance in which a vetting subject disputes the details contained in the relevant Garda Vetting disclosure. The procedure may be activated by the vetting subject by indicating the basis of their dispute in writing to the authorised signatory who received the Garda Vetting disclosure. The authorised signatory then resubmits the complete application file to the Garda Central Vetting Unit for the conduct of further checks.

d) Probation Act 1907 and Vetting

In instances where, in the court outcome, the court applies the provisions of the Probation Act 1907, the charges are dismissed. However, in order to avail of the provisions of the Probation Act 1907, the case is marked as "proved". While individuals often consider that they do not have a formal criminal record, when a person gives their written authorisation for vetting to be conducted the authorised signatory for theregistered organisation is informed of the charge as a "non-conviction" rather than a formal conviction.

e) Age

There is no Garda Vetting for people under the age of 16. However, if a candidate is aged 16/17 and requires vetting (e.g. to enter a child care course in college) the consent of a parent or guardian is sought by An Garda Síochána.

f) Retention of vetting forms by An Garda Síochána Central Vetting Unit

When the Garda Vetting Unit has complied with a vetting request, the original vetting application form is returned to the authorised signatory for the registered organisation. The Garda Vetting Unit does not retain a copy of this documentation. Information about the retention of these forms by registered organisations is dealt with in the next section.

3. Important data protection guidance regarding the use/storage and retention of information received by an organisation which carries out vetting

a) Can information received as part of the vetting process be shared by one organisation with another?

As mentioned previously, the Office of the Data Protection Commissioner supports the current procedure for managing requests for vetting in this jurisdiction.

As outlined in Section 2 of this guidance note, the consent given by an individual for vetting is specifically linked to the disclosure of their information to a specific registered organisation to allow the organisation to make an assessment decision about allowing that individual to take on a particular role within that organisation. The Office of the Data Protection Commissioner does not consider it appropriate that information disclosed to one named organisation for this sole purpose would be shared by that organisation subsequently with any other organisation, even with consent (except where the registered organisation is clearly undertaking the vetting on behalf of a related organisation). There are a number of data protection reasons for this.

Firstly, as the vetting process may involve the provision of sensitive personal information about a person, it is absolutely imperative that there is no drift in terms of the use to which such information may be put or in terms of the identity of the organisation using the information (other than within the restricted context outlined previously).

Secondly, An Garda Síochána ensures that confidentiality and data protection requirements are met by restricting vetting disclosures to persons trained as authorised signatories. The further disclosure of such information to other parties, even with the consent of the vetting subject, would not be appropriate and will increase the potential for breaches of data protection rights.

Aside from data protection concerns, An Garda Síochána wish to ensure the integrity of the vetting process. To achieve this it is necessary that each organisation should separately vet each person rather than share potentially dated information that was supplied as part of a previous vetting request.

b) Secure storage of vetting information
The secure storage of vetting disclosures made by An Garda Síochána to authorised signatories is another key data protection consideration in this area. The content of such disclosures constitute sensitive personal data. Therefore they must be held in a secure manner with access restricted to a small number of authorised personnel.

Vetting disclosures may only be used for the purpose for which they were provided to an organisation in accordance with the consent of the vetting subject. They cannot be further processed or disclosed to other parties.

c) Retention of vetting information
Personal data must be destroyed when the purpose for which it was sought has expired. This can be problematic in relation to the continued holding of vetting disclosures as the Data Protection Commissioner is concerned that their long-term retention creates the potential for unauthorised access and use. Accordingly, the Office of the Data Protection Commissioner recommends that vetting disclosures should be routinely deleted one year after they are received except in exceptional circumstances. In case of future queries or issues in relation to a vetting disclosure, the reference number

and date of disclosure may be retained on file and this can be checked with An Garda Síochána. This practice is sufficient for all organisations engaged in vetting, including organisations subject to external statutory inspection of staff vetting practices.

In regard to all unsuccessful employment applications, the vetting disclosure and all other personal data collected in the recruitment process should be deleted after a year in line with standard advice in this area. It is important that organisations are aware that an individual has the right to make a request for a copy of information held about them.

This requirement that an organisation does not share with another organisation information on individuals received as part of the vetting process does not prevent the supply of the vetting response to the vetting subject. It is good practice to give it to them and in any case they would have a right to access a copy of their personal data under section 4 of the Data Protection Acts 1988 [and] 2003.

4. Can Garda Vetting be carried out by employers in sectors other than those mentioned in Section 2 of this guidance note?

In general, An Garda Síochána will only carry out vetting for approved organisations in designated sectors. Such a service is not generally available to other employers. While An Garda Síochána are required to provide information from their records in response to *access requests* from individuals, the responses to such requests are not of the standard applied to vetting applications. Furthermore, it is a clear abuse of the right of access for an employer to attempt to require a prospective employee to reveal the result of such an access request. This Office considers that such practices constitute a breach of the Acts as the consent given cannot be considered to be free. Furthermore, any such action by an employer will be a criminal offence when Section 4(13) of the Data Protection Acts comes into effect.[6]

The Data Protection Commissioner also provides further guidance in relation to what type of background checks an organisation can carry out on potential employees.[7] The Data Protection Commissioner states that the key to compliance with data protection requirements in this area is to inform the potential employee of any potential checks that may be undertaken and seek their specific consent for certain types of checks, e.g. release of transcripts by a university. Information that is *legitimately* in the public domain can also be accessed within the context of data protection requirements. Certain sectors, where employees have contact with children or vulnerable adults, are permitted to make use of Garda vetting checks that are carried out with the consent of the person.

---

6.   *ibid.*
7.   See DPC, available athttp://www.dataprotection.ie/viewdoc.asp?DocID=636, last accessed 11 January 2013.

Data Protection Commissioner – Monitoring Employees

The Data Protection Commissioner has provided detailed guidance in relation to the issue of monitoring and employees.[8] The guidance states that:

Guidance Notes – Monitoring of Staff

The Data Protection Commissioner accepts that organisations have a legitimate interest to protect their business, reputation, resources and equipment. To achieve this, organisations may wish to monitor staff's use of email, the internet, and the telephone. However, it should be noted that the collection, use or storage of information about workers, the monitoring of their email or internet access or their surveillance by video cameras (which process images) involves the processing of personal data and, as such, data protection law applies to such processing. The processing of sound and image data in the employment context falls within the scope of the Data Protection Laws.

The Article 29 Working Party has adopted a Working Document (WP55) on the surveillance of electronic communications in the workplace. Its main guiding principle is that you do not lose your privacy and data protection rights just because you are an employee. Any limitation of the employee's right to privacy should be proportionate to the likely damage to the employer's legitimate interests. An acceptable usage policy should be adopted reflecting this balance and employees should be notified of the nature, extent and purposes of the monitoring specified in the policy.

In principle, there is nothing to stop an employer specifying that use of equipment is prohibited for personal purposes but the likelihood is that most employers will allow a limited amount of personal use. In the absence of a clear policy, employees may be assumed to have a reasonable expectation of privacy in the workplace.

The following points need to be addressed by data controllers:

- the legitimate interests of the employer – to process personal data that is necessary for the normal development of the employment relationship and the business operation – justify certain limitations to the privacy of individuals at the workplace. However, these interests cannot take precedence over the principles of data protection, including the requirement for transparency, fair and lawful processing of data and the need to ensure that any encroachment on an employee's privacy is fair and proportionate. A worker can always object to processing on the grounds that it is causing or likely to cause substantial damage or distress to an individual.

- monitoring, including employees' email or internet usage, surveillance by camera, video cameras or location data must comply with the transparency requirements of data protection law. Staff must be informed of the existence

8.   See DPC, available at http://www.dataprotection.ie/viewdoc.asp?DocID=208, last accessed 11 January 2013.

of the surveillance, and also the purposes for which personal data are to be processed. If CCTV cameras are in operation, and public access is allowed, a notice to that effect should be displayed. Any monitoring must be carried out in the least intrusive way possible. Only in exceptional circumstances associated with a criminal investigation, and in consultation with the Gardaí, should resort be made to covert surveillance.

- monitoring and surveillance, whether in terms of email use, internet use, video cameras or location data, are subject to data protection requirements. Any monitoring must be a proportionate response by an employer to the risk he or she faces taking into account the legitimate privacy and other interests of workers.

- at a very minimum, staff should be aware of what the employer is collecting on them (directly or from other sources). Staff have a right of access to their data under Section 4 of the Data Protection Acts.

- any personal data processed in the course of monitoring must be adequate, relevant and not excessive and not retained for longer than necessary for the purpose for which the monitoring is justified.[9]

The Data Protection Commissioner's guidance then refers to employee computer, email and internet use, as follows:

> *Use of the Computer Network, Email and Internet*
>
> Private use of the Internet in the workplace and the monitoring of private emails pose certain challenges. A workplace policy should be in place in an open and transparent manner to provide that:
>
> - A balance is required between the legitimate rights of employers and the personal privacy rights of employees;
>
> - Any monitoring activity [is] transparent to workers;
>
> - Employers should consider whether [or not] they would obtain the same results with traditional measures of supervision; [and]
>
> - Monitoring should be fair and proportionate, with prevention being more important than detection.[10]

DPC Guidance Template

The Data Protection Commissioner's guidance in relation to monitoring and employee issues also sets out an illustrative template.[11] Of course, no template fits all

---

9. *ibid.*
10. *ibid.*
11. *ibid.*

situations as all organisatiosn are different. The risks and issues to be considered and balanced will vary for each organisation. The template is set out below.

Template for Acceptable Usage Policy – Email and Internet

The following is the Office Policy of the Data Protection Commissioner and may serve as a template for organisations wishing to develop Acceptable Usage Policies in relation to email and the internet.

- Material you receive (email, fax, cd, diskette, download)

- Email has the same status as incoming paper and fax. It must be opened, read and evaluated and responded to within the timelines set out in the offices business plan.

1. Potentially dangerous material

Do not launch, detach or save any executable file (i.e. those ending in 'exe' or 'vbs') under any circumstances. Contact [the] IT Division immediately.

All incoming attachments must be virus checked by [the] IT Division. Please note that all floppy disks and CDs brought into the office from home PCs should also be virus checked. The safer option is to forward these attachments by email from your home [PC] as they will be automatically screened by the mailsweeper software.

Do not open, detach or save any unofficial file attachments to your hard disk or any network drive. Official attachments should be placed in the relevant document [l]ibrary or detached to a shared drive. Please beware of saving any documentation to the hard drive of you[r] [PC] as this will not be backed up and will be irretrievable in the event of your [PC] breaking down.

2. Obscenity, child pornography and incitement to hate

You are subject to all legislation regulating Internet use, including the provisions regarding obscenity, child pornography, sedition and the incitement of hate. In particular, persons have obligations under the Irish Child Trafficking and Pornography Act 1997, not to allow any of its systems (mail, Internet, etc.) to be used for downloading or distributing offensive material.

3. Other offensive and time-wasting material

Unsolicited material can arrive from anywhere. Should you receive material which you find offensive or abusive or time-wasting, respond to it just as you would an offensive letter: complain directly to the sender and bring it to the attention of the sender's employing organisation/IT and HR managers as appropriate.

In the case of any Spam mail do not issue any reply.

4. Misleading information

Always be aware that the Internet is an unregulated, world wide environment. It contains information and opinions that range in scope from reliable and authoritative to controversial and extremely offensive. It is your responsibility to assess the validity of the information found on the Internet.

Material you send

Remember that email is effectively on official headed paper and can be traced back to place, date and time of sending. Make sure you are satisfied with its content and that it has been approved at the appropriate level. Double check the address of the intended recipient. Once the "send" key is pressed, email cannot be stopped or retrieved. Deleting mail from your system does not make it untraceable.

Do not send any unofficial graphics or executable files under any circumstances. Do not instigate or forward "unofficial mail" to users either within or outside the Office or send any material which may be offensive or disruptive to others or which may be construed as harassment. Do not make derogatory comments regarding gender, marital status, family status, sexual orientation, religion, age, disability, race or membership of the travelling community.

Remember that screensavers can be a means of causing offence.

Do not use another's email account.

All emails are automatically backed up and are recoverable. All emails leaving the Office should have the following text or equivalent automatically appended:

> The information transmitted is intended only for the person or entity to which it is addressed and may contain confidential and/or privileged material. Any review, retransmission, dissemination or other use of, or taking of any action in reliance upon, this information by persons or entities other than the intended recipient is prohibited. If you received this in error, please contact the sender and delete the material from any computer. It is the policy of [insert employer's name] to disallow the sending of offensive material and should you consider that the material contained in the message is offensive you should contact the sender immediately and also your IT manager.

In general: think before you send.

Screening procedures

A suitable IT screening system should automatically screen all mail for known viruses, attachments, etc.

[The] IT Division does not normally read individual's mail or open mail boxes except:

(1) where the screening software or a complaint from an individual indicates that a particular mailbox contains material which is dangerous or offensive;

(2) where a legitimate work reason exists to open the email.

Opening mailboxes for investigation requires authorisation by (Senior manager) on a case-by-case basis. The individual's mailbox, hard disk, network drive and relevant backups are then searched.

Where investigation proves that a problem exists it will be reported to the sender, their organisation, the staff member concerned, [the] Head of Division and HR Manager for appropriate action. Where the problem concerns material such as a virus or an unauthorised .exe file, which can damage the network, [the] IT Division may immediately close down an account pending further investigation and action.

Blocked messages either inbound or outbound are deleted after 21 days if a request for release is not received. Messages containing virus files are not retained.

Time-wasting and resources

Network resources such as storage space and capacity to carry traffic are not unlimited. However, your time and that of your colleagues is the most valuable resource available to the Office.

You must not deliberately perform acts which waste your own and your colleagues' time or computer resources. These acts include:

• Playing games;
• Online chat groups;
• Uploading/Downloading large, unofficial files, which create unnecessary non-business related loads on network traffic;
• Accessing streaming audio/video files, for example, listening to music or watching movie clips;
• Forwarding audio/video files to colleagues;
• Participating in mass non-business related mailings such as chain letters; [and]
• Sending unofficial attachments.

Financial Implications

Do not download any material/software from the Internet for which a registration fee is charged without first obtaining the express permission of the Office. Only the software installed by [the] IT Division, and therefore listed on the Offices Assets Register, is deemed to be legally sourced by the Office and covered by the appropriate licence agreement. No other software is approved for use on any of the Office's computers or laptops.

Security

You are responsible for the use of the facilities granted in your name. The main protection at present is your password. Make it difficult to guess and above all, do not share your password with anyone, write it down or give it out over the phone. If you think someone knows your password, ask for it to be changed as soon as possible. Maintaining the privacy of your password is your responsibility and consequently you are responsible for any abuses taking place using your name and password.

In general do not leave your computer unattended without securing the session by password or signing off.

When leaving your [PC] unattended press Ctrl Alt Del (in the same way as logging into your [PC]) and click the "Lock workstation / Lock computer" box. On return press Ctrl Alt Del and enter your password to log back into the [PC].

Users accessing the Internet through a computer attached to the Office's network must do so through an approved Internet firewall or other security device. Bypassing the Office's computer network security by accessing the Internet directly by modem or other means is strictly prohibited.

You are reminded that files obtained from sources outside the Office, including disks brought from home, files downloaded from the Internet, news groups, bulletin boards or other online services and files attached to email messages may contain computer viruses that may damage the Office's computer network. While the Office is continually upgrading its virus protection infrastructure, the potential introduction of viruses on the Office system always remains a threat. All incoming material, regardless of origin, should be virus checked before being used on any PC on the Office's network. This is not paranoia: a wide variety of viruses from a wide range of individuals and organisations have been blocked over the last 12 months. This threat is real and will not be diminishing. If you suspect that a virus has been introduced into the Office's network, notify the IT [Division] immediately.

The Internet is not secure. Whether by email or via the World Wide web, do not give out more information than is necessary to fulfil your purpose. Beware of demands for unnecessary information. Be wary of sites which request more data than is necessary for accessing the site or for making a transaction, or which do not tell you why they require this data from you. In particular, no information on IT systems or resources should be disclosed over the Internet or through email without authorisation from IT Division.

External email should only be used to transmit unclassified information to individuals outside the Office. Classified or confidential material should not be sent by email unless it is encrypted.

Weblogs

All web browsing is logged. Screening software prevents access to certain non-work related sites. The logs of web browsing will only be accessed with management authorisation, where there are reasonable grounds to believe that this policy has been contravened.

Personal Use

Just as with the phone, a small amount of limited personal use of email and internet facilities is permitted if such use does not otherwise infringe this policy.

Freedom of Information and Archives Acts (only applies to public bodies)

Incoming and outgoing email's which are of "enduring organisational interest" are records under the above Acts and must not be kept in your email account. They must be transferred to the appropriate document library or file.[12]

The Canadian Supreme Court recently held that employees have privacy interests in work-related activities.[13]

The Data Protection Commissioner also provides further guidance in relation to whether or not an organisation can access employee email or internet usage. The Data Protection Commissioner states that:

> The advice of this Office is that every employee has a legitimate right to expect a certain amount of privacy in a work context. The key point is that the employer needs to have a clear policy that is made available to all employees in relation to whether personal use of employee equipment such as email or the internet is allowable. If an employer does not allow any such use then the employee should not use these systems for their own use. Such a policy will allow more ready access to an employee's email and internet records by an employer as the employee should not be making use of them for a personal purpose. However, even in such circumstances ongoing monitoring is never considered proportionate and access should be in response to a reasonable suspicion.
>
> If the employer's usage policy does allow some use of equipment for personal purposes then ongoing monitoring of that usage will likely give rise to data protection concerns as the employee is entitled to privacy in relation to that limited personal use. Any specific access to emails or internet usage should be in response to a specific and reasonable suspicion of inappropriate use of the facilities provided.[14]

---

12. *ibid.*
13. *R v Cole*, Canadian Supreme Court, available at http://scc.lexum.org/decisia-scc-csc/scc-csc/scc-csc/en/item/12615/index.do, last accessed 11 January 2013.
14. See DPC, available at http://www.dataprotection.ie/viewdoc.asp?DocID=634, last accessed 11 January 2013.

Data Protection Commissioner – Enforced Access

The Data Protection Commissioner has also commented in relation to enforced subject access requests, i.e. the practice where an employer forces their potential employee to make an access request to An Garda Síochána so that the employer can access the records of any criminal convictions.

The Data Protection Commissioner states that s 4(13) of the Data Protection Acts provides that it is an offence for an employer to require a prospective or current employee to seek their personal data in conjunction with applying for a job or continuing to hold their job. Unfortunately, the Data Protection Commissioner comments, this provision has not been commenced and at present there is nothing in Data Protection legislation to prevent this happening.[15]

Data Protection Commissioner Checklist

The Data Protection Commissioner has provided a general checklist[16] for compliance purposes, as follows:

Data Protection Checklist
- Are the individuals whose data you collect aware of your identity?

- Have you told the data subject what use you make of his or her data?

- Are the disclosures you make of that data legitimate ones?

- Do you have appropriate security measures in place, both internally and externally, to ensure all access to data is appropriate?

- Do you have appropriate procedures in place to ensure that each data item is kept up-to-date?

- Do you have a defined policy on retention periods for all items of personal data?

- Do you have a data protection policy in place?

- Do you have procedures for handling access requests from individuals?

- Are you clear on whether or not you should be registered?

- Are your staff appropriately trained in data protection?

- Do you regularly review and audit the data you hold and the manner in which they are processed?

---

15. See DPC, available at http://www.dataprotection.ie/viewdoc.asp?DocID=638, last accessed 11 January 2013.
16. See DPC, available at http://www.dataprotection.ie/ViewDoc.asp?fn=/documents/guidance/Guide_Data_Contollers.htm&CatID=90&m=y, last accessed 11 January 2013.

UK ICO Codes

Organisations may, in addition, also wish to consult the UK ICO guidance and codes in terms of implanting, or tailoring, its data processing and data protection compliance practices.[17]

Responsible Person for Data Protection Compliance

Organisations will have to appoint a particular identified person in the organisation to deal with and be responsible for all data protection processes and related compliance issues. This includes ensuring that the organisation is data protection compliant in accordance with the Data Protection Acts[18] (and, for example, EU Article 29 Working Party on Data Protection recommendations).

In addition to a data protection supervisor or officer, it is also recommended that an individual at board level be appointed to be responsible for overseeing and dealing with data protection compliance within the organisation. The contemporary importance and significance of data protection ensures that it is now clearly a boardroom issue.

Responsibilities include ongoing compliance, policies, strategies, processes, training, monitoring, reviewing and updating, co-ordinating, engaging appropriate expertise and advice, audits, privacy by design (PbD), education, courses, notification and registration, incident response, etc., as regards data protection.

HR and Contracts

The organisation's contracts of employment need to incorporate appropriate notifications, consent clauses (only if appropriate), and references to the organisational policies relevant to data protection, such as corporate communications usage policies, internet policies, devices, security, breaches, etc. There may also be reference to where these policies are located and where the latest and most up-to-date version will always be available. This might be a staff handbook, intranet, etc.

These documents will all be different depending on the organisation, the sector and the data protection practices, i.e. the types of personal data, what it is used for and why.

Issues such as compliance, security and confidentiality should be emphasised.

---

17. ICO Employment Practices Code, available at http://www.ico.gov.uk/upload/documents/ library/data_protection/detailed_specialist_guides/employment_practices_code.pdf, last accessed 11 January 2013.
18. Data Protection Act 1988 and Data Protection (Amendment) Act 2003.

Training

Staff induction sessions as well as ongoing staff training should all incorporate guidance in relation to dealing with and handling personal data.

Employee Handbooks

Most organisations provide an employee handbook to their employees. These handbooks should contain guidance and polices on data protection, corporate communications, usage policies, etc.

Notices, Communications, Internet, Intranet

All of these provide an opportunity for the organisation to set out and reinforce the organisational requirements regarding the data protection regime. These can be user friendly and instantaneous, and hence provide an easy means of notifying new and urgent changes, notices, etc.

HR Department

While the HR department or HR director will be required to be familiar with data protection, the role and responsibility of operating data protection compliance is not an HR role. It needs to be someone outside of the employment and HR function. However, the person responsible for data protection will need to liaise regularly with the HR department, including training and keeping HR personnel up to date in relation to new developments in data protection compliance.

Data Protection Acts: Employees and Security

The security of employee personal data is an essential obligation under the data protection regime.

The data controller must take reasonable steps to ensure the reliability of any employees of the organisation who have access to personal data.[19]

Lynda MacDonald[20] refers to security, indicating that the following would be required to be checked, namely:

---

19. *ibid.*
20. MacDonald, *Data Protection: Legal Compliance and Good Practice for Employers* (London: Tottel, 2008) pp 11–12.

- access to buildings, computer rooms and offices where personal data is held;

- access to computer and other equipment where unauthorised access could have a detrimental effect on security;

- that manual records are put away at night in locked filing cabinets before the cleaners arrive;

- that passwords are not written down so that others can access them;

- that strict rules are in force within the business about what personal information can be accessed by which organisations, for example, the information that line managers can access about their staff should be different to (and less than) that which an HR manager can access;

- that there is an efficient and effective security system in place to prevent employees from seeing other employees' data;

- that mechanisms are in place to detect any breach of security, and procedures in place to investigate such breaches;

- that all staff have undergone training on the organisation's data protection policy and how it works in practice, either as part of their induction or at specialist sessions that are appropriate to their job role, position and function.[21]

Even where an employee is working off site or at home, or indeed travelling, it is still the organisation's responsibility to ensure appropriate security measures and processes are in place.

These scenarious are increasingly prominent but the organisation should ensure that they occur on a planned and permission basis. Unregulated activities enhance the level of risk as well as increasing the level of unknown, uncontrollable activities.

Access Requests by Employees

Employees are individuals and are hence able to rely upon their data protection rights, such as requesting a copy of the personal data relating to them. In the instance of an employee access request being made, the organisation should assess the request to see if the appropriate fee has to be paid (if any) and whether any exemptions apply that would prevent a disclosure being made. In addition, while the employee's personal data may have to be disclosed, any third party personal data may be taken out or redacted. It may also be the case that clarification may have to be obtained as to the particular personal data being sought. It should not be, however, a mere mechanism to avoid so complying.

---

21. *ibid.*

The access request must be complied with within 40 calendar days.

MacDonald[22] refers to some examples of the types of employee-related personal data that may relate to access requests, such as:

- performance reviews or appraisals;
- sickness records;
- warnings or minutes of disciplinary interviews;
- training records;
- statements about pay;
- emails or electronic documents of which they are the subject;
- expressions of opinion regarding e.g. prospects for promotion.

Information relating to automated individual decisions regarding employees are also relevant and may be requested.

Conclusion

Organisations need to have actively considered data protection compliance issues. Compliance issues arise even before an employee is engaged. Data protection and personal data are gathered at recruitment, selection and interview stages. Personal data and issues of notifying relevant policies are important issues for organisations to sytematically deal with. Unless data protection issues and policy issues are properly incorporated into the employment relationship, the organisation may be noncompliant. In addition, it may not be able to enforce and rely upon particular contract terms, policies, employee obligations, disciplinary rules and such like.

---

22. MacDonald, *op cit*, p 51.

CHAPTER 14

Employee Data Protection Rights

Introduction

Employees (etc.) have data subject rights just as well as other individual data subjects whose personal data is being collected and processed by the organisation.

The Data Protection Rights of Employees

The rights of employees (etc.) can be summarised as including:

- to expect the prior information requirements to be satisfied (s 2D Data Protection Acts[1]);
- to expect the data protection principles and legitimate processing conditions to be complied with, including fair processing;
- to expect adequate security requirements;
- the right to establish the existence of personal data (s 3 Data Protection Acts);
- the right of access to personal data (s 4 Data Protection Acts[2]);
- the right of data subjects to object to processing likely to cause damage or distress (s 6A Data Protection Acts);
- the right to prevent processing for direct marketing (s 2(7) Data Protection Acts);
- the right to not be subjected to automated decision taking processes (s 6B Data Protection Acts); and
- the right of rectification, blocking or erasure (s 6 Data Protection Acts).

---

1. Data Protection Act 1988 and Data Protection (Amendment) Act 2003.
2. *ibid.*

Employee Access Right

Sections 3–6B of the Data Protection Acts refers to the rights of data subjects and others. In particular, s 4 refers to the right of access to personal data. This applies to data subjects. It is an individual data subject's right.

Section 4 provides an individual shall, if he or she so requests a data controller by notice in writing:

- be informed by the data controller whether or not the data processed by or on behalf of the data controller include personal data relating to the individual;

- if it does, be supplied by the data controller with a description of:

    - the categories of data being processed by or on behalf of the data controller;

    - the personal data constituting the data of which that individual is the data subject;

    - the purpose or purposes of the processing; and

    - the recipients or categories of recipients to whom the data are or may be disclosed;

- have communicated to him or her in intelligible form:

    - the information constituting any personal data of which that individual is the data subject; and

    - any information known or available to the data controller as to the source of those data unless the communication of that information is contrary to the public interest; and

    - where the processing by automatic means of the data of which the individual is the data subject has constituted or is likely to constitute the sole basis for any decision significantly affecting him or her, be informed free of charge by the data controller of the logic involved in the processing,

as soon as may be and in any event not more than 40 days after compliance by the individual with the provisions of this section and, where any of the information is expressed in terms that are not intelligible to the average person without explanation, the information shall be accompanied by an explanation of those terms.

However, under s 4A(a) where personal data relating to a data subject consist of an expression of opinion about the data subject by another person, the data may be disclosed to the data subject without obtaining the consent of that person to the disclosure (unless given in confidence, s 4A(b)).

The obligations imposed by s 4(1)(a)(iii) shall be complied with by supplying the data subject with a copy of the information concerned in permanent form unless:

- the supply of such a copy is not possible or would involve disproportionate effort; or
- the data subject agrees otherwise.

Where a data controller has previously complied with a request under s 4(1), the data controller is not obliged to comply with a subsequent identical or similar request under that subsection by the same individual unless, in the opinion of the data controller, a reasonable interval has elapsed between compliance with the previous request and the making of the current request.

In determining for the purposes of s 4(10) whether the reasonable interval specified in that subsection has elapsed, regard shall be had to the nature of the data, the purpose for which the data are processed and the frequency with which the data are altered.

In determining for the purposes of s 4(10) whether the reasonable interval specified in that subsection has elapsed, regard shall be had to the nature of the data, the purpose for which the data are processed and the frequency with which the data are altered.

Section 4(1)(a)(iv) is not to be regarded as requiring the provision of information as to the logic involved in the taking of a decision if and to the extent only that such provision would adversely affect trade secrets or intellectual property (in particular any copyright protecting computer software).

Therefore, an employee is entitled to access as set out above.

DP Directive 95: Access Right

Article 12 of the DP Directive 95[3] provides for the right of access, and states that Member States shall guarantee every data subject the right to obtain from the controller:

(a) without constraint at reasonable intervals and without excessive delay or expense:

- confirmation as to whether or not data relating to him are being processed and information at least as to the purposes of the

---

3.   EU Data Protection Directive 1995 (Directive 95/46/EC of the European Parliament and of the Council of 24 October 1995 on the protection of individuals with regard to the processing of personal data and on the free movement of such data).

processing, the categories of data concerned, and the recipients or categories of recipients to whom the data are disclosed;

- communication to him in an intelligible form of the data undergoing processing and of any available information as to their source;

- knowledge of the logic involved in any automatic processing of data concerning him at least in the case of the automated decisions referred to in Article 15(1);

(b) as appropriate the rectification, erasure or blocking of data the processing of which does not comply with the provisions of the Directive, in particular because of the incomplete or inaccurate nature of the data;

(c) notification to third parties to whom the data have been disclosed of any rectification, erasure or blocking carried out in compliance with (b), unless this proves impossible or involves a disproportionate effort.

DP Regulation: Access Right

Article 15 of the DP Regulation[4] relates to the right of access for the data subject. Article 15(1) provides that the data subject shall have the right to obtain from the data controller at any time, on request, confirmation as to whether or not personal data relating to the data subject are being processed. Where such personal data are being processed, the data controller shall provide the following information:

(a) the purposes of the processing;

(b) the categories of personal data concerned;

(c) the recipients or categories of recipients to whom the personal data are to be or have been disclosed, in particular to recipients in third countries;

(d) the period for which the personal data will be stored;

(e) the existence of the right to request from the data controller rectification or erasure of personal data concerning the data subject or to object to the processing of such personal data;

(f) the right to lodge a complaint to the supervisory authority and the contact details of the supervisory authority;

(g) communication of the personal data undergoing processing and of any available information as to their source; and

---

4. EU draft Data Protection Regulation (Proposal for a Regulation of the European Parliament and of the Council on the protection of individuals with regard to the processing of personal data and on the free movement of such data (General Data Protection Regulation) COM (2012) 11 final).

(h) the significance and envisaged consequences of such processing, at least in the case of measures referred to in Article 20.

The data subject shall have the right to obtain from the data controller communication of the personal data undergoing processing. Where the data subject makes the request in electronic form, the information shall be provided in electronic form, unless otherwise requested by the data subject.[5]

The Commission shall be empowered to adopt delegated acts for the purpose of further specifying the criteria and requirements for the communication to the data subject of the content of the personal data referred to in Article 15(1)(g).[6]

The Commission may specify standard forms and procedures for requesting and granting access to the information referred to in Article 15(1), including for verification of the identity of the data subject and communicating the personal data to the data subject, taking into account the specific features and necessities of various sectors and data processing situations. Those implementing acts shall be adopted in accordance with the examination procedure referred to in Article 87(2).[7]

Data Protection Acts: Right to Prevent Data Processing Likely to Cause Damage or Distress

Section 6A of the Data Protection Acts refers to the right to prevent processing likely to cause damage or distress.

Data Protection Acts: Right to Prevent Data Processing for DM

Section 2(7) of the Data Protection Acts relates to the right to prevent processing for the purposes of direct marketing.

Data Protection Acts: Automated Decision Taking/Making Processes

Data Controllers may not take decisions that produce legal effects concerning a data subject or that otherwise significantly effect a data subject and are based solely on processing by automatic means of personal data and are intended to evaluate certain personal matters relating to the data subject, such as performance at work, credit worthiness, reliability of conduct (s 6B).

---

5.   art 15(2) *ibid.*
6.   art 15(3) *ibid.*
7.   art 15(4) *ibid.*

DP Directive 95: Right Against Automated Individual Decisions

Article 15 of the DP Directive 95 provides for the right against automated individual decisions. Article 15(1) states that Member States shall grant the right to every person not to be subject to a decision that produces legal effects concerning him or significantly affects him and that is based solely on automated processing of data intended to evaluate certain personal aspects relating to him, such as his or her performance at work, creditworthiness, reliability, conduct, etc.

Article 15(2) states that subject to the other Articles of the Directive, Member States shall provide that a person may be subjected to a decision of the kind referred to in paragraph 1 if that decision:

- is taken in the course of the entering into or performance of a contract, provided the request for the entering into or the performance of the contract, lodged by the data subject, has been satisfied or that there are suitable measures to safeguard his or her legitimate interests, such as arrangements allowing him to put his or her point of view; or

- is authorised by a law that also lays down measures to safeguard the data subject's legitimate interests.

DP Directive 95: Right to Object

Article 14 of the DP Directive 95 provides for the data subject's right to object. It states that Member States shall grant the data subject the right:

- at least in the cases referred to in Article 7(e) and (f), to object at any time on compelling legitimate grounds relating to his or her particular situation to the processing of data relating to him, save where otherwise provided by Member State legislation. Where there is a justified objection, the processing instigated by the data controller may no longer involve those data;

- to object, on request and free of charge, to the processing of personal data relating to him that the data controller anticipates being processed for the purposes of direct marketing, or to be informed before personal data are disclosed for the first time to third parties or used on their behalf for the purposes of direct marketing, and to be expressly offered the right to object free of charge to such disclosures or uses.

It also provides that Member States shall take the necessary measures to ensure that data subjects are aware of the existence of the right.

DP Regulation: Rectification Right

Article 3 of the DP Regulation refers to rectification and erasure. Article 16 refers to the right to rectification. It provides that the data subject shall have the right to obtain from the data controller the rectification of personal data relating to them that are inaccurate. The data subject shall have the right to obtain completion of incomplete personal data, including by way of supplementing a corrective statement.

DP Regulation: Erasure Right/Right to be Forgotten

Article 17 of the DP Regulation refers to the right to be forgotten and to erasure. Article 17(1) provides that the data subject shall have the right to obtain from the data controller the erasure of personal data relating to them and the abstention from further dissemination of such data, especially in relation to personal data that are made available by the data subject while he or she was a child, where one of the following grounds applies:

- the data are no longer necessary in relation to the purposes for which they were collected or otherwise processed;

- the data subject withdraws consent on which the processing is based according to Article 6(1)(a), or when the storage period consented to has expired, and where there is no other legal ground for the processing of the data;

- the data subject objects to the processing of personal data pursuant to Article 19;

- the processing of the data does not comply with the Regulation for other reasons.

Article 17(2) provides that where the data controller referred to in Article 17(1) above has made the personal data public, it shall take all reasonable steps, including technical measures, in relation to data for the publication of which the data controller is responsible, to inform third parties that are processing such data, that a data subject requests them to erase any links to, or copy or replication of that personal data. Where the data controller has authorised a third-party publication of personal data, the data controller shall be considered responsible for that publication.

Article 17(3) provides that the data controller shall carry out the erasure without delay, except to the extent that the retention of the personal data is necessary:

- for exercising the right of freedom of expression in accordance with Article 80;

- for reasons of public interest in the area of public health in accordance with Article 81;

- for historical, statistical and scientific research purposes in accordance with Article 83;

- for compliance with a legal obligation to retain the personal data by EU or Member State law to which the data controller is subject; Member State laws shall meet an objective of public interest, respect the essence of the right to the protection of personal data and be proportionate to the legitimate aim pursued; and

- in the cases referred to in Article 17(4).

Article 17(4) provides that instead of erasure, the data controller shall restrict processing of personal data where:

- their accuracy is contested by the data subject, for a period enabling the data controller to verify the accuracy of the data;

- the data controller no longer needs the personal data for the accomplishment of its task but they have to be maintained for purposes of proof;

- the processing is unlawful and the data subject opposes their erasure and requests the restriction of their use instead;

- the data subject requests to transmit the personal data into another automated processing system in accordance with Article 18(2).

Personal data referred to in Article 17(4) may, with the exception of storage, only be processed for purposes of proof, or with the data subject's consent, or for the protection of the rights of another natural or legal person or for an objective of public interest.[8]

Article 17(6) provides that where processing of personal data is restricted pursuant to Article 17(4), the data controller shall inform the data subject before lifting the restriction on processing.

The data controller shall implement mechanisms to ensure that the time limits established for the erasure of personal data and/or for a periodic review of the need for the storage of the data are observed.[9]

Where the erasure is carried out, the data controller shall not otherwise process such personal data.[10]

Article 17(9) provides that the Commission shall be empowered to adopt delegated acts for the purpose of further specifying:

---

8. art 17(5) *ibid.*
9. art 17(7) *ibid.*
10. art 17(8) *ibid.*

- the criteria and requirements for the application of Article 17(1) for specific sectors and in specific data processing situations;

- the conditions for deleting links, copies or replications of personal data from publicly available communication services as referred to in Article 17(2);

- the criteria and conditions for restricting the processing of personal data referred to in Article 17(4).[11]

Data Protection Acts: Rectification, Blocking, Erasure and Destruction Rights

Section 6 of the Data Protection Acts provides user rights in relation to rectification, blocking, erasure and destruction.

DP Directive 95: Rectification, Erasure and Blocking

Article 12, which relates to the right of access, also provides for rectification, erasure and blocking. It states that Member States shall guarantee every data subject the right to obtain from the data controller:

(b) as appropriate the rectification, erasure or blocking of data the processing of which does not comply with the provisions of [the] Directive, in particular because of the incomplete or inaccurate nature of the data;

(c) notification to third parties to whom the data have been disclosed of any rectification, erasure or blocking carried out in compliance with (b), unless this proves impossible or involves a disproportionate effort.

DP Regulation: Right to Portability

Article 18 refers to the right to data portability. The data subject shall have the right, where personal data are processed by electronic means and in a structured and commonly used format, to obtain from the data controller a copy of data undergoing processing in an electronic and structured format that is commonly used and allows for further use by the data subject.[12]

Where the data subject has provided the personal data and the processing is based on consent or on a contract, the data subject shall have the right to transmit those personal data and any other information provided by the data subject and retained by an automated processing system, into another one, in an electronic format that

---

11.   art 17(9) *ibid.*
12.   art 18(1) EU draft Data Protection Regulation.

is commonly used, without hindrance from the data controller from whom the personal data are withdrawn.[13]

Article 18(3) provides that the Commission may specify the electronic format referred to in Article 18(1) and the technical standards, modalities and procedures for the transmission of personal data pursuant to Article 18(2). Those implementing acts shall be adopted in accordance with the examination procedure referred to in Article 87(2).

DP Regulation: Right to Object and Profiling

Section 4 of the DP Regulation refers to the right to object and profiling. Article 19 of the DP Regulation refers to the right to object. Article 19(1) provides that the data subject shall have the right to object, on grounds relating to their particular situation, at any time to the processing of personal data which is based on Article 6(1)(d), (e) and (f), unless the data controller demonstrates compelling legitimate grounds for the processing that override the interests or fundamental rights and freedoms of the data subject.

Where personal data are processed for direct marketing purposes, the data subject shall have the right to object free of charge to the processing of their personal data for such marketing.[14] This right shall be explicitly offered to the data subject in an intelligible manner and shall be clearly distinguishable from other information.

Article 19(3) provides that where an objection is upheld pursuant to Article 19(1) and (2), the data controller shall no longer use or otherwise process the personal data concerned.

DP Regulation: Right re Profiling

Article 20 of the DP Regulation refers to measures based on profiling. Article 20(1) provides that every natural person shall have the right not to be subject to a measure that produces legal effects concerning this natural person or significantly affects this natural person, and which is based solely on automated processing intended to evaluate certain personal aspects relating to this natural person or to analyse or predict in particular the natural person's performance at work, economic situation, location, health, personal preferences, reliability or behaviour.

Subject to the other provisions of the Regulation, a person may be subjected to a measure of the kind referred to in Article 20(1) only if the processing:

---

13.   art 18(2) *ibid.*
14.   art 19(2) *ibid.*

- is carried out in the course of the entering into, or performance of, a contract, where the request for the entering into or the performance of the contract, lodged by the data subject, has been satisfied or where suitable measures to safeguard the data subject's legitimate interests have been adduced, such as the right to obtain human intervention; or

- is expressly authorised by an EU or Member State law that also lays down suitable measures to safeguard the data subject's legitimate interests; or

- is based on the data subject's consent, subject to the conditions laid down in Article 7 and to suitable safeguards.[15]

Automated processing of personal data intended to evaluate certain personal aspects relating to a natural person shall not be based solely on the special categories of personal data referred to in Article 9.[16]

In the cases referred to in Article 20(2), the information to be provided by the data controller under Article 14 shall include information as to the existence of processing for a measure of the kind referred to in Article 20(1) and the envisaged effects of such processing on the data subject.[17]

The Commission shall be empowered to adopt delegated acts in accordance with Article 86 for the purpose of further specifying the criteria and conditions for suitable measures to safeguard the data subject's legitimate interests referred to in Article 20(2).[18]

Data Protection Acts: Requiring Data Disclosure

Section 4 of the Data Protection Acts[19] prohibits an organisation from forcing or requiring the production by data subjects of personal data records to them in relation to recruitment or employment. For example, an organisation may be prohibited from forcing employees to disclose genetic data.

Compensation for Data Subjects

Section 7 of the Data Protection Acts provides for a duty of care to data subjects and which would include compensation for failure to comply with certain obligations and requirements. Article 22 of the DP Directive 95 provides that "Member States shall provide for the right of every person to a judicial remedy for any breach of the rights guaranteed [them] by the national law applicable to the processing in question."

---

15. art 20(2) *ibid.*
16. art 20(3) *ibid.*
17. art 20(4) *ibid.*
18. art 20(5) *ibid.*
19. Data Protection Act 1988 and Data Protection (Amendment) Act 2003.

Article 23 of the DP Directive 95 provides that "Member States shall provide that any person who has suffered damage as a result of an unlawful processing operation or of any act incompatible with the national provisions adopted pursuant to [the] Directive is entitled to receive compensation from the controller for the damage suffered."

Conclusion

Organisations need to respect the data protection rights of their employees, and even potential employees. In addition, particular care and attention needs to be paid to access requests from employees. Compliance is an ongoing issue as new changes and business practices will always present new challenges internally. New ways of working and new ways of monitoring and managing employees all create the need for careful data protection compliance assessments.

CHAPTER 15

Employee Considerations

Introduction

A large number of issues arise in terms of dealing with employee personal data, both in terms of audits, planning and compliance.

Contract

The starting point for informing and appraising employees of the importance of data protection, confidentiality and security in the organisation, and in relation to the employee's personal data, should be begin with the employment contract. There should be clauses referring to data protection and also to security.

Policies

There should also be policies relating to data protection furnished to all actual and prospective employees as appropriate. These need to be updated regularly as the issues covered change constantly.

These policies may be separate or may be incorporated into an employee handbook.

Organisations need to be aware that if there is an important change made, unless this is notified and recorded to employees, the organisation may not be able to rely upon the changed clause. For example, if there is a new activity banned or regulated in an updated policy but the new policy is not notified to employees, it may be impossible to use the new policy to discipline an errant employee. They and their lawyers will strongly argue that the new policy was not notified, is not part of the employment relationship, and would be unlawful to apply. There are many examples of this problem occurring in practice.

Data Protection Policy

In considering what policies to implement, the organisation will have to consider many issues and separate policies, with data protection being just one. Others include health and safety, environmental, etc. The data protection policy will perhaps be the most dynamic given the wide range of data, individuals, processes, activities and technologies involved, and which are ever-changing. Someone within the organisation needs to be responsible for examining and implementing ongoing changes as the requirement arises.

Internet Usage Policy

In addition to a general data protection policy, further specific data protection related policies will be required. The foremost of these relates to the employees' use of the internet on the organisation's systems.

Mobile and Device Usage Policies

Increasingly employees use not just desktop computers but also laptops, mobile phones, smart phones, handheld devices, Blackberrys, iPads, etc. Unless explicitly incorporated into one of the above policies, then additional, or extended, policies need to be implemented. One particular issue for an organisation to consider is the employees' own devices but which usage bill is paid by the organisation. Devices can also be supplied and paid for by the organisation. Somewhat different considerations may need to be applied.

Vehicle Use Policy

Vehicles must also be considered by organisations in terms of policy and employee usage. Increasingly tracking and other data from vehicles can be related to identified employees. Sometimes this may be as a result of the organisation furnishing a vehicle to the employee for work-related business. However, this need not be the case. Even where an employee is using their own vehicle, it is possible for the organisation to be collecting or accessing personal data. In addition, organisations must also be aware that vehicle technology, both in-built and added, can result in greater collections of data, including personal data, being potentially accessible. Tracking, incident and accident reports, etc., are just some examples. It is important for organisations to consider these personal data issues.

Evidence

Disputes naturally arise between employers and employees from time to time. In such disputes the organisation may need to rely upon documents, information and materials that contain personal data. While this may fit under the legitimate interests and legal interests provisions, employers should be careful about using less-obvious personal data. This might include private email communications over which an employee may argue privacy and confidentiality. Particular concerns arise where covert monitoring has been used. Before commencing covert activities of this type the organisation should seek legal advice. Otherwise, any evidence gathered may possibly be ruled inadmissible.

Organisations also need to be careful in that computer, electronic and mobile data can be changed, expire and or be amended quickly. It can be important to act quickly. Advance policies, procedures and protocols assist in this regard.

Conclusion

Employee data protection compliance is a complicated and ongoing obligation for organisations. It needs to involve the data protection officers, appropriate board member, human resources, IT personnel, legal (in-house and or external) and on occasion others may also have to become involved.

CHAPTER 16

Employee Monitoring Issues

Introduction

One of the more contentious areas of employee data protection practice relates to the issue of the monitoring of employee email, internet, etc., usage.

Often employers may not always be familiar with the obligations and restrictions to monitoring under the data protection regime. The more common reason that employers are concerned to seek to monitor is that certain risks can arise as result of the activities of employees in the workplace.

Sample Legal Issues

Some examples of the legal issues, risks and concerns that can arise for employers and organisations as a result of the actions of their employees include:

- vicarious liability;
- defamation;
- copyright and intellectual property infringement;
- confidentiality breaches and leaks;
- data protection;
- contract;
- inadvertent contract formation;
- harassment;
- abuse and online abuse;
- discrimination;
- computer crime;
- interception offences;
- criminal damage;
- data loss and data breach;

- data damage and data loss;
- contempt of court;
- criminal damage;
- ecommerce law;
- arms and dual use good export restrictions;
- non-fatal offences against the person; and
- child pornography.

These are examples of an expanding list (for example, online abuse) of concerns for organisations. Obviously, some of these will be recalibrated in importance depending on the type of organisation, the business sector and what its activities are. Confidentiality, for example, may be critically important for certain organisations, but less important for others.

Employee Misuse of Email, Internet, etc.

Even before the recent increase in data breach and data loss examples, there have been a significant number of examples where problems have arisen for organisations as a result of the activities of certain employees. Increasingly, organisations face the problem that the activity of an errant employee on the internet, television or social networks can go viral instantly on a global scale, with adverse reputational damage for the organisation. Vicarious liability, etc., is also a risk.

There are many instances where organisations have felt the need to discipline or dismiss employees.[1]

Security

The frequency and scale of recent breaches of security, e.g. Sony Playstation (70 million individuals' personal data[2] and 25 million in another[3]), make the topicality and importance of data security compliance ever more important. The largest UK data loss appears to be from Revenue and Customs' loss of discs with the names, dates

---

1. Some examples include Norwich Union Healthcare; Lois Franxhi; Royal & Sun Alliance Liverpool (77); C&W Birmingham (6); Rolls Royce Bristol (5); a shannon based company (24); Claire Swire/Bradley Chait; Ford; Weil Gotshal; Sellafield; iBBC. As these instances are ever-expanding, it would be impossible to provide a definitive list.
2. See, for example, Martin, "Sony Data Loss Biggest Ever" *Boston Herald* (27 April 2011), available at http://bostonherald.com/business/technology/general/view/2011_0427sony_data_loss_biggest_ever, last accessed 11 January 2013.
3. See, for example, Arthur, "Sony Suffers Second Data Breach With Theft of 25m More User Details" *Guardian* (3 May 2011), available at http://www.guardian.co.uk/technology/blog/2011/may/03/sony-data-breach-online-entertainment, last accessed 11 January 2013.

of birth, bank and address details for 25 million individuals.[4] Marks and Spencer was also involved in a data breach.

There are many new UK cases involving substantial fines for data protection breaches. The Brighton and Sussex University Hospitals NHS Trust had a fine of £325,000 imposed by the ICO in relation a data loss incident.[5] Zurich Insurance was fined £2.3m for losing data in relation to 46,000 individual customers.[6] The Data Protection Commissioner has also acted in relation to data breaches and other breaches under the data protection regime.

HP suspended 150 employees in one instance, which is one of the potential actions available. In a more creative solution, Ford issued a deletion amnesty to 20,000 employees to delete objected to material before a new or amended policy would kick in. Employees must contribute to, as well as help, maintain organisational security.

Online Abuse

The issue of the online abuse problem (and its various forms) is increasingly prominent. However, what issues arise for employers if they are associated with an event of online abuse, or worse, it transpires that an online abuser is an employee? This could occur on site, or off site with the organisation's devices. What liability arises if online abuse is circulated/endorsed on the organisation's systems by employees? Organisations will have to increasingly assess these issues in future.

Contract

It is possible for employees to agree and enter into contracts via electronic communications. This is increasingly a concern since the legal recognition of electronic contract in the ecommerce legislation.[7] This can include the inadvertent creation of legally binding contracts for the organisation. In addition, it is possible that an employee may create or agree to particular contract terms, delivery dates, etc., electronically that they would not otherwise do. These can all be contracts, or terms, the

---

4. See, for example, 'Brown Apologises for Record Loss: Prime Minister Gordon Brown has said he 'Profoundly Regrets' the Loss of 25 Million Child Benefit Records" *BBC* (21 November 2007), available at http://news.bbc.co.uk/2/hi/7104945.stm, last accessed 11 January 2013.

5. See, for example, "Largest Ever Fine for Data Loss Highlights Need for Audited Data Wiping" *ReturnOnIt*, available at http://www.returnonit.co.uk/largest-ever-fine-for-data-loss-highlights-need-for-audited-data-wiping.php, last accessed 11 January 2013.

6. See, for example, Oates, "UK Insurer Hit With Biggest Ever Data Loss Fine" *The Register*, 24 August 2010, available at http://www.theregister.co.uk/2010/08/24/data_loss_fine/, last accessed 11 January 2013. This was imposed by the Financial Services Authority (FSA).

7. For example, Directive 2000/31/EC of the European Parliament and of the Council of 8 June 2000 on certain legal aspects of information society services, in particular electronic commerce, in the Internal Market (Directive on electronic commerce).

organisation would not like to be bound by. It is also possible that breach of contract issues could arise.

Employment Equality

It can be illegal to discriminate, or permit discrimination, on grounds of, for example:

- gender;
- race;
- age;
- sexual orientation;
- family status;
- religious beliefs;
- disability; or
- being a member of a minority group.

Instances of such discrimination can occur on the organisation's computer systems and now social networking and related websites. Even though the organisation may not be initially aware of the instance, it can still have legal and other consequences.

Harassment

Harassment via the organisation's computer systems is also something that could cause consequences for an organisation. Examples could include the circulation of written words, pictures or other material a person may reasonably regard as offensive. The organisation could be held liable for employees' discriminatory actions unless it took reasonable steps to prevent them, or to deal with them appropriately once they arose.

Child Pornography

There is a serious risk and concern for organisations where this could occur on the organisation's computer systems or devices. Note, for example, the Status of Children Act 1987, Children Act 1989, Children Act 1997, Protection of Children (Hague Convention) Act 2000, Children Act 2001, Criminal Justice Act, Child Trafficking and Pornography Act 1998 and the Constitutional Amendment in relation to childrens' rights.

Dealing with the Employee Risks

It is important for all organisations to engage in a process of risk assessment of exposures that can be created as a result of their employees' use of its computer systems and devices. The scope of such assessments now increase with social networking and related websites.

Organisations should:

- identify the areas of risk;
- assess and evaluate those risks;
- engage in a process to eliminate/reduce the risks identified as appropriate;
- formalise an overall body of employee–corporate communications usage policies;
- implement appropriate and lawful technical solutions appropriate to dealing with the identified risks;
- implement an ongoing strategy to schedule reviews of the new and emerging risks, and to update and/or implement appropriate procedures and policies, including the update of existing employee–corporate communications usage policies.

Employee–Corporate Communications Usage Policies

Given the general risks, and the risks specific to an organisation identified in a review process, it is critical that the organisation implement appropriate policies in an overall body of employee–corporate communications usage policies.

It is important to note that there is no one fixed solution, or one single policy on its own that is sufficient to deal with these issues. Equally, a single policy on its own would not be sufficient to give comfort to the organisation in terms of (a) dealing with the risks and issues, and (b) ensuring that the organisation has implemented sufficient policies that allow it to act appropriately to meet specific issues as they arise.

For example, if an organisation discovers a particular instance of unauthorised activity on its computer systems undertaken by one of its employees, e.g. illegal file sharing or an employee hosting an illegal gambling website on its servers, it may decide that it wishes to dismiss the errant employee. But can it legally dismiss the employee? In the first instance, the organisation should ideally be in the position of being able to point to a specific clause in the employee's written contract of employment and a specific breach, or breaches, of one or more of the organisation's employee–corporate communications usage policies.

If such a clause exists, then the likelihood is that the organisation's legal advisors would be comfortable recommending that the dismissal is likely warranted, justified and lawful. However, if the answer is no, in that there is no written clause that is clearly breached as a result of the specific activities, even though carried out during the hours of employment, at the organisation's office, on the organisation's computer system and utilising the organisation's computer servers, the organisation would not have any legal comfort in dismissing the employee.

The organisation may not be able to obtain comfort for the dismissal in legal advices. If the company decided to proceed in any event in the dismissal it could run the legal risk that the employee may decide to legally challenge the dismissal under employment law. The employee would be assisted in that there is no express written clause breached. Unfortunately, the organisation may have to defend such an action and prove justification. Injunctions can also arise.

Focus of Organisational Communications Usage Policies

Organisations have a need for a comprehensive suite of organisational communications usage policies. This includes use of the organisation's telephone, voicemail, email and internet usage policy. The policies need to address:

- telephone;
- email;
- internet;
- mobile and portable devices;
- home and off-site usage; and
- vehicle usage.

This will be an ongoing task. Now, issues of social networking and related websites must be added.

Key Issues to Organisational Communications Usage Policies

The key aspects to consider in relation to the employee–corporate communications usage policies include:

- ownership;
- usage;
- authorisation;
- confidentiality;
- authentication;

- retention and storage;
- viruses;
- disciplinary matters;
- risk, security, etc.; and
- awareness.

These will vary depending on each organisation. Increasingly now, off site issues need to be considered.

From a data protection regime perspective, one of the key issues for an organisation is the ability to investigate or monitor employees or issues: can they? The answer is complex.

Data Protection and Employee Monitoring

Organisations may wish to monitor for various reasons, including:

- continuity of operations during staff illness;
- maintenance;
- preventing/investigating allegations of misuse;
- assessing/verifying compliance with software licensing obligations; and
- complying with legal and regulatory requests for information.

Organisations may also wish to monitor in order to prevent risks and to identify problems as they arise. When issues arise they will wish to deal appropriately with the employee.

Employers and agencies recruiting them need to carefully consider the legality of internet and social networking monitoring of employees and applicants. While it is a growing practice by all accounts, and appears more permissible in the US than the EU, organisations should not assume that they are permitted to monitor, record, keep files, and make decisions based upon personal information and personal data gathered online unbenownst to the individual employee or applicant.[8]

---

8. See, for example, Brandenburg, "The Newest Way to Screen Job Applicants: A Social Networker's Nightmare" (2007–2008)(60) *Federal Communications Law Journal* 597; Gersen, "Your Image: Employers Investigate Job Candidates Online more than ever. What Can you Do to Protect Yourself?" (2007–2008) *Student Law* 24; Levinson, "Industrial Justice: Privacy Protection for the Employed" (2009)(18) *Cornell Journal of Law and Public Policy* 609–688; Byrnside, "Six Degrees of Separation: The Legal Ramifications of Employers Using Social Networking Sites to Research Applicants" (2008)(2) *Vanderbilt Journal of Entertainment and Technology Lawn* 445–477; and Maher, "You've Got Messages: Modern Technology Recruiting Through Text Messaging and the Intrusiveness of Facebook" (2007)(8) *Texas Review of Entertainment and Sports Law* 125–151.

The issue of the right to privacy of the employee and the rights and interests of the organisation arise. The issue of the right to privacy is a complex subject beyond the scope of this discussion. However, it is an expanding area, particularly after the introduction of the European Convention on Human Rights Act 2003. Monitoring raises interlinking issues of privacy, human rights and data protection.

In Canada the Supreme Court has recently decided that employees have privacy interests in relation to their work-related activities.[9] There are various DPC case studies.

Human Rights

The European Convention on Human Rights Act 2003 means that the European Convention for the Protection of Human Rights and Fundamental Freedoms[10] is now incorporated into and applicable in Ireland. This means that Article 8 of European Convention for the Protection of Human Rights and Fundamental Freedoms is an important consideration. It provides that everyone has a right to privacy in relation to their family life, their home and correspondence. It states that:

- Everyone has the right to respect for their private and family life, their home and their correspondence;

- There shall be no interference by a public authority with the exercise of this right except such as is in accordance with the law and is necessary in a democratic society in the interests of national security, public safety or the economic well-being of the country, for the prevention of disorder or crime, for the protection of health or morals, or for the protection of the rights and freedoms of others.[11]

This was also a factor in the *Halford* case in the UK.

Application of Data Protection Regime

In terms of employee monitoring, employers are entitled to exercise reasonable control and supervision over their employees and their use of organisational resources. Employers are also entitled to have policies to protect their property and good name and to ensure that they do not become inadvertently liable for the misbehaviour of employees (this is increasingly relevant in relation to social networking, etc.).

---

9. *R v Cole*, Canadian Supreme Court, available at http://scc.lexum.org/decisia-scc-csc/scc-csc/scc-csc/en/item/12615/index.do, last accessed 24 October 2012.
10. Available at http://www.echr.coe.int/NR/rdonlyres/D5CC24A7-DC13-4318-B457-5C9014916 D7A/0/CONVENTION_ENG_WEB.pdf, last accessed 11 January 2013. See also Balla, "Constitutionalism – Reform on Data Protection Law and Human Rights" *Cerentul Juridic* 61–74.
11. *ibid.*

Equally, however, employees do retain privacy rights and data protection rights that must be respected by the organisation. Organisations must consider:

- the culture of the organisation;

- whether there is an understanding and expectation that employees can use the organisation's computers for personal use; and

- whether or not the organisation accessing the employee's communications without permission would be unfair and unlawful obtaining of information.

Monitoring involves careful consideration of policy and practice, as well as the inter-related legal issues of privacy/human rights/data protection.

Monitoring or acessing employee emails or tracking of employee web browsing without permission could easily be unfair obtaining. It is important, therefore, that the organisation has appropriate mechanisms and policies to reduce the risks and also to deal with issues as they arise. Reactively responding and trying to set up policies once a problem has arisen should be avoided. As pointed out above, it is difficult if not impossible to enforce contracts, terms or policies, if they are not explicitly in place before the incident in question. Retrospective terms cannot generally be relied upon in invoking particular sanctions against the employee.

Where it is discovered that there are no policies or inadequate provision in place, immediate advise should be sought in terms of the best course of action in order to deal with the situation to the extent possible.

ILO Code

Organisations should also consider the ILO code recommendations. The ILO Code of Practice on Protection of Workers Personal Data[12] recommends that:

- employees must be informed in advance of reasons, time schedule, methods and techniques used and the personal data collected;

- the monitoring must minimise the intrusion on the privacy of employees;

- secret monitoring must be in conformity with legislation or on foot of suspicion of criminal activity or serious wrongdoing;

- continuous monitoring should only occur if required for health and safety or protection of property.

---

12. Available at http://www.ilo.org/wcmsp5/groups/public/---ed_protect/---protrav/---safework/documents/normativeinstrument/wcms_107797.pdf, last accessed 11 January 2013.

Article 29 and Employment Processing

The EU Article 29 Working Party on Data Protection has long been concerned about employee monitoring and surveillance issues in terms of privacy and personal data. It issued an opinion in September 2001 entitled Opinion 8/2001 on the Processing of Personal Data in the Employment Context,[13] which states that "no business interest may ever prevail on the principles of transparency, lawful processing, legitimisation, proportionality, necessity and others contained in data protection laws".

The EU Article 29 Working Party on Data Protection states that when processing employee personal data, employers should always bear in mind fundamental *data protection principles* such as the following:

Finality

Data must be collected for a specified, explicit and legitimate purpose and not further processed in a way incompatible with those purposes.[14]

Transparency

As a very minimum, employees need to know which data the employer is collecting about them (directly or from other sources), which are the purposes of processing operations envisaged or carried out with these data presently or in the future. Transparency is also assured by granting the data subject the right to access to his or her personal data and with the data controllers' obligation of notifying supervisory authorities as provided in Member State law.[15]

Legitimacy

The processing of workers' personal data must be legitimate. Article 7 of the Directive lists the criteria that make the processing legitimate.[16]

Proportionality

The personal data must be adequate, relevant and not excessive in relation to the purposes for which they are collected and/or further processed. Assuming that employees have been informed about the processing operation and assuming that such processing activity is legitimate and proportionate, such processing still needs to be fair to the employee.[17]

---

13. Opinion 8/2001 on the processing of personal data in the employment context. Available at http://ec.europa.eu/justice/policies/privacy/workinggroup/wpdocs/2001_en.htm, last accessed 11 January 2013.
14. Available at http://ec.europa.eu/justice/policies/privacy/docs/wpdocs/2001/wp48en.pdf, last accessed 11 January 2013.
15. *ibid.*
16. *ibid.*
17. *ibid.*

Accuracy and Retention of the Data

Employment records must be accurate and, where necessary, kept up to date. The employer must take every reasonable step to ensure that data that are inaccurate or incomplete, having regard to the purposes for which they were collected or further processed, are erased or rectified.[18]

Security

The employer must implement appropriate technical and organisational measures at the workplace to guarantee that the personal data of his or her employees is kept secure. Particular protection should be granted as regards unauthorised disclosure or access.[19]

Awareness of the Staff

Staff in charge or with responsibilities in the processing of personal data of other employees need to know about data protection and receive proper training. Without adequate training of the staff handling personal data, there cannot be appropriate respect for the privacy of employees in the workplace.[20]

In relation to consent, the EU Article 29 Working Party on Data Protection adds that it has taken the view that where as a necessary and unavoidable consequence of the employment relationship an employer has to process personal data it is misleading if it seeks to legitimise this processing through consent.[21] Reliance on consent should be confined to cases where the employee has a genuine free choice and is subsequently able to withdraw the consent without detriment.[22]

EU Article 29 Working Party on Data Protection: Electronic Communications

The EU Article 29 Working Party on Data Protection also issued an opinion in 2008 on the review of the Directive 2002/58/EC on privacy and electronic communications.[23] It was entitled Opinion 2/2008 on the Review of the Directive 2002/58/EC on Privacy and Electronic Communications (ePrivacy Directive) and was adopted on 15 May 2008.

Under the heading "Privacy by Design" it states that it advocates the application of the principle of data minimisation and the deployment of Privacy Enhancing

---

18. *ibid.*
19. *ibid.*
20. *ibid.*
21. *ibid.*
22. *ibid.*
23. Opinion 2/2008 on the review of the Directive 2002/58/EC on privacy and electronic communications (ePrivacy Directive), available at http://ec.europa.eu/justice/policies/privacy/docs/wpdocs/2008/wp150_en.pdf, last accessed 11 January 2013.

Technologies (PETs) by data controllers. It also calls upon European legislators to make provision for a re-enforcement of that principle, by reiterating Recitals 9 and 30 of the ePrivacy Directive in a new paragraph in Article 1 of the Directive.[24]

It also notes that Article 5(1) imposes an obligation to ensure confidentiality of communications irrespective of the nature of the network and whether or not the communication crosses borders to non-EU Member States.[25]

Electronic communications were also considered in EU Article 29 Working Party on Data Protection Opinion 8/2006 on the Review of the Regulatory Framework for Electronic Communications and Services, with focus on the ePrivacy Directive.[26]

The EU Article 29 Working Party on Data Protection also issued a working document on the surveillance of electronic communications in the workplace on 29 May 2002.[27]

It also issued Opinion 4/2007 on the concept of personal data, which is relevant in considering the definition of personal data.[28]

In relation to employee health records it is worth examining the Working Document on the Processing of Personal Data Relating to Health in Electronic Health Records (EHR).[29]

When outsourcing and dealing with data processors it is worth considering Opinion 1/2010 on the concepts of data "controller" and data "processor".[30]

In relation to video surveillance, the EU Article 29 Working Party on Data Protection issued Opinion 4/2004 on the Processing of Personal Data by means of Video Surveillance.[31]

---

24. *ibid* p 6.
25. *ibid*.
26. Available at http://ec.europa.eu/justice/policies/privacy/docs/wpdocs/2006/wp126_en.pdf, last accessed 11 January 2013.
27. Working document on the surveillance of electronic communications in the workplace, WP 55, adopted 29 May 2002, available at http://ec.europa.eu/justice/policies/privacy/docs/wpdocs/2002/wp55_en.pdf, last accessed 11 January 2013.
28. Available at http://ec.europa.eu/justice/policies/privacy/docs/wpdocs/2007/wp136_en.pdf, last accessed 11 January 2013.
29. Available at http://ec.europa.eu/justice/policies/privacy/docs/wpdocs/2007/wp131_en.pdf, last accessed 11 January 2013.
30. Available at http://ec.europa.eu/justice/policies/privacy/docs/wpdocs/2010/wp169_en.pdf, last accessed 11 January 2013.
31. Available at http://ec.europa.eu/justice/policies/privacy/docs/wpdocs/2004/wp89_en.pdf, last accessed 11 January 2013.

Employment Contracts, Terms, Policies

As indicated above, organisations need to consider contracts. Particular matters are:

- whether the contract provision has been properly incorporated;
- issues of limitation of liability;
- issues of exclusion of warranties;
- disclaimers;
- graduated disclaimers;
- ongoing risk assessment; and
- continual review and updating.

Registration Requirements

The data protection regime imposes registration requirements with the Data Protection Commissioners.

Possible guidance questions in relation to assessing an organisation's registration requirements, including employee data, include:

- Is the organisation processing personal information?
- Is any of the processing on computer?
- Is the organisation a data controller?
- Is the organisation only processing personal information for personal, family or household affairs (including recreational purposes)?
- Is it processing personal information for any of the following purposes?
- Is the organisation only processing personal information to maintain a public register?
- Is the organisation a not-for-profit organisation?
- Is the organisation a not-for-profit organisation? Is the processing covered by the following descriptions? Is there an exemption?

UK ICO

The ICO in the UK asks the following guidance questions:

- Does the organisation really need this information about an individual?

- Does the organisation know what it is going to use it for?

- Do the employees know what information the organisation has, and what it will be used for?

- If the organisation is asked to pass on personal information, would the people about whom the organisation hold information expect the organisation to do this?

- Is the organisation satisfied that the information is being held securely, whether on paper or on computer?

- Is the organisation website secure?

- Does the organisation need to notify the ICO, and if so, is the notification up to date?

The ICO has also issued a useful data protection notification handbook, *A Complete Guide to Notification*.[32] This is available online.

Registration Exemptions

Section 16(1) of the Data Protection Acts provides that registration would not be required where the organisation carries out

- processing whose sole purpose is the keeping in accordance with the law of a register that is intended to provide information to the public and is open to consultation either by the public in general or by any person demonstrating a legitimate interest;

- processing of manual data (other than such categories, if any, of such data as may be prescribed); or

- any combination of the foregoing categories of processing;

- the data controller is a body that is not established or conducted for profit and is carrying out processing for the purposes of establishing or maintaining membership of or support for the body or providing or administering activities for individuals who are either members of the body or have regular contact with it.

However, even if exempt from registration, the other obligations and compliance rules set out in the data protection regime still apply once there is personal data being processed.

---

32. Available at http://www.ico.gov.uk/for_organisations/data_protection/notification/need_to_notify.aspx, last accessed 11 January 2013.

The Data Protection Act 1988 (Section 16(1)) Regulations 2007 refers to various exemptions.[33] Regulation 3 provides that, subject to Regulation 4 below, the following categories of data controller and data processor are specified for the purposes of s 16(1) of the Data Protection Acts:

- a data controller who processes personal data relating to the data controller's past, existing or prospective employees in the ordinary course of personnel administration and not for any other purpose, where the data are not processed other than where it is necessary to carry out such processing in the ordinary course of personnel administration;

- a data controller, being a person who is seeking or intends to seek nomination as a candidate for election to a political office where the data are not processed other than where it is necessary to carry out such processing for the purpose of electoral activities, for political purposes or providing such advice or assistance to a data subject, as the case may be;

- a data controller, being an educational establishment that is:

    - a preschool service as defined;

    - a primary school;

    - a post-primary school;

    - an institution providing adult, continuing or further education; or

    - a university or any other third-level or higher-level institution;

- a data controller, being a solicitor who, for the purpose of providing legal services to their clients, processes personal data for the purpose of providing legal services;

- a data controller, being a barrister who processes personal data for legal professional purposes, where the data are not processed other than where it is necessary to carry out such processing for legal professional purposes;

- a data controller, other than a health professional who processes personal data relating to the physical or mental health or condition of a data subject for medical purposes, who processes personal data relating to the past, existing or prospective customers or suppliers of the data controller for the purposes of:

    (i) advertising or marketing the data controller's business, activity, goods or services;

    (ii) keeping accounts relating to any business or other activity carried on by the data controller;

---

33. SI 657/2007.

(iii) deciding whether or not to accept any person as a customer or supplier;

(iv) keeping records of purchases, sales or other transactions for the purpose of ensuring that the requisite payments and deliveries are made or services provided by or to the data controller in respect of those transactions;

(v) making financial or management forecasts to assist in the conduct of the business or other activity carried on by the data controller; or

(vi) performing a contract with a data subject,

where the data are not processed other than where it is necessary to carry out such processing for any of the purposes specified in the above Regulation (3)(i) to (vi) above;

- a data controller, being a company that processes personal data relating to the past or existing shareholders, directors or other officers of the company for the purpose of compliance with the Companies Acts, where the data are not processed other than where it is necessary to carry out such processing for that purpose;

- a data controller who processes personal data with a view to the publication of any journalistic, literary or artistic material, where the data are not processed other than where it is necessary to carry out such processing for journalistic, literary or artistic purposes;

- a data controller or a data processor to whom a code of practice in respect of which a resolution approving of it has been passed by each House of the Oireachtas under s 13(3) of the Data Protection Acts apply;

- a data processor who processes personal data on behalf of a data controller insofar as the processing of the data would, if undertaken by the data controller, fall under any one or more of the paragraphs above.[34]

Regulation 4 provides that the following categories of data controller and data processor are not specified for the purposes of s 16(1) of the Data Protection Acts, even if such a data controller or data processor falls under any one or more points of Regulation 3(1)(a) to (k). Data controllers and data processors to whom Regulation 3 does not apply are exempted from the registration requirement. These are namely:

- a data controller, being a financial institution other than an institution referred to in paragraphs s 7(4)(a) and (f) of the Central Bank Act 1971 (as amended);

---

34. Regulation 3, Data Protection Act 1988 (Section 16(1)) Regulations 2007.

- a data controller, being a person authorised in accordance with the European Communities (Licensing and Supervision of Credit Institutions) Regulations 1992[35] to carry on business in the State;

- a data controller, being an insurance undertaking within the meaning of s 2 of the Insurance Act 1989 (as amended);

- a data controller, being a person whose business consists wholly or mainly in direct marketing, providing credit references or collecting debts;

- a data controller, being an internet access provider whose business consists wholly or partly in the connection of persons to the Internet and who holds personal data relating to such persons;

- a data controller, being an authorised undertaking within the meaning of the European Communities (Electronic Communications Networks and Services) (Authorisation) Regulations 2003[36] who processes personal data relating to persons to whom electronic communications networks or electronic communications services are provided;

- a data controller who processes genetic data within the meaning of s 41 of the Disability Act 2005;

- a data processor who processes personal data on behalf of a data controller who falls under any one or more of the above paragraphs of Regulation 4.

Registration Issues

Some of the registration and registration planning issues to consider are:

- the data controller;
- the legal entity of the data controller;
- the categories of general personal data collected and processed;
- the categories of sensitive personal data collected and processed;
- the purposes and uses for the collection and processing;
- where there are two or more related purposes, separate registration details must be supplied;
- where there are two or more unrelated purposes, separate registrations may be required;
- whether or not there are any data processors involved;
- location of personal data;

---

35. SI 395/1992.
36. SI 306/2003.

- trans-border data flows with the personal data;

- disclosures of personal data to third parties, if so occurring;

- security requirements apply;

- annual renewal; and

- update if there are significant changes.

Processing Compliance Rules

If an organisation is collecting and processing personal data, it must comply with the DP Directive 95[37] and data protection regime in respect of:

- data protection principles;

- non-sensitive personal data legitimate processing conditions;

- sensitive personal data legitimate processing conditions;

- direct marketing (DM) requirements;

- security requirements;

- registration requirements;

- data processor contract requirements; and

- transfer requirements.

Suggested Guidelines

Some suggested guidelines to consider generally are set out below. However, it is always recommended that appropriate professional legal and technical advice be sought in particular circumstances.

- comply with the processing compliance rules set out above;

- ensure fair obtaining, collecting and processing of personal data;

- compliance must be ensured at the time of data capture NOT subsequently;

- implement appropriate procedures in the first instance;

- the lessons of *British Gas* and other examples are that in a worst case scenario an organisation may have to delete the database and start again from the beginning, or re-do the collection and notification process;

---

37. EU Data Protection Directive 1995 (Directive 95/46/EC of the European Parliament and of the Council of 24 October 1995 on the protection of individuals with regard to the processing of personal data and on the free movement of such data).

- consider and decide upon opt-in or op-out consent;

- consider the purpose or purposes for the data collection and which must be specified;

- provide information to the data subject when collecting;

- consider whether the data subject is the source (direct) or whether a third-party is the source (indirect);

- specifying in the registration may not be enough, it may have to be earlier;

- processing must be specified and lawful;

- the use or purpose to which the data collected will be put must be clear and defined. Otherwise it could be deemed too vague and unfair and ultimately an unfair collection, which would undermine the initial consent given;

- if disclosure occurs, it must be specified, clear and defined;

- security measures must be assessed and implemented;

- security includes physical security;

- security also includes technical security;

- measures must be put in place to prevent loss, alteration or destruction;

- other legislation may also apply such as in relation to hacking, criminal damage, etc.;

- the personal data must be kept accurate and up to date;

- personal data must be kept for no longer than is necessary;

- consider that there are many different types of personal data;

- the organisational or business needs requirement must be identified;

- how personal data is collected must be considered, planned and recorded;

- check principles;

- check legitimate processing conditions;

- explicit consent is required for collecting and processing sensitive personal data;

- identify and deal with new processes and procedures in advance to ensure data protection compliance. One cannot assume that the organisation can obtain a fair and lawful consent after a go-live;

- identify new contracts, collections and consents in advance to ensure data protection compliance; and

- identify direct marketing changes and campaigns in advance to ensure data protection compliance.

These all take on particular significance in the employment context.

Conclusion

Organisations at different times may feel a temptation to engage in monitoring of employees. No matter how tempting, this needs to be checked in order to be data protection compliant. While there are naturally risks and issues to deal with, the starting point should be one of proportionate responses that ensure data protection compliance.

CHAPTER 17

Case Studies

Data Protection Commissioner Employment Complaint Decisions and Case Studies

Set out below are some of the relevant case studies of complaints and decisions by the Data Protection Commissioner.

Case Study 9/2011: Unlawful use of CCTV to remotely monitor an employee

In October 2010, I received a complaint from an individual who stated that he considered that his personal privacy was being affected in his workplace through the inappropriate use of a CCTV system which his employer had installed. The complainant was employed by Westwood Swimming Ltd in Leopardstown as an administrator. In support of his complaint the individual cited two separate occasions, three months apart, when he received phone calls from his employer who was not on the premises at the time. In both of these phone calls the employer allegedly described to him what he had been doing at a particular time, i.e. that he was conversing with and working on a computer used by an individual from the office next door (who had a different employer). The complainant stated that subsequent to these incidents he had received two separate written warnings. He also stated that the CCTV system was installed without prior staff notification as to the reason for its installation or its purpose.

My Office contacted Westwood Swimming Ltd and we informed it of its obligations under the Acts in respect of CCTV usage. We advised that any monitoring must be a proportionate response by an employer to the risk he or she faces taking into account the legitimate privacy and other interests of workers. We further advised that in terms of meeting transparency requirements, staff must be informed of the existence of the CCTV surveillance and also of the purposes for which personal data are to be processed by CCTV systems. We provided it with copies of our guidance material on the use of CCTV and staff monitoring. It was asked to outline how the processing of personal data as complained of complied with the Acts and to give details of any signage that was in place on the premises informing individuals that there was CCTV in operation and its purpose.

Westwood Swimming Ltd in response stated that the CCTV system was installed with the priority focus being security of the office due to the amount of cash and credit card slips with customer information on hand. It informed us that a secondary purpose for the CCTV was the fact that it had received numerous complaints from its customers stating that the office was not open or that the office was open and unattended which gave it further concern for the security of cash/credit cards. It confirmed that its staff had not been informed in writing of the installation and purpose of the CCTV. However, it indicated that staff were well aware of the reasons behind the new system as the cameras were overt and the recorder and screen showing views and recordings were in the office in full view of both staff and clients. It stated that the system was installed during working hours in full view of the staff and no query, question or complaint was received from either the staff or clients. It also referred to having signage in place informing people of CCTV being in operation. In this regard, it provided us with a copy of a notice posted at its main entrance listing the various services available at the centre. While it was noted on the bottom of the signage that CCTV cameras were in operation it gave no indication as to its purpose.

Westwood Swimming Ltd acknowledged that the CCTV footage had been reviewed by it in respect of the incidents cited by the complainant.

After consideration of the response received from Westwood Swimming Ltd, my Office informed it that we were satisfied that it had used a CCTV system to monitor an employee and that such monitoring was in breach of the Data Protection Acts. We asked that it immediately confirm to us that it would cease the practice of monitoring employees by remotely accessing the system from a live feed or by any other means. In response, it provided us with a commitment that its employees would not be monitored remotely or by other means using CCTV. It confirmed that the cameras in the office would be removed, any disciplinary actions taken against the employee concerned on foot of the use of CCTV would be discarded, and that it would ensure that the employee would not suffer as a result of any information seen on camera.

At the request of the complainant, I issued a formal decision on this matter in March 2011 which stated that the leisure centre contravened Section 2(1)(c)(ii) of the Data Protection Acts by the further processing of CCTV images which were stated to have been obtained for security purposes in a manner incompatible with that purpose. These contraventions occurred in the two instances when the CCTV was used to monitor the performance of the complainant in the course of their employment.

The improper use of CCTV to monitor employees is a matter of increasing concern to me. Even where employers have sought to legitimise the use of CCTV to monitor staff by referring to it in their company handbook, the position remains that transparency and proportionality are the key points to be considered by any data controller before using CCTV in this manner. We would only expect CCTV footage to be reviewed to examine the actions of individual staff members in exceptional circumstances of a serious nature where the employer could legitimately invoke the provisions of Section

2A (1)(d) of the Acts ('the processing is necessary for the purposes of the legitimate interests pursued by the data controller ... except where the processing is unwarranted in any particular case by reason of prejudice to the fundamental rights and freedoms or legitimate interests of the data subject.'). This was clearly not the case in the circumstances which formed the basis of this complaint.[1]

Case study 10/2010: Use of CCTV & biometrics

In late 2009, we received a number of separate complaints from employees of Boran Plastic Packaging Ltd located at Millennium Park, Naas. These complaints concerned the alleged use by management of CCTV on the factory floor for the purpose of monitoring staff and the use of a biometric system for recording employees' time and attendance. As both CCTV and biometric systems process personal data, their use is governed by the Data Protection Acts. We decided that the most effective course of investigation was to carry out an unannounced inspection at the premises in question to establish the facts.

> In November 2009 two authorised officers carried out an unannounced inspection. While we use such powers sparingly, this is a useful means of establishing compliance with the Data Protection Acts. In general, authorised officers are treated courteously and receive full cooperation in the course of such inspections. Unfortunately that was not the case on this occasion. From the outset of the inspection the factory manager made every effort to frustrate the work of the authorised officers. It was made clear to them that their presence on the site was not welcome. Such was the level of discourtesy displayed towards the authorised officers in the performance of their functions that they considered issuing a caution against the factory manager with a view to formally charging him with obstruction – a criminal offence under Section 24 of the Data Protection Acts. However, the level of cooperation increased as the inspection continued. During the inspection Boran Plastic Packaging Limited denied that one of the purposes of the CCTV was to monitor staff. The company informed us that the main purpose of the CCTV system related to security and health and safety. On inspection of the factory, my authorised officers noted the location of the CCTV cameras. Based on information provided during the inspection, they noted that the individual who had access to monitor the CCTV images was a non-staff member. The individual in question was a member of the owner's family and had off-site access to real-time CCTV views. It was also clear from our inspection that the company had no data protection policies in place in relation to the use of CCTV and biometrics. Following the inspection, the investigation progressed in the normal manner.

> In our subsequent communications with the company we found Boran Plastic Packaging Ltd to be cooperative with our investigation. As a result of our extensive engagements with the company in the following weeks, it drew up a comprehensive data protection policy document. This document includes, among other things, its

---

1.   See DPC, available at http://dataprotection.ie/viewdoc.asp?m=c&fn=/documents/caseStudies/ Case_Studies_2011.htm, last accessed 11 January 2013.

policy on the use of CCTV and biometrics in the workplace. The company's CCTV policy includes confirmation that there will be no live monitoring of images captured on CCTV and that recorded images will be viewed only following the rare occasions when a security breach, employee personal protection or health and safety incident occurs. In relation to our concerns about access to the CCTV system, the company confirmed that access had now been restricted to two members of staff who had on-site access only. At our instruction, its policy on the use of the biometric system includes the provision that, should an employee have a legitimate privacy concern or any other concern in relation to the biometric hand scanner, they can contact a specific member of staff in the HR Department about their concerns. My Office informed the company that, if a legitimate privacy concern about the use of the biometric system is expressed by any employee to the HR Department, that employee has a right to opt out of using the system. We made it clear the onus is on the company to offer such an employee an alternative means of recording time and attendance. We informed Boran Plastic Packaging Ltd that, if it was to refuse such an employee the right to opt-out, he/she would have a right to make a complaint to our Office. Boran Plastic Packaging Ltd also confirmed that staff would be informed of the availability of a copy of its data protection policy documents.

The proliferation of CCTV and biometric systems in workplaces, without due regard to the data protection rights of employees and others, is a matter of great concern. Elsewhere in this Annual Report and in previous Annual Reports we have commented at length on these issues.

This case study also highlights the difficulties which my authorised officers face from time to time in carrying out their statutory functions. In most cases they receive cooperation from data controllers and their staff. We acknowledge that for a data controller or data processor an unannounced inspection can be a trying and anxious experience. However, for our part, we tend not to conduct such inspections unless we have solid reasons based on complaints about breaches of the Data Protection Acts. Whatever the reason for the inspection, data controllers, data processors and their employees would be well-advised to cooperate fully with authorised officers. Authorised officers, in the exercise of their functions, have considerable powers conferred on them by law. Any obstruction or impediment placed in the way of the exercising of those powers is an offence and we will have no hesitation in prosecuting any individual, data controller or data processor who commits such an offence.[2]

---

2.   See DPC, available at http://dataprotection.ie/viewdoc.asp?m=c&fn=/documents/caseStudies/ CaseStudies2010.htm#10, last accessed 11 January 2013.

Case study 11/2010: Lawful use of CCTV cameras by an employer

We received a complaint in September 2010 from solicitors acting on behalf of a data subject. The complaint stated that CCTV cameras were installed in the data subject's workplace without her knowledge and that the purpose of the cameras was to identify disciplinary issues relating to staff. The complaint also stated that CCTV evidence was obtained and used to dismiss the data subject for gross misconduct.

Recognisable images captured by CCTV systems are personal data. Therefore they are subject to the provisions of the Data Protection Acts. To satisfy the fair obtaining principle of the Data Protection Acts with regard to the use of CCTV cameras, those people whose images are captured on camera must be informed about the identity of the data controller and the purpose(s) of processing the data. This can be achieved by placing easily-read signs in prominent positions. A data controller must be able to justify obtaining and using personal data by means of a CCTV system.

With regard to the installation of covert CCTV cameras, our position is that the use of recording mechanisms to obtain data without an individual's knowledge is generally unlawful. Covert CCTV surveillance is normally only permitted on a case-by-case basis where the information is kept for the purposes of preventing, detecting or investigating offences, or apprehending or prosecuting offenders. This provision automatically implies an actual involvement of An Garda Síochána or an intention to involve An Garda Síochána. Covert surveillance must be focused and of short duration and only specific (and relevant) individuals/locations should be recorded. If no evidence is obtained within a reasonable period, the surveillance should cease.

If the surveillance is intended to prevent crime, overt cameras may be a more appropriate measure, and less invasive of individual privacy.

In this case we requested the data subject's solicitors to provide us with a copy of all correspondence that was exchanged in relation to the matter. On examining this correspondence, we noted that the data subject's employer considered it necessary to install the covert CCTV cameras because some members of staff informed the employer that money had gone missing from their purses. We also noted the involvement of An Garda Síochána in the decision to install the covert cameras. We subsequently informed the data subject's solicitors that we did not consider that a basis arose in the Data Protection Acts to progress an investigation.

This case demonstrates the use of covert CCTV by a data controller in compliance with the Data Protection Acts. For personal data captured on covert CCTV to be fairly obtained and fairly processed under the Data Protection Acts, the installation of covert CCTV must involve An Garda Síochána or a clear intention to involve An Garda Síochána, as was the case in this instance.[3]

---

3.   *ibid.*

Case study 16/2010: Employee obtains data from customer file for his or her own use

In March 2010 we received a complaint regarding an alleged inappropriate access to customer personal information by an employee of Aviva (an insurance company). The complainant informed us that, in March 2010, he was telephoned by an individual who accused him of scratching his car on the previous evening while parking in University College Dublin. As the complainant knew nothing of this incident, he asked the caller how he had obtained his phone number. He was informed by the caller that he had noticed that the car was insured with Aviva and, as he worked for that company, he had sourced the phone number from the Aviva system. The caller stated that he had left a business card on the car windscreen. When the data subject checked, he found the business card with the name of the individual concerned and his job title.

We commenced our investigation of this complaint by writing to Aviva, drawing their attention to the obligation to keep personal data for specified, explicit and lawful purposes and use it only in ways compatible with these purposes. On this basis, we asked Aviva to outline the circumstances in which the complainant's personal data was processed in the manner outlined in his complaint. In its response Aviva assured us that it has very stringent procedures in place regarding the safeguarding of customers' personal data from unauthorised access and the protection of this data from processing for purposes other than for which it was collected. In relation to the specifics of this complaint, Aviva investigated the matter and raised it with the employee concerned. The employee confirmed that he accessed the policyholder's data for the purpose of contacting him to discuss the incident and to see if he wished to settle the matter directly with him. Aviva acknowledged that the incident should have been pursued in the normal manner through its claims procedure. If the correct procedure had been followed, the complainant's personal information would have been accessed by claims personnel and used to alert him of the allegation. Aviva informed us that the staff member in question had been made aware in no uncertain terms of the seriousness of the incident. In addition, the issues raised by this complaint [were] used to draw the attention of other staff members to the importance of complying with data protection obligations.

In an effort to amicably resolve this complaint, Aviva issued a letter to the complainant explaining what had occurred and apologising for the distress and inconvenience caused. The company also offered the complainant a voucher for €100 towards his next renewal premium. The complainant accepted this amicable resolution.

This complaint raised a serious data protection issue. Organisations are entrusted with a huge amount of personal data which they have a responsibility to keep safe and secure. The message that customer personal information can only be accessed on a 'need to know' basis must be continually reinforced. While safeguards are required to protect customer data from disclosure to third parties outside the organisation, similar protection must be afforded to protect the data from internal misuse. This theme is raised again elsewhere in this report in relation to insurance companies. We must also acknowledge that we received full co-operation from Aviva in this matter and the company takes its data protection responsibilities seriously.[4]

Note also the *Davies* case in the UK regarding conviction for unlawful access by a bank employee.

Case study 7/2009: Recruitment companies sharing CVs

In April 2009 I received a complaint against a recruitment company (company A) regarding an alleged disclosure of the complainant's curriculum vitae (CV) to another recruitment company (company B). The complainant submitted his CV to company A for a particular job which was advertised on a recruitment website. However, he was subsequently contacted by company B asking for further details in relation to his CV. In a phone call, company B confirmed to the complainant that it had received his CV from company A. The complainant claimed that the company to whom he sent his CV did not obtain his consent to disclose his CV to another company.

My Office commenced an investigation into the matter and we wrote to company A and asked it to demonstrate the consent it considered it had in place to disclose the complainant's CV to company B. A key principle of data protection is that personal data should be used and disclosed only in ways compatible with the purposes for which it was obtained. Company A explained that it and company B, although they were separate legal entities and registered separately with the Companies Registration Office, were effectively run as one company. They both shared, among other things, the same office space, databases, IT infrastructure, telephone system and management. However, one of the companies handled recruitment of middle and senior management while the other one handled recruitment of office and customer support staff. In this case, when the complainant submitted his CV to Company A, the consultant who received it passed it to a consultant in Company B as possible skills were identified from the CV which may have been of interest to the other consultant's clients.

My Office advised Company A that the companies were two separate entities and therefore, individuals using the services of either one should be made fully aware, prior to submitting their personal information, that it would be shared between the two companies. We also noted that the privacy policy on its website did not contain any reference to the fact that both companies share information and we advised that it should contain a statement which informed individuals using the website how their information would be processed and that their information would be shared between the two companies. My Office also advised that, if it was unable to do this, the only alternative was to separate out the two entities completely and cease sharing personal information.

---

4. *ibid.*

As a result of our investigation, we received an assurance from Company A that it would insert a statement on both of the companies' websites to inform individuals using the websites how their personal information would be processed and of the fact that it would be shared between both companies. It also indicated that it would no longer have separate entities and that, although this would take some time to arrange, both companies would trade as one company in future.

I welcome the fact that the data controller immediately put in place the measures needed to bring it into compliance with the Acts. It is important for any data controller to make individuals fully aware at the outset as to how their personal data will be processed and to whom it may be disclosed. As a general rule personal data may not be shared between two legal entities without the consent of the individual about whom the data relates.[5]

Case study 14/2009: Employer breaches Acts by covert surveillance using a private investigator

In October 2008, I received a complaint from an individual concerning the processing, without his knowledge or consent, of both his and his children's personal data by his employer. The complaint involved the obtaining and processing of his personal data and that of his children by way of a private investigator producing footage of his movements and his children's movements on a DVD for the company without his knowledge or consent.

My Office commenced an investigation into the matter by writing to the company. We informed it of its obligations under the Data Protection Acts and we asked for its comments on the complaint. The company informed my Office of the circumstances which led to it hiring a private investigator to check on the employee's activities. According to it, the complainant was employed as a sales representative and, as such, spent virtually all of his time away from the company's premises. It stated it became concerned that the employee was not carrying out his duties as required by his contract of employment and it decided it was necessary to check on his activities in his sales territory. A private investigator was engaged to check on the employee's activities in order to establish whether or not he was performing his duties. The private investigator recorded the movements of the employee for a period of approximately one week and produced a DVD of those movements which he provided to the company. Some of the recordings produced on the DVD also contained images of the employee's children.

My Office remained concerned about the justification for the processing of the employee's personal data by way of the private investigator recording his movements. We asked that the company review any documentation it had which it believed may suggest that

---

5. See DPC, available at http://www.dataprotection.ie/viewdoc.asp?DocID=1068#7, last accessed 11 January 2013.

the processing of the employee's personal data in this way was justified. We subsequently received a range of documents in that regard. My Office also asked if it had taken any steps to address the concerns it had about the employee's activities prior to the hiring of the private investigator – to which it replied that it believed there were no other steps it could have taken. It also informed my Office that it felt it needed to make observations of the employee's company car over a period of at least a week before it could be satisfied that the employee had a case to answer. The company stated that it did not have the resources internally to check this over such a period of time and for that reason the private investigator was asked to check and report. Having considered the case put forward by the company and the documentation submitted, my Office informed it that we considered that the processing of the employee's personal data by way of a private investigator recording the employee's movements was not justified as it had not taken appropriate steps to highlight its concerns to the employee prior to making the decision to hire a private investigator to record his movements. My Office also requested that the DVD in question be destroyed and we subsequently received confirmation of its destruction from the company.

The complainant subsequently requested a decision under Section 10 of the Acts. My decision found that the company had contravened Section 2(1)(a) of the Acts by the processing of the employee's personal data and that of his children, in the recording of images by a private investigator acting on its behalf, without his knowledge or consent.

Covert surveillance of individuals is very difficult to reconcile with the Data Protection Acts. As a minimum and this may not even make such surveillance legal, there must be strong and evidence based justification for such surveillance in the first instance.[6]

Case study 10/2008: An employer attempts to use CCTV for disciplinary purposes

In February 2008 I received complaints from two employees of the same company regarding their employer's intention to use CCTV recordings for disciplinary purposes.

In this case, the employer had used CCTV images to compile a log that recorded the employees' pattern of entry and exit from their place of work. The employer then notified a trade union representative that this log would be used at a disciplinary meeting. It also supplied a copy of the log to the union representative. The employer sent letters to each employee requesting that they attend a disciplinary meeting to discuss potential irregularities in their attendance. The letters indicated that this was a very serious matter of potential gross misconduct and that it could result in disciplinary action, up to and including dismissal.

The employees immediately lodged complaints with my Office. They stated that they had never been informed of the purpose of the CCTV cameras on the campus where

---

6.   *ibid.*

they were employed. They pointed out that there were no signs visible about the operation of CCTV. On receipt of the complaints, my Office contacted the employer and we outlined the data protection implications of using CCTV footage without having an appropriate basis for doing so. We informed the company that, to satisfy the fair obtaining principle of the Data Protection Acts with regard to the use of CCTV cameras, those people whose images are captured on camera must be informed about the identity of the data controller and the purpose(s) of processing the data. This can be achieved by placing easily read signs in prominent positions. A sign at all entrances will normally suffice. If an employer intends to use cameras to identify disciplinary (or other) issues relating to staff, as in this instance, staff must be informed of this before the cameras are used for these purposes.

The employer accepted the views of my Office. It informed the two employees that it was not in a position to pursue the matter of potential irregularities in attendance as it could not rely on CCTV evidence obtained in contravention of the Data Protection Acts.

This case demonstrates how data controllers are tempted to use personal information captured on CCTV systems for a whole range of purposes. Many businesses have justifiable reasons, related to security, for the deployment of CCTV systems on their premises. However, any further use of personal data captured in this way is unlawful under the Data Protection Acts unless the data controller has made it known at the time of recording that images captured may be used for those additional purposes. Transparency and proportionality are the key points to be considered by any data controller before they install a CCTV system. Proportionality is an important factor in this respect since the proposed use must be justifiable and reasonable if it is not to breach the Data Protection Acts. Notification of all proposed uses will not be enough if such uses are not justifiable.

Substantial guidance is available on our website in relation to the use of CCTV in a business or in a workplace. I would encourage all data controllers, particularly those who may already have such recording systems in place, to familiarise themselves with our guidance on this important issue.[7]

Case Study 6/2007 Data Controller breaches data protection law in regard to use of covert CCTV footage

I received a complaint in October 2006 from a data subject regarding the unfair obtaining by her employer of her personal information and its subsequent use as evidence to terminate her employment. The data subject had been employed in a supervisory capacity at the Gresham Hotel in Dublin for a number of years. In January 2005 she was called to a meeting by hotel management, at which she was

7. See DPC, available at http://www.dataprotection.ie/ViewDoc.asp?fn=/documents/casestudies/CaseStudies_2008.htm&CatID=96&m=c#10, last accessed 11 January 2013.

informed that covert cameras had been installed some time previously in the hotel for the purposes of an investigation. The investigation was initiated on foot of a complaint received by the hotel regarding cash handling at the bar. The data subject was not the subject of the investigation, she was not made aware of the investigation nor was she informed of the covert CCTV recordings. At the meeting, the data subject was confronted with a series of questions and was asked to explain some of her actions which had been recorded by the covert cameras. Later in 2005, she was dismissed from her employment with the hotel. Evidence taken from the covert CCTV recordings was used in the decision to terminate the data subject's employment. No criminal prosecutions took place following the hotel's investigation nor was the data subject interviewed by An Garda Síochána.

As part of the detailed investigation into this complaint, my Office initially sought the observations of The Gresham Hotel regarding this issue, drawing particular attention to the fair obtaining principle of the Data Protection Acts 1988 & 2003. The use of recording mechanisms to obtain data without an individual's knowledge is generally unlawful. Such covert surveillance is normally only permitted on a case by case basis where the data is gathered for the purposes of preventing, detecting or investigating offences, or apprehending or prosecuting offenders. This provision automatically implies an actual involvement of An Garda Síochána or an intention to involve An Garda Síochána.

In response to our initial queries, the hotel stated that the cameras were installed for a legitimate and specified purpose – the investigation of a complaint regarding cash handling in this area. It stated that it was of the opinion that the processing of this information was necessary for the protection of a legitimate legal interest, the protection of property of the hotel in response to a specific concern it had. The hotel also emphasised in its early correspondence with my Office that at no point were the cameras hidden or covert and it presumed that all employees would have seen them.

During our investigation, the data subject supplied photographs of electrical type data boxes/sockets that were located in the bar area of the hotel as it was her understanding that the covert cameras were hidden within these boxes. My Office forwarded copies of these photographs to the hotel requesting clarification on the matter. In response it indicated that these electrical type data boxes were telephone connections, microphone connections and internet connections and were never used as a means to record images for CCTV footage.

As part of our investigation, my Office visited the Gresham Hotel for the purpose of viewing the CCTV footage in question and to inspect the area in which the CCTV footage had been recorded. During this inspection, as well as viewing the footage, we were shown two electrical type boxes located just below ceiling level in the bar area and these boxes were identified as having been the location for the covert cameras. The location of the boxes also matched the views of the bar area which could be seen in the CCTV footage. The boxes were marked '1' and '2' and they appeared to be the same as the electrical boxes which appeared in the photographs which were previously supplied by the data subject. This clearly conflicted with the earlier information which the hotel had supplied to my Office as part of its investigation. Following this inspection, my Office was satisfied, on the basis of all of the information which had been compiled during our investigation, that the data protection rights of the data subject had been breached. Covert CCTV cameras had been installed to investigate specific incidents. The data subject was not the subject matter of this investigation. The personal data of the persons captured on the footage was obtained for one purpose – the investigation of specific incidents in the hotel. In the case of this data subject, her personal data was further processed in a manner incompatible with the original purpose. Furthermore, the data subject's personal data was not processed in accordance with the requirements of "fair processing" as she had not been informed by the data controller, at the time when the data controller first processed her data, of the purpose for which it intended to process her personal data.

As the Acts require me to try to arrange, within a reasonable time, for the amicable resolution by the parties concerned of the matter which is the subject of a complaint, my Office asked both parties to consider this approach. Within a few weeks, a settlement was agreed between the parties. I was pleased that my Office was able to close its investigation file on the basis that an amicable resolution had been reached.[8]

Case Study 7/2007: Disclosure of employee information

Early in 2007, my Office received a significant number of complaints from employees of Aer Lingus regarding an alleged disclosure of their personal information by Aer Lingus to a third party without their consent. According to the complainants, the Human Resources Division of Aer Lingus had passed on the names, staff numbers and place of employment of its staff to HSA Ireland without the knowledge or consent of the employees concerned. Staff of Aer Lingus had become aware of this matter when they received personally addressed promotional literature from HSA Ireland, a healthcare organisation offering a range of health care plans. In this promotional literature, a copy of which was received in my Office, HSA Ireland informed the Aer Lingus employees that Aer Lingus had agreed to allow it to directly distribute the information to them.

Section 2 of the Data Protection Acts, 1988 and 2003 sets out the position in relation to the collection, processing, keeping, use and disclosure of personal data. It provides that data should be obtained and processed fairly, kept for only one or more specified purposes and it should be used and disclosed only in ways compatible with that purpose or those purposes. It also provides that personal data should not be processed by a data controller unless at least one of a number of conditions is met – one of those conditions being the consent of the data subject to the processing.

---

8.   See DPC, available at http://www.dataprotection.ie/ViewDoc.asp?fn=/documents/casestudies/CaseStudies2007.htm&CatID=91&m=c#6, last accessed 11 January 2013.

In response to initial contact from my Office regarding the alleged disclosure of personal information, Aer Lingus confirmed that it had passed on the personal data of its staff to HSA Ireland and it set out the background to how it had occurred. It explained that the company had previously operated and administered a Staff Welfare Fund to assist employees in certain circumstances in relation to personal and family medical expenses. As this fund had closed, Aer Lingus committed to putting another scheme in place and it negotiated with HSA Ireland to offer a replacement scheme to employees. In order to increase staff awareness of this new scheme, it was decided that it would be in the best interests of staff to write to them directly at their place of employment. Employee names and staff numbers were provided to HSA Ireland by means of a mail merge file. Aer Lingus was of the opinion that this disclosure was legitimate in accordance with what it regarded as a bona fide employment purpose. It also confirmed that consent had not been sought or obtained from its employees prior to the forwarding of the employee details to HSA Ireland.

My Office reminded Aer Lingus of its obligations under Section 2 of the Data Protection Acts with regard to the processing of personal data and it pointed out that the personal data of its staff should not have been disclosed to a third party without the consent of the employees concerned. In the circumstances, my Office sought and obtained confirmation from Aer Lingus that it had now destroyed the mail merge file containing the names and staff numbers which it had forwarded to HSA Ireland. Confirmation was also received from HSA Ireland that it had not retained records of Aer Lingus employee names, addresses, payroll or payslip numbers on any database.

My Office was satisfied by the steps taken by Aer Lingus and HSA Ireland in terms of corrective action. By way of clarification, we pointed out that the key issue from a data protection perspective was that Aer Lingus had facilitated contact from a third party to its employees concerning the availability of a staff welfare scheme while the same information could have been promulgated to those employees without raising any data protection concerns had Aer Lingus sent it directly to its employees instead.

I fully recognise that employers may, from time to time, wish to communicate details of various schemes to their employees. This can easily be achieved without infringing on the data protection rights of employees if the employer supplies the information directly to its employees or by some other means in conformity with the Data Protection Acts. My Office had only in the weeks before these complaints were received conducted an audit of Aer Lingus which had generally found a high level of compliance with data protection requirements. The occasion of the audit could have been used to seek advice from my Office on this issue.

My Office is always available to give advice to data controllers and the public alike in relation to data protection responsibilities and rights.[9]

---

9.   *ibid.*

PART 3

Organisations and Outward-Facing Obligations

CHAPTER 18

Outward-Facing Issues

Introduction

Beyond the inward-facing employee related sphere, organisations also need to consider the outward-facing sphere. For many organisations the outward-facing data protection issues frequently dominate more. They can also be the most contentious. These issues raise significant data protection concerns and compliance issues to be dealt with.

Some of the queries that can arise include:

- What are the forms of outward-facing personal data to consider?
- How can the organisation comply with the data protection regime when dealing with existing customers?
- How do organisations contact potential customers yet remain data protection compliant?
- Can an organisation engage in direct marketing (DM)?
- Do users who are not customers raise additional issues?
- Do security considerations still arise?
- Are there higher security obligations for customers and users?

Types of Outward-Facing Personal Data: Customers, Prospects and Users

What forms of outward-facing personal data must organisations be concerned with? The types of personal data to be considered relate to:

- current customers;
- past customers;
- prospective customers;
- users who may be registered customers.

Organisations will be often concerned with collecting personal preferences, account details, etc., from customers and leads. Direct marketing (DM) and additional avenues for commercialisation are also a frequent business imperative, yet if misman-aged can breach the data protection regime.

In addition, there may be individuals who access the organisation's website but who are not actual customers. Indeed, they may never become customers. Yet, certain personal data may still be collected by the organisation. In this instance, it is also necessary for the organisation to comply with the *data protection principles* and related obligations.

How to be Outward-Facing Compliant: Customers, Prospects and Users

How can an organisation focus on the elements that will ensure data protection compliance when dealing with the personal data of customers, prospects and/or users? In terms of personal data collected and processed relating to the above catego-ries, the following must be complied with:

- prior information requirements;
- data protection principles;
- legitimate processing conditions;
- sensitive personal data legitimate processing conditions;
- security requirements; and
- notification/registration requirements.

Particular considerations can also arise in relation to users who may not be customers in the normal and contractual sense.

What Prior Information Requirements?

The organisation is obliged to inform customers, etc., in a fair and transparent manner that it is intending to collect and process their personal data. It must identify exactly who the data controller is, i.e. the legal entity collecting and processing the personal data. The categories of personal data being collected must be outlined, as well as the linking of each purpose with the categories of personal data. If any third parties will be involved in processing the personal data, these must be referred to and identified, at least by category, when the personal data is being collected. Particular information must also be produced where it is envisaged that the personal data may be transferred outside of the EEA.

Compliance with the Outward-Facing Data Protection Principles

In dealing with customer personal data, as well as potential customers, etc., it is necessary for the organisation to comply with the *data protection principles*.

The *data protection principles* require that personal data are:

- obtained and processed, fairly;
- accurate, complete and kept up to date;
- obtained only for one specified, explicit and legitimate purpose;
- not further processed in a manner incompatible with that purpose;
- adequate, relevant and not excessive in relation to the purpose;
- kept for longer than is necessary for that purpose;
- protected by appropriate security measures.

Data controllers must also give a copy of personal data to any individual on request (i.e. an access request).

Compliance with the *data protection principles* applies to all customers' personal data collected and/or processed by an organisation. It also applies regardless of registration notification requirements. This requires that each of the *data protection principles* must be considered separately and individually assessed by the organisation to ensure that each data collection is legally compliant. Compliance must be maintained and accross each of the fields or categories of personal data collected.

This will involve particular consideration of the contracting model with customers, how contracts are formed, the instant that they are formed and how records are maintained in the event that these need to be examined and evidenced subsequently e.g. to prove compliance. Integral to this contract model process is how the data protection elements, data protection policies, data protection clauses, data protection prior information requirements and customers' consent, as appropriate, are complied with. Is the organisation proposing to ask questions that are not strictly required for the provision of the service or goods? Are questions being asked that are wholly unrelated to the actual service or product? If so, the third *data protection principle* may be breached. If the product or service is time limited, and no further product or service is envisaged, it would be difficult for the organisation to permanently keep the personal data. This could conflict with the second, third and/or fifth *data protection principles*.

Depending on the type of service, products and/or relationship with customers, etc., whether physical or online, can mean that even more attention needs to be paid to fulfilling compliance with certain *data protection principles*.

Customers, etc., and Ordinary Personal Data Legitimate Processing Conditions

What are the *legitimate processing conditions* when an organisation is processing personal data regarding customers, users, etc. (collectively referred to as "customers")? The *legitimate processing conditions* are required to be complied with, in addition to the *data protection principles*. Section 2A of the Data Protection Acts[1] contains the general *legitimate processing conditions*. In order to collect and process personal data, in addition to complying with the above *data protection principles*, organisations must comply or fall within one of the following general personal data *legitimate processing conditions* in dealing with customers' personal data:

(a) the data subject has given his or her consent to the processing or, if the data subject, by reason of his or her physical or mental incapacity or age, is or is likely to be unable to appreciate the nature and effect of such consent, it is given by a parent or guardian or a grandparent, uncle, aunt, brother or sister of the data subject and the giving of such consent is not prohibited by law;

(b) the processing is necessary:

   (i)   for the performance of a contract to which the data subject is a party;

   (ii) in order to take steps at the request of the data subject prior to entering into a contract;

   (iii) for compliance with a legal obligation to which the data controller is subject other than an obligation imposed by contract; or

   (iv) to prevent:

      (I) injury or other damage to the health of the data subject; or

      (II) serious loss of or damage to property of the data subject;

or otherwise to protect his or her vital interests where the seeking of the consent of the data subject or another person referred to in paragraph (a) of this subsection is likely to result in those interests being damaged;

(c) the processing is necessary:

   (i)   for the administration of justice;

   (ii) for the performance of a function conferred on a person by or under an enactment;

   (iii) for the performance of a function of the government or a minister of the government; or

---

1.   Data Protection Act 1988 and Data Protection (Amendment) Act 2003.

      (iv) for the performance of any other function of a public nature performed in the public interest by a person;

   (d) the processing is necessary for the purposes of the legitimate interests pursued by the data controller or by a third party or parties to whom the data are disclosed, except where the processing is unwarranted in any particular case by reason of prejudice to the fundamental rights and freedoms or legitimate interests of the data subject;

(2) The Minister may, after consultation with the Data Protection Commissioner, by regulations specify particular circumstances in which subsection (1)(d) of this section is, or is not, to be taken as satisfied.

These additional compliance criteria are be summarised as follows:

- the data subject has given consent;

- the processing is necessary for the performance of a contract;

- to take steps at the request of the data subject prior to entering into a contract;

- compliance with a legal obligation;

- to prevent injury or other damage to the health of data subject, or serious loss of or damage to property of data subject, or otherwise to protect his or her vital interests;

- necessary for the administration of justice;

- necessary under an enactment;

- official function;

- necessary for the purposes of the legitimate interests pursued by the data controller or by a third party or parties to whom the data are disclosed, unless unwarranted by reason of prejudice to the fundamental rights and freedoms or legitimate interests of the data subject.

Organisations prior to collecting and processing customers' personal data should identify what personal data it is seeking, why, and which of the *legitimate processing conditions* it will be complying with. This will differ according to the organisation, sector and particular activity envisaged.

Frequently, an organisation may wish to rely upon the consent option. In that instance, there should be documented policies and/or contact whereby the customer, is informed and appraised of the proposed data processing and freely consents to same. The manner of consent should be recorded. If it is not recorded, it could present difficulties subsequently where it is needed to be proven that consent was obtained for a particular customer, or for a whole database of customers.

A further issue arises. Many organisations over a long period of time will make changes to their business activities. There may also be changes to the contract and transaction models that can mean changes to the processing activities and contacts, policies, etc., relating to data protection and consent. The details of the changeover, the nature of the changes, and means of recording and maintaining a record of the consent also needed to be maintained by the organisation in an easily accessible manner.

These issues are more pronounced for organisations that change their business models and processes more frequently. Many internet companies will, therefore, have frequent additional challenges.

As noted above an organisation would often seek to fall within the contract consent condition above in relation to customers, etc.

However, an organisation may seek to maintain compliance based on the legitimate interests condition. This could mean, on occasion, that an organisation seeks to legitimise the processing activities by saying the customer has entered a contact and that the processing is a legitimate and necessary consequence of that. However, an organisation seeking to adopt this model should seek professional advice beforehand. It is quite easy for an organisation to feel that it is compliant, but for certain activities, additional activities, commercialisation and/or direct marketing, to be undertaken which may not be transparent, fair, warranted or legally compliant.

In any event, the *data protection principles* must be complied with regardless of the particular *legitimate processing condition*.

Customers', etc., Sensitive Personal Data Legitimate Processing Conditions

Organisations generally, or more frequently organisations involved in particular sectors, may wish to know certain information that falls within the sensitive personal data categories, e.g. health data or sexual data. In the case of customers' sensitive personal data, an organisation must, in addition to the *data protection principles*, be able to comply or fall within one of the *sensitive personal data legitimate processing conditions*.

Section 2B of the Data Protection Acts sets out conditions relevant for the purposes of the first *data protection principle*, in particular in relation to the *sensitive personal data legitimate processing conditions*. It states:

(i) the consent referred to in subsection s 2A(1)(a) of the Acts is explicitly given;

(ii) the processing is necessary for the purpose of exercising or performing any right or obligation that is conferred or imposed by law on the data controller in connection with employment;

(iii) the processing is necessary to prevent injury or other damage to the health of the data subject or another person or serious loss in respect of, or damage to, property or otherwise to protect the vital interests of the data subject or of another person in a case where:

   (I)   consent to the processing cannot be given by or on behalf of the data subject in accordance with s 2A(1)(a)of the Acts; or

   (II) the data controller cannot reasonably be expected to obtain such consent, or the processing is necessary to prevent injury to, or damage to the health of, another person, or serious loss in respect of, or damage to, the property of another person, in a case where such consent has been unreasonably withheld;

(iv) the processing:

   (I)   is carried out in the course of its legitimate activities by any body corporate, or any unincorporated body of persons, that:

      (A) is not established, and whose activities are not carried on, for profit; and

      (B) exists for political, philosophical, religious or trade union purposes;

   (II) is carried out with appropriate safeguards for the fundamental rights and freedoms of data subjects;

   (III) relates only to individuals who either are members of the body or have regular contact with it in connection with its purposes; and

   (IV) does not involve disclosure of the data to a third party without the consent of the data subject;

(v) the information contained in the data has been made public as a result of steps deliberately taken by the data subject;

(vi) the processing is necessary:

   (I)   for the administration of justice;

   (II) for the performance of a function conferred on a person by or under an enactment; or

   (III) for the performance of a function of the government or a minister of the government;

(vii) the processing:

   (I)   is required for the purpose of obtaining legal advice or for the purposes of, or in connection with, legal proceedings or prospective legal proceedings; or

(II) is otherwise necessary for the purposes of establishing, exercising or defending legal rights;

(viii) the processing is necessary for medical purposes and is undertaken by:

(I) a health professional; or

(II) a person who in the circumstances owes a duty of confidentiality to the data subject that is equivalent to that which would exist if that person were a health professional;

(ix) the processing is necessary in order to obtain information for use, subject to and in accordance with the Statistics Act 1993, only for statistical, compilation and analysis purposes;

(x) the processing is carried out by political parties, or candidates for election to, or holders of, elective political office, in the course of electoral activities for the purpose of compiling data on people's political opinions and complies with such requirements (if any) as may be prescribed for the purpose of safeguarding the fundamental rights and freedoms of data subjects;

(xi) the processing is authorised by regulations that are made by the Minister and are made for reasons of substantial public interest;

(xii) the processing is necessary for the purpose of the assessment, collection or payment of any tax, duty, levy or other moneys owed or payable to the State and the data has been provided by the data subject solely for that purpose;

(xiii) the processing is necessary for the purposes of determining entitlement to or control of, or any other purpose connected with the administration of any benefit, pension, assistance, allowance, supplement or payment under the Social Welfare (Consolidation) Act 1993, or any non-statutory scheme administered by the Minister for Social, Community and Family Affairs.

These customers' *sensitive personal data legitimate processing conditions* may be summarised as follows:

- explicit consent is given; necessary for a legal obligation;

- necessary to prevent injury or other damage to health or serious loss or damage to property or protect the vital interests of the data subject:

    (I) consent to the processing cannot be given by or on behalf of the data subject in accordance with s 2A(1)(a) of the Acts; or

    (II) the data controller cannot reasonably be expected to obtain such consent, or the processing is necessary to prevent injury to, or damage to the health of, another person, or serious loss in respect of, or damage to, the property of another person, in a case where such consent has been unreasonably withheld;

- not for profit organisation for political, philosophical, religious or trade union purposes with appropriate safeguards;

- the information contained in the data has been made public as a result of steps deliberately taken by the data subject;

- administration of justice;

- legal function; or

- government function;

- obtaining legal advice or in connection with legal proceedings; or establishing, exercising or defending legal rights;

- medical purposes and is undertaken by a health professional;

- in accordance with the Statistics Act 1993;

- political parties or electoral activities;

- authorised by Ministerial regulations for substantial public interest;

- tax purposes;

- determining official benefits, pensions, etc.

Furthermore, regulations enacted also set out further obligations in relation to the processing of sensitive personal data.

It should be noted that the ability of an organisation to actually come within one of the *sensitive personal data legitimate processing conditions* is more restricted than the general personal data conditions. This is because the data protection regime considers that organisations have less legitimate interest in the processing of sensitive personal data. It also recognises the greater importance that legislators and individuals attach to the sensitive categories of personal data.

Customers, etc., and Security Requirements

What security issues arise for customer-related personal data? Customers will be concerned to ensure that their personal data is not inadvertently disclosed or used in a manner they have not consented to and are unaware of. This is a legal requirement under the data protection regime. Appropriate security measures must be established.

In the case of outward-facing personal data, such categories will generally present significant differences to employee-related personal data. Generally there will be more customer-related personal data. It will also be more widely accessible within the organisation. Fewer people within an organisation need to have access to employee files and personal data. Customers' personal data tends to be spread across more than one single location or database. Frequently, customers' personal data is obtained through a variety of sources, which are more diverse than inward-facing personal data. This all means that there are greater security issues and access issues to be considered by the organisation.

Increasingly, attacks and breaches that come to public attention tend to relate to outward-facing personal data. This means that there are greater reasons to maintain and/or enhance these security measures to avoid the consequences of publicity, official enquiries, enforcement proceedings, or complaints and/or proceedings from data subjects. Sony, for example, was fined £250,000 for data breach.

Notification Requirements

Organisations collecting and processing customers' personal data will also have to consider notification requirement issues. The notification registration details will have to specify the categories of customers' personal data being collected, for what purposes and activities, and also whether or not there are any third party recipients and transfers (TBDFs). The notification also needs to outline details of the security measures.

Direct Marketing (DM)

Most commercial organisations will wish to engage in direct marketing (DM). For some organisations this will be an important core activity. Section 2(7) of the Data Protection Acts provides that "direct marketing" means the communication (by whatever means) of any advertising or marketing material that is directed to particular individuals.

The Data Protection Acts and data protection regime have extensive provisions dealing with direct marketing. There are requirements to inform the data subject that they may object by a written request and free of charge to their personal data being used for direct marketing purposes.

If the data controller anticipates that personal data kept by it will be processed for purposes of direct marketing it must inform the persons to whom the data relates that they may object by means of a request in writing to the data controller and free of charge.

However, s 2(7) of the Data Protection Acts provides a right to prevent processing for purposes of direct marketing. A customer is entitled at any time by notice in writing to a data controller to require the data controller at the end of such period as is reasonable in the circumstances to cease, or not to begin, processing for the purposes of direct marketing personal data in respect of which he or she is the data subject.

Consequences of Non-Compliance

If the organisation fails to assess and organise compliance procedures in advance of undertaking the collection and processing of personal data of customers, it will likely be operating in breach of the data protection regime. Any personal data collected will be non-compliant.

Equally, if data processing is originally compliant, but becomes non complaint whereby one of the *data protection principles, legitimate processing conditions,* and/ or security requirements are breached, the personal data processed will be questionable. This is particularly so if new personal data is involved or new activities and uses occur. Lawful data processing can become unlawful.

What are the consequences? The collection and/or processing are illegal. The organisation, as a data controller, can be the subject of complaints, investigations and enforcement proceedings from the Data Protection Commissioner. Depending on the severity of the non-compliance, prosecutions can also involve the directors and employees of the organisation in addition to the organisation itself.

If convicted, the organisation could face significant fines. These will be in addition to the adverse publicity and media attention a prosecution can bring.

There can be other consequences too. If the organisation relies heavily on direct marketing (DM) or is a particular type of internet company, the customer database of personal data can be one of the most significant assets of the organisation. If the database is collected in breach of the data protection regime, the organisation will not be able to establish compliant data collections and consents. It could, therefore, be ordered to delete the database.

Alternatively, an organisation may wish to sell its business or to seek investors for the business. This is frequently the case in the technology sector. However, a potential purchaser or investor assessing whether or not to proceed, will undertake a due diligence examination of the processes, procedures and documentation of the organisation. It will request to see documented evidence of data protection compliance and that the valuable database(s), etc., are fully data protection compliant. If this cannot be established, questions will arise and potentially also the transaction may not proceed.

Users Versus Customers

Do separate issues arise for users and their personal data? Where someone is a customer, there is more direct contact and therefore more direct means to engage with the customer in a measured contract formation process. Consequently, it is possible to ensure compliance though a considered and documented data protection compliance process and to engage consent appropriately at an early stage from the individual customer or potential customer.

Users, however, may not be customers. Therefore, customer contract models that incorporate consent or other data protection legitimising procedures for customers may leave a gap where non-customer users are not presented with the same documentation, notices and sign-up document sets. Organisations, therefore, need to consider users as separate from normal customers. They must assess where the organisation interacts with such users, physically or online, and what personal data may be collected. Where personal data is collected from users, the organisation needs to ensure transparent compliance. This may mean that the organisation needs to have a separate and additional set of notices, policies and consent documentation in relation to users.

Conclusion

When organisations begin to look outwards, a separate range of data collection possibilities will arise. The avenues for data collection are more diverse. In addition, the intended uses of this type of personal data will be potentially greater. The *data protection principles* and *legitimate processing conditions* require particular consideration and configuration if the intended data processing activities of customers' personal data. Different security and enforcement risks can arise and need to be protected against. It cannot be assumed that everyone that the organisation may wish to collect personal data from will be an actual customer. Therefore, organisations need to consider how to ensure separate transparency, consent and notifications to this category of person. An example of this may be cookies that may obtain personal data (see Chapter 19).

CHAPTER 19

Cookies and Electronic Communications

Introduction

Cookies are technical software devices that can help to speed up interactions with websites. They can also be used to track, profile and undertake direct marketing (DM) of individuals, given that they can collect information on the online activities of individuals.[1]

The permissibility and transparency of the use of cookies has been somewhat controversial. There have been increasing calls for the abuse or non-transparent use of cookies to be regulated by the data protection regime.

The ePD was amended by Directive 2000/136/EC and Directive 2009/136/EC.[2] In particular, Article 5(3) as amended refers to cookies and sets out a consent requirement.

The Data Protection Commissioner is contacting organisations to ensure that they are complying with the new cookie rules. Organisations must respond within 21 days.[3] Prosecution could arise for non-compliance. The Deputy Data Protection Commissioner states that there will be "enforcement action where websites fail to engage with us and meet their legal obligations".[4]

---

1.   See, for example, Newson, Duffy and Cheng, "Cookies Compliance: The Practicalities" (29 February 2012) SCL *Computers and Law*.

2.   Directive 2002/58/EC of the European Parliament and of the Council of 12 July 2002 concerning the processing of personal data and the protection of privacy in the electronic communications sector (Directive on privacy and electronic communications)(as amended by Directives 2006/24/EC and 2009/136/EC).

3.   See Data Protection Commissioner press statement, "Data Protection Commissioner Commences Action On 'Cookie' Law", December 2012, available at www.dataprotection.ie/viewdoc.asp?DocID=1274&m=f, accessed on 1 January 2013.

4.   *ibid.*

ePrivacy Directive: Cookie Amendment

The concern in relation to cookies and data protection has led to Article 5(3) of ePD[5] being amended by Directive 2009/136/EC[6] in relation to how cookies can be used. The amended Article 5(3) reads:

> Member States shall ensure that the storing of information, or the gaining of access to information already stored, in the terminal equipment of a subscriber or user is only allowed on condition that the subscriber or user concerned has given his or her consent, having been provided with clear and comprehensive information, in accordance with [DP Directive 95[7]], *inter alia*, about the purposes of the processing. This shall not prevent any technical storage or access for the sole purpose of carrying out the transmission of a communication over an electronic communications network, or as strictly necessary in order for the provider of an information society service explicitly requested by the subscriber or user to provide the service.

ePrivacy Regulations

The ePrivacy Regulations[8] give effect to the ePrivacy Directive,[9] and the amendments to that Directive as introduced by Directive 2009/136/EC of the European Parliament and of the Council of 25 November 2009.

As well as transposing the amendments made by Directive 2009/136/EC, the Regulations consolidate the provisions of the existing Statutory Instruments transposing the ePrivacy Directive, namely, the European Communities (Electronic Communications Networks and Services)(Data Protection and Privacy) Regulations 2003[10] and the European Communities (Electronic Communications Networks and Services)(Data Protection and Privacy)(Amendment) Regulations 2008,[11] which have been revoked by the Regulations.

---

5. Directive 2002/58/EC, the ePrivacy Directive.
6. Directive 2009/136/EC of the European Parliament and of the Council of 25 November 2009 amending Directive 2002/22/EC on universal service and users' rights relating to electronic communications networks and services, Directive 2002/58/EC concerning the processing of personal data and the protection of privacy in the electronic communications sector and Regulation (EC) No 2006/2004 on co-operation between national authorities responsible for the enforcement of consumer protection laws.
7. EU Data Protection Directive 1995 (Directive 95/46/EC of the European Parliament and of the Council of 24 October 1995 on the protection of individuals with regard to the processing of personal data and on the free movement of such data).
8. The European Communities (Electronic Communications Networks and Services)(Privacy and Electronic Communications) Regulations 2011 (SI 336/2011).
9. Directive 2002/58/EC of the European Parliament and of the Council of 12 July 2002 concerning the processing of personal data and the protection of privacy in the electronic communications sector (ePrivacy Directive).
10. SI 535/2003.
11. SI 526/2008.

The ePrivacy Regulations[12] provide for data protection and privacy connected with electronic communications networks and services and to enhance the security and reliability of such networks and services.

Definitions

The definitions include the following, namely:

Automated Calling Machine

"Automated calling machine" means an automatic calling machine or system that, when activated, operates to make calls without human intervention.

Blocking

"Blocking", in relation to data, means so marking the data that it is not possible to process it for purposes in relation to which it is marked.

Communication

"Communication" means any information exchanged or conveyed between a finite number of parties by means of a publicly available electronic communications service, but does not include any information conveyed as part of a broadcasting service to the public over the electronic communications network except to the extent that the information can be related to the identifiable subscriber or user receiving the information.

Consent

"Consent" by a user or subscriber means a data subject's consent in accordance with the Data Protection Acts and these Regulations.

Data

"Data" means automated data and manual data.

Directory

"Directory" means a directory of subscribers in printed or electronic form:

---

12. ePrivacy Regulations 2011 of the European Communities (Electronic Communications Networks and Services)(Privacy and Electronic Communications) Regulations 2011 (SI 336/2011) implementing the ePrivacy Directive (as amended by Directives 2006/24/EC and 2009/136/EC) dealing with data protection for phone, email, SMS text and Internet.

(a) that is available to members of the public, or

(b) information from which is available to members of the public by way of a directory enquiry service.

Electronic Mail

"Electronic mail" means any text, voice, sound or image message including an SMS message sent over a public communications network that can be stored in the network or in the recipient's terminal equipment until it is collected by the recipient.

Enforcement Notice

"Enforcement notice" means a notice served under Regulation 17(4).

Framework Regulations

"Framework Regulations" means European Communities (Electronic Communications Networks and Services)(Framework) Regulations 2011 (SI 33/2011).

Information Notice

"Information notice" means a notice served under Regulation 18(1).

Interconnection

"Interconnection" means the physical and logical linking of public communications networks used by the same or a different undertaking in order to allow the users of one undertaking to communicate with users of the same or another undertaking, or to access services provided by another undertaking. Services may be provided by the parties involved or other parties who have access to the network. Interconnection is a specific type of access implemented between the public network operators.

Location Data

"Location data" means any data processed in an electronic communications network or by an electronic communications service, indicating the geographic position of the terminal equipment of a user of a publicly available electronic communications service.

National Directory Database

"National Directory Database" means the record of all subscribers of publicly available telephone services in the State, including those with fixed, personal or mobile numbers, who have not refused to be included in that record, kept in accordance with Regulation 19(4) of the Universal Service Regulations and these Regulations.

Operator

"Operator" means a person designated by the regulator under Regulation 7(1) of the Universal Service Regulations to provide a universal service (within the meaning of those Regulations) in respect of directory services referred to in Regulation 4 of those Regulations.

Personal Data Breach

"Personal data breach" means a breach of security leading to the accidental or unlawful destruction, loss, alteration, unauthorised disclosure of, or access to, personal data transmitted, stored or otherwise processed in connection with the provision of a publicly available electronic communications service in the European Union.

Regulations of 2003

"Regulations of 2003" means European Communities (Electronic Communications Networks and Services)(Data Protection and Privacy) Regulations 2003 (SI 535/2003).

Traffic Data

"Traffic data" means any data processed for the purpose of the conveyance of a communication on an electronic communications network or for the billing thereof.

Unsolicited Call

"Unsolicited call" means a call that is not requested by the called party.

Unsolicited Communication

"Unsolicited communication" means a communication that is not requested by the contacted party.

User

"User" means any natural person using a publicly available electronic communications service, for private or business purposes, without necessarily having subscribed to this service.

Value Added Service

"Value added service" means any service that requires the processing of traffic data or location data other than traffic data beyond what is necessary for the transmission of a communication or the billing thereof.

Services Covered

The ePrivacy Regulations[13] provide as follows. Regulation 3(1) states that the Regulations apply to the processing of personal data in connection with the provision of publicly available electronic communications services in public communications networks in the State and where relevant the EU, including public communications networks supporting data collection and identification devices.

Regulation 3(2) provides that s 1(3B) of the Act of 1988 (inserted by s 2 of the Act of 2003) applies in relation to personal data referred to in paragraph 3(1).

Security of Processing

The ePrivacy Regulations[14] at Regulation 4(1) provides that with respect to network security and, in particular, the requirements of the Regulation 4(2) below, an undertaking providing a publicly available electronic communications network or service shall take appropriate technical and organisational measures to safeguard the security of its services, if necessary, in conjunction with undertakings upon whose networks such services are transmitted. These measures shall ensure the level of security appropriate to the risk presented having regard to the state of the art and the cost of their implementation. (Note also proposed security Directive announced.)

Regulation 4(2) provides that without prejudice to the Data Protection Acts, the measures referred to in Regulation 4(1) shall at least:

(a) ensure that personal data can be accessed only by authorised personnel for legally authorised purposes;

(b) protect personal data stored or transmitted against accidental or unlawful destruction, accidental loss or alteration, and unauthorised or unlawful storage, processing, access or disclosure; and

(c) ensure the implementation of a security policy with respect to the processing of personal data.

Regulation 4(3) provides that the Data Protection Commissioner may audit the measures taken by an undertaking providing publicly available electronic communications services and issue recommendations about best practices concerning the level of security those measures should achieve.

Regulation 4(4) provides that in the case of a particular risk of a breach of the security of the public communications network, the undertaking providing the publicly available electronic communications service shall inform its subscribers concerning

---

13. *ibid.*
14. *ibid.*

such risk without delay and, where the risk lies outside the scope of the measures to be taken by the relevant service provider, any possible remedies including an indication of the likely costs involved.

Regulation 4(5) provides that an undertaking whose public communications network is used by another undertaking for the supply of a publicly available electronic communications service shall comply with any reasonable request made by the undertaking using the public communications network for the purpose of complying with the Regulation.

Regulation 4(6) provides that where there has been a personal data breach, the undertaking shall, without undue delay:

(a) notify the Data Protection Commissioner of the breach; and

(b) where the breach is likely to adversely affect the personal data or privacy of a subscriber or individual, notify the subscriber or individual of the breach.

Regulation 4(7) provides that a notification under Regulation 4(6)(b) shall not be required if the undertaking has demonstrated to the satisfaction of the Data Protection Commissioner that it has implemented appropriate technological protection measures that render the data unintelligible to any person who is not authorised to access it and that those measures were applied to the data affected by the security breach.

Regulation 4(8) provides that without prejudice to Regulation 4(6) and (7), where the undertaking has not notified the subscriber or individual of the personal data breach, the Data Protection Commissioner may, having considered the likely adverse effects of the breach, require the undertaking to do so by serving an enforcement notice on the undertaking in accordance with Regulation 17(4).

Regulation 4(9) provides that notification under Regulation 4(6) shall, at least, contain:

(a) a description of the nature of the personal data breach;

(b) a description of the contact points where more information can be obtained;

(c) a recommendation on measures to mitigate the possible adverse effects of the personal data breach; and

(d) where the notification is under Regulation 4(6)(a), a description of the consequences of, and the measures proposed to be taken by the undertaking to address, the personal data breach.

Regulation 4(10) provides that subject to any technical implementing measures adopted by the European Commission under Article 4(5) of the Directive on privacy and electronic communications, the Data Protection Commissioner may adopt guidelines concerning the circumstances in which undertakings are required to notify personal data breaches, the format of such notification and the manner in which such notification is to be made. Where necessary the Data Protection Commissioner may, for the purpose of this paragraph, issue such instructions as he considers necessary.

Regulation 4(11) provides that the Data Protection Commissioner may conduct an audit to determine compliance with guidelines and instructions issued under Regulation 4(10).

Regulation 4(12) provides that undertakings shall maintain an inventory of personal data breaches, which shall comprise the following information:

(a) the facts surrounding the breach;

(b) the effects of the breach; and

(c) any remedial action taken, and shall be sufficient to enable the Data Protection Commissioner to verify compliance with Regulation 3(6) to (10).

Regulation 4(13) provides that an undertaking that:

(a) fails to comply with the requirements of paragraph (1);

(b) fails to comply with the requirements of paragraph (4);

(c) subject to Regulation 4(7), fails to comply with the requirements of Regulation 4(6);

(d) refuses to co-operate with an audit referred to in Regulation 4(3) or (11); or

(e) fails to comply with the requirements of Regulation 4(12), commits an offence.

Regulation 4(14) provides that:

(a) An undertaking that commits an offence under the Regulation (other than under paragraph 13(a) or (c)) is liable on summary conviction to a class A fine;

(b) An undertaking that commits an offence under paragraph 13(a) or (c) is liable, on summary conviction, to a class A fine or, on indictment:

    (i) in the case of a body corporate, to a fine not exceeding €250,000; or

    (ii) in the case of a natural person, to a fine not exceeding €50,000.

Confidentiality of Communications

The ePrivacy Regulations[15] provide that without prejudice to s 98 of the Act of 1983 and s 2 of the Act of 1993 and except where legally authorised under a provision

---

15. *ibid.*

adopted in accordance with Article 15(1) of the Directive on privacy and electronic communications, the listening, tapping, storage or other kinds of interception or surveillance of communications and the related traffic data by persons other than users, without the consent of the users concerned, is prohibited.[16]

Regulation 5(1) above does not:

- prevent the technical storage of communications and the related traffic data that is necessary for the conveyance of a communication without prejudice to the principle of confidentiality; and

- affect any legally authorised recording of communications and the related traffic data when carried out in the course of lawful business practice for the purpose of providing evidence of a commercial transaction or of any other business communication.[17]

A person shall not use an electronic communications network to store information, or to gain access to information already stored in the terminal equipment of a subscriber or user; unless

- the subscriber or user has given his or her consent to that use; and

- the subscriber or user has been provided with clear and comprehensive information in accordance with the Data Protection Acts that:

  - is both prominently displayed and easily accessible; and

  - includes, without limitation, the purposes of the processing of the information.[18]

For the purpose of Regulation 5(3), the methods of providing information and giving consent should be as user-friendly as possible. Where it is technically possible and effective, having regard to the relevant provisions of the Data Protection Acts, the user's consent to the storing of information or to gaining access to information already stored may be given by the use of appropriate browser settings or other technological application by means of which the user can be considered to have given his or her consent.[19]

Regulation 5(3) does not prevent any technical storage of, or access to, information for the sole purpose of carrying out the transmission of a communication over an electronic communications network or which is strictly necessary in order to provide an information society service explicitly requested by the subscriber or user.[20]

---

16. Regulation 5(1).
17. Regulation 5(2).
18. Regulation 5(3).
19. Regulation 5(4).
20. Regulation 5(5).

Traffic Data

Regulation 6 of the ePrivacy Regulations[21] provide as follows.

Regulation 6(1) provides that subject to Regulation 6(2), (3), (4) and (5) and the provisions of the Act of 2011, an undertaking shall ensure that traffic data relating to subscribers and users processed and stored for the purpose of the transmission of a communication shall be erased or made anonymous when it is no longer needed for that purpose.

Regulation 6(2)(a) provides that an undertaking may process traffic data necessary for the purpose of subscriber billing and interconnection payments only up to the end of the period in which the bill may be lawfully challenged and payment pursued or where such proceedings are brought during that period until those proceedings are finally determined. An undertaking shall inform its subscribers of the types of traffic data that are processed and of the duration of such processing.

Regulation 6(2)(b) provides that legal proceedings shall be deemed, for the purpose of this paragraph, to be finally determined:

(i) if no appeal is brought within the ordinary time for an appeal by either party to the proceedings, upon the expiry of that time;

(ii) if an appeal is brought within that time or such extended time as the court to which the appeal is brought may allow, upon the date of the determination of the appeal or any further appeal from it or the ordinary time for instituting any further appeal has expired or such other date as may be determined by the court hearing any such appeal, whichever is the latest; or

(iii) if an appeal has been brought and is withdrawn, upon the date of the withdrawal of the appeal.

Regulation 6(3) provides that:

(a) An undertaking may process traffic data referred to in paragraph (1) for the purpose of marketing electronic communications services or for the provision of value added services to the extent and for the duration necessary for such services or marketing, provided the subscriber or user to whom the data relates has given his or her prior consent in accordance with s 2A(1)(a) of the Data Protection Acts.

---

21. ePrivacy Regulations 2011 of the European Communities (Electronic Communications Networks and Services)(Privacy and Electronic Communications) Regulations 2011 (SI 336/2011) implementing the ePrivacy Directive (as amended by Directives 2006/24/EC and 2009/136/EC) dealing with data protection for phone, email, SMS text and Internet.

(b) Prior to obtaining consent, the undertaking shall inform the subscriber or user of the types of traffic data that are processed and of the duration of such processing.

(c) An undertaking shall ensure that users or subscribers are informed of and given the possibility to withdraw their consent for processing of traffic data for the purpose of this paragraph at any time.

Regulation 6(4) provides that an undertaking shall ensure that the processing of traffic data in accordance with Regulation 6(1), (2) and (3) is restricted to persons acting under its authority in accordance with s 2C(3) of the Acts handling billing or traffic management, customer enquiries, fraud detection, the marketing of electronic communication services or providing a value added service, and such processing is restricted to what is necessary for the purpose of such activities.

Regulation 6(5) nothing in these Regulations precludes a court or any other body involved in the settlement of disputes (whether by way of legal proceedings or otherwise) under any enactment from being informed of traffic data for the purpose of settling such disputes, in particular, disputes relating to billing or interconnection.

Itemised Billing

The ePrivacy Regulations[22] at Regulation 7 provide that:

- An undertaking shall comply with a request of a subscriber to that undertaking to give him or her bills that are not itemised in respect of the electronic communications service supplied by the undertaking to the subscriber;

- The Regulator and the Data Protection Commissioner shall, in the performance of their functions, have regard to the need to reconcile the rights of subscribers to receive itemised bills with the right to privacy of calling users and called subscribers.

Presentation and Restriction of Calling and Connected Line Identification

The ePrivacy Regulations[23] Regulation 8(1) provides that where presentation of calling line identification is offered by an undertaking, the undertaking shall:

(a) offer the calling user the possibility, using a simple means and free of charge, of preventing the presentation of the calling line identification on a per call

---

22. *ibid.*
23. *ibid.*

basis. The undertaking shall offer the calling subscriber this option on a per-line basis;

(b) offer the called subscriber the possibility, using a simple means and free of charge for reasonable use of this function, of preventing the presentation of the calling line identification of incoming calls; and

(c) where the calling line identification is presented prior to the call being established, offer the called subscriber the possibility, using simple means, of rejecting incoming calls where the presentation of the calling line identification has been prevented by the calling user or subscriber.

Regulation 8(2) provides that where presentation of connected line identification is offered, the undertaking shall offer the called subscriber the possibility, using a simple means and free of charge, of preventing the presentation of the connected line identification to the calling user.

Regulation 8(3) provides that whereRegulation 8(1)(a) also applies with regard to calls to third countries originating in the EU.

Regulation 8(4) provides that Regulation 8(2) and Regulation 8(1)(b) and (c) also apply to incoming calls originating in third countries.

Regulation 8(5) provides that an undertaking that offers the presentation of calling line or connected line identification shall inform the public of it and of the possibilities contained in Regulation 8(1) and (2) by publishing a notice regularly, at intervals not more than annually, stating how that information may be obtained.

Regulation 8(6) provides that an undertaking to whom Regulation 8(1) or (2) applies shall display the information referred to in Regulation 8(5) on the undertaking's website and, where appropriate, in a directory.

Location Data other than Traffic Data

The ePrivacy Regulations[24] at Regulation 9(1) provides that no person shall process location data other than traffic data relating to users or subscribers of undertakings unless:

(a) such data are made anonymous; or

(b) they have obtained the consent of the users or subscribers in accordance with section 2A(1)(a) of the Act of 1988 (inserted by section 4 of the Act of 2003) to the extent and for the duration necessary for the provision of a value added service.

---

24. *ibid.*

Regulation 9(2) provides that an undertaking that has not already done so shall inform its users or subscribers, prior to obtaining their consent in accordance with s 2A(1)(a) of the Acts, of:

(a) the type of location data other than traffic data that will be processed;

(b) the purposes and duration of the processing; and

(c) whether or not the data will be transmitted to a third party for the purpose of providing the value added service.

Regulation 9(3) provides that an undertaking shall give users or subscribers the possibility to withdraw their consent for the processing of location data other than traffic data at any time by making a request that such processing be stopped.

Regulation 9(4) provides that where the consent of users or subscribers has been obtained for the processing of location data other than traffic data, an undertaking shall give the user or subscriber the possibility, using a simple means and free of charge, of temporarily refusing the processing of such data for each connection to the public communications network or for each transmission of a communication.

Regulation 9(5) provides that an undertaking shall ensure that the processing of location data other than traffic data in accordance with paragraphs 9(1), (2) and (4) is restricted to persons acting under the authority of the undertaking or of the third party providing the value added service based on data provided by that undertaking and shall be restricted to what is necessary for the purpose of providing the value added service.

Exceptions

The ePrivacy Regulations[25] provide the following exemptions at Regulation 10. An undertaking that has not already done so shall ensure that a general description is prepared, and available for any person who requests it, of the circumstances in which the undertaking may override:

- the elimination of the presentation of calling line identification in respect of a line, on a temporary basis, following a complaint by a subscriber and investigation by a member of An Garda Síochána of a suspected offence under s 13 of the Post Office (Amendment) Act 1951, requesting the tracing of malicious or nuisance calls. In such a case, the data containing the identification of the calling subscriber will be stored and will be made available in accordance with the Data Protections Acts and s 98(2) of the Act of 1983 by the undertaking to An Garda Síochána; and

---

25. *ibid.*

- the elimination of the presentation of calling line identification in respect of a line and the temporary denial or absence of consent of a subscriber or user for the processing of location data on a per-line basis, for calls to the emergency services including law enforcement agencies, ambulance services, fire brigades using the national emergency call number 999 or the single European emergency call number 112 or for the purpose of responding to such calls and bodies dealing with such calls for the purposes of answering them.

Automatic Call Forwarding

The ePrivacy Regulations[26] provide at Regulation 11(1)(a) that an undertaking shall ensure that calls automatically forwarded to a subscriber's terminal as a result of action by a third party shall, without charge upon a request being made to the undertaking by the subscriber to do so, cease to be so forwarded as soon as practicable after receipt of such a request. An undertaking that has not already done so shall inform its subscribers of the requirements of subparagraph (a). Also, an undertaking whose network is interconnected with the network to which the line of the subscriber concerned is connected shall, within 48 hours, comply with any reasonable request made by another undertaking for the purpose of complying with Regulation 11(1).

Directories of Subscribers

Regulation 12(1) of the ePrivacy Regulations[27] provides that an undertaking referred to in Regulation 19(1) or (2) of the Universal Service Regulations shall ensure that all its subscribers are, without charge:

(a) informed, before they are included in any directory for which the undertaking provides relevant information in accordance with that Regulation and in which their personal data can be included, about the purpose of such a directory and any further usage possibilities based on search functions embedded in electronic versions of that directory;

(b) given the opportunity to determine whether their personal data are included in that directory; and

(c) given the opportunity to determine which of their personal data are included in that directory to the extent that such data are relevant for the purpose of the directory as determined by the provider of the directory and to verify, correct or withdraw such data.

Regulation 12(2) provides that any other person responsible for the collection and making available of a subscriber's data for inclusion in any other directory of subscribers shall ensure that the subscribers are, without charge:

---

26. *ibid.*
27. *ibid.*

(a) informed, before they are included in any such directory in which their personal data can be included, about the purpose of such a directory and any further usage possibilities based on search functions embedded in electronic versions of the directory;

(b) given the opportunity to determine whether or not their personal data are included in that directory; and

(c) given the opportunity to determine which of their personal data are included in that directory to the extent that such data are relevant for the purpose of the directory as determined by the provider of the directory and to verify, correct or withdraw such data.

Regulation 12(3)(a) provides that an undertaking referred to in Regulation 19(1) or (2) of the Universal Service Regulations shall ensure that its subscribers other than natural persons are, without charge, provided with the information referred to in Regulation 12(1)(a) and the opportunities referred to in Regulation 12(1)(b) and (c) notwithstanding the fact that the data may not be personal data.

Regulation 13(3)(b) provides that any other person responsible for the collection and making available of data for inclusion in any other directory of subscribers shall ensure that subscribers other than natural persons are, without charge, provided with the information referred to in Regulation 13(2)(a) and the opportunities referred to in Regulation 13(2)(b) and (c) notwithstanding the fact that the data may not be personal data.

Regulation 13(4) provides that a subscriber may request the relevant undertaking or person to disregard or reverse the effect of a determination previously made by the subscriber to the undertaking or person under Regulation 13(2) or (3).

Regulation 13(5) provides that the relevant undertaking or person shall comply with any notification of a determination made, or deemed to have been made, to that undertaking or that person under Regulation 13(1), (2) or (4).

Unsolicited Communications/Spam

The ePrivacy Regulations[28] at Regulation 13(1) provides that subject to Regulation 13(2), a person shall not use or cause to be used any publicly available electronic communications service to send to a subscriber or user who is a natural person an unsolicited communication for the purpose of direct marketing by means of:

(a) an automated calling machine;

(b) a facsimile machine; or

(c) electronic mail,

---

28. *ibid.*

unless the person has been notified by that subscriber or user that he or she consents to the receipt of such a communication.

Regulation 13(2) provides that notwithstanding Regulation 13(1) and subject to Reguation 13(4), the use of electronic mail to send an unsolicited communication for the purpose of direct marketing to a natural person does not include an electronic mail to an email address that reasonably appears to the sender to be an email address used mainly by the subscriber or user in the context of their commercial or official activity and the unsolicited communication relates solely to that commercial or official activity.

Regulation 13(3) provides that a person shall not use or cause to be used any publicly available electronic communications service to send an unsolicited communication for the purpose of direct marketing by means of an automated calling machine or a facsimile machine to a subscriber or user, other than a natural person, where:

(a) the subscriber or user has notified the person that the subscriber or user does not consent to the receipt of such a communication; or

(b) subject to Regulation 13(9), the relevant information referred to in Regulation 14(3) is recorded in respect of the subscriber or user in the National Directory Database.

National Directory Database

The ePrivacy Regulations[29] provide as follows. Regulation 13(4) provides that a person shall not use or cause to be used any publicly available electronic communications service to send an unsolicited communication for the purpose of direct marketing by means of electronic mail, to a subscriber or user other than a natural person, where the subscriber or user has notified the person that the subscriber or user does not consent to the receipt of such a communication.

Regulation 13(5) provides that a person shall not use or cause to be used any publicly available electronic communications service to make an unsolicited telephone call for the purpose of direct marketing to a subscriber or user, where:

(a) the subscriber or user has notified the person that the subscriber or user does not consent to the receipt of such a call; or

(b) subject to paragraph (9), the relevant information referred to in Regulation 14(3) is recorded in the National Directory Database.

Regulation 13(6) provides that a person shall not use or cause to be used any publicly available electronic communications service to make an unsolicited communication

---

29. *ibid.*

for the purpose of direct marketing by means of a telephone call or automated calling machine to the mobile telephone of a subscriber or user unless:

(a) the person has been notified by that subscriber or user that he or she consents to the receipt of such communication on his or her mobile telephone; or

(b) the subscriber or user has consented to receiving such communication and such consent stands recorded on the date of such communication in the National Directory Database in respect of his or her mobile phone number.

Regulation 13(7) provides that a person shall not use or cause to be used any publicly available electronic communications service to send to a subscriber or user an SMS message for a non-marketing purpose that includes information intended for the purpose of direct marketing unless the person has been notified by that subscriber or user that he or she consents to the receipt of such a communication.

Regulation 13(8) provides that a subscriber or user shall be able to make a notification under paragraph 13(3)(a), (5)(a) or (6)(a) or make a request to record relevant information in the National Directory Database without charge.

Regulation 13(9) provides that a person will not contravene paragraph 13(3)(b) or (5)(b) if the unsolicited communication concerned is made during the period of 28 days after a request or notification under Regulation 14 is received and recorded in the National Directory Database by the operator in respect of the subscriber or user concerned.

Regulation 13(10) provides that a person who uses, or causes to be used, any publicly available electronic communications service to make a call or send a communication for the purpose of direct marketing shall:

(a) in the case of a call, include the name of the person making the call and, if applicable, the name of the person on whose behalf the call is made;

(b) in the case of a communication by means of an automated calling machine or a facsimile machine include the name, address and telephone number of the person making the communication and, if applicable, the name, address and telephone number of the person on whose behalf the communication is made; or

(c) in the case of a communication by electronic mail, include a valid address at which that person may be contacted.

Regulation 13(11) provides that a person who, in accordance with the Data Protection Acts, obtains from a customer the customer's contact details for electronic mail, in the context of the sale of a product or service, shall not use those details for direct marketing unless:

(a) the product or service being marketed is the person's own product or service;

(b) the product or service being marketed is of a kind similar to that supplied to the customer in the context of the sale by the person;

(c) the customer is clearly and distinctly given the opportunity to object, in an easy manner and without charge, to the use of those details:

   (i) at the time the details are collected; and

   (ii) if the customer has not initially refused that use, each time the person sends a message to the customer; and

(d) the sale of the product or service occurred not more than 12 months prior to the sending of the direct marketing communication or, where applicable, the contact details were used for the sending of electronic mail for the purposes of direct marketing within that 12 month period.

Regulation 13(12) provides that a person shall not send or cause to be sent electronic mail for the purposes of direct marketing, which:

(a) disguises or conceals the identity of the sender on whose behalf the communication was made;

(b) encourages recipients to visit websites or otherwise contravenes Regulation 8 of the European Communities (Directive 2000/31/EC) Regulations 2003 (SI 68/2003); or

(c) does not have a valid address to which the recipient may send a request that such communication shall cease.

Regulation 13(13)(a) provides that a person who:

   (i) contravenes the requirements of paragraph 13(1), (3), (4), (5), (6), (7), (11) or (12); or

   (ii) fails to comply with the requirements of paragraph (10), commits an offence.

Regulation 13(13)(b) provides that for the purposes of subparagraph (a) the sending of each unsolicited communication or electronic mail or the making of each unsolicited call constitutes a separate offence.

Regulation 13(14) provides that if, in proceedings for an offence under the Regulation, the question of whether or not a subscriber or user consented to receiving an unsolicited communication or call is in issue, the onus of establishing that the subscriber or user concerned unambiguously consented to receipt of the communication or call lies on the defendant.

Regulation 13(15) provides that a person who commits an offence under the Regulation is liable:

    (a) on summary conviction, to a class A fine; or

    (b) on conviction on indictment;

        (i) in the case of a body corporate, to a fine not exceeding €250,000; or

        (ii) in the case of a natural person, to a fine not exceeding €50,000.

Regulation 13(16) provides that where a person is convicted of an offence under the Regulation, the court may order any data material or data, which appears to the court to be connected with the offence, to be forfeited or destroyed and any relevant data to be erased.

Regualtion 13(17) provides that the court shall not make an order under paragraph (16) in relation to data material or data where it considers that some person other than the person convicted of the offence concerned may be the owner of, or otherwise interested in, the data material or data unless such steps as are reasonably practicable have been taken for notifying that person and giving him or her an opportunity to show cause why the order should not be made.

Regulation 13(18) provides that for the purpose of the Regulation, personal data shall be deemed to include a phone number or an email address of a subscriber or user.

National Directory Database (NDD)

The ePrivacy Regulations,[30] Regulation 14(1) provides as follows.

An undertaking referred to in Regulation 19(1) or (2) of the Universal Service Regulations shall, for the purpose of Regulation 13(3)(b) or (5)(b), record or cause to be recorded in the National Directory Database the relevant information specified in paragraph (3) in respect of a line of any one of its subscribers who:

    (a) is, upon the making of these Regulations, an ex-directory subscriber in respect of that line who, in the absence of any express instructions to the contrary, shall be taken not to consent to unsolicited calls for the purpose of direct marketing or to such calls by means of an automated calling machine or a facsimile machine; or

    (b) had, at any time after the establishment of that Database, made a request to the operator or notified the relevant undertaking that the subscriber does not consent to unsolicited calls for the purpose of direct marketing or to such calls

---

30. *ibid.*

by means of an automated calling machine or a facsimile machine to a line of that subscriber.

Regulation 14(2) provides that an undertaking referred to in Regulation 19(1) or (2) of the Universal Service Regulations that has not already done so shall ensure that its subscribers are provided with information regarding their entitlements under Regulation 13(1), (3)(b) and (5)(b) and the possibilities referred to in paragraph (1).

Regulation 14(3) provides that an undertaking referred to in Regulation 19(1) or (2) of the Universal Service Regulations shall, for the purpose of Regulation 13(3)(b) and (5)(b) and when so notified by any one of its subscribers, make available to the operator the following relevant information in respect of a line of that subscriber to be recorded in the entry in the National Directory Database in relation to that subscriber:

   (a) the fact that the subscriber does not consent to unsolicited telephone calls for the purpose of direct marketing or to such calls by means of automated calling machines or facsimile machines; and

   (b) if appropriate, the date on which a notification under Regulation 13(3)(b) and (5)(b) was received by the operator;

Regulation 14(4)(a) provides that an undertaking, for the purpose of Regulation 13(3)(b) or (5)(b), shall, as soon as practicable after having been notified under paragraph (3) that a subscriber does not consent to unsolicited telephone calls for the purpose of direct marketing or to such calls by means of automated calling machines or facsimile machines, transmit particulars of such notification to the operator or other person who publishes a directory to whom the undertaking supplies relevant information relating to its subscribers for inclusion in that directory.

Regulation 14(4)(b) provides that when the operator or other person who publishes a directory receives particulars of a notification under paragraph 14(1), the notification shall be deemed, for the purpose of the Regulation, to have been made to the operator or that other person at the time the operator or that other person receives particulars of the notification.

Regulation 14(5) provides that the operator shall record the relevant information referred to in paragraph 14(3) in respect of a line of a subscriber in the entry in the National Directory Database in relation to that subscriber when it is made available to the operator.

Regulation 14(6)(a) provides that for the purpose of complying with Regulation 13(3)(b) and (5)(b) a person may, on such terms and conditions as may be approved under Regulation 19(4) of the Universal Service Regulations and on payment to the operator of such fee as may be required by the operator:

(i) be allowed access to the National Directory Database at all reasonable times and take copies of, or of extracts from, entries in that Database; or

(ii) obtain from the operator a copy (certified by the operator or by a member of the operator's staff to be a true copy) of, or of an extract from, any entry in the National Directory Database, or both, but the operator shall refuse such inspection or copying of, or of extracts from, entries in the National Directory Database if the operator has reasonable grounds to believe that the person will not comply with the Data Protection Acts and these Regulations in respect of the information in that Database;

(b) A subscriber, or other person with the written consent of the subscriber, may:

(i) be allowed access to the entry in the National Directory Database in relation to that subscriber in respect of a particular line of the subscriber at all reasonable times and, on payment to the operator of such fee as may be required by the operator, take a copy of that entry; or

(ii) on payment to the operator of such fee as may be required by the operator, obtain from the operator a copy (certified by the operator or by a member of the operator's staff to be a true copy) of that entry, or both.

(c) In any proceedings:

(i) a copy of, or of an extract from, an entry in the National Directory Database certified by the operator or by a member of the operator's staff to be a true copy is evidence of the entry or extract on the date that it is so certified; and

(ii) a document purporting to be such a copy, and to be certified as aforesaid, is deemed to be such a copy and to be so certified unless the contrary is proved;

(d) In any proceedings:

(i) a certificate signed by the operator or by a member of the operator's staff of an entry in the National Directory Database in relation to a specified subscriber in respect of a particular line is evidence of the entry on the date that it is so certified; and

(ii) a document purporting to be such a certificate, and to be signed as aforesaid, is deemed to be such a certificate and to be so signed unless the contrary is proved;

Regulation 14(7)(a) provides that subject to subparagraph (c), the operator may require the payment of fees in respect of the matters referred to in paragraph 14(6)(a) or (b) and the amount of those fees shall be designed to secure, as nearly as may be and taking one year with another, that the aggregate amount of fees received, or reasonably expected to be received, equals the costs incurred, or reasonably expected to be incurred, by the operator in performing the functions conferred on the operator by the Regulation.

Regulation 14(7)(b) provides that different fees may be required in respect of the matters referred to in paragraph (6)(a) and (b).

Regulation 14(7)(c) provides that the amount of the fees required under subparagraph (a) is subject to the approval of the Regulator.

Regulation 14(8) provides that for the purpose of his or her functions under Regulation 17, the Data Protection Commissioner:

(a) shall be allowed access to the National Directory Database at all reasonable times and take copies of, or extracts from, entries in that Database; and

(b) may obtain from the operator a copy (certified by the operator or a member of the operator's staff to be a true copy) of, or an extract from, any entry in the National Directory Database, without payment of a fee to the operator.

Technical Features and Standardisation

The ePrivacy Regulations[31] at Regulation 15 provides:

(1) In implementing these Regulations, the Regulator shall ensure, subject to paragraphs 15(2) and (3), that no mandatory requirements for specific technical features are imposed on terminal or other electronic communication equipment that could impede the placing of equipment on the market and the free circulation of such equipment in the European Union;

(2) Where these Regulations can be implemented only by requiring specific technical features in electronic communications networks, the Regulator shall inform the Commission in accordance with the procedure provided for by Directive 98/34/EC of the European Parliament and of the Council of 22 June 1998;

(3) The Regulator shall issue such instructions as may be necessary for the purpose of requiring any specific technical features on terminal or other electronic communication equipment necessary under paragraph 15(1). Internal procedures where the scope of rights and obligations are restricted and damages for contravention of Regulations.

---

31.   *ibid.*

Under Regulation 16 it is provided that:

(1)(a) Where a legislative measure has been adopted in accordance with Article 15(1) of the Directive on privacy and electronic communications that restricts the scope of the rights and obligations provided for under Regulations 5, 6, 8(1), 8(2) and 9, providers shall establish internal procedures for responding to requests for access to users' personal data having regard to the legislative measures adopted;

(b) The provider shall, when requested to do so by the Data Protection Commissioner, provide the Data Protection Commissioner with information about the internal procedures referred to in subparagraph (a), the number of requests received, the legal justification invoked and the provider's response to the requests;

(c) The Data Protection Commissioner may seek the information referred to in subparagraph (b) in writing and the provider shall supply the information sought in writing within 28 days of receipt of the request;

(d) A person who, without reasonable excuse, fails or refuses to comply with a requirement specified in a request for information under subparagraph (b) or in purported compliance with such a requirement gives information to the Data Protection Commissioner that the person knows to be false or misleading in a material respect commits an offence;

(2) A person who suffers loss and damage as a result of a contravention of any of the requirements of these Regulations by any other person shall be entitled to damages from that other person for that loss and damage;

(3) In legal proceedings seeking damages against a person under these Regulations, it is a defence for a person to provide that he or she had taken all reasonable care in the circumstances to comply with the requirement concerned.

Data Protection Commissioner Powers of Enforcement

The ePrivacy Regulations[32] at Regulation 17 provide as follows:

Regulation 17(1) provides that the Data Protection Commissioner may investigate, or cause to be investigated, whether any prescribed provision of these Regulations has been, is being or is likely to be contravened or not complied with. The power may be exercised either as a result of a complaint made by or on behalf of the person or on the Commissioner's own initiative as a result of forming an opinion that there may be such a contravention.

---

32. *ibid.*

Regulation 17(2) provides that unless the Commissioner is of the opinion that a complaint referred to in Regulation 17(1) is frivolous or vexatious, as soon as practicable after the complaint is received the Data Protection Commissioner shall ensure that the complaint is investigated having regard to the Data Protection Commissioner's responsibilities under the Data Protection Acts.

Regulation 17(3) provides that if, after a reasonable time, the Data Protection Commissioner is unable to bring about an amicable resolution of the matter to which a complaint relates (other than a complaint giving rise to the commission of an offence), the Data Protection Commissioner shall notify the complainant in writing of the Data Protection Commissioner's decision in relation to the matter. The notice must include a statement to the effect that, if the complainant is dissatisfied with the Data Protection Commissioner's decision, the complainant has a right to appeal to the Circuit Court under Regulation 21 against the decision within 21 days after the date on which the decision is notified to the complainant under this paragraph.

Regulation 17(4) provides that if the Data Protection Commissioner is of the opinion that a person has contravened or not complied with, or is contravening or not complying with, a prescribed provision of these Regulations (other than one giving rise to the commission of an offence), the Data Protection Commissioner may serve on the person an enforcement notice requiring the person to take, within a specified period, such steps as are specified in the enforcement notice.

Regulation 17(5) provides that if an enforcement notice:

(a) shall specify the prescribed provision of these Regulations (if any) that, in the opinion of the Data Protection Commissioner, has been or is being contravened or not complied with and the reasons for having formed that opinion; and

(b) subject to Regulation 17(7), shall state that the person concerned has a right to appeal to the Circuit Court under Regulation 21 against the requirement specified in the notice within 21 days from the date of service of the enforcement notice on that person.

Regulation 17(6) provides that subject to Regulation 17(7), the time specified in an enforcement notice for compliance with a specified requirement may not be expressed to expire until after the period of 21 days from the date of service of the enforcement notice referred to in Regulation 17(5)(b). If the requirement subsequently becomes the subject of an appeal, the requirement specified in the enforcement notice need not be complied with, and Regulation 17(10) does not apply in relation to it, pending the determination or withdrawal of the appeal.

Regulation 17(7) provides that Regulation 17(5)(b) and (6) do not apply to an enforcement notice if the Data Protection Commissioner:

(a) because of special circumstances, is of the opinion that a requirement specified in the enforcement notice should be complied with without delay; and

(b) includes a statement to that effect in the enforcement notice. In that case,
however, the enforcement notice shall contain a statement specifying the
effect of Regulation 21, Regulation 17(3) and (4) excepted, and may not
require compliance with the requirement before the expiry of seven days
beginning on the date on which the notice was served.

Regulation 17(8) provides that as soon as practicable after complying with Regulation
17(4), and in any case not later than 40 days after so complying, a data controller
shall notify the blocking, rectification, erasure, destruction or statement concerned:

(a) to the data subject concerned; and

(b) if compliance materially modifies the data concerned and notification is not
impossible and does not involve disproportionate effort, to any person to
whom the data was disclosed during the period beginning 12 months before
the date of the service of the relevant enforcement notice and ending immediately before that compliance.

Regulation 17(9) provides that the Data Protection Commissioner may cancel an
enforcement notice and, on doing so, shall by notice in writing notify the cancella-
tion to the person concerned.

Regulation 17(10) provides that a person who, without reasonable excuse, fails or
refuses to comply with a requirement specified in an enforcement notice commits
an offence.

Regulation 17(11) provides that for the purpose of the Regulation, Regulations 4, 5, 6,
9, 12, 13, 14 and 16(1) are prescribed provisions.

Power to Require Information

The ePrivacy Regulations[33] provide as follows.

The Data Protection Commissioner may serve an information notice on a person
requiring the person to give to the Data Protection Commissioner in writing such
information in relation to matters specified in the information notice as is necessary
or expedient for the performance of the Data Protection Commissioner's functions
(18(1)).

Regulation 18(2) provides that an information notice shall state that the person
concerned has a right to appeal to the Circuit Court under Regulation 21 against

---

33. *ibid.*

the requirement specified in the information notice and that, if that right is to be exercised, it must be exercised within 21 days from the date on which the information notice is served on that person.

Regulation 18(3) provides that a person to whom an information notice is served under paragraph 18(1) shall, to the extent that it is possible to do so, comply with the information notice within the period specified in the information notice. That period may not be less than 21 days from the giving of the information notice.

Regulation 18(4) provides that if an appeal is brought under Regulation 21 against a requirement specified in the information notice then, pending the determination or withdrawal of the appeal:

(a) the requirement need not be complied with; and

(b) paragraph (8) does not apply to a failure to comply with the requirement.

Regulation 18(5) provides that paragraph 18(4) does not apply to an information notice if the Data Protection Commissioner:

(a) because of special circumstances is of the opinion that a requirement specified in the information notice ought to be complied with without delay; and

(b) includes in the information notice a statement to that effect. In that case, the information notice shall contain a statement specifying the effect of Regulation 21, paragraphs 18(3) and (4) excepted, and provide that compliance with the requirement may not be required before the expiry of seven days beginning on the date on which the information notice was served.

Regulation 18(6) provides that no enactment or rule of law prohibiting or restricting the disclosure of information precludes a person from giving to the Data Protection Commissioner information necessary or expedient for the performance or exercise of the Data Protection Commissioner's functions.

Regulation 18(7) provides that paragraph 18(6) does not apply to information that in the opinion of the Minister for Justice and Equality or the Minister for Defence is, or at any time was, kept for the purpose of safeguarding the security of the State or information that is privileged from disclosure in proceedings in a court.

Regulation 18(8) provides that a person who:

(a) without reasonable excuse, fails or refuses to comply with a requirement specified in an information notice; or

(b) in purported compliance with such a requirement, gives information to the Data Protection Commissioner that the person knows to be false or misleading in a material respect, commits an offence.

Powers of Authorised Officers

The ePrivacy Regulations,[34] at Regulation 19(1), provides that in the Regulations, "authorised officer" means a person authorised in writing by the Data Protection Commissioner under the Data Protection Acts to exercise the powers conferred by s 24 of the Act of 1988 or these Regulations, or both.

Regulation 19(2) provides that an authorised officer may, for the purpose of obtaining information that is necessary or expedient for the performance of the Data Protection Commissioner's functions under these Regulations, do all or any of the following:

(a) at any reasonable time:

    (i) subject to paragraph 19(4), enter a premises that the officer reasonably believes to be occupied by a data controller or a data processor;

    (ii) inspect the premises and any data located on the premises (other than data consisting of information specified in Regulation 18(7)); and

    (iii) inspect, examine, operate and test any data equipment located on the premises,

(b) require any relevant person (data controller or data processor, or an employee of either of them):

    (i) to disclose to the officer any such data and produce to the officer any data material (other than data material consisting of information specified in Regulation 18(7)) that is within the power or under the control of that person; and

    (ii) to give to the officer such information as the officer reasonably requires in relation to the data or material;

(c) either on the premises or elsewhere, inspect and copy or extract information from those data, or inspect and copy or take extracts from that material; or

(d) require any relevant person to give to the officer such information as the officer reasonably requires in relation to:

    (i) the procedures employed for complying with these Regulations and the Data Protection Acts;

    (ii) the sources from which those data are obtained;

    (iii) the purposes for which they are kept;

    (iv) the persons to whom they are disclosed; and

    (v) the data equipment kept on the premises.

---

34. *ibid.*

Regulation 19(3) provides that a person commits an offence if the person:

(a) obstructs or impedes an authorised officer in the exercise of a power conferred by the Regulation;

(b) without reasonable excuse, does not comply with a requirement imposed by such an officer under the Regulation; or

(c) in purported compliance with such a requirement, gives information to such an officer that the person knows to be false or misleading in a material respect.

Regulation 19(4) provides that an authorised officer shall not, other than with the consent of the occupier, enter a premises that is a private dwelling unless he or she has obtained a warrant from the District Court under paragraph 19(6) authorising such entry.

Regulation 19(5) provides that an authorised officer appointed under these Regulations, when exercising any powers conferred on an authorised officer by these Regulations, may be accompanied by such other authorised officers or members of An Garda Síochána or both as he or she considers necessary.

Regulation 19(6) provides that without prejudice to the powers conferred on an authorised officer by or under any provision of the Regulation, if a judge of the District Court is satisfied on the sworn information of an authorised officer that there are reasonable grounds for suspecting that there is information required by an authorised officer under the Regulation held on or at any, or any part of any, premises, the judge may issue a warrant authorising an authorised officer (accompanied by such other authorised officers or members of An Garda Síochána or both as provided for in paragraph 19(5)) at any time or times within one month from the date of issue of the warrant, on production if so requested of the warrant, to enter the premises, using reasonable force where necessary, and exercise all or any of the powers conferred on an authorised officer under the Regulation.

Circumstances Where there is no Need to Comply with an Enforcement/Information Notice

The ePrivacy Regulations,[35] Regulation 22, provides that if:

- a person appeals to the Circuit Court under Regulation 21;

- the appeal is brought within the period specified in the relevant enforcement or information notice; and

- the Data Protection Commissioner has included in that notice a statement to the effect that, because of special circumstances, the Data Protection

---

35. *ibid.*

Commissioner is of the opinion that the person should comply with the requirement specified in that notice urgently and that that notice should therefore have immediate effect, the Circuit Court may, on application made to it for the purpose, make an order determining that non-compliance by the person with the requirement does not constitute an offence pending determination or withdrawal of the appeal or during such other period as may be specified in the order. An order may be made under the Regulation despite any other provision of these Regulations to the contrary.

Evidence in Legal Proceedings

The ePrivacy Regulations[36] provide at Regulation 23(1) that in any legal proceedings:

(a) a certificate signed by the Minister for Justice and Equality or the Minister for Defence and stating that in the opinion of the Minister concerned personal data are, or at any time were, kept for the purpose of safeguarding the security of the State; or

(b) a certificate signed by an authorised person and stating that, in the authorised person's opinion, a disclosure of personal data is required for that purpose, is evidence of that opinion.

Regulation 23(2) provides that a document purporting to be a certificate under paragraph 23(1)(a) or (b) and to be signed by a person specified in the relevant paragraph is taken to be such a certificate and to be so signed unless the contrary is proved.

Regulation 23(3) provides that information supplied by a person in compliance with a requirement under Regulation 18 or a direction of a court in proceedings under these Regulations is not admissible in evidence against the person or the person's spouse in proceedings for an offence under these Regulations.

Regulation 23(4) provides that for the purpose of Regulation 23(1)(b), a person is an authorised person if the person is:

(a) a member of An Garda Síochána not below the rank of chief superintendent; or

(b) an officer of the Permanent Defence Forces who holds an army rank not below that of colonel and is designated by the Minister for Defence under s 8(a) of the Data Protection Acts.

---

36. *ibid.*

Offences by Officers of Bodies Corporate

The ePrivacy Regulations,[37] Regulation 25(1), provide that if an offence under these Regulations:

(a) has been committed by a body corporate; and

(b) is proved to have been committed with the consent or connivance of, or to be attributable to any neglect on the part of, an officer of the body corporate, that officer commits a separate offence and is liable to be proceeded against and punished as if that person had committed the first mentioned offence.

Regulation 25(2) provides that if the affairs of a body corporate are managed by its members, paragraph 25(1) applies to the acts and defaults of a member in connection with the member's functions of management as if the member were a director or manager of the body corporate.

Regulation 25(3) provides that an officer of a body corporate may be proceeded against for an offence under paragraph 25(1) whether or not the body corporate has been proceeded against or been convicted of the offence committed by the body.

Regulation 25(4) provides that in the Regulations, "officer", in relation to a body corporate, means a director, manager, secretary or other similar officer of the body, or a person who is purporting to act in any such capacity.

Prosecution of Offences

The ePrivacy Regulations[38] at Regulation 26 provide:

- (1) The Data Protection Commissioner may bring and prosecute proceedings for an offence under these Regulations that is to be tried summarily;

- (2) Paragraph (1) above does not limit any other power conferred by law to prosecute an offence under these Regulations;

- (3) If of the opinion that the circumstances relating to a complaint investigated under Regulation 17 involves the commission of an offence under these Regulations, the Data Protection Commissioner may bring and prosecute proceedings for the offence without attempting to bring about an amicable resolution of the complaint.

---

37. *ibid.*
38. *ibid.*

Penalties

The ePrivacy Regulations[39] provide the following in relation to penalties:

(1) Except as provided by Regulations 4 and 13, a person who commits an offence under these Regulations is liable on summary conviction to a class A fine;

(2) If a person is convicted of an offence under these Regulations, the court may order any data material or data that appears to it to be connected with the commission of the offence to be forfeited or destroyed and any relevant data to be erased;

(3) The court may not make such an order in relation to data material or data if it considers that some person other than the person convicted of the offence concerned might be the owner of, or have a proprietary interest in, the data material or data unless all reasonably practicable steps have been taken:

(a) to notify the person who reasonably appears to be the owner of the data material or data of the proposed forfeiture, destruction or erasure; and

(b) to give that person an opportunity to show cause why the order should not be made.

There is also a power to include requirements under these Regulations in codes of practice under the Acts (Regulation 28).

Enforcement of Regulations by the Regulator

The ePrivacy Regulations[40] provide at Regulation 30(1) that subject to the performance by the Data Protection Commissioner of the functions under Regulation 17, it shall be a function of the Regulator to monitor compliance with Regulation 7, 8, 9, 10, 11, 12, 13, 14 or 15 and to issue such directions as may be necessary, from time to time, for their effective implementation. The Regulator, in consultation with the Data Protection Commissioner, may also specify the form and any other requirements regarding the obtaining, recording and rescinding of consent of subscribers for the purpose of these Regulations.

Regulation 30(2) provides that the functions of the Regulator under the Regulation shall be deemed to be included in the functions conferred on the Regulator under the Act of 2002.

Regulation 30(3) provides that the Regulator may give directions to an undertaking to which Regulation 7, 8, 9, 10, 11, 12, 13, 14 or 15 applies requiring the undertaking to

39. *ibid.*
40. *ibid.*

take specified measures or to refrain from taking specified measures for the purpose of complying with the provision.

Regulation 30(4) provides that an undertaking to whom Regulation 7, 8, 9, 10, 11, 12, 13, 14 or 15 applies shall furnish the Regulator with such information as the Regulator may reasonably require for the purpose of its functions under these Regulations.

Regulation 30(5) provides that where the Regulator issues a direction under the Regulation, such direction shall be in writing, state the reasons on which it is based and be addressed to the undertaking concerned and, as soon as practicable, be sent or given in any of the following ways:

(a) by delivering it to the undertaking;

(b) by leaving it at the address at which the undertaking ordinarily carries on business;

(c) by sending it by pre-paid registered post addressed to the undertaking at the address at which the undertaking ordinarily carries on business;

(d) if an address for the service of directions has been furnished by the undertaking to the Regulator, by leaving it at, or sending it by prepaid registered post to, that address; or

(e) in any case where the Regulator considers that the immediate giving of the direction is required, by sending it, by means of a facsimile machine or by electronic mail, to a device or facility for the reception of facsimiles or electronic mail located at the address at which the undertaking ordinarily carries on business or, if an address for the service of notices has been furnished by the undertaking, that address, but only if:

(i) the sender's facsimile machine generates a message confirming successful delivery of the total number of pages of the direction; or

(ii) the recipient's facility for the reception of electronic mail generates a message confirming receipt of the electronic mail, and it is also given in one of the other ways mentioned in subparagraphs (a) to (d).

Regulation 30(6) provides that in Regulation 30(5) and Regulation 20, a company within the meaning of the Companies Acts is deemed to be ordinarily resident at its registered office and every other body corporate and every unincorporated body of persons shall be deemed to be ordinarily resident at its principal office or place of business.

Application to the High Court

The ePrivacy Regulations[41] provide as follows in relation to court applications. At Regulation 31(1) it is provided that where the Regulator finds that an undertaking has not complied with an obligation or requirement under these Regulations or a direction under Regulation 29, 30(1) or (3), the Regulator shall notify the undertaking of those findings and give the undertaking an opportunity to state its views or, if the non-compliance can be remedied, to remedy the non-compliance within a reasonable time limit as specified by the Regulator.

Regulation 31(2) provides that the Regulator may publish, in such manner as it thinks fit, any notification given by it under the Regulation subject to the protection of the confidentiality of any information the Regulator considers confidential. Regulation 31(3) provides that the Regulator may amend or revoke any notification under the Regulation.

Regulation 31(4) provides that where, at the end of the period specified by the Regulator under paragraph 31(1), the Regulator is of the opinion that the undertaking concerned has not complied with the obligation, requirement or direction, the Regulator may, whether or not the non-compliance is continuing, apply to the High Court for such order as the Regulator considers appropriate including:

(a) a declaration of non-compliance;

(b) an order directing compliance with the obligation, requirement or direction;

(c) an order directing the remedy of any non-compliance with the obligation, requirement or direction; or

(d) an order as provided for in Regulation 31(8).

Regulation 31(5) provides that the High Court may, on the hearing of the application referred to in paragraph 31(4), make such order as it thinks fit, which may include:

(a) a declaration of non-compliance;

(b) an order directing compliance with the obligation, requirement or direction;

(c) an order directing the remedy of any non-compliance with the obligation, requirement or direction; or

(d) an order as provided for in Regulation 31(8), or refuse the application. An order of the High Court compelling compliance may stipulate that the obligation, requirement or direction must be complied with immediately or may specify a reasonable time limit for compliance and may also stipulate appropriate and proportionate measures aimed at ensuring compliance.

---

41. *ibid.*

Regulation 31(6) provides that the High Court when dealing with an application under Regulation 31(4) may make such interim or interlocutory order as it considers appropriate.

Regulation 31(7) provides that the High Court shall not deny any interim or interlocutory relief, referred to in Regulation 31(6), solely on the basis that the Regulator may not suffer any damage if such relief were not granted pending conclusion of the action.

Regulation 31(8)(a) provides that an application for an order under Regulation 31(4) may be for, or include an application for, an order to pay to the Regulator such amount, by way of financial penalty, which may include penalties having effect for periods of non-compliance with the obligation, requirement or direction, as the Regulator may propose as appropriate in the light of the non-compliance or any continuing non-compliance. Such an application for an order in respect of a financial penalty for a period of non-compliance may be made even if there since has been compliance with the obligation, requirement or direction;

    (b) In deciding on such an application, the High Court shall decide the amount, if any, of the financial penalty that should be payable and shall not be bound by the amount proposed by the Regulator;

    (c) Any financial penalty ordered by the High Court to be paid by an undertaking against whom an order may be sought shall be retained by the Regulator as income;

    (d) In deciding what amount, if any, should be payable, the High Court shall consider the circumstances of the non-compliance, including:

        (i) its duration;

        (ii) the effect on consumers, users and other operators;

        (iii) the submissions of the Regulator on the appropriate amount; and

        (iv) any excuse or explanation for the non-compliance.

UK ICO Cookie Guidance

The UK ICO updated its guidance in relation to cookies in May 2012, entitled *Privacy and Electronic Communications Regulations, Guidance on the Rules on Use of Cookies and Similar Technologies.*[42] The ICO indicated that "prior" consent means

---

42. *Privacy and Electronic Communications Regulations, Guidance on the Rules on Use of Cookies and Similar* Technologies, ICO, 2012. Available at http://www.ico.gov.uk/for_organisations/ privacy_and_electronic_communications/the_guide/cookies.aspx, last accessed 11 January 2013.

that consent be obtained prior to the cookie being used.[43] The use of cookies should be delayed until users have had the opportunity to understand what cookies may be used and to make their choice. Where this is not possible at present websites should be able to demonstrate that they are doing as much as possible to reduce the amount of time before the user receives information about cookies and is provided with options. Prior information should be clear and comprehensive.[44] If users make a one-off visit to a website a persistent cookie may not be needed. Organisations should shorten the lifespan of these cookies or, make them temporary session cookies.[45]

The ICO indicates that, while explicit consent might allow for regulatory certainty, it does not mean that implied consent cannot be compliant. As always, website organisations collecting sensitive personal data such as information about an identifiable individual's health, require explicit consent.[46]

Consent (implied or express) has to be a freely given, specific and informed indication of the individual's wishes. For implied consent, there has to be some action taken by the consenting individual from which their consent can be inferred. This might for example be visiting a website, moving from one page to another or clicking on a particular button. In this instance, the individual has to have a reasonable understanding that by doing so they are agreeing to cookies being set.[47]

Merely visiting a website is not sufficient consent.[48] A user cannot "give" consent if unaware that their actions are being interpreted as a consent. If the user is not informed, there is no valid consent.[49]

The ICO gives the analogy of a patient visiting a doctor. This act of visiting alone would not indicate that the patient consents to treatment or recording of health information.[50]

To rely on implied consent for cookies, it is important that the organisation seeking consent satisfy themselves that the user's actions are not only an explicit request for content or services but also an indirect expression of the user's agreement that the organisation may store or access information on the user's device.[51]

Organisations must ensure that clear and relevant information is readily available to users explaining what is likely to happen while the user is accessing the site and what

---

43. *ibid.*
44. *ibid.*
45. *ibid.*
46. *ibid.*
47. *ibid.*
48. *ibid.*
49. *ibid.*
50. *ibid.*
51. *ibid.*

choices the user has in terms of controlling what happens.[52] Important factors to bear in mind might include the following:

The nature of the intended audience of the site: Some websites might be aimed at an audience who are technically aware enough to have a reasonable understanding of what is going on. These sites would not necessarily need to provide very basic information about what cookies are but they might still want to give their users detailed explanation of how the site uses cookies and similar technology.[53]

The way in which users expect to receive information from and on the website: The more the information about cookies fits with the rest of the site, the more likely users are to read it and, in turn, the more likely the website operator is able to assume that users understand and accept how the website works.[54]

Make sure that the language used is appropriate for the audience: See the advice of the International Chambers of Commerce.[55]

The ePrivacy regulations/PECR Amendment Regulations state that consent for a cookie should be obtained from the subscriber or user. The subscriber means the person who pays the bill for the use of the line. The user is the person using the computer or other device to access a website.[56]

Those setting cookies must:

- tell people that the cookies are there;
- explain what the cookies are doing; and
- obtain their consent to store a cookie on their device.[57]

Since 2003 anyone using cookies has been required to provide clear information about those cookies. In May 2011 the existing rules were amended. Under the revised UK PECR Amendment Regulations the requirement is not just to provide clear information about the cookies but also to obtain consent from users or subscribers to store a cookie on their device.[58]

There is an exception to the requirement to provide information about cookies and to obtain consent, namely, where the use of the cookie is:

---

52. *ibid.*
53. *ibid.*
54. *ibid.*
55. *ibid.*
56. *ibid.*
57. *ibid.*
58. *ibid.*

- for the sole purpose of carrying out the transmission of a communication over an electronic communications network; or

- where such storage or access is strictly necessary for the provision of an information society service requested by the subscriber or user.[59]

In defining an "information society service" the Electronic Commerce (EC Directive) Regulations 2002 refer to "any service normally provided for remuneration, at a distance, by means of electronic equipment for the processing (including digital compression) and storage of data, and at the individual request of a recipient of a service".[60]

The term "strictly necessary" means that such storage of or access to information should be essential, rather than reasonably necessary, for this exemption to apply. However, it will also be restricted to what is essential to provide the service requested by the user, rather than what might be essential for any other uses the service provider might wish to make of that data. It will also include what is required to comply with any other legislation the person using the cookie might be subject to, e.g. the security requirements of the seventh *data protection principle*.[61]

This exception is likely to apply, for example, to a cookie used to ensure that when a user of a website has chosen the goods they wish to buy and clicks "add to basket"/"proceed to checkout" button, the website "remembers" what they chose on a previous page. This cookie is strictly necessary to provide the service the user requests (taking the purchase they want to make to the checkout) and so the exception would apply and no consent is required.[62]

The intention of the legislation is clearly that this exemption is narrow.[63]

The UK ICO provides the following practical advice. It is not enough simply to continue to comply with the 2003 requirement to tell users about cookies and allow them to opt out. The ICO states that the law has changed and whatever solution an organisation implements has to do more than comply with the previous requirements in this area.[64]

An organisation may consider the following steps:

- check what type of cookies and similar technologies it uses and how it uses them;

---

59. *ibid.*
60. *ibid.*
61. *ibid.*
62. *ibid.*
63. *ibid.*
64. *ibid.*

- assess how intrusive the organisation's use of cookies is;
- where the organisation needs consent, decide what solution to obtain consent is best in the circumstances.[65]

Organisations should already know what cookies they are using but should recheck. This might be part of a comprehensive audit of the website.[66] Organisations should analyse which cookies are strictly necessary and therefore might not need consent.[67]

The more intrusive the use of cookies, the more priority organisations will need to give to considering changing how they use it.[68]

Some uses of cookies can involve creating detailed profiles of an individual's browsing activity.[69] If doing this, or allowing it to happen, on a website or across a range of websites, it is clear that the organisations are doing something that could be quite intrusive – the more privacy intrusive the activity, the more priority the organisations will need to give to getting meaningful consent.[70]

Privacy neutral cookies are at one end of the scale and more intrusive uses of the technology at the other. More information and detailed choices are required at the intrusive end of the scale.[71]

Once the organisation knows what they do, how and for what purpose, the organisations will need to consider the best method for obtaining such consent. The more privacy-intrusive the activity, the greater the need to obtain meaningful consent.[72]

An audit of cookies could involve the following:

- identify which cookies are operating on or through the organisation's website;
- confirm the purpose(s) of each of these cookies;
- confirm whether or not the organisation links cookies to other information held about users – such as usernames;
- identify what data each cookie holds;
- confirm the type of cookie – session or persistent;

---

65. *ibid.*
66. *ibid.*
67. *ibid.*
68. *ibid.*
69. *ibid.*
70. *ibid.*
71. *ibid.*
72. *ibid.*

- identify if it is a persistent cookie, ansd how long the lifespan is;

- identify if it is it a first or third party cookie?;

- identify if it is a third party cookie and who is setting it;

- check if the privacy policy/statement provides accurate and clear information about each cookie.[73]

Article 29 and Online Behavioural Advertising Opinion

The EU Article 29 Working Party on Data Protection adopted an Opinion[74] on 22 June 2010, which relates to online behavioural advertising ("OBA"). It notes that behavioural advertising involves the tracking of users when they surf the internet and profiles are built, which are later used to provide them with advertising deemed to match their interests.[75] The Article 29 Working Party states that such practice must not be carried out at the expense of data subject's rights.[76]

The data protection regime, safeguards and rights must be respected. The Opinion provides some guidance for those organisations considering OBA.

The Opinion states that advertising network providers are obliged to comply with Article 5(3) of ePrivacy Directive,[77] which provides that placing cookies or similar devices on users' terminal equipment, or obtaining information through such devices, is only lawful once the informed consent of the users is obtained.[78] Frequently, the settings of the current generation of internet browsers and opt-out mechanisms only permit consent in limited circumstances.[79] Advertising network providers must create prior opt-in mechanisms requiring an affirmative consent action by the data subjects which indicated their willingness to receive cookies, similar devices and the subsequent monitoring of their internet surfing activities for the advertising purposes.[80] Sometimes a single consent acceptance regarding cookies may be sufficient for subsequent cookies, and hence monitoring of their internet browsing.[81] Article 5(3) may not need consent for each reading of the cookie.[82] However, in order "to keep data

---

73. *ibid.*
74. WP29, Opinion 2/2010 on Online Behavioural Advertising (WP 171).
75. *ibid.*
76. *ibid.*
77. Directive 2002/58/EC of the European Parliament and of the Council of 12 July 2002 concerning the processing of personal data and the protection of privacy in the electronic communications sector (Directive on privacy and electronic communications) (as amended by Directives 2006/24/EC and 2009/136/EC).
78. *ibid.*
79. *ibid.*
80. *ibid.*
81. *ibid.*
82. *ibid.*

subjects aware of the monitoring, ad network providers should: i) limit in time the scope of the consent; ii) offer the possibility to revoke it easily; and iii) create visible tools to be displayed where the monitoring takes place".[83]

OBA involves "the creation of very detailed user profiles which, in most cases, will be deemed personal data".[84] The data protection regime including DP Directive 95[85] applies. The Opinion states that advertising network providers must adhere to the Directive, including rights of access, rectification, erasure, retention, etc.[86] Publishers also share responsibility for OBA data processing.[87] Therefore, publishers share with ad network providers, the responsibility to provide information to users.[88] Transparency is a key condition for individuals in order to be able to consent to the collection and processing of their personal data and the exercising of an effective choice.[89]

The Opinion refers to the information obligations for advertising network providers and publishers in relation to data subjects, referring to the ePrivacy Directive, which requires that users are provided with "clear and comprehensive information".[90]

Article 29 Opinion 2/2010: OBA Context

The growing practice of behavioural advertising raises important data protection and privacy-concerns.[91] The tracking data subjects internet activities, and across different websites and over time, is increasing. Such data is gathered and analysed in order to build extensive profiles about individual data subjects and their interests.[92] Such profiles can be used to provide data subjects with tailored advertising, both of the data controller and of third parties, as well as to sell profile databases, or access to such databases. Ever increasing amounts and fields of data, and the linking of such data from different activities and sources, is possible. This developing area has significant implications for users, regulators and industry.

The Article 29 Working Party states that:

> Given the increasing use of behavioural advertising based on the use of tracking cookies and similar devices and its high level of intrusiveness into people's privacy, the EU Article 29 Working Party on Data Protection has decided to focus this Opinion

---

83. *ibid.*
84. *ibid.*
85. EU Data Protection Directive 1995 *supra.*
86. *ibid.*
87. *ibid.*
88. *ibid.*
89. *ibid.*
90. *ibid.*
91. *ibid.*
92. *ibid.*

on online behavioural advertising across several websites, without prejudice to future opinions, which may analyse other advertising technologies.[93]

It will continue to evaluate the situation and states that it will "take any measures necessary and appropriate to ensure [data protection] compliance".[94]

Article 29 Opinion 2/2010: OBA Detail

The Opinion notes that interactive media advertising refers to a broad range of methods aimed at creating "more relevant advertisements".[95] Examples include contextual advertising, segmented advertising and behavioural advertising.

Behavioural advertising is referred to as "advertising ... based on ... observation of the [online] behaviour of individuals over time".[96] It studies the characteristics of this behaviour through their actions (e.g. repeated site visits, interactions, keywords, online content production, etc.) to develop a specific profile and thus tailored advertisements tailored to match their users' inferred interests.[97]

The Opinion notes that OBA "gives advertisers a very detailed picture of a data subject's online life, with many of the websites and specific pages they have viewed, how long they viewed certain articles or items, in which order, etc.".[98]

The Opinion refers to the OBA process, which includes the

> delivery of ads through advertising networks ... as follows: the publisher reserves visual space on its website to display an ad and relinquishes the rest of the advertising process to one or more advertising network providers. The ad network providers are responsible for distributing advertisements to publishers with the maximum effect possible. The ad network providers control the targeting technology and associated databases.[99]

It also increasingly incorporates a bidding system.[100]

---

93. *ibid.*
94. *ibid.*
95. *ibid.*
96. *ibid.*
97. *ibid.*
98. *ibid.*
99. *ibid.*
100. *ibid.*

Article 29 Opinion 2/2010: Tracking Technologies

The main OBA tracking technology is based on "tracking cookies".[101]

A cookie is, the Opinion notes "a short alphanumeric text, … stored … on the data subject's terminal equipment by a network provider".[102] The cookie enables the ad network provider to recognise visitors to the website or (related) websites.[103]

Some browsers allow blocking or deletion of cookies.[104] However, new enhanced tracking technologies (e.g. Flash Cookies) cannot be deleted through browser privacy settings.[105]

In the Opinion, "cookies" refers to all technologies that are based on the principle of storing and accessing information on the user's terminal equipment.[106]

While a separate issue from the current Opinion, the Article 29 Working Party notes that a partnership between an ad network and ISP in order to monitor the user browsing content and using tracking cookies in all unencrypted web traffic, "raises serious legal issues [even] beyond the processing of personal data, regardless of the purpose".[107]

Article 29 Opinion 2/2010: Profiles and Identifiers

Ad networks can construct predictive non-explicit profiles with a combination of tracking techniques, cookie-based technologies and data-mining software.[108] Gender and age ranges can be guaged.[109]

The location of the data subject can also be guaged, e.g. from the IP addresses of the terminals and WiFi access points.[110]

Article 29 Opinion 2/2010: Legal Framework Introduction

Article 5(1) of Directive 2002/58 protects the confidentiality of communications. The protection of the confidentiality regarding cookies and similar devices is primarily provided in the amended Article 5(3).[111]

---

101. *ibid.*
102. *ibid.*
103. *ibid.*
104. *ibid.*
105. *ibid.*
106. *ibid.*
107. *ibid.*
108. *ibid.*
109. *ibid.*
110. *ibid.*
111. *ibid.*

Member States must ensure that the use of electronic communications networks to store information, or to gain access to information already stored, in user terminal equipment is only lawful if the user has given their consent, after being provided with clear and comprehensive information, in accordance with DP Directive 95. The information to be provided includes information about the purposes of the processing, and the right to refuse such processing.[112] However, technical storage or access for the sole purpose of carrying out the transmission of a communication over an electronic communications network, or as strictly necessary in order to provide an information society service explicitly requested by the user is permitted.[113]

Article 29 Opinion 2/2010: Article 5(3) and DP Directive 95

Organisations using behavioural advertising must comply with Article 5(3) of the ePrivacy Directive[114] and the DP Directive 95.

WP29 Opinion 2/2010: Substantive Scope of Article 5(3)

Article 5(3) requires organisations to obtain informed consent in order to lawfully store user information, or to gain access to information stored in user terminal equipment.[115] Any storage of cookies and similar devices (of any type) must comply with Article 5(3).[116]

Article 5(3) does not require that the information is personal data within the meaning of DP Directive 95. The private sphere triggers the obligations contained in Article 5(3), not that the information is, or is not, personal data.[117]

Article 5(3) also applies to data controllers and data processors.[118]

WP29 Opinion 2/2010: Scope and DP Directive 95

If the cookie or similar device is personal data then, in addition to Article 5(3), the DP Directive 95 applies.[119]

Tracking users to specific computers identifies personal data.[120]

---

112. *ibid.*
113. *ibid.*
114. *ibid.*
115. *ibid.*
116. *ibid.*
117. *ibid.* See also Recital 24.
118. *ibid.*
119. *ibid.*
120. *ibid.*

Recital 10 of ePrivacy Directive states that DP Directive 95 applies "to all matters concerning protection of fundamental rights and freedoms which are not specifically covered by the provisions of the Directive, including the obligations on the [data] controller and the rights of individuals".

Article 5(3) of the ePrivacy Directive, which deals with informed consent, is directly applicable.[121] DP Directive 95 is fully applicable - except for issues specifically addressed in the ePrivacy Directive.[122] The DP Directive 95, e.g. data quality, data subject's rights (such as access, erasure, right to object), confidentiality, security and international transfers, fully apply.[123]

WP29 Opinion 2/2010: Ad Network Providers

Article 5(3) of the ePrivacy Directive applies to those who place cookies and/ or retrieve information from cookies.[124] Article 5(3) puts the obligation to obtain informed consent on ad network providers.[125]

When behavioural advertising involves processing personal data, the ad network provider is also a data controller.[126] The Opinion notes that ad network providers have complete control over the purposes and means of the processing.[127] It notes, for example, that they

> "rent" space from publishers' websites to place advertisements; ... set and read cookie-related information ... collect ... IP address[es] and ... other data that the browser may reveal ... use the information gathered on Internet users' surfing behaviour to build profiles and to select and deliver the ads to be displayed on the basis of this profile ... they clearly act as data controllers.[128]

WP29 Opinion 2/2010: Publishers

Publishers, the Opinion notes, will rent out space on their websites for ad networks to place advertisements.[129]

---

121. *ibid.*
122. Directive 2002/58/EC of the European Parliament and of the Council of 12 July 2002 concerning the processing of personal data and the protection of privacy in the electronic communications sector (Directive on privacy and electronic communications) (as amended by Directives 2006/24/EC and 2009/136/EC).
123. *ibid.*
124. *ibid.*
125. *ibid.*
126. *ibid.*
127. *ibid.*
128. *ibid.*
129. *ibid.*

Their websites are configured in a way that visitors' browsers automatically redirect to the ad network provider's webpage (which will then send a cookie and serve tailored advertising).[130]

The Opinion states that publishers have a responsibility for the data processing, which derives from the Member State implementation of DP Directive 95 and/or other national legislation.[131] Publishers have some responsibility as data controllers.[132]

Publishers must comply with some of the Directive obligations e.g. the obligation to inform individuals of the data processing.[133]

Publishers will be joint data controllers if they collect and transmit personal data regarding visitor' name, address, age, location, etc., to the ad network provider.[134] If publishers act as data controllers, they are bound by the DP Directive 95 obligations.[135] Ad network providers and publishers "shall ensure that the complexity and the technicalities of the behavioural advertising system do not prevent them from finding appropriate ways to comply with data controllers' obligations and to ensure data subjects' rights".[136]

By entering into contracts with ad networks whereby the personal data of their visitors are available to ad network providers, publishers take some responsibility towards their visitors. This must be examined on a case-by-case basis.[137] Contracts, service agreements, etc. between publishers and ad network providers should establish the clear roles and responsibilities of the parties.[138]

WP29 Opinion 2/2010: Advertisers

Advertisers can track which marketing campaign resulted in the user click-through.[139] If targeted information (e.g. demographics or interests) is combined with the data subject's onsite surfing behaviour or registration data, the advertiser is an independent data controller.[140]

---

130. *ibid.*
131. *ibid.*
132. *ibid.*
133. *ibid.*
134. *ibid.*
135. *ibid.*
136. *ibid.*
137. *ibid.*
138. *ibid.*
139. *ibid.*
140. *ibid.*

WP29 Opinion 2/2010: Prior Informed Consent Obligation

The general rule contained in the first paragraph of Article 5(3) requires Member States to:

> ensure that the storing of information, or the gaining of access to information already stored, in the terminal equipment of a subscriber or user is only allowed on condition that the subscriber or user concerned has given [their] consent, having been provided with clear and comprehensive information, in accordance with DP Directive 95, *inter alia* about the purposes of the processing.

This provision was changed when the ePrivacy Directive was amended in 2009. The changes reinforce the need for users' informed prior consent.[141]

The Opinion discusses various ways of satisfying the requirements of Article 5(3). There is also guidance on the obligation to provide information.[142]

WP29 Opinion 2/2010: Prior Consent to Engage in Behavioural Advertising

Pursuant to Article 5(3), an ad network provider who wishes to store or gain access to information stored in a user's terminal equipment is allowed to do so if:

- it has provided the user with clear and comprehensive information in accordance with DP Directive 95, *inter alia*, about the purposes of the processing; and

- it has obtained the user's consent to the storage of or access to information on their terminal equipment, after having provided the prior information above.[143]

Consent must be obtained before the cookie is placed and/or information stored in the user's terminal equipment is collected, i.e. prior consent.[144] Informed consent can only be obtained if prior information (about the sending and purposes of the cookie) has been given to the user.[145] For consent to be valid, it must be freely given, specific and constitute an informed indication of the data subject's wishes.[146] The consent must be obtained before the personal data are collected.[147] Furthermore, the consent must be revocable.[148]

---

141. *ibid.*
142. *ibid.*
143. *ibid.*
144. *ibid.*
145. *ibid.*
146. *ibid.*
147. *ibid.*
148. *ibid.*

WP29 Opinion 2/2010: Consent Via Browser Settings

Publishers and ad network providers often provide information in their general terms and conditions and/or privacy policies/statements about third-party cookies used for behavioural advertising.[149] The information may include the purposes of such cookies and how they can be avoided by browser settings.[150] However, this practice does not meet the requirements of Article 5(3), particularly which requires prior information and obtaining prior consent (prior to the starting of the processing).[151]

Recital 66 of the amended ePrivacy Directive indicates that user's consent may be expressed by using the appropriate browser settings or other application, "where it is technically possible and effective" in accordance with the relevant provisions of DP Directive 95 i.e. consent can be given in different ways – where technically possible, effective and in accordance with the other relevant requirements for valid consent.[152]

However, browser settings will only meet the requirements of DP Directive 95, and a valid consent in very limited circumstances.[153]

Data subjects cannot be deemed to consent simply because they used a browser or defaulted to enable the data collection.[154] Most data subjects are unaware of the tracking of their online behaviour, purposes of the tracking, how to use browser settings to reject cookies, etc.[155]

As pointed out in WP29 Opinion 1/2008, the "responsibility for [cookie] processing cannot be reduced to the responsibility of the user for taking or not taking certain precautions in [their] browser settings".[156] The Opinion notes that three of four major browsers have as a default setting to allow all cookies.[157]

For browser's settings to deliver informed consent, it should not be possible to bypass the user's choice (e.g. respawning).[158]

Consent in bulk for any future processing without knowing the circumstances surrounding the processing cannot be valid consent.

---

149. *ibid.*
150. *ibid.*
151. *ibid.*
152. *ibid.*
153. *ibid.*
154. *ibid.*
155. *ibid.*
156. *ibid.*
157. *ibid.*
158. *ibid.*

In order for browsers or any other application to be able to deliver valid consent, they must overcome the above problems. Effectively, this means that:

- Browsers or other applications which by default reject 3rd-party cookies and which require the data subject to engage in an affirmative action to accept both the setting of and continued transmission of information contained in cookies by specific websites may be able to deliver valid and effective consent. By contrast, if the browser settings were predetermined to accept all cookies, such consent would not comply with Article 5(3) insofar as, in general, such consent cannot constitute a true indication of the data subject's wishes. Such consent would neither be specific nor prior (to the processing). Whereas a given data subject could indeed have decided to keep the settings to accept all 3rd-party cookies, it would not be realistic for ad network providers to assume that the vast majority of data subjects who have their browsers 'set' to accept cookies, effectively exercised this choice[159];

- Browsers, together or in combination with other information tools, including the co-operation of ad network providers and publishers, should convey clear, comprehensive and fully visible information in order to ensure that consent is fully informed. To meet the requirements of DP Directive 95 browsers should convey, on behalf of the ad network provider, the relevant information about the purposes of the cookies and the further processing. So, generic warnings without explicit references to the ad network which is placing the cookie are unsatisfactory.[160]

Unless the above requirements are met, providing information and, facilitating the user's ability to reject cookies (and by explaining how this can be done), there cannot generally be informed consent per Article 5(3) of the ePrivacy Directive (and per Article 2(h) of DP Directive 9).[161]

The Article 29 Working Party states that it is "of paramount importance for browsers to be provided with default privacy-protective settings".[162] This requires settings of "non-acceptance and non-transmission of third-party cookies" and a privacy wizard when users first install or update the browser aswell as an easy way of exercising choice during use.[163]

WP29 Opinion 2/2010: Consent and Opt-Out Options

Ad network provider opt-out mechanisms where the data subject must go to the website and indicate that they wish to opt-out from being tracked for the purposes of being served targeted advertisements are welcome, according to the Opinion.[164]

---

159. *ibid.*
160. *ibid.*
161. *ibid.*
162. *ibid.*
163. *ibid.*
164. *ibid.*

However, such opt-out mechanisms do not, in principle deliver consent.[165] It is not an adequate mechanism to obtain average users informed consent.[166]

Cookie-based opt-out mechanisms do not provide average users with the effective means to consent to receiving behavioural advertising.[167] They "fail to fulfil the requirement of Article 5(3)".[168]

WP29 Opinion 2/2010: Prior Opt-In Consent Better For Informed Consent

Prior opt-in mechanisms which require an affirmative data subject's action to indicate consent before the cookie is sent to the data subject, are closer to Article 5(3).[169]

A previous Opinion recommended the use of specific messages, e.g.

> [i]n the case of cookies, the user should be informed when a cookie is intended to be received, stored or sent ... The message should specify, in generally understandable language, which information is intended to be stored in the cookie, for what purpose as well as the period of validity of the cookie.[170]

After receiving such information, the data subject should be offered the possibility to indicate whether or not they wants to be profiled for the purposes of behavioural advertising.[171] To avoid practical problems, in accordance with Recital 25 of the ePrivacy Directive ("the right to refuse [cookies] may be offered once for the use of various devices to be installed on the user's terminal equipment ... during subsequent connections"), users' acceptance of a cookie could be understood to be valid not only for the sending of the cookie but also for subsequent collection of data arising from such a cookie.[172]

Organisations should limit the scope of the consent in terms of time.[173] After a period, the ad network providers would need to obtain a new consent.[174] Cookies can have a limited lifespan.[175]

---

165. *ibid.*
166. *ibid.*
167. *ibid.*
168. *ibid.*
169. *ibid.*
170. *ibid.*
171. *ibid.*
172. *ibid.*
173. *ibid.*
174. *ibid.*
175. *ibid.*

Freely given user consent can always be revoked.[176] Therefore, data subjects should be offered the possibility to easily revoke their consent to being monitored for behavioural advertising purposes.[177] Clear information is essential.[178]

WP29 Opinion 2/2010: Informed Consent and Children

Opinion 2/2009 the WP29 refers to the protection of personal data of children.[179] Obtaining informed consent for children is a particular issue. In addition to the cookie requirements, in some cases children's consent must be provided by a parent or legal guardian.[180] That means ad network providers may need to provide notice to parents about the collection and the use of children's information and obtain their consent before collecting and further using their information for the purposes of engaging in behavioural targeting of children.[181]

The Article 29 Working Party feels that ad network providers should not offer "interest categories intended to serve behavioural advertising or influence children".[182]

WP29 Opinion 2/2010: Obligation to Provide Information for OBA

Transparency is a key condition for individuals to be able to consent.[183] They may not know, or understand, the technology of behavioural advertising.[184] The Opinion states that "it is therefore of paramount importance to ensure that sufficient and effective information is provided in a way that will reach internet users. Only if data subjects are informed will they be in a position to exercise their choices."[185]

WP29 Opinion 2/2010: What Information Provided by Whom?

Article 5(3) states that the user must be provided with information, "in accordance with [DP Directive 95], *inter alia* about the purposes of the processing". Article 10 of DP Directive 95 deals with the provision of this information.

As regards behavioural advertising, data subjects should informed, *inter alia*, about the identity of the advertising network provider and the processing purposes.[186]

---

176. *ibid.*
177. *ibid.*
178. *ibid.*
179. *ibid.*
180. *ibid.*
181. *ibid.*
182. *ibid.*
183. *ibid.*
184. *ibid.*
185. *ibid.*
186. *ibid.*

The data subject must be clearly informed that the cookie will allow the advertising provider to collect information about their visits to other websites, the advertisements they see, which advertisements they click on, timing, etc.[187]

"There should be a simple explanation on the uses of the cookie to create profiles in order to serve targeted advertising."[188] Recital 25 of the ePrivacy Directive requires such notices to be provided in a "clear and comprehensive" manner.[189] The Opinion makes clear that statements such as "advertisers and other third parties may also use their own cookies or action tags" are "clearly" not sufficient.[190]

Recital 25 requires the information to be provided in "as user friendly [a manner] as possible".[191] Providing "a minimum of information directly on the screen, interactively, easily visible and understandable, would be the most effective way to comply with this principle".[192] Information must be easily accessible and highly visible.[193] The essential information must not be hidden in general terms and conditions and or privacy statements.[194]

Ad network providers must inform users periodically that the monitoring is taking place.[195] If not given clear and unambiguous reminders, by easy means, of the monitoring, it is "likely that after a certain period of time, [users] may no longer be aware that it is still taking place and that they consented to it".[196]

The obligation to provide the necessary information and obtain data subjects' consent ultimately lies with the entity that sends and reads the cookie, frequently the ad network provider.[197] Where publishers are joint-controllers, they are also bound by the obligation to provide information to data subjects about the data processing.[198]

Publishers also share with ad network providers certain responsibility for the data processing that happens in the context of serving behavioural advertising.[199] This covers the first stage of the processing, i.e. the transfer of the IP address to ad network providers once individuals are re-directed to the ad network provider's website.[200]

---

187. *ibid.*
188. *ibid.*
189. *ibid.*
190. *ibid.*
191. *ibid.*
192. *ibid.*
193. *ibid.*
194. *ibid.*
195. *ibid.*
196. *ibid.*
197. *ibid.*
198. *ibid.*
199. *ibid.*
200. *ibid.*

Publishers, therefore, have certain obligations to data subjects from the DP Directive 95. They are bound by the obligation to provide information to data subjects about the data processing occurring as a result of the redirected browser and the advertising processing purposes,[201] and any further data processing carried out by the ad network providers, including cookie set up.[202]

WP29 Opinion 2/2010: Other Obligations from DP Directive 95

In addition to Article 5(3), data controllers must ensure compliance with all the obligations that arise from DP Directive 95 not overlapping with Article 5(3).

WP29 Opinion 2/2010: Obligations and Special Categories of Data

Data revealing racial or ethnic origin, political opinions, religious or philosophical beliefs, trade-union membership or data concerning health or sex life is considered sensitive (Article 8 of DP Directive 95). Targeting of data subjects based on sensitive personal data opens the possibility of abuse.[203] Such use is discouraged.[204]

However, if sensitive data is revealed to ad network providers, they must comply with Article 8 of DP Directive 95. Article 8 of DP Directive 95 prohibits the processing of sensitive data except in certain, specific circumstances. In this context, according to the Opinion, the only available legal ground that would legitimise such data processing would be explicit, separate prior opt-in consent (Article 8(2)(a)). The requirement of a separate, affirmative prior indication of the data subjects' agreement means that an opt-out consent mechanism would not meet the legal requirement.[205] Consent could not be obtained through browser settings. To lawfully collect and process such data, ad network providers need mechanisms to obtain explicit prior consent, separate from other consent obtained for processing in general.[206]

WP29 Opinion 2/2010: Compliance with Data Protection Principles

Behavioural advertising profiles could potentially be used for purposes other than advertising.[207]

---

201. *ibid.*
202. *ibid.*
203. *ibid.*
204. *ibid.*
205. *ibid.*
206. *ibid.*
207. *ibid.*

However, the purpose limitation principle (Article 6 of DP Directive 95) prohibits processing of personal data that is not compatible with the purposes that legitimised the initial collection.[208] Incompatible secondary uses of the information behavioural advertising data would breach Article 6(b) of DP Directive 95.[209]

If ad network providers want to use behavioural advertisement data for secondary, incompatible purposes, they need additional legal grounds to do so.[210] They will need to inform data subjects and, in most cases, obtain their additional consent (Article 7(a)).

Article 6(1)(e) requires data to be deleted when no longer necessary for the purpose for which the data were originally collected (the retention principle). This requires time limiting the storage of information, and ultimate deletion.

The information about users' behaviour has to be eliminated if it is no longer needed for the development of a profile.[211] Indefinite or overly long retention periods breach Article 6(1)(e) of the Directive.

Ad network providers should have policies to ensure that information collected each time a cookie is read is immediately deleted or anonymised once the necessity has expired.[212] The data controller needs to justify the necessity for any given retention period.[213]

If an individual asks for a deletion of their profile or if they exercise their right to withdraw their consent, the ad network provider must erase or delete promptly the data subject's information.[214] The ad network provider ceases to have the necessary legal grounds (i.e. the consent) required for the processing.[215]

WP29 Opinion 2/2010: Data Subjects' Rights

Individuals must be allowed to exercise their rights of access, rectification, erasure and to object to processing as set out in Articles 12 and 14 of the DP Directive 95.[216]

The Opinion refers to the development and rollout of new tools in this regard.[217]

---

208. *ibid.*
209. *ibid.*
210. *ibid.*
211. *ibid.*
212. *ibid.*
213. *ibid.*
214. *ibid.*
215. *ibid.*
216. *ibid.*
217. *ibid.*

WP29 Opinion 2/2010: Other Obligations

Article 17 of the Directive requires technical and organisational measures to protect personal data against accidental or unlawful destruction loss, disclosure, and other forms of unlawful processing. Compliance with the security obligations requires ad network providers to implement state-of-the-art technical and organisational measures to ensure the security and confidentiality of the information.[218]

If the data is transferred outside the EU, for example, to servers located in third countries, ad network providers must ensure compliance with the provisions on transfers of personal data to third countries (Articles 25 and 26 DP Directive 95).[219]

WP29 Opinion 2/2010: Recommendations

The Opinion notes that:

> Behavioural advertising techniques enable advertisers, mainly ad providers, to track individuals when they surf the internet, to build profiles and to use them to serve tailored advertising. In most cases, individuals are simply unaware that this is happening.[220]

It is "deeply concerned about ... this increasingly widespread practice".[221] It is "doubtful whether average individuals are aware of, much less that they consent to, being monitored to receive tailored advertising".[222]

Policies or notices provided in general terms and conditions and/or privacy policies, "often drafted in rather obscure ways, fall short of the requirements of data protection legislation".[223]

Article 5(3) applies whenever information such as a cookie is stored or retrieved from user terminal equipment.[224] "It is not a prerequisite that this information is personal data."[225]

In addition, the DP Directive 95[226] applies to matters not specifically covered by the

---

218. *ibid.*
219. *ibid.*
220. *ibid.*
221. *ibid.*
222. *ibid.*
223. *ibid.*
224. *ibid.*
225. *ibid.*
226. EU Data Protection Directive 1995 *supra.*

ePrivacy Directive whenever personal data are processed.[227] Behavioural advertising includes use of personal data.[228]

WP29 Opinion 2/2010: Roles and Responsibilities

Ad network providers must comply with Article 5(3) of the ePrivacy Directive as they place cookies and/or retrieve information from cookies already stored in the data subjects' terminal equipment.[229] They are also data controllers as they determine the purposes and the essential means of the processing of data.[230]

Publishers have data controller-responsibilities regarding the first phase of the processing, i.e. when by virtue of the way they configure their websites to trigger the transfer of the IP address to ad network providers (enabling the further processing).[231] If publishers transfer directly identifiable personal data to ad network providers themselves, they will be deemed joint controllers.[232]

WP29 Opinion 2/2010: Obligations and Rights Regarding Ad Network Providers

The Article 5(3) of the ePrivacy Directive obligation to obtain prior informed consent, applies to ad network providers.

Browsers must either alone or in combination with other means effectively convey clear, comprehensive and fully visible information about the proposed processing.[233]

Cookie-based opt-out mechanisms generally do not constitute an adequate mechanism to obtain informed user consent.[234]

Ad network providers must move away from opt-out mechanisms and create prior opt-in mechanisms.[235] Mechanisms to deliver informed, valid consent should require an affirmative action by the data subject indicating their agreement to receive cookies and also the subsequent monitoring of their surfing behaviour for the purposes of sending tailored advertising.[236]

---

227. *ibid.*
228. *ibid.*
229. *ibid.*
230. *ibid.*
231. *ibid.*
232. *ibid.*
233. *ibid.*
234. *ibid.*
235. *ibid.*
236. *ibid.*

To ensure that data subjects remain aware of the monitoring over time, ad network providers should:

> i) limit in time the scope of the consent; ii) offer the possibility to easily revoke their consent to being monitored for the purposes of serving behavioural advertising and iii) create a symbol or other tools which should be visible in all the websites where the monitoring takes place (the website partners of the ad network provider). This symbol would not only remind individuals of the monitoring but also help them to control whether they want to continue being monitored or wish to revoke their consent.[237]

Network providers should also ensure compliance with the DP Directive 95 requirements that do not directly overlap with Article 5(3), namely, the purpose limitation principle and security obligations.

Ad network providers should also allow individuals to exercise their rights of access, rectification and erasure.[238]

Ad network providers must implement retention policies that ensure that information collected each time a cookie is read, are automatically deleted after the justified time period.[239] This also applies for alternative tracking technologies used for behavioural advertising e.g. JavaScript.[240]

Ad network providers and publishers should note that providing highly visible information is a precondition for consent to be valid.[241]

Ad network providers and publishers must provide information to users in compliance with Article 10 of the DP Directive 95. Individuals at a minimum must be told which entity is responsible for serving the cookie and collecting the related information.[242] They must also be informed in simple ways that:

> (a) the cookie will be used to create profiles; (b) what type of information will be collected to build such profiles; (c) the fact that the profiles will be used to deliver targeted advertising and (d) the fact that the cookie will enable the user's identification across multiple websites.[243]

Network providers and publishers should provide the information directly on the website screen, interactively, if needed, and through layered notices.[244] They should be easily accessible and highly visible.[245]

---

237. *ibid.*
238. *ibid.*
239. *ibid.*
240. *ibid.*
241. *ibid.*
242. *ibid.*
243. *ibid.*
244. *ibid.*
245. *ibid.*

WP29: Opinion 16/2011 on OBA

The Article 29 Working Party Opinion 16/2011 on EASA/IAB Best Practice Recommendation on Online Behavioural Advertising (WP 188) was adopted on 8 December 2011. It comments on suggested policies by EASA/IAB.

It notes that Directive 2009/136/EC revises the ePrivacy Directive. One of the key changes concerns the mechanisms for implanting information in the user's terminal device.[246] The existing opt-out regime, where a user can object to the processing of information collected via terminal equipment (e.g. "cookies") was rejected.[247]

The standard became one of informed consent.[248] This includes the online behavioural advertising industry.[249] This reflects the growing concern with technical possibilities to track individual's internet behaviour over time and across different websites.[250] Policymakers had doubts the advertising industry increasing public awareness and user choice regarding online behavioural advertising.[251] The Opinion notes that the "rapid replacement of 'fixed' internet access by mobile access has even further complicated the ability of internet users to protect themselves with technical means".[252]

Opinion 2/2010 on Online Behavioural Advertising (OBA) describes the roles and responsibilities of the different actors engaged in online behavioural advertising.

In April 2011 the European Advertising Standards Alliance (EASA) and the Internet Advertising Bureau Europe (IAB), adopted a self-regulatory Best Practice Recommendation on online behavioural advertising ("EASA/IAB Code").[253] The Article 29 Working Party was concerned with the opt-out approach suggested within the EASA/IAB Code.[254] While welcome, the Opinion notes that the EASA/IAB Code is not adequate to ensure compliance with the European data protection regime.[255]

The Opinion focuses on the first two principles of the EASA/IAB Code, namely, Principle I (Notice) and Principle II (User Choice). Some examples of possibly exempted cookies are also discussed.[256]

---

246. Article 29 Working Party Opinion 16/2011 on EASA/IAB Best Practice Recommendation on Online Behavioural Advertising (WP 188).
247. *ibid.*
248. *ibid.*
249. *ibid.*
250. *ibid.*
251. *ibid.*
252. *ibid.*
253. *ibid.*
254. *ibid.*
255. *ibid.*
256. *ibid.*

Under Article 5(3), the relevant information notice must be provided directly to the users in a clear and understandable form before the processing takes place.[257] It is not enough for information to be "available" somewhere on the website.[258]

Opinion 2/2010 stated that:

> from the literal wording of Article 5(3): i) consent must be obtained before the cookie is placed and/or information stored in the user's terminal equipment is collected, which is usually referred to as prior consent and ii) informed consent can only be obtained if prior information about the sending and purposes of the cookie has been given to the user. In this context, it is important to take into account that for consent to be valid whatever the circumstances in which it is given, it must be freely given, specific and constitute an informed indication of the data subject's wishes. Consent must be obtained before the personal data are collected, as a necessary measure to ensure that data subjects can fully appreciate that they are consenting and what they are consenting to. Furthermore, consent must be revocable.[259]

The EASA/IAB "choice" is "not" consistent with Article 5(3) of the revised ePrivacy Directive,[260] as the data are processed without the user's consent and without providing the user with information before the processing takes place.[261]

The Opinion clarifies that consent is not required for every type of cookie, as there are different ways to use cookies with different purposes and requirements associated with them.[262] According to Article 5(3) of the revised ePrivacy Directive, a cookie may be exempted from informed consent if it is "necessary to carry out the transmission of an electronic communications network" or if "it is strictly necessary in order to provide an information society service explicitly requested by the subscriber or user to provide that service".[263]

The opinion provides examples of cookies that could be exempted from informed consent:

- A secure login session cookie. This type of cookie is designed to identify the user once [they have] logged in to an information society service and is necessary to recognise him or her, maintaining the consistency of the communication with the server over the communication network;

- A shopping-basket cookie. On a shopping website, this type of cookie is typically used to store the reference of items the user has selected by clicking on a button

---

257. *ibid.*
258. *ibid.*
259. *ibid.*
260. *ibid.*
261. *ibid.*
262. *ibid.*
263. *ibid.*

(e.g. "add to my shopping cart"). This cookie is thus necessary to provide an information society service explicitly requested by the user;

- Security cookies. Cookies which provide security that are essential to comply with the security requirements of the ePrivacy Directive for an information society service explicitly requested by the user. For example, a cookie may be used to store a unique identifier to allow the information society service to provide additional assurance in the recognition of returning users. Attempted logins from previously unseen devices could prompt for additional security questions.[264]

However, while some cookies may be exempted from the informed consent required by Article 5(3) of the ePrivacy Directive, they may still be used for data processing that must comply with the DP Directive 1995. Providers of information society services still have to comply with the obligation to inform users.[265]

Pop up screens are not the only way to obtain consent. Other examples of user-friendly ways to obtain consent are:

- A static information banner on top of a website requesting the user's consent to set some cookies, with a hyperlink to a privacy statement with a more detailed explanation about the different data controllers and the purposes of the processing...;

- A splash screen on entering the website explaining what cookies will be set by what parties if the user consents. Such splash screens are being used by, for example, breweries that wish to ensure their visitors are old enough to be allowed to visit the website;

- A default setting prohibiting the transfer of data to external parties, requiring a user click to indicate consent for tracking purposes. A practical technical solution has been developed by the German ezine Heise with regard to cookies set and read by Facebook with the help of its 'Like' button. By default, the button is light-grey. Only if the user clicks on the button, it will be highlighted and become able to set and receive user data;

- A default setting in browsers that would prevent the collection of behavioural data (Do not collect). Recital 66 of the amended DP Directive 95suggests browser settings as a way to obtain consent, provided that they are 'technically possible and effective, in accordance with the relevant provisions of' [DP Directive 95].[266]

Data subjects cannot be deemed to have consented simply because they acquired/used a browser or other application.[267] For browsers or any other application to deliver valid and effective consent, they must require the data subject to engage in

---

264. *ibid.*
265. *ibid.*
266. *ibid.*
267. *ibid.*

an affirmative action to accept both the setting of and continued transmission of information contained in cookies by specific websites.[268]

Users should receive the relevant information on data processing as a preliminary step to installing the specific "advertising" plug-in. One might argue that a prerequisite for this opt-in mechanism to work appropriately consists in ensuring that third-party cookies are not accepted by default in browser settings.

The Opinion welcomes recent initiatives such as Do Not Track.[269]

The Opinion states that the EASA/IAB website www.youronlinechoices.eu approach could be reengineered to provide an "opt-in" approach.[270] The following example is given:

- The first time a user comes in contact with an OBA provider (through a website visit), no cookie has been set, and thus no cookie will be sent to the ad network provider. The ad provider can display a message in any type of information area (including the area where the advertisement would appear) to propose a choice to the user:
  - accept an "opt-in" cookie for the purpose of future behavioural advertising;
  - refuse cookies for the purpose of behavioural advertising, at the same time accepting a cookie containing the word "Refuse" so that this refusal can be recorded going forward;
  - store no cookie at all. In that case, the user will be asked again about their choice during the next visit;

- When the user comes into contact with the same OBA provider again, the ad provider could adjust its behaviour according to three possible scenarios:
  - if there is an "opt-in" cookie, the OBA provider can access and store cookies on the user's terminal and provide behavioural advertising;
  - if there is a "Refuse" cookie, the OBA provider will know that the user refuses future cookies (and thus behavioural advertising), and will stick to untargeted ads;
  - if there is no cookie at all, the OBA provider will consider that this is the user's first contact with him and will ask him about their choice.[271]

---

268. *ibid.*
269. *ibid.*
270. *ibid.*
271. *ibid.*

WP29: Opinion on ePrivacy Directive Cookie Amendment

The WP29, for example, issued an opinion on cookies. *Opinion 04/2012 on Cookie Consent Exemption* was issued on 7 June 2012.[272]

WP29 states that the new amendment has:

> reinforced the protection of users of electronic communication networks and services by requiring informed consent before information is stored or accessed in the user's (or subscriber's) terminal device. The requirement applies to all types of information stored or accessed in the user's terminal device although the majority of discussion has centred on the usage of cookies.[273]

Generally customers' informed consent is required. However, now under Article 5.3, exemptions from requiring informed consent can apply to cookies if either:

- the cookie is used "for the sole purpose of carrying out the transmission of a communication over an electronic communications network" (Condition A); OR

- the cookie is "strictly necessary in order for the provider of an information society service explicitly requested by the subscriber or user to provide the service" (Condition B).[274]

WP29: Condition A

The phrase "sole purpose" in Condition A limits the types of processing using cookies. Simply using a cookie to assist, speed up or regulate the transmission over an electronic communications network is not sufficient. The transmission "must *not be possible without* the use of the cookie".[275]

Three elements arise in considering the strictly necessary criteria, namely:

- the ability to route the information over the network, notably by identifying the communication endpoints;

- the ability to exchange data items in their intended order, notably by numbering data packets; and

---

272. Opinion 04/2012 on Cookie Consent Exemption, art 9 Working Party, 7 June 2012, available at http://ec.europa.eu/justice/data-protection/article-29/documentation/opinion-recommendation/files/2012/wp194_en.pdf, last accessed 12 September 2012.

273. *ibid.* The Opinion explains how revised art 5.3 impacts on the use of cookies but and potentially similar technologies.

274. *ibid.*

275. *ibid.*

- the ability to detect transmission errors or data loss.[276]

Condition A "encompasses cookies that fulfil at least one of the properties defined above for Internet communications".[277]

WP29: Condition B

The Opinion states that the Condition B exemption criteria must remain high.[278] A cookie matching CRITERION B has to pass two tests simultaneously, namely:

- the information society service is explicitly requested by the user: the user (or subscriber) by positive action requested a service with a clearly defined perimeter; and

- the cookie is strictly needed to enable the information society service: if cookies are disabled, the service will not work.[279]

Recital 66 of Directive 2009/136/EC underlines that:

> Exceptions to the obligation to provide information and offer the right to refuse should be limited to those situations where the technical storage or access is strictly necessary for the legitimate purpose of enabling the use of a specific service explicitly requested by the subscriber or user.

The Opinion states that there has to be a clear link between the strict necessity of a cookie and the delivery of the service explicitly requested by the user for the exemption to apply.

A cookie matching Condition B would need to pass the following tests:

- a cookie is necessary to provide a specific functionality to the user (or subscriber): if cookies are disabled, the functionality will not be available; and

- this functionality has been explicitly requested by the user (or subscriber), as part of an information society service.[280]

---

276. *ibid.*
277. *ibid.*
278. *ibid.*
279. *ibid.*
280. *ibid.*

WP29: Characteristics of a Cookie

Cookies are, according to the Opinion, often categorised according to whether they are "session cookies" or "persistent cookies";[281] or whether they are "third-party cookies" or not.[282]

A cookie exempted from consent should have a lifespan in direct relation to the purpose it is used for, and must be set to expire once not needed, reflecting the reasonable expectations of users.

Third-party cookies are usually not "strictly necessary" and relate to a service distinct from the service "explicitly requested" by the user. Therefore, first-party session cookies are more likely exempted from consent than third-party persistent cookies. The Opinion states that ultimately the purpose and the specific processing will determine whether or not a cookie can be exempted from consent according to Condition A or B. Permanent cookies on the user's computer are unlikely to be exempted.

WP29: Multipurpose Cookies

A cookie for several purposes may only be exempted from consent if all the distinct purposes for which the cookie is used are individually exempted from consent.

Tracking is unlikely to meet Condition A or B. A website would need to seek user consent for the tracking purpose.

The Opinion refers to some examples of cookie use, such as:

- user-input cookies;
- authentication cookies;
- field code changed;
- user centric security cookies;
- multimedia player session cookies;
- UI customisation cookies; and
- social plug-in content sharing cookies.[283]

---

281. A "session cookie" is a cookie that is automatically deleted when the user closes his browser. A "persistent cookie" is a cookie that remains stored in the user's terminal device until it reaches a defined expiration date (which can be minutes, days or several years in the future).
282. The Opinion uses the term "third party cookie" to describe cookies that are set by data controllers that do not operate the website currently visited by the user.
283. *ibid.*

WP29: Non-Exempted Cookies

Some cookie-usage scenarios do not fall in the exemption afforded under Condition A or B. Examples include:

- social plug-in tracking cookies;
- third-party advertising; and
- first-party analytics.

Social plug-in tracking cookies can also be used to track individuals, both members and non-members, with third-party cookies for additional purposes such as behavioural advertising, analytics or market research, for example. These cookies are not "strictly necessary" to provide functionality explicitly requested by the user. Such tracking cookies cannot be exempted under Condition B. Without consent, there is unlikely a legal basis for social networks collecting data through social plug-ins about non-members of their network. By default, social plug-ins should thus not set a third-party cookie in pages displayed to non-members.[284]

As regards third-party advertising, the Opinion states that third-party cookies used for behavioural advertising are not exempted from consent.[285] Consent is required for all related third-party operational cookies.[286]

WP29: Opinion Summary and Guidelines

The Opinion provides the following guide of cookies that can be exempted from informed consent under certain conditions and if they are not used for additional purposes:

- user input cookies (session-id), for the duration of a session or persistent cookies limited to a few hours in some cases;
- authentication cookies, used for authenticated services, for the duration of a session;
- user-centric security cookies, used to detect authentication abuses, for a limited persistent duration;
- multimedia content player session cookies, such as flash player cookies, for the duration of a session;
- load balancing session cookies, for the duration of session;
- UI customisation persistent cookies, for the duration of a session (or slightly more); and

---

284. *ibid.*
285. This is already noted in Opinion 2/2010 and Opinion 16/2011.
286. *ibid.*

- third-party social plug-in content sharing cookies, for logged in members of a social network.[287]

In relation to social networks, the WP29 notes that the use of third-party social plug-in cookies for other purposes than to provide a functionality explicitly requested by their own members requires consent, notably if these purposes involve tracking users across websites.[288]

The WP29 notes[289] that third-party advertising cookies cannot be exempted from consent, and further clarifies that consent would also be needed for operational purposes related to third-party advertising such as frequency capping, financial logging, ad affiliation, click-fraud detection, research and market analysis, product improvement and debugging.

While some operational purposes may distinguish one user from another, in principle these purposes do not justify the use of unique identifiers. This is relevant in the context of the discussions regarding the implementation of the Do Not Track standard in Europe.[290]

Some primary guidelines offered by the Opinion include:

- when applying Condition B, it is important to examine what is strictly necessary from the point of view of the user, not the service provider;
- if a cookie is used for several purposes, it can only benefit from an exemption to informed consent if each distinct purpose individually benefits from such an exemption; and
- first-party session cookies are far more likely to be exempted from consent than third-party persistent cookies. However, the purpose of the cookie should always be the basis for evaluating if the exemption can be successfully applied rather than a technical feature of the cookie.[291]

Ultimately, the Opinion recommends that to decide if a cookie is exempt from the principle of informed consent it is important to verify carefully if it fulfils one of the two exemption criteria defined in Article 5.3 as modified by Directive 2009/136/EC. After a careful examination, if substantial doubts remain on whether or not an exemption criterion applies, websites should closely examine if there is not in practice an opportunity to gain consent from users in a simple, unobtrusive way, thus avoiding any legal uncertainty.[292]

---

287. *ibid.*
288. *ibid.*
289. *ibid.*
290. *ibid.*
291. *ibid.*
292. *ibid.*

Conclusion

In relation to cookies and the new amending Regulations the UK ICO recommends that organisations:

- check what type of cookies and similar technologies the organisation uses and how it uses them;

- assess how intrusive the organisation's use of cookies is; and

- where the organisation needs consent, decide what solution to obtain consent will be best in the circumstances.[293]

As stated in its Opinion 2/2010, the WP29 does not question the economic benefits that behavioural advertising may bring, but it firmly believes that such practices must not be carried out at the expense of individuals' rights to privacy and data protection. The EU data protection regulatory framework sets forth specific safeguards that must be respected.

Adherence to the EASA/IAB Code on online behavioural advertising and participation in the website www.youronlinechoices.eu may not result in compliance with the current ePrivacy Directive. Moreover, the Code and the website create the wrong presumption that it is possible to choose not be tracked while surfing the web. This wrong presumption can be damaging to users but also to the industry if organisations believe that by applying the Code they meet the data protection requirements.

The advertising industry needs to comply with the precise requirements of the ePrivacy Directive[294] and the Opinion shows that many practical solutions are available to ensure a good level of compliance together with a good user experience.

While the technicalities of cookies can be a little complex, and it is sometimes easy for an organisation to look straight at the potential data available via the use of cookies, it is critical for organisations to consider the new rules. Some cookie use may be permitted, but clearly some are not. Organisations and those responsible for web development need to reassess their current online practices to ensure full compliance. It may mean a period of adjustment as organisations, and developers, come to grips with understanding what personal data is required and what may be gathered legitimately by permitted cookies.

---

293. *Privacy and Electronic Communications Regulations, Guidance on the Rules on Use of Cookies and Similar Technologies*, ICO (May 2012), available at http://www.ico.gov.uk/for_organisations/privacy_and_electronic_communications/the_guide/cookies.aspx, last accessed 25 August 2012.

294. Directive 2002/58/EC of the European Parliament and of the Council of 12 July 2002 concerning the processing of personal data and the protection of privacy in the electronic communications sector (Directive on privacy and electronic communications)(as amended by Directives 2006/24/EC and 2009/136/EC).

More recently the Data Protection Commissioner has begun to directly contact organisations to query their implementing of the new cookie rules. The websites and organisations targeted must respond within 21 days outlining their compliance arrangements.[295] The first set of letters were aimed at eighty organisations. This may be expanded in later phases. In either event, the importance of compliance is being highlighted, including the possibility of prosecution for non-compliance. The Deputy Data Protection Commissioner has indicated that "we will be obliged to take enforcement action where websites fail to engage with us and meet their legal obligations".[296]

---

295. See Data Protection Commissioner press statement, "Data Protection Commissioner Commences Action On 'Cookie' Law", December 2012, available at www.dataprotection.ie/viewdoc.asp?DocID=1274&m=f, accessed on 1 January 2013.

296. *ibid.*

CHAPTER 20

Enforcement Powers

Introduction

What happens if an organisation does not comply with the data protection regime when dealing with customers', etc. (referred to collectively as "customers") personal data?

As indicated previously there can be consequences in terms of due diligence, value and the ability to maintain a customer database.

When things go wrong, there can be legal and publicity consequences for the organisation. The impact of a data protection breach can mean an immediate multi team effort to deal with the data protection breach.

In dealing with an incident, and in planning for compliance with customers' personal data, organisations should be aware of the various Data Protection Commissioner enforcement powers. These emphasise the importance of consequences for non-compliance. Enforcement proceedings can be issued by the Data Protection Commissioner. Significant fines and penalties can result. Also, potentially individual customers may decide to sue for damage, loss and breach of their personal data rights.

Enforcement Powers of Data Protection Commissioner

The Data Protection Commissioner has a number of powers of enforcement available to him. These include the following.[1]

Investigations by the Data Protection Commissioner

Under s 10 of the Data Protection Acts,[2] the Data Protection Commissioner will investigate any complaints he receives from individuals who feel that personal

---

1. See DPC, available at http://www.dataprotection.ie/viewdoc.asp?DocID=569, last accessed 24 October 2012.
2. Data Protection Act 1988 and Data Protection (Amendment) Act 2003.

information about them is not being treated in accordance with the Acts, unless he is of the opinion that such complaints are "frivolous or vexatious". The Data Protection Commissioner notifies the complainant in writing of his decision regarding the complaint. The Data Protection Commissioner's decision can be appealed to the Circuit Court.

The Data Protection Commissioner may also launch investigations on his own initiative, where he is of the opinion that there might be a breach of the Data Protection Acts,[3] or he considers it appropriate in order to ensure compliance with the Data Protection Acts.[4]

Power to Obtain Information

Under s 12 of the Data Protection Acts,[5] the Data Protection Commissioner may require any person to provide him with whatever information the Data Protection Commissioner needs to carry out his functions, such as to pursue an investigation. The Data Protection Commissioner exercises this power by providing a written notice, called an "information notice", to the person.

A person who receives an information notice has the right to appeal it to the Circuit Court. Failure to comply with an information notice without reasonable excuse is an offence. Knowingly to provide false information, or information that is misleading in a material respect, in response to an information notice is an offence. No legal prohibition may stand in the way of compliance with an information notice. The only exceptions to compliance with an information notice are (i) where the information in question is or was, in the opinion of the Minister for Justice, Equality and Law Reform, or in the opinion of the Minister for Defence, kept for the purpose of safeguarding the security of the State, and (ii) where the information is privileged from disclosure in proceedings in any court.

Power to Enforce Compliance with the Data Protection Acts

Under s 10 of the Data Protection Acts, the Data Protection Commissioner may require a data controller or data processor to take whatever steps the Commissioner considers appropriate to comply with the terms of the Data Protection Acts. Such steps could include correcting the data, blocking the data from use for certain purposes, supplementing the data with a statement that the Commissioner approves, or erasing the data altogether. The Data Protection Commissioner exercises this power by providing a written notice, called an enforcement notice, to the data controller or data processor. A person who receives an enforcement notice has the right to appeal it

---

3.   *ibid.*
4.   *ibid.*
5.   *ibid.*

to the Circuit Court. It is an offence to fail or refuse to comply with an enforcement notice without reasonable excuse.

Power to Prohibit Overseas Transfer of Personal Data

Under s 11 of the Data Protection Acts, the Data Protection Commissioner may prohibit the transfer of personal data from the State to a place outside the State. The Data Protection Commissioner exercises this power by providing a written notice, called a prohibition notice, to the data controller or data processor. In considering whether to exercise this power, the Data Protection Commissioner must have regard to the need to facilitate international transfers of information.

A prohibition notice may be absolute, or may prohibit the transfer of personal data until the person concerned takes certain steps to protect the interests of the individuals affected. A person who receives an enforcement notice has the right to appeal it to the Circuit Court. It is an offence to fail or refuse to comply with a prohibition specified in a prohibition notice without reasonable excuse.

Powers of Authorised Officers to Enter and Examine

Under s 24 of the Data Protection Acts, the Data Protection Commissioner may appoint an authorised officer to enter and examine the premises of a data controller or data processor, to enable the Data Protection Commissioner to carry out his functions, such as to pursue an investigation. The authorised officer, upon production of written authorisation from the Data Protection Commissioner, has the power to:

- enter the premises and inspect any data equipment there;
- require the data controller, data processor or staff to assist in obtaining access to data, and to provide any related information;
- inspect and copy any information; and
- require the data controller, data processor or staff to provide information about procedures on complying with the Act, sources of data, purposes for which personal data are kept, persons to whom data are disclosed, and data equipment on the premises.

It is an offence to obstruct or impede an authorised officer; to fail to comply with any of the requirements set out above; or knowingly to give false or misleading information to an authorised officer.

Prosecution of Offences

Section 30 of the Data Protection Acts provides that the Data Protection Commissioner may bring summary proceedings for an offence under the Data Protection Acts. The Data Protection Commissioner also has the power to prosecute offences in relation to unsolicited marketing under SI 535/2003 (Electronic Communications Regulations) (as amended by SI 526/2008).

Conclusion

Even general personal data is considered important and sensitive to customers. This should be respected by organisations. Organisations are not permitted to collect nor process customers' personal data without being data protection compliant. It is in this context that there can be severe consequences for an organisation for non-compliance, whether in collecting personal data initially or in the subsequent processing of the personal data. The Data Protection Commissioner can prosecute for non-compliance. Alternatively, enforcement notices can be imposed that specify certain actions that must be implemented by the organisation. Certain types of organisations can be the recipient of separate types of notices, namely assessment notices. In any of these events, customers will be particularly concerned that their personal data has been collected, is being processed in a certain manner and/or may have been subject to a breach event. This can have its own consequences. Overall, it should also be noted that the consequences of breach or non-compliance are becoming increasingly important as enforcement actions and penalties are increasing in number and financial scale.

CHAPTER 21

Trans-Border Data Flows/Transfers of Personal Data

Introduction

Organisations are under ever-increasing pressure to reduce costs. This can sometimes involve consideration of outsourcing to countries outside of the EEA. Personal data transfers, unless specifically excepted, can be restricted.

In addition, the global nature of commercial activities means that organisations as part of normal business processes may seek to transfer particular sets of personal data to group entities who may be located outside of the EEA. There can be similar situations where an organisation wishes to make trans-border data flows to agents, partners or outsourced data processors.

The data protection regime controls and regulates the transfers of personal data[1] from Ireland to jurisdictions outside of the EEA. The transfer of personal data outside of the EU/EEA are known as Trans-Border Data Flows (TBDFs).[2] Frequently organisations would have transferred personal data to other sections within their international organisations, e.g. banks. This could be personal data in relation to customers as well as employees (e.g. where the HR or payroll section may be in a different country).

This trend of TDBFs has increased, however, as more and more activity is carried out online, such as eCommerce and social networking. Personal data is frequently transferred or mirrored on computer servers in more than one country as a matter of

---

1. See Nugter, *Transborder Flow of Personal Data within the EC* (Boston: Kluwer Law and Taxation Publishers, 1990).

2. Beling, "Transborder Data Flows: International Privacy Protection and the Free Flow of Information" (1983)(6) *Boston College International and Comparative Law Review* 591–624; "Declaration on Transborder Data Flows" (1985)(24) *International Legal Materials* 912–913; "Council Recommendation Concerning Guidelines Governing the Protection of Privacy and Transborder Flows of Personal Data" (1981)(20) *International Legal Materials* 422–450; "Draft Recommendation of the Council Concerning Guidelines the Protection of Privacy and Transborder Flows of Personal Data" (1980)(19) *International Legal Materials* 318–324.

technical routine.

However, organisations need to be aware that any transfer of personal data of EU citizens needs to be in compliance with the EU data protection regime. One of the restrictions is that TBDFs of personal data may not occur.[3] This default position can be derogated from if one of a limited number of criteria are satisfied.

Transfer Ban

Section 11 of the Data Protection Acts[4] and the DP Directive 95[5] provides a default position of banning the export or trans-border data flows to countries outside of the EEA.

Section 11 of the Data Protection Acts provides as follows:

(1) The transfer of personal data to a country or territory outside the European Economic Area may not take place unless that country or territory ensures an adequate level of protection for the privacy and the fundamental rights and freedoms of data subjects in relation to the processing of personal data, having regard to all the circumstances surrounding the transfer and, in particular, but without prejudice to, the generality of the foregoing, to:

   (a) the nature of the data;

   (b) the purposes for which and the period during which the data are intended to be processed;

   (c) the country or territory of origin of the information contained in the data;

   (d) the country or territory of final destination of that information;

   (e) the law in force in the country or territory referred to in paragraph (d);

   (f) any relevant codes of conduct or other rules that are enforceable in that country or territory;

   (g) any security measures taken in respect of the data in that country or territory; and

   (h) the international obligations of that country or territory.

---

3. For one article noting the difficulties that the data protection regime creates in terms of trans border data flows, see Kong, "Data Protection and Trans Border Data Flow in the European and Global Context" (2010)(21) *European Journal of International Law* 441–456.
4. Data Protection Act 1988 and Data Protection (Amendment) Act 2003.
5. EU Data Protection Directive 1995 (Directive 95/46/EC of the European Parliament and of the Council of 24 October 1995 on the protection of individuals with regard to the processing of personal data and on the free movement of such data).

Article 25 of the DP Directive 95 prohibits the transfer of data outside of the EEA unless:

- the third country ensures appropriate levels of protection (Article 25); or

- the transfer can come within one of the exemptions (Article 26).

The regime created under DP Directive 95 means transfers are prohibited *per se* and is thus focused upon privacy protection and the dangers of uncontrolled transfers of personal data.

The Data Protection Acts sets out in the eighth Data Protection Principle that the:

> Transfer of personal data to a country or territory outside the European Economic Area [EEA] may not take place unless that country or territory ensures an adequate level of protection for the privacy and the fundamental rights and freedoms of data subjects in relation to the processing of personal data. (section 11)

Data protection compliance practice for organisations means that they will have to include a compliance assessment as well as an assessment of the risks associated with transfers of personal data outside of the EEA. This applies to transfers from parent to subsidiary or to a branch office in the same way as a transfer to an unrelated company or entity.

Data Protection Acts: Adequate Protection Exception

If the recipient country has been deemed by the EU to already have an adequate level of protection for personal data, then the transfer is permitted. It is provided that a transfer can occur where there has been a positive Community finding in relation to the type of transfer proposed. A Community finding means a finding of the European Commission, under the procedure provided for in Article 31(2) of the DP Directive 95, that a country or territory outside the European Economic Area does, or does not, ensure an adequate level of protection within the meaning of Article 25(2) of the Directive (see s 11(2) of the Data Protection Acts).

The EU Commission provides a list of Commission decisions on the adequacy of the protection of personal data in third countries.[6] The EU Commission has thus far recognised that Switzerland, Canada, Argentina, Guernsey, Isle of Man, the US Department of Commerce's Safe Harbor Privacy Principles, and the transfer of air passenger name records to the United States Bureau of Customs and Border Protection as providing adequate protection.

---

6.   Available at http://ec.europa.eu/justice/policies/privacy/thridcountries/index_en.htm, last accessed 11 January 2013.

Exceptions

If the recipient country's protection is not adequate, or perhaps not ascertainable, but a transfer is still preferred, the organisation should then ascertain if the transfer comes within one of the other excepted categories.

Transfers of personal data from Ireland to outside the EEA cannot occur unless exempted, such as:

- the data subject has given consent;

- the transfer is necessary for performance of contract between data subject and controller;

- the transfer is necessary for taking steps at the request of data subject with a view to entering into contract with the data controller;

- the transfer is necessary for the conclusion of a contract between the data controller and a person other than the data subject that is entered into at the request of the data subject and is in the interests of the data subject;

- the transfer is necessary for the performance of such a contract;

- the transfer is required or authorised under any enactment or instrument imposing international obligations on Ireland;

- the transfer is necessary for reasons of substantial public interest;

- the transfer is necessary for purposes of or in connection with legal proceedings or prospective legal proceedings;

- the transfer is necessary in order to prevent injury or damage to the health of the data subject or serious loss of or damage to the property of the data subject or serious loss of or damage to the property of the data subject or otherwise to protect vital interests;

- subject to certain conditions, the transfer is only part of the personal data on a register established by or under an enactment;

- the transfer has been authorised by data protection commissioners where the data controller adduces adequate safeguards;

- the transfer is made to a country that has been determined by the EU Commission as having "adequate levels of protection";

- the transfer is made to a US entity that has signed up to the EU/US "Safe Harbour" arrangements; or

- the EU Commission contract provisions (i.e. the Model Contract clauses issues by the Commission) apply.

Therefore, for example, where a customer books a hotel in New York through an agent in Dublin, it is necessary for the ultimate performance of the contract for the personal data to be transferred to the hotel in New York from Ireland. The transfer of the personal data is likely permitted.

However, when an Irish company transfers its employee payroll personal data to a US parent company, such a transfer is for the convenience of the company and is not strictly necessary for the performance of a contract.

Creating Adequacy through Consent, Contract

One solution involves "creating adequacy" through consent. Under Article 26 of DP Directive 95, transfers can be made to a non-EEA country where the unambiguous consent of the data subject to that transfer is obtained. Transfers of data to a third country may be made even though there is not adequate protection in place, *if* the data controller secures the necessary level of protection through contractual obligations. This refers to the model contract clauses from Commission. The Commission has issued what it considers to be adequate clauses which, incorporated into the contract relationship of the data exporter and data importer, should then provide an adequate level of consent.

Section 11(6) of the Data Protection Acts also provides that if data controller adduces the safeguards for the data subject concerned referred to in subsection (4)(a)(ix) of the section by means of a contract embodying the contractual clauses referred to in Article 26(2) or (4) of the Directive, the data subject shall have the same right, (a) to enforce a clause of the contract conferring rights on him or relating to such rights, and (b) to compensation or damages for breach of such a clause, that he would have if he were a party to the contract.

Binding Corporate Rules

The Commission and the WP29[7] also developed a policy of recognising adequate protection of the policies of multinational organisations transferring personal data that satisfy the determined binding corporate rules, pursuant to DP Directive 95 Article 26(2).[8] Organisations that have contracts, policies and procedures that satisfy

---

7. Article 29 Working Party Recommendation 1/2007 on the Standard Application for Approval of Binding Corporate Rules for the Transfer of Personal Data; Working Document setting up a table with the elements and principles to be found in Binding Corporate Rules, WP 153 (2008); Working Document Setting up a framework for the structure of Binding Corporate Rules, WP154 (2008); Working Document on Frequently Asked Questions (FAQs) related to Binding Corporate Rules, WP155 (2008).
8. See http://ec.europa.eu/justice/policies/privacy/binding_rules/index_en.htm, last accessed 13 September 2012; Moerel, *Binding Corporate Rules, Corporate Self-Regulation of Global Data Transfers* (Oxford: OUP, 2012).

the binding corporate rules and are so accepted as doing so after a review process with the Commission or one of the Member State data protection authorities can transfer personal data outside of the EU within the organisation. Recently, Intel and its binding corporate rules have been examined and approved by the Data Protection Commissioner.[9] This now provides a passporting type recognition in the EU Member States.

DP Directive 95: Transfers Ban in Detail

DP Directive 95 Article 25 refers to the principles. Article 25(1) provides that the Member States shall provide that the transfer to a third country of personal data that are undergoing processing or are intended for processing after transfer may take place only if, without prejudice to compliance with the Member State provisions adopted pursuant to the other provisions of the Directive, the third country in question ensures an adequate level of protection.

Article 25(2) provides that the adequacy of the level of protection afforded by a third country shall be assessed in the light of all the circumstances surrounding a data transfer operation or set of data transfer operations; particular consideration shall be given to the nature of the data, the purpose and duration of the proposed processing operation or operations, the country of origin and country of final destination, the rules of law, both general and sectoral, in force in the third country in question, and the professional rules and security measures that are complied with in that country.

Article 25(3) provides that the Member States and the Commission shall inform each other of cases where they consider that a third country does not ensure an adequate level of protection within the meaning of paragraph 2.

Article 25(4) provides that where the Commission finds, under the procedure provided for in Article 31 (2), that a third country does not ensure an adequate level of protection within the meaning of paragraph 2 of this Article, Member States shall take the measures necessary to prevent any transfer of data of the same type to the third country in question.

Article 25(4) provides that at the appropriate time, the Commission shall enter into negotiations with a view to remedying the situation resulting from the finding made pursuant to paragraph 4.

Article 25(6) provides that the Commission may find, in accordance with the procedure referred to in Article 31 (2), that a third country ensures an adequate level of protection within the meaning of paragraph 2 of this Article, by reason of its domestic law or of the international commitments it has entered into, particularly

---

9.   See DPC, available at http://www.dataprotection.ie/docs/20/1/12_Commissioner_approves_
     Intel_Corporation_Binding_Corp/1190.htm, last accessed 11 January 2013.

upon conclusion of the negotiations referred to in paragraph 5, for the protection of the private lives and basic freedoms and rights of individuals. In addition, Member States shall take the measures necessary to comply with the Commission's decision.

DP Regulation: The New Transfers Regime

Chapter V of the DP Regulation[10] refers to the transfer of personal data to third countries or international organisations. This is the proposed change to the data protection regime.

Article 40 sets out general principles for transfers. It provides that any transfer of personal data that are undergoing processing or are intended for processing after transfer to a third country or to an international organisation may only take place if, subject to the other provisions of the Regulation, the conditions laid down in this Chapter are complied with by the data controller and data processor, including for onward transfers of personal data from the third country or an international organisation to another third country or to another international organisation.

Article 41 refers to transfers with an adequacy decision. Article 41(1) provides that a transfer may take place where the Commission has decided that the third country, or a territory or a processing sector within that third country, or the international organisation in question, ensures an adequate level of protection. Such a transfer shall not require any further authorisation.

Article 41(2) provides that when assessing the adequacy of the level of protection, the Commission shall give consideration to the following elements:

- the rule of law, relevant legislation in force, both general and sectoral, including concerning public security, defence, national security and criminal law, the professional rules and security measures that are complied with in that country or by that international organisation, as well as the effective and enforceable rights including effective administrative and judicial redress for data subjects, in particular for those data subjects residing in the EU whose personal data are being transferred;

- the existence and effective functioning of one or more independent supervisory authorities in the third country or international organisation in question responsible for ensuring compliance with the data protection rules, for assisting and advising the data subjects in exercising their rights and for co-operation with the supervisory authorities of the EU and of Member States; and

10. EU draft Data Protection Regulation (Proposal for a Regulation of the European Parliament and of the Council on the protection of individuals with regard to the processing of personal data and on the free movement of such data (General Data Protection Regulation) COM (2012) 11 final).

- the international commitments the third country or international organisation in question has entered into.

Article 41(3) provides that the Commission may decide that a third country, or a territory or a processing sector within that third country, or an international organisation ensures an adequate level of protection within the meaning of Article 41(2). Those implementing acts shall be adopted in accordance with the examination procedure referred to in Article 87(2).

Article 41(4) provides that the implementing act shall specify its geographical and sectoral application, and, where applicable, identify the supervisory authority mentioned in paragraph Article 41(2)(b). Article 41(5) provides that the Commission may decide that a third country, or a territory or a processing sector within that third country, or an international organisation, does not ensure an adequate level of protection within the meaning of Article 41(5)(2), in particular in cases where the relevant legislation, both general and sectoral, in force in the third country or international organisation, does not guarantee effective and enforceable rights including effective administrative and judicial redress for data subjects, including for those data subjects residing in the EU whose personal data are being transferred. Those implementing acts shall be adopted in accordance with the examination procedure referred to in Article 87(2), or, in cases of extreme urgency for individuals with respect to their right to personal data protection, in accordance with the procedure referred to in Article 87(3).

Article 41(6) provides that where the Commission decides pursuant to Article 41(5), any transfer of personal data to the third country, or a territory or a processing sector within that third country, or the international organisation in question, shall be prohibited, without prejudice to arts 42 to 44. At the appropriate time, the Commission shall enter into consultations with the third country or international organisation with a view to remedying the situation resulting from the Decision made pursuant to Article 41(5).

Article 41(7) provides that the Commission shall publish in the Official Journal of the European Union a list of those third countries, territories and processing sectors within a third country and international organisations where it has decided that an adequate level of protection is or is not ensured.

Article 41(8) provides that decisions adopted by the Commission on the basis of Articles 25(6) or 26(4) of DP Directive 95 shall remain in force, until amended, replaced or repealed by the Commission.

Article 42 refers to transfers by way of appropriate safeguards. Article 42(1) provides that where the Commission has taken no decision pursuant to Article 41, a data controller or data processor may transfer personal data to a third country or an international organisation only if the data controller or data processor has adduced appropriate safeguards with respect to the protection of personal data in a legally binding instrument.

Article 42(2) provides that the appropriate safeguards referred to in paragraph 1 shall be provided for, in particular, by:

- binding corporate rules in accordance with Article 43 (transfers in accordance with binding corporate rules); or
- standard data protection clauses adopted by the Commission;[11] or
- standard data protection clauses adopted by a supervisory authority in accordance with the consistency mechanism as between national authorities and which is referred to in Article 57[12]; or
- contractual clauses between the data controller or data processor and the recipient of the data authorised by a supervisory authority.[13]

Article 42(3) provides that a transfer based on standard data protection clauses or binding corporate rules as referred to in Article 42(2)(a), (b) or (c) shall not require any further authorisation.

Article 42(4) provides that where a transfer is based on contractual clauses as referred to in point (d) of paragraph 2 of the Article, the data controller or data processor shall obtain prior authorisation of the contractual clauses according to point (a) of Article 34(1) from the supervisory authority. If the transfer is related to processing activities that concern data subjects in another Member State or other Member States, or substantially affect the free movement of personal data within the Union, the supervisory authority shall apply the consistency mechanism referred to in Article 57.

Article 42(5) provides that where the appropriate safeguards with respect to the protection of personal data are not provided for in a legally binding instrument, the data controller or data processor shall obtain prior authorisation for the transfer, or a set of transfers, or for provisions to be inserted into administrative arrangements providing the basis for such transfer. Such authorisation by the supervisory authority shall be in accordance with point (a) of Article 34(1). If the transfer is related to processing activities that concern data subjects in another Member State or other Member States, or substantially affect the free movement of personal data within the EU, the supervisory authority shall apply the consistency mechanism referred to in Article 57. Authorisations by a supervisory authority on the basis of Article 26(2) of Directive 95/46/EC shall remain valid, until amended, replaced or repealed by that supervisory authority.

---

11. The examination procedure is referred to in Article 87(2) *ibid.*
12. See also Article 62(1)(b) *ibid* as to when these measures may be declared valid by the Commission.
13. In accordance with Article 42(4).

Article 43 refers to transfers by way of binding corporate rules. Article 43(1) provides that a supervisory authority shall, in accordance with the consistency mechanism set out in Article 58, approve binding corporate rules, provided that they:

- are legally binding and apply to and are enforced by every member within the data controller's or data processor's group of undertakings, and include their employees;

- expressly confer enforceable rights on data subjects; and

- fulfil the requirements laid down in paragraph 2.

Article 43(2) provides that the binding corporate rules shall at least specify:

(a) the structure and contact details of the group of undertakings and its members;

(b) the data transfers or set of transfers, including the categories of personal data, the type of processing and its purposes, the type of data subjects affected and the identification of the third country or countries in question;

(c) their legally binding nature, both internally and externally;

(d) the general *data protection principles*, in particular purpose limitation, data quality, legal basis for the processing, processing of sensitive personal data; measures to ensure data security; and the requirements for onward transfers to organisations that are not bound by the policies;

(e) the rights of data subjects and the means to exercise these rights, including the right not to be subject to a measure based on profiling in accordance with Article 20, the right to lodge a complaint before the competent supervisory authority and before the competent courts of the Member States in accordance with Article 75, and to obtain redress and, where appropriate, compensation for a breach of the binding corporate rules;

(f) the acceptance by the data controller or data processor established on the territory of a Member State of liability for any breaches of the binding corporate rules by any member of the group of undertakings not established in the EU; the data controller or the data processor may only be exempted from this liability, in whole or in part, if he proves that that member is not responsible for the event giving rise to the damage;

(g) how the information on the binding corporate rules, in particular on the provisions referred to in points (d), (e) and (f) of this paragraph is provided to the data subjects in accordance with Article 11;

(h) the tasks of the data protection officer designated in accordance with Article 35, including monitoring within the group of undertakings the compliance with the binding corporate rules, as well as monitoring the training and complaint handling;

(i)   the mechanisms within the group of undertakings aiming at ensuring the verification of compliance with the binding corporate rules;

(j)   the mechanisms for reporting and recording changes to the policies and reporting these changes to the supervisory authority;

(k)   the co-operation mechanism with the supervisory authority to ensure compliance by any member of the group of undertakings, in particular by making available to the supervisory authority the results of the verifications of the measures referred to in point (i) of this paragraph.

Article 43(3) provides that the Commission shall be empowered to adopt delegated acts in accordance with Article 86 for the purpose of further specifying the criteria and requirements for binding corporate rules within the meaning of the Article, in particular as regards the criteria for their approval, the application of points (b), (d), (e) and (f) of paragraph 2 to binding corporate rules adhered to by data processors and on further necessary requirements to ensure the protection of personal data of the data subjects concerned.

Article 43(4) provides that the Commission may specify the format and procedures for the exchange of information by electronic means between data controllers, data processors and supervisory authorities for binding corporate rules within the meaning of this Article. Those implementing acts shall be adopted in accordance with the examination procedure set out in Article 87(2).

Article 44 refers to derogations. Article 44(1) provides that in the absence of an adequacy decision pursuant to Article 41 or of appropriate safeguards pursuant to Article 42, a transfer or a set of transfers of personal data to a third country or an international organisation may take place only on condition that:

(a)   the data subject has consented to the proposed transfer, after having been informed of the risks of such transfers due to the absence of an adequacy decision and appropriate safeguards; or

(b)   the transfer is necessary for the performance of a contract between the data subject and the data controller or the implementation of pre-contractual measures taken at the data subject's request; or

(c)   the transfer is necessary for the conclusion or performance of a contract concluded in the interest of the data subject between the data controller and another natural or legal person; or

(d)   the transfer is necessary for important grounds of public interest; or

(e)   the transfer is necessary for the establishment, exercise or defence of legal claims; or

(f)   the transfer is necessary in order to protect the vital interests of the data subject or of another person, where the data subject is physically or legally incapable of giving consent; or

(g)   the transfer is made from a register which, according to EU or Member State law, is intended to provide information to the public and which is open to consultation either by the public in general or by any person who can demonstrate legitimate interest, to the extent that the conditions laid down in EU or Member State law for consultation are fulfilled in the particular case; or

(h)   the transfer is necessary for the purposes of the legitimate interests pursued by the data controller or the data processor, which cannot be qualified as frequent or massive, and where the data controller or data processor has assessed all the circumstances surrounding the data transfer operation or the set of data transfer operations and based on this assessment adduced appropriate safeguards with respect to the protection of personal data, where necessary.

Article 44(2) provides that a transfer pursuant to Article 44(1)(g) shall not involve the entirety of the personal data or entire categories of the personal data contained in the register. When the register is intended for consultation by persons having a legitimate interest, the transfer shall be made only at the request of those persons or if they are to be the recipients.

Article 44(3) provides that where the processing is based on Article 44(1)(h) of paragraph 1, the data controller or data processor shall give particular consideration to the nature of the data, the purpose and duration of the proposed processing operation or operations, as well as the situation in the country of origin, the third country and the country of final destination, and adduced appropriate safeguards with respect to the protection of personal data, where necessary.

Article 44(4) provides that Article 44(1)(b), (c) and (h) shall not apply to activities carried out by public authorities in the exercise of their public powers.

Article 44(5) provides that the public interest referred to in Article 44(1)(d) must be recognised in EU law or in the law of the Member State to which the controller is subject.

Article 44(6) provides that the data controller or data processor shall document the assessment as well as the appropriate safeguards adduced referred to in Article 44(1)(h) of this Article in the documentation referred to in Article 28 and shall inform the supervisory authority of the transfer.

Article 44(7) provides that the Commission shall be empowered to adopt delegated acts in accordance with Article 86 for the purpose of further specifying "important grounds of public interest" within the meaning of Article 44(1)(d) of as well as the criteria and requirements for appropriate safeguards referred to in Article 44(1)(h).

Article 45 refers to international co-operation for the protection of personal data. Article 45(1) provides that in relation to third countries and international organisations, the Commission and supervisory authorities shall take appropriate steps to:

(a) develop effective international co-operation mechanisms to facilitate the enforcement of legislation for the protection of personal data;

(b) provide international mutual assistance in the enforcement of legislation for the protection of personal data, including through notification, complaint referral, investigative assistance and information exchange, subject to appropriate safeguards for the protection of personal data and other fundamental rights and freedoms;

(c) engage relevant stakeholders in discussion and activities aimed at furthering international co-operation in the enforcement of legislation for the protection of personal data; and

(d) promote the exchange and documentation of personal data protection legislation and practice.

Article 45(2) provides that for the purposes of Article 45, the Commission shall take appropriate steps to advance the relationship with third countries or international organisations, and in particular their supervisory authorities, where the Commission has decided that they ensure an adequate level of protection within the meaning of Article 41(3).

DP Directive 95: Derogations

Article 26 of the DP Directive 95 refers to derogations. Article 26(1) provides that by way of derogation from Article 25 and save where otherwise provided by domestic law governing particular cases, Member States shall provide that a transfer or a set of transfers of personal data to a third country that does not ensure an adequate level of protection within the meaning of Article 25(2) may take place on condition that:

- the data subject has given his or her consent unambiguously to the proposed transfer; or

- the transfer is necessary for the performance of a contract between the data subject and the data controller or the implementation of pre-contractual measures taken in response to the data subject's request; or

- the transfer is necessary for the conclusion or performance of a contract concluded in the interest of the data subject between the data controller and a third party; or

- the transfer is necessary or legally required on important public interest grounds, or for the establishment, exercise or defence of legal claims; or

- the transfer is necessary in order to protect the vital interests of the data subject; or

- the transfer is made from a register that, according to laws or regulations, is intended to provide information to the public and that is open to consultation either by the public in general or by any person who can demonstrate legitimate interest, to the extent that the conditions laid down in law for consultation are fulfilled in the particular case.

Article 26(2) provides that without prejudice to Article 26(1), a Member State may authorise a transfer or a set of transfers of personal data to a third country that does not ensure an adequate level of protection within the meaning of Article 25(2), where the data controller adduces adequate safeguards with respect to the protection of the privacy and fundamental rights and freedoms of individuals and as regards the exercise of the corresponding rights; such safeguards may in particular result from appropriate contractual clauses.

Article 26(3) provides that the Member State shall inform the Commission and the other Member States of the authorisations it grants pursuant to Article 26(2). If a Member State or the Commission objects on justified grounds involving the protection of the privacy and fundamental rights and freedoms of individuals, the Commission shall take appropriate measures in accordance with the procedure laid down in Article 31(2). Member States shall take the necessary measures to comply with the Commission's decision.

Article 26(4) provides that where the Commission decides, in accordance with the procedure referred to in Article 31(2), that certain standard contractual clauses offer sufficient safeguards as required by Article 26(2), Member States shall take the necessary measures to comply with the Commission's decision.

DP Regulation: Derogations and Restriction

Section 5 of the DP Regulation[14] refers to restrictions. Article 21(1) provides that EU or Member State law may restrict by way of a legislative measure the scope of the obligations and rights provided for in points (a) to (e) of Article 5 and Articles 11 to 20 and Article 32, when such a restriction constitutes a necessary and proportionate measure in a democratic society to safeguard:

(a) public security;

(b) the prevention, investigation, detection and prosecution of criminal offences;

(c) other public interests of the EU or of a Member State, in particular an important economic or financial interest of the EU or of a Member State, including

---

14. EU draft Data Protection Regulation.

monetary, budgetary and taxation matters and the protection of market stability and integrity;

(d) the prevention, investigation, detection and prosecution of breaches of ethics for regulated professions;

(e) a monitoring, inspection or regulatory function connected, even occasionally, with the exercise of official authority in cases referred to in (a), (b), (c) and (d);

(f) the protection of the data subject or the rights and freedoms of others.

Article 21(2) provides that in particular, any legislative measure referred to in paragraph 1 shall contain specific provisions at least as to the objectives to be pursued by the processing and the determination of the data controller.

Issues

Certain issues may arise in relation to:

- What is a "transfer"? Is there a difference between transfer versus transit?
- "Data" and anonymised data: is there a restriction on TBDFs of anonymised data? For example, can certain anonymised data fall outside the definition of personal data?
- "Third country" currently includes the EU countries and EEA countries of Iceland, Norway, Liechtenstein. The EU countries are expanding over time. In addition, the list of permitted additional third countries is also expanding over time, for example, safe harbour.

Establishing if the Ban Applies

Criteria for assessing if the ban applies include the following issues:

- identifying whether the organisation transfers personal data;
- identifying if there is a transfer;
- identifying if there is a transfer to a "third country";
- identifying if that third country has an adequate level of protection;
- identifying in relation to transfers to the US – if the "Safe Harbour" rules apply;
- identifying whether any of the white list countries are recipients; considering what constitutes adequacy;
- identifying the nature of the data; Identify how it is to be used;

- consider the laws and practices in place in the third country; Identify if there is a transfer by a data controller to a data processor. Under Article 7 DP Directive 95 such a transfer requires a contract to be put in place relating to security measures to date. The data controller retains control of the personal data so that the risk to the data subject is minimal; identify if there is a ransfer within an international or multinational company or group of companies where an internal privacy code or agreement is in place; identify if there is a transfer within a consortium established to process international transactions, for example, banking; identify if there is a transfers between professionals such as lawyers or accountants where a client's business has on international dimension; The European Commission has identified core principles that must be present in the foreign laws or codes of practice or regulations in order to achieve the requisite standard of "adequacy" in third-party countries. Identify whether these are applicable in the particular instance; Personal data must be processed for a specific purpose. Identify what this purpose is;

- ensure that personal data must be accurate and kept up to date. Ensure that this applies; The data subject must be provided with adequate information in relation to the transfer. Ensure that this principle is compled with; Technical and organisational security measures should be taken by the data controller;

- ensure that there must be a right of access to the data by the data subject; There should be a prohibition on onward transfer of data along the lines of Article 25 of the DP Directive 95; and

- ensure that there should be an effective procedure or mode of enforcement.

Checklist and Guidance

The Data Protection Commissioner provides the following guidance[15] to data controllers who must be able to point to one or more of the following legitimising exemption alternatives, in order for the transfer of personal data to the third country may proceed lawfully:

- The transfer of personal data is required or authorised by law. Data Protection Commissioner Comment: If a data controller is subject to a requirement under Irish law to transfer personal data to a third country, or is clearly authorised by Irish law to make the transfer, then the transfer may proceed.[16]

---

15. See DPC, available at http://www.dataprotection.ie/ViewDoc.asp?fn=/documents/responsibilities/3ma.htm&CatID=56&m=y, last accessed 11 January 2013.
16. *ibid.*

- The data subject (i.e. the individual to whom the personal data relates) has given his consent to the transfer.

Data Protection Commissioner Comment: If the organisation wishes to transfer a database containing records about many individuals to a third country, then – in order to rely on this provision – the organisation needs to obtain the consent of each one of these individuals before the organisation can transfer their data. In interpreting what is meant by the word "consent", the Data Protection Commissioner will have regard to relevant provisions of the DP Directive 95,[17] which refers to the "unambiguous consent" of individuals in this context. The Directive also requires that "consent" must be freely given and informed. Data controllers should therefore be extremely cautious about relying on consent as a basis for data transfer since, in practice, demonstrating that such consent is clear, unambiguous, freely given and specific is likely to be problematic.[18]

- The transfer is necessary for the performance of a contract to which the data subject is party, or the transfer is necessary for the taking of steps – at the request of the data subject – with a view to his entering into a contract with the data controller.[19]
- The transfer is necessary to conclude a contract (or to perform a contract) between the data controller and someone other than the data subject, in cases where the contract is entered into at the request of the data subject, or where the contract is in the interests of the data subject.

Data Protection Commissioner Comment: Data controllers should be cautious about relying on provisions (iii) and (iv) since the "necessity" test rules out use of these provisions other than in very specific circumstances. For example, it would not be prudent to rely solely on these provisions for the transfer of employee data within a multinational company.[20]

- The transfer is necessary for reasons of substantial public interest.

Data Protection Commissioner Comment: This basis is only likely to be relevant to public sector data controllers and only in circumstances where they can show that there is a substantial Irish public interest in the transfer of personal data.[21]

- The transfer is necessary for obtaining legal advice or for legal proceedings. Data Protection Commissioner Comment: This provision appears to be of relevance only in two situations. The first situation is where a data controller

---

17. *ibid.*
18. *ibid.*
19. *ibid.*
20. *ibid.*
21. *ibid.*

wishes to obtain legal advice from a legal adviser located in a third country, and where the data controller needs to make personal data available to the adviser for this purpose. The second situation is where a data controller in Ireland is involved as a party in legal proceedings in a third country, and the data controller needs to make personal data available in that third country for the purpose of the legal proceedings.[22]

- The transfer is necessary to prevent injury or other damage to the data subject's health, or to prevent serious damage to his property, or to protect his vital interests in some other way – provided that it is not possible to inform the data subject, or obtain his consent, without harming his vital interests.

Data Protection Commissioner Comment: Naturally, data protection considerations are sometimes outweighed by other considerations, such as the protection of life and limb. This provision allows data controllers to transfer personal data to third countries in such situations. However, before relying on this provision, data controllers must first establish whether or not it is possible to obtain the person's consent. Only if this is not possible – for example due to urgency of time – can this provision be invoked.[23]

- The personal data to be transferred are an extract from a statutory public register, i.e. a register established by law as being available for public consultation, or as being available for consultation by persons with a legitimate interest in its contents. In the latter case, the transfer must be made to a person having such a legitimate interest, and subject to compliance by that person with any relevant conditions.

Data Protection Commissioner Comment: It is permissible to make personal data, derived from a public register, available in a third country. It is not permissible to transfer the whole of such a register to a third country. If a statutory register is available for inspection by persons demonstrating a legitimate interest, then this condition – and any other conditions – must be fully complied with before the personal data can be made available;[24] or

- The transfer is authorised by the Data Protection Commissioner where the data controller can point to adequate data protection safeguards, such as approved contractual provisions. The EU Commission has approved model contracts to assist data controllers in this regard, and such contracts would automatically fall under this provision. The Data Protection Commissioner also has the power to endorse "model contracts" specific to Irish circumstances, as well as the power to approve particular contracts or other arrangements that provide satisfactory safeguards. In practice, it is likely that

22. *ibid.*
23. *ibid.*
24. *ibid.*

most transfers to "unapproved" third countries will be on the basis of model contracts.[25]

The Data Protection Commissioner also states that in the case of multinational companies with operations inside and outside the EU, the use of so-called binding corporate rules – legally enforceable privacy/data protection codes of practice – can offer an alternative or complementary mechanism for approved international transfers within the global corporate entity. A company interested in this option should apply for approval of its rules to the data protection authority of the EU Member State where its headquarters, or main EU centre of activity, is based.[26] The UK ICO has also published materials.[27]

Conclusion

Data protection compliance practice for organisations means that they will have to include a compliance assessment as well as an assessment of the risks associated with transfers of personal data outside of the EEA. This applies to transfers from parent to subsidiary or to a branch office in the same way as a transfer to an unrelated company or entity.

Organisations should at least be aware that if they wish to transfer personal data outside of the EEA, that additional considerations arise and that unless there is a specific exemption process, then the transfer may not be permitted. Once a transfer possibility arises, the organisation should undertake a compliance exercise to assess if the transfer can be permitted, and if so, how. Additional compliance documentation may be required.

---

25. *ibid.*
26. *ibid.*
27. The ICO also provides useful guidance in relation to Assessing Adequacy; Model Contract Clauses; Binding Corporate Rules; and Outsourcing. See ICO, available at http://www.ico. gov.uk/for_organisations/data_protection/overseas.aspx, last accessed 11 January 2013. There is also the following ICO guidance which can be a useful reference for organisations, namely, the, *Data Protection Act 1998, The Eighth Data Protection Principle and International Data Transfers, The Information Commissioner's Recommended Approach to Assessing Adequacy Including Consideration of the Issue of Contractual Solutions, Binding Corporate Rules and Safe Harbor.*

CHAPTER **22**

ePrivacy and Electronic Communications

Introduction

There is increasing use of electronically transmitted personal data. This is protected and regulated in certain respects separate from the general data protection regime under the DP Directive 95[1] (and DP Regulation[2]).

While originally the regulation of telecommunications-related personal data centred on telecoms companies, it is now recognised as encompassing telecoms companies and other companies engaged in activities involving the collection or transmission of particular personal data over electronic communications networks, including the internet.

Organisations undertaking marketing, email marketing, text marketing, telephone marketing, fax marketing, and using location-based data, cookies and identification regarding telephone calls need to comply with the rules in relation to eprivacy and electronic communications.

Background

There has been a separation between the data protection of general personal data, in the DP Directive 95, and the regulation of personal data in (tele)communications networks. The latter were legislated for in the Data Protection Directive of 1997.[3]

---

1. EU Data Protection Directive 1995 (Directive 95/46/EC of the European Parliament and of the Council of 24 October 1995 on the protection of individuals with regard to the processing of personal data and on the free movement of such data).
2. EU draft Data Protection Regulation (Proposal for a Regulation of the European Parliament and of the Council on the protection of individuals with regard to the processing of personal data and on the free movement of such data (General Data Protection Regulation) COM (2012) 11 final).
3. Directive 97/66/EC.

This was later replaced with the ePrivacy Directive.[4] More recently, the ePrivacy Directive was amended by Directives 2006/24/EC and 2009/136/EC.

The ePrivacy Directive concerns the processing of personal data and the protection of privacy in the electronic communications sector. It is also known as the Directive on privacy and electronic communications, hence the ePrivacy Directive. One of the concerns has been how electronic communications and electronic information are increasingly used for profiling for marketing purposes, including by electronic means.[5]

Scope of the ePrivacy Directive

The ePrivacy Directive broadly relates to and encompasses the following:

- definitions;
- security;
- confidentiality;
- traffic data;
- non-itemised bills;
- call and connected line identification;
- location data;
- exceptions;
- directories;
- unsolicited communications; and
- technical features.

It also provides rules in relation to:

- email marketing;
- text marketing;
- telephone marketing;
- fax marketing; and
- cookies (see Chapter 19).

---

4. Directive 2002/58/EC of the European Parliament and of the Council of 12 July 2002 concerning the processing of personal data and the protection of privacy in the electronic communications sector (Directive on privacy and electronic communications)(as amended by Directives 2006/24/EC and 2009/136/EC).

5. See, for example, McGeveran, "Disclosure, Endorsement, and Identity in Social Marketing" (2009)(4) *University of Illinois Law Review* 1105–1166.

Marketing

How should organisations go about data protection compliance for direct marketing? When is DM permitted? All organisations should carefully assess compliance issues when considering any direct marketing activities. Getting it wrong can be costly and can have DPC enforcement and investigation consequences.

Article 13 of the ePrivacy Directive refers to unsolicited communications. Article 13(1) in particular provides that the use of automated calling systems without human intervention (automatic calling machines), facsimile machines (fax), or electronic mail, for the purposes of direct marketing, may *only* be allowed in respect of subscribers who have given their *prior consent*.

This means that there is a default rule prohibiting direct marketing (DM) without prior consent. Many marketing orientated organisations may be surprised, if not dismayed, by this.

Existing Customers' Email

However, in the context of existing customers, there is a possibility to direct market using emails. Article 13(2) of the ePrivacy Directive provides that notwithstanding paragraph 13(1), where an organisation obtains from its customers their electronic contact details for electronic mail, in the context of the sale of a product or a service, in accordance with DP Directive 95, the organisation may use these electronic contact details for direct marketing (DM) of its own similar products or services provided that customers clearly and distinctly are given the opportunity to object, free of charge and in an easy manner, to such use of electronic contact details when they are collected and on the occasion of each message in case the customer has not initially refused such use.

Therefore, once the email details are obtained at the time of a product or service transaction, it will be possible to use that email for direct marketing purposes. Conditions or limitations apply, however. First, the organisation is only permitted to market and promote similar products or services. This, therefore, rules out unrelated, non-identical and non-similar products and services. Secondly, at the time of each subsequent act of direct marketing (DM), the customer must be given the opportunity in an easy manner to opt-out or cancel the direct marketing (DM). Effectively, they must be taken off of the DM list.

National Opt-out Registers

Article 13(3) of ePrivacy Directive provides that Member States shall take appropriate measures to ensure that, free of charge, unsolicited communications for purposes of direct marketing, in cases other than those referred to in paragraphs 1 and 2, are not allowed either without the consent of the subscribers concerned or in respect of subscribers who do not wish to receive these communications; the choice between these options to be determined by national legislation. This means that each Member State must determine and provide a means for individuals to opt-out of receiving direct marketing (DM) in advance.[6]

Marketing Emails Must Not Conceal their Identity

Article 13(4) of ePrivacy Directive provides that the practice of sending electronic mail for purposes of direct marketing (DM) disguising or concealing the identity of the sender on whose behalf the communication is made shall be prohibited. This means that organisations cannot conceal their identity if permitted to engage in direct marketing. If these are not complied with, what might otherwise be permissible direct marketing (DM) can be deemed to be impermissible. Complaints, investigations or enforcement proceedings can thus arise.

Marketing Emails Must Have an Opt-Out

In addition, Article 13(4) of ePrivacy Directive provides that the practice of sending electronic mail for purposes of direct marketing (DM) without a valid address to which the recipient may send a request that such communications cease shall be prohibited. This means that organisations must also include an easy contact address or other details the recipient can use if he or she wishes to object to receiving any further direct marketing (DM). If these are not complied with, what might otherwise be permissible direct marketing (DM) can be deemed to be impermissible. Complaints, investigations or enforcement proceedings can thus also arise.

Marketing Protection for Organisations

Article 13(5) of ePrivacy Directive provides that Article 13(1) and (3) shall apply to subscribers who are natural persons. Member States shall also ensure, in the framework of Community law and applicable Member State legislation, that the legitimate interests of subscribers other than natural persons with regard to unsolicited communications are sufficiently protected. This means that protection from unsolicited direct marketing (DM) can also be extended to organisations.

---

6. See ICO website, available at http://www.ico.gov.uk/for_the_public/topic_specific_guides/ marketing.aspx, last accessed 11 January 2013.

Background: ePrivacy Directive

Directive Recitals sometimes provide background and contextual details useful to understanding the purpose and interpretation of the Directive. ePrivacy Directive Recital 1 notes that DP Directive 95 requires Member States to ensure the rights and freedoms of natural persons with regard to the processing of personal data, and in particular their right to privacy, in order to ensure the free flow of personal data in the Community.

ePrivacy Directive Recital 2 notes that the Directive seeks to respect the fundamental rights and observes the principles recognised in particular by the Charter of Fundamental Rights of the European Union. In particular, the Directive seeks to ensure full respect for the rights set out in Articles 7 and 8 of that Charter.

ePrivacy Directive Recital 3 notes that confidentiality of communications is guaranteed in accordance with the international instruments relating to human rights, in particular the European Convention for the Protection of Human Rights and Fundamental Freedoms, and the constitutions of the Member States.

ePrivacy Directive Recital 4 notes that Directive 97/66/EC of the European Parliament and of the Council of 15 December 1997 concerning the processing of personal data and the protection of privacy in the telecommunications sector translated the principles set out in DP Directive 95 into specific rules for the telecommunications sector. Directive 97/66/EC has to be adapted to developments in the markets and technologies for electronic communications services in order to provide an equal level of protection of personal data and privacy for users of publicly available electronic communications services, regardless of the technologies used. That Directive should, therefore, be repealed and replaced.

ePrivacy Directive Recital 5 notes that new advanced digital technologies are currently being introduced in public communications networks in the Community, which give rise to specific requirements concerning the protection of personal data and privacy of the user. The development of the information society is characterised by the introduction of new electronic communications services. Access to digital mobile networks has become available and affordable for a large public. These digital networks have large capacities and possibilities for processing personal data. The successful cross-border development of these services is partly dependent on the confidence of users that their privacy will not be at risk.

ePrivacy Directive Recital 6 notes that the internet is overturning traditional market structures by providing a common, global infrastructure for the delivery of a wide range of electronic communications services. Publicly available electronic communications services over the internet open new possibilities for users but also new risks for their personal data and privacy.

ePrivacy Directive Recital 7 notes that in the case of public communications networks, specific legal, regulatory and technical provisions should be made in order to protect fundamental rights and freedoms of natural persons and legitimate interests of legal persons, in particular with regard to the increasing capacity for automated storage and processing of data relating to subscribers and users.

ePrivacy Directive Recital 8 notes that notes that legal, regulatory and technical provisions adopted by the Member States concerning the protection of personal data, privacy and the legitimate interest of legal persons, in the electronic communication sector, should be harmonised in order to avoid obstacles to the internal market for electronic communication in accordance with Article 14 of the Treaty. Harmonisation should be limited to requirements necessary to guarantee that the promotion and development of new electronic communications services and networks between Member States are not hindered.

ePrivacy Directive Recital 9 notes that the Member States, providers and users concerned, together with the competent Community bodies, should co-operate in introducing and developing the relevant technologies where this is necessary to apply the guarantees provided for by the Directive and taking particular account of the objectives of minimising the processing of personal data and of using anonymous or pseudonymous data where possible.

ePrivacy Directive Recital 10 notes that in the electronic communications sector, DP Directive 95 applies in particular to all matters concerning protection of funda-mental rights and freedoms that are not specifically covered by the provisions of the Directive, including the obligations on the data controller and the rights of indi-viduals. DP Directive 95applies to non-public communications services.

ePrivacy Directive Recital 11 notes that, like DP Directive 95, the Directive does not address issues of protection of fundamental rights and freedoms related to activities that are not governed by Community law. Therefore, it does not alter the existing balance between the individual's right to privacy and the possibility for Member States to take the measures referred to in Article 15(1) of the Directive. Such meas-ures must be necessary for the protection of public security, defence, State security (including the economic well-being of the State when the activities relate to State security matters) and the enforcement of criminal law. Consequently, the Directive does not affect the ability of Member States to carry out lawful interception of elec-tronic communications, or take other measures, if necessary for any of these purposes and in accordance with the European Convention for the Protection of Human Rights and Fundamental Freedoms, as interpreted by the rulings of the European Court of Human Rights. Such measures must be appropriate, strictly proportionate to the intended purpose and necessary within a democratic society and should be subject to adequate safeguards in accordance with the European Convention for the Protection of Human Rights and Fundamental Freedoms.

ePrivacy Directive Recital 12 notes that subscribers to a publicly available electronic communications service may be natural or legal persons. By supplementing DP Directive 95, the Directive is aimed at protecting the fundamental rights of natural persons and particularly their right to privacy, as well as the legitimate interests of legal persons. The Directive does not entail an obligation for Member States to extend the application of DP Directive 95 to the protection of the legitimate interests of legal persons, which is ensured within the framework of the applicable Community and Member State legislation.

ePrivacy Directive Recital 13 notes that the contractual relation between a subscriber and a service provider may entail a periodic or a one-off payment for the service provided or to be provided. Prepaid cards are also considered as a contract.

ePrivacy Directive Recital 14 notes that location data may refer to the latitude, longitude and altitude of the user's terminal equipment, to the direction of travel, to the level of accuracy of the location information, to the identification of the network cell in which the terminal equipment is located at a certain point in time and to the time the location information was recorded.

ePrivacy Directive Recital 15 notes that a communication may include any naming, numbering or addressing information provided by the sender of a communication or the user of a connection to carry out the communication. Traffic data may include any translation of this information by the network over which the communication is transmitted for the purpose of carrying out the transmission. Traffic data may, *inter alia*, consist of data referring to the routing, duration, time or volume of a communication, to the protocol used, to the location of the terminal equipment of the sender or recipient, to the network on which the communication originates or terminates, to the beginning, end or duration of a connection. They may also consist of the format in which the communication is conveyed by the network.

ePrivacy Directive Recital 16 notes that information that is part of a broadcasting service provided over a public communications network is intended for a potentially unlimited audience and does not constitute a communication in the sense of the Directive. However, in cases where the individual subscriber or user receiving such information can be identified, for example with video-on-demand services, the information conveyed is covered within the meaning of a communication for the purposes of the Directive.

ePrivacy Directive Recital 17 notes that for the purposes of the Directive, consent of a user or subscriber, regardless of whether the latter is a natural or a legal person, should have the same meaning as the data subject's consent as defined and further specified in DP Directive 95. Consent may be given by any appropriate method enabling a freely given specific and informed indication of the user's wishes, including by ticking a box when visiting a website.

ePrivacy Directive Recital 18 notes that value added services (VAS) may, for example, consist of advice on least expensive tariff packages, route guidance, traffic information, weather forecasts and tourist information.

ePrivacy Directive Recital 19 notes that the application of certain requirements relating to presentation and restriction of calling and connected line identification and to automatic call forwarding to subscriber lines connected to analogue exchanges should not be made mandatory in specific cases where such application would prove to be technically impossible or would require a disproportionate economic effort. It is important for interested parties to be informed of such cases and the Member States should therefore notify them to the Commission.

ePrivacy Directive Recital 20 notes that service providers should take appropriate measures to safeguard the security of their services, if necessary in conjunction with the provider of the network, and inform subscribers of any special risks of a breach of the security of the network. Such risks may especially occur for electronic communications services over an open network such as the internet or analogue mobile telephony. It is particularly important for subscribers and users of such services to be fully informed by their service provider of the existing security risks that lie outside the scope of possible remedies by the service provider. Service providers who offer publicly available electronic communications services over the internet should inform users and subscribers of measures they can take to protect the security of their communications, for instance by using specific types of software or encryption technologies. The requirement to inform subscribers of particular security risks does not discharge a service provider from the obligation to take, at its own costs, appropriate and immediate measures to remedy any new, unforeseen security risks and restore the normal security level of the service. The provision of information about security risks to the subscriber should be free of charge except for any nominal costs the subscriber may incur while receiving or collecting the information, for instance by downloading an electronic mail message. Security is appraised in the light of Article 17 of DP Directive 95.

ePrivacy Directive[7] Recital 21 notes that measures should be taken to prevent unauthorised access to communications in order to protect the confidentiality of communications, including both the contents and any data related to such communications, by means of public communications networks and publicly available electronic communications services. National legislation in some Member States only prohibits intentional unauthorised access to communications.

ePrivacy DirectiveRecital 22 notes that the prohibition of storage of communications and the related traffic data by persons other than the users or without their consent is not intended to prohibit any automatic, intermediate and transient storage

---

7.   Directive 2002/58/EC of the European Parliament and of the Council of 12 July 2002 concerning the processing of personal data and the protection of privacy in the electronic communications sector.

of this information insofar as this takes place for the sole purpose of carrying out the transmission in the electronic communications network and provided that the information is not stored for any period longer than is necessary for the transmission and for traffic management purposes, and that during the period of storage the confidentiality remains guaranteed. Where this is necessary for making more efficient the onward transmission of any publicly accessible information to other recipients of the service upon their request, the Directive does not prevent such information from being further stored, provided that this information would in any case be accessible to the public without restriction and that any data referring to the individual subscribers or users requesting such information are erased.

ePrivacy Directive Recital 23 notes that confidentiality of communications should also be ensured in the course of lawful business practice. Where necessary and legally authorised, communications can be recorded for the purpose of providing evidence of a commercial transaction. DP Directive 95 applies to such processing. Parties to the communications should be informed prior to the recording about the recording, its purpose and the duration of its storage. The recorded communication should be erased as soon as possible and in any case at the latest by the end of the period during which the transaction can be lawfully challenged.

ePrivacy Directive Recital 24 notes that terminal equipment of users of electronic communications networks and any information stored on such equipment are part of the private sphere of the users, requiring protection under the European Convention for the Protection of Human Rights and Fundamental Freedoms. So-called spyware, web bugs, hidden identifiers and other similar devices can enter the user's terminal without their knowledge in order to gain access to information, to store hidden information or to trace the activities of the user and may seriously intrude upon the privacy of these users. The use of such devices should be allowed only for legitimate purposes, with the knowledge of the users concerned.

ePrivacy Directive Recital 25 notes, however, that such devices, for instance "cookies", can be a legitimate and useful tool, for example, in analysing the effectiveness of website design and advertising, and in verifying the identity of users engaged in online transactions. Where such devices are intended for a legitimate purpose, such as to facilitate the provision of information society services, their use should be allowed on condition that users are provided with clear and precise information in accordance with DP Directive 95 about the purposes of cookies or similar devices so as to ensure that users are made aware of information being placed on the terminal equipment they are using. Users should have the opportunity to refuse to have a cookie or similar device stored on their terminal equipment. This is particularly important where users other than the original user have access to the terminal equipment and thereby to any data containing privacy-sensitive information stored on such equipment. Information and the right to refuse may be offered once for the use of various devices to be installed on the user's terminal equipment during the same connection and also covering any further use that may be made of those devices during subsequent connections. The methods for giving information, offering a right to refuse or requesting consent should be made as user-friendly as possible. Access to specific website content may still be made conditional on the well-informed acceptance of a cookie or similar device, if it is used for a legitimate purpose.

ePrivacy Directive Recital 26 notes that the data relating to subscribers processed within electronic communications networks to establish connections and to transmit information contain information on the private life of natural persons and concern the right to respect for their correspondence or concern the legitimate interests of legal persons. Such data may only be stored to the extent that is necessary for the provision of the service for the purpose of billing and for interconnection payments, and for a limited time. Any further processing of such data that the provider of the publicly available electronic communications services may want to perform, for the marketing of electronic communications services or for the provision of value added services, may only be allowed if the subscriber has agreed to this on the basis of accurate and full information given by the provider of the publicly available electronic communications services about the types of further processing it intends to perform and about the subscriber's right not to give or to withdraw his consent to such processing. Traffic data used for marketing communications services or for the provision of value added services should also be erased or made anonymous after the provision of the service. Service providers should always keep subscribers informed of the types of data they are processing and the purposes and duration for which this is done.

ePrivacy Directive Recital 27 notes that the exact moment of the completion of the transmission of a communication, after which traffic data should be erased except for billing purposes, may depend on the type of electronic communications service that is provided. For instance, for a voice telephony call the transmission will be completed as soon as either of the users terminates the connection. For electronic mail the transmission is completed as soon as the addressee collects the message, typically from the server of his service provider.

ePrivacy Directive Recital 28 notes that the obligation to erase traffic data or to make such data anonymous when it is no longer needed for the purpose of the transmission of a communication does not conflict with such procedures on the internet as the caching in the domain name system of IP addresses or the caching of IP addresses to physical address bindings or the use of log-in information to control the right of access to networks or services.

ePrivacy Directive Recital 29 notes that the service provider may process traffic data relating to subscribers and users where necessary in individual cases in order to detect technical failure or errors in the transmission of communications. Traffic data necessary for billing purposes may also be processed by the provider in order to detect and stop fraud consisting of unpaid use of the electronic communications service.

ePrivacy Directive Recital 30 notes that systems for the provision of electronic communications networks and services should be designed to limit the amount of personal data necessary to a strict minimum. Any activities related to the provision of the electronic communications service that go beyond the transmission of a communication and the billing thereof should be based on aggregated, traffic data that cannot be related to subscribers or users. Where such activities cannot be based on aggregated data, they should be considered as value added services for which the consent of the subscriber is required.

ePrivacy Directive Recital 31 notes that whether the consent – to be obtained for the processing of personal data with a view to providing a particular value added service – should be that of the user or of the subscriber will depend on the data to be processed and on the type of service to be provided and on whether it is technically, procedurally and contractually possible to distinguish the individual using an electronic communications service from the legal or natural person having subscribed to it.

ePrivacy Directive Recital 32 notes that where the provider of an electronic communications service or of a value added service subcontracts the processing of personal data necessary for the provision of these services to another entity, such subcontracting and subsequent data processing should be in full compliance with the requirements regarding data controllers and data processors of personal data as set out in DP Directive 95. Where the provision of a value added service requires that traffic or location data are forwarded from an electronic communications service provider to a provider of value added services, the subscribers or users to whom the data are related should also be fully informed of this forwarding before giving their consent for the processing of the data.

ePrivacy Directive Recital 33 notes that the introduction of itemised bills has improved the possibilities for the subscriber to check the accuracy of the fees charged by the service provider but, at the same time, it may jeopardise the privacy of the users of publicly available electronic communications services. Therefore, in order to preserve the privacy of the user, Member States should encourage the development of electronic communication service options such as alternative payment facilities that allow anonymous or strictly private access to publicly available electronic communications services, for example calling cards and facilities for payment by credit card. To the same end, Member States may ask the operators to offer their subscribers a different type of detailed bill in which a certain number of digits of the called number have been deleted.

ePrivacy Directive Recital 34 notes that it is necessary, as regards calling line identification, to protect the right of the calling party to withhold the presentation of the identification of the line from which the call is being made and the right of the called party to reject calls from unidentified lines. There is justification for overriding the elimination of calling line identification presentation in specific cases. Certain subscribers, in particular help lines and similar organisations, have an interest in guaranteeing the anonymity of their callers. It is necessary, as regards connected line identification, to protect the right and the legitimate interest of the called party to withhold the presentation of the identification of the line to which the calling party is actually connected, in particular in the case of forwarded calls. The providers of publicly available electronic communications services should inform their subscribers of the existence of calling and connected line identification in the network and of all services that are offered on the basis of calling and connected line identification as well as the privacy options available. This will allow the subscribers to make an informed choice about the privacy facilities they may want to use. The privacy options that are offered on a per-line basis do not necessarily have to be available as an automatic network service but may be obtainable through a simple request to the provider of the publicly available electronic communications service.

ePrivacy Directive Recital 35 notes that in digital mobile networks, location data giving the geographic position of the terminal equipment of the mobile user are processed to enable the transmission of communications. Such data are traffic data covered by Article 6 of the ePrivacy Directive. However, in addition, digital mobile networks may have the capacity to process location data, which are more precise than is necessary for the transmission of communications and which are used for the provision of value added services, such as services providing individualised traffic information and guidance to drivers. The processing of such data for value added services should only be allowed where subscribers have given their consent. Even in cases where subscribers have given their consent, they should have a simple means to temporarily deny the processing of location data, free of charge.

ePrivacy Directive Recital 36 notes that Member States may restrict the users' and subscribers' rights to privacy with regard to calling line identification where this is necessary to trace nuisance calls and with regard to calling line identification and location data where this is necessary to allow emergency services to carry out their tasks as effectively as possible. For these purposes, Member States may adopt specific provisions to entitle providers of electronic communications services to provide access to calling line identification and location data without the prior consent of the users or subscribers concerned.

ePrivacy Directive Recital 37 notes that safeguards should be provided for subscribers against the nuisance that may be caused by automatic call forwarding by others. Moreover, in such cases, it must be possible for subscribers to stop the forwarded calls being passed on to their terminals by simple request to the provider of the publicly available electronic communications service.

ePrivacy Directive Recital 38 notes that directories of subscribers to electronic communications services are widely distributed and public. The right to privacy of natural persons and the legitimate interest of legal persons require that subscribers are able to determine whether or not their personal data are published in a directory and if so, which. Providers of public directories should inform the subscribers to be included in such directories of the purposes of the directory and of any particular usage that may be made of electronic versions of public directories especially through search functions embedded in the software, such as reverse search functions enabling users of the directory to discover the name and address of the subscriber on the basis of a telephone number only.

ePrivacy Directive Recital 39 notes that the obligation to inform subscribers of the purpose(s) of public directories in which their personal data are to be included should be imposed on the party collecting the data for such inclusion. Where the data may be transmitted to one or more third parties, the subscriber should be informed of this possibility and of the recipient or the categories of possible recipients. Any transmission should be subject to the condition that the data may not be used for other purposes than those for which they were collected. If the party collecting the data from the subscriber or any third party to whom the data have been transmitted wishes to use the data for an additional purpose, the renewed consent of the subscriber is to be obtained either by the initial party collecting the data or by the third party to whom the data have been transmitted.

ePrivacy Directive Recital 40 notes that safeguards should be provided for subscribers against intrusion of their privacy by unsolicited communications for direct marketing purposes, in particular by means of automated calling machines, telefaxes, and emails, including SMS messages. These forms of unsolicited commercial communications may, on the one hand, be relatively easy and cheap to send, and on the other, may impose a burden and/or cost on the recipient. Moreover, in some cases their volume may also cause difficulties for electronic communications networks and terminal equipment. For such forms of unsolicited communications for direct marketing, it is justified to require that prior explicit consent of the recipients is obtained before such communications are addressed to them. The single market requires a harmonised approach to ensure simple, Community-wide rules for businesses and users.

ePrivacy Directive Recital 41 notes that within the context of an existing customer relationship, it is reasonable to allow the use of electronic contact details for the offering of similar products or services, but only by the same company that has obtained the electronic contact details in accordance with DP Directive 95. When electronic contact details are obtained, the customer should be informed about their further use for direct marketing in a clear and distinct manner, and be given the opportunity to refuse such usage. This opportunity should continue to be offered with each subsequent direct marketing message, free of charge, except for any costs for the transmission of this refusal.

ePrivacy Directive Recital 42 notes that other forms of direct marketing that are more costly for the sender and impose no financial costs on subscribers and users, such as person-to-person voice telephony calls, may justify the maintenance of a system giving subscribers or users the possibility to indicate that they do not want to receive such calls. Nevertheless, in order not to decrease existing levels of privacy protection,

Member States should be entitled to uphold national systems, only allowing such calls to subscribers and users who have given their prior consent.

ePrivacy Directive Recital 43 notes that to facilitate effective enforcement of Community rules on unsolicited messages for direct marketing, it is necessary to prohibit the use of false identities or false return addresses or numbers while sending unsolicited messages for direct marketing purposes.

ePrivacy Directive Recital 44 notes that certain electronic mail systems allow subscribers to view the sender and subject line of an electronic mail, and also to delete the message, without having to download the rest of the electronic mail's content or any attachments, thereby reducing costs that could arise from downloading unsolicited electronic mails or attachments. These arrangements may continue to be useful in certain cases as an additional tool to the general obligations established in the Directive.

ePrivacy Directive Recital 45 notes that the Directive is without prejudice to the arrangements Member States make to protect the legitimate interests of legal persons with regard to unsolicited communications for direct marketing purposes. Where Member States establish an opt-out register for such communications to legal persons, mostly business users, the provisions of Article 7 of Directive 2000/31/EC of the European Parliament and of the Council of 8 June 2000 on certain legal aspects of information society services, in particular electronic commerce, in the internal market (Directive on electronic commerce) are fully applicable.

ePrivacy Directive Recital 46 notes that the functionalities for the provision of electronic communications services may be integrated in the network or in any part of the terminal equipment of the user, including the software. The protection of the personal data and the privacy of the user of publicly available electronic communications services should be independent of the configuration of the various components necessary to provide the service and of the distribution of the necessary functionalities between these components. DP Directive 95 covers any form of processing of personal data regardless of the technology used. The existence of specific rules for electronic communications services alongside general rules for other components necessary for the provision of such services may not facilitate the protection of personal data and privacy in a technologically neutral way. It may therefore be necessary to adopt measures requiring manufacturers of certain types of equipment used for electronic communications services to construct their product in such a way as to incorporate safeguards to ensure that the personal data and privacy of the user and subscriber are protected. The adoption of such measures in accordance with Directive 1999/5/EC of the European Parliament and of the Council of 9 March 1999 on radio equipment and telecommunications terminal equipment and the mutual recognition of their conformity will ensure that the introduction of technical features of electronic communication equipment, including software for data protection purposes, is harmonised in order to be compatible with the implementation of the internal market.

ePrivacy Directive Recital 47 notes that where the rights of the users and subscribers are not respected, Member State legislation should provide for judicial remedies. Penalties should be imposed on any person, whether governed by private or public law, who fails to comply with the national measures taken under the Directive.

Recital 48 notes that it is useful, in the field of application of the Directive, to draw on the experience of the WP29.

ePrivacy Directive Recital 49 notes that to facilitate compliance with the provisions of the Directive, certain specific arrangements are needed for processing of data already underway on the date that Member State implementing legislation pursuant to the Directive enters into force.

ePrivacy Directive: Scope

ePrivacy Directive Article 1 refers to the scope and aim. Article 1(1) provides that the Directive harmonises the provisions of the Member States to ensure an equivalent level of protection of fundamental rights and freedoms, and in particular the right to privacy, with respect to the processing of personal data in the electronic communications sector and to ensure the free movement of such data and of electronic communications equipment and services in the EU.

Article 1(2) provides that the provisions of the Directive particularise and complement DP Directive 95 for the purposes mentioned in Article 1(1). Moreover, they provide for protection of the legitimate interests of subscribers who are legal persons.

Article 1(3) provides that the ePrivacy Directive shall not apply to activities that fall outside the scope of the Treaty establishing the European Community, such as those covered by Titles V and VI of the Treaty on European Union, and in any case to activities concerning public security, defence, State security (including the economic well-being of the State when the activities relate to State security matters) and the activities of the State in areas of criminal law.

ePrivacy Directive: Definitions

Article 2 of the ePrivacy Directive refers to definitions. The definitions in the DP Directive 95 and in the ePrivacy Directive shall apply. The following additional definitions shall also apply.

User

"User'" means any natural person using a publicly available electronic communications service, for private or business purposes, without necessarily having subscribed to this service.

Traffic Data

"Traffic data" means any data processed for the purpose of the conveyance of a communication on an electronic communications network or for the billing thereof.

Location Data

"Location data" means any data processed in an electronic communications network, indicating the geographic position of the terminal equipment of a user of a publicly available electronic communications service.

Communication

"Communication" means any information exchanged or conveyed between a finite number of parties by means of a publicly available electronic communications service. This does not include any information conveyed as part of a broadcasting service to the public over an electronic communications network except to the extent that the information can be related to the identifiable subscriber or user receiving the information.

Call

"Call" means a connection established by means of a publicly available telephone service allowing two-way communication in real time.

Consent

"Consent" by a user or subscriber corresponds to the data subject's consent in DP Directive 95.

Value Added Service

"Value added service" means any service that requires the processing of traffic data or location data other than traffic data beyond what is necessary for the transmission of a communication or the billing thereof.

Electronic Mail

"Electronic mail" means any text, voice, sound or image message sent over a public communications network that can be stored in the network or in the recipient's terminal equipment until it is collected by the recipient.

ePrivacy Directive: Services

Article 3 relates to the services concerned. Article 3(1) provides that the ePrivacy Directive shall apply to the processing of personal data in connection with the provision of publicly available electronic communications services in public communications networks in the EU.

Article 3(2) provides that Articles 8, 10 and 11 shall apply to subscriber lines connected to digital exchanges and, where technically possible and if it does not require a disproportionate economic effort, to subscriber lines connected to analogue exchanges.

Article 3(3) provides that cases where it would be technically impossible or require a disproportionate economic effort to fulfil the requirements of Articles 8, 10 and 11 shall be notified to the Commission by the Member States.

ePrivacy Directive: Unsolicited Communications/Spam

Article 13 refers to unsolicited communications. Article 13(1) provides that the use of automated calling systems without human intervention (automatic calling machines), facsimile machines (fax) or electronic mail for the purposes of direct marketing may only be allowed in respect of subscribers who have given their prior consent.

However, Article 13(1), where a natural or legal person obtains from its customers their electronic contact details for electronic mail, in the context of the sale of a product or a service, in accordance with DP Directive 95, the same natural or legal person may use these electronic contact details for direct marketing of its own similar products or services provided that customers clearly and distinctly are given the opportunity to object, free of charge and in an easy manner, to such use of electronic contact details when they are collected and on the occasion of each message in case the customer has not initially refused such use.[8]

Member States shall take appropriate measures to ensure that, free of charge, unsolicited communications for purposes of direct marketing, in cases other than those referred to in Article 13(1) and (2), are not allowed either without the consent of the subscribers concerned or in respect of subscribers who do not wish to receive these communications, the choice between these options to be determined by national legislation.[9]

In any event, the practice of sending electronic mail for purposes of direct marketing disguising or concealing the identity of the sender on whose behalf the communication is made, or without a valid address to which the recipient may send a request that such communications cease, shall be prohibited.[10]

Article 13(1) and (3) shall apply to subscribers who are natural persons. Member States shall also ensure, in the framework of Community law and applicable Member State legislation, that the legitimate interests of subscribers other than natural persons with regard to unsolicited communications are sufficiently protected.[11]

---

8.   art 13(2) *ibid*.
9.   art 13(3) *ibid*.
10. art 13(4) *ibid*.
11. art 13(5) *ibid*.

ePrivacy Directive: Security

Article 4 relates to security. Article 4(1) provides that the provider of a publicly available electronic communications service must take appropriate technical and organisational measures to safeguard security of its services, if necessary in conjunction with the provider of the public communications network with respect to network security. Having regard to the state of the technology and the cost of their implementation, these measures shall ensure a level of security appropriate to the risk presented.

In case of a particular risk of a breach of the security of the network, the provider of a publicly available electronic communications service must inform the subscribers concerning such risk and, where the risk lies outside the scope of the measures to be taken by the service provider, of any possible remedies, including an indication of the likely costs involved.[12]

ePrivacy Directive: Confidentiality

Article 5 refers to confidentiality of the communications. Article 5(1) provides that Member States shall ensure the confidentiality of communications and the related traffic data by means of a public communications network and publicly available electronic communications services, through Member State legislation. In particular, they shall prohibit listening, tapping, storage or other kinds of interception or surveillance of communications and the related traffic data by persons other than users, without the consent of the users concerned, except when legally authorised to do so in accordance with Article 15(1). This paragraph shall not prevent technical storage that is necessary for the conveyance of a communication without prejudice to the principle of confidentiality.

Paragraph 5(1) shall not affect any legally authorised recording of communications and the related traffic data when carried out in the course of lawful business practice for the purpose of providing evidence of a commercial transaction or of any other business communication.[13]

Member States shall ensure that the use of electronic communications networks to store information or to gain access to information stored in the terminal equipment of a subscriber or user is only allowed on condition that the subscriber or user concerned is provided with clear and comprehensive information in accordance with DP Directive 95, *inter alia* about the purposes of the processing, and is offered the right to refuse such processing by the data controller. This shall not prevent any technical storage or access for the sole purpose of carrying out or facilitating the transmission of a communication over an electronic communications network, or as strictly

---

12.   art 4(2) *ibid.*
13.   art 5(2) *ibid.*

necessary in order to provide an information society service explicitly requested by the subscriber or user.[14]

ePrivacy Directive: Traffic Data

Article 6 refers to traffic data. Article 6(1) provides that traffic data relating to subscribers and users processed and stored by the provider of a public communications network or publicly available electronic communications service must be erased or made anonymous when it is no longer needed for the purpose of the transmission of a communication without prejudice to Article 6(2), (3) and (5) and Article 15(1).

Traffic data necessary for the purposes of subscriber billing and interconnection payments may be processed. Such processing is permissible only up to the end of the period during which the bill may lawfully be challenged or payment pursued.[15]

Article 6(3) provides that for the purpose of marketing electronic communications services or for the provision of value added services, the provider of a publicly available electronic communications service may process the data referred to in paragraph 1 to the extent and for the duration necessary for such services or marketing, if the subscriber or user to whom the data relates has given his consent. Users or subscribers shall be given the possibility to withdraw their consent for the processing of traffic data at any time.

The service provider must inform the subscriber or user of the types of traffic data that are processed and of the duration of such processing for the purposes mentioned in paragraph 2 and, prior to obtaining consent, for the purposes mentioned in paragraph 6(3).[16]

Processing of traffic data, in accordance with Article 6(1), (2), (3) and (4), must be restricted to persons acting under the authority of providers of the public communications networks and publicly available electronic communications services handling billing or traffic management, customer enquiries, fraud detection, marketing electronic communications services or providing a value added service, and must be restricted to what is necessary for the purposes of such activities.[17]

Article 6(1), (2), (3) and (5) shall apply without prejudice to the possibility for competent bodies to be informed of traffic data in conformity with applicable legislation with a view to settling disputes, in particular interconnection or billing disputes.[18]

---

14.   art 5(3) *ibid.*
15.   art 6(2) *ibid.*
16.   art 6(3) *ibid.*
17.   art 6(3) *ibid.*
18.   art 6(6) *ibid.*

ePrivacy Directive: Non-Itemised Billing

Article 7 relates to itemised billing. Article 7(1) provides that subscribers shall have the right to receive non-itemised bills. Article 7(2) provides that Member States shall apply national provisions in order to reconcile the rights of subscribers receiving itemised bills with the right to privacy of calling users and called subscribers, for example by ensuring that sufficient alternative privacy enhancing methods of communications or payments are available to such users and subscribers.

ePrivacy Directive: Calling and Connected Line Identification

Article 8 relates to presentation and restriction of calling and connected line identification.

Where presentation of calling line identification is offered, the service provider must offer the calling user the possibility, using a simple means and free of charge, of preventing the presentation of the calling line identification on a per-call basis.[19] The calling subscriber must have this possibility on a per-line basis.

Where presentation of calling line identification is offered, the service provider must offer the called subscriber the possibility, using a simple means and free of charge for reasonable use of this function, of preventing the presentation of the calling line identification of incoming calls.[20]

Where presentation of calling line identification is offered and where the calling line identification is presented prior to the call being established, the service provider must offer the called subscriber the possibility, using a simple means, of rejecting incoming calls where the presentation of the calling line identification has been prevented by the calling user or subscriber.[21]

Where presentation of connected line identification is offered, the service provider must offer the called subscriber the possibility, using a simple means and free of charge, of preventing the presentation of the connected line identification to the calling user.[22]

Article 8(1) shall also apply with regard to calls to third countries originating in the Community. Article 8(2), (3) and (4) shall also apply to incoming calls originating in third countries.[23]

---

19. art 8(1) *ibid.*
20. art 8(2) *ibid.*
21. art 8(3) *ibid.*
22. art 8(4) *ibid.*
23. art 8(5) *ibid.*

Member States shall ensure that where presentation of calling and/or connected line identification is offered, the providers of publicly available electronic communications services inform the public thereof and of the possibilities set out in Article 8(1), (2), (3) and (4).[24]

ePrivacy Directive: Location Data other than Traffic Data

Article 9 of the ePD relates to location data other than traffic data. Article 9(1) provides that where location data other than traffic data, relating to users or subscribers of public communications networks or publicly available electronic communications services can be processed, such data may only be processed when they are made anonymous, or with the *consent* of the users or subscribers to the extent and for the duration necessary for the provision of a value added service. The service provider must inform the users or subscribers, prior to obtaining their consent, of the type of location data other than traffic data that will be processed, of the purposes and duration of the processing and whether the data will be transmitted to a third party for the purpose of providing the value added service. Users or subscribers shall be given the possibility to withdraw their consent for the processing of location data other than traffic data at any time.

This is increasingly important as more and more smart phones and electronic devices permit the capture of location-based data relating to individuals and or their personal equipment.

Where consent of the users or subscribers has been obtained for the processing of location data other than traffic data, the user or subscriber must continue to have the possibility, using a simple means and free of charge, of temporarily refusing the processing of such data for each connection to the network or for each transmission of a communication.[25]

Processing of location data other than traffic data in accordance with Article 9(1) and (2) must be restricted to persons acting under the authority of the provider of the public communications network or publicly available communications service or of the third party providing the value added service, and must be restricted to what is necessary for the purposes of providing the value added service.[26]

ePrivacy Directive: Exceptions

Article 10 relates to exceptions. Member States shall ensure that there are transparent procedures governing the way in which a provider of a public communications network and/or a publicly available electronic communications service may override:

---

24.   art 8(6) *ibid.*
25.   art 9(1) *ibid.*
26.   art 9(1) *ibid.*

- the elimination of the presentation of calling line identification, on a temporary basis, upon application of a subscriber requesting the tracing of malicious or nuisance calls. In this case, in accordance with Member State law, the data containing the identification of the calling subscriber will be stored and be made available by the provider of a public communications network and/or publicly available electronic communications service;

- the elimination of the presentation of calling line identification and the temporary denial or absence of consent of a subscriber or user for the processing of location data, on a per-line basis for organisations dealing with emergency calls and recognised as such by a Member State, including law enforcement agencies, ambulance services and fire brigades, for the purpose of responding to such calls.

Article 11 refers to automatic call forwarding. It provides that Member States shall ensure that any subscriber has the possibility, using a simple means and free of charge, of stopping automatic call forwarding by a third party to the subscriber's terminal.

ePrivacy Directive: Directories

Article 12 refers to directories of subscribers. Article 12(1) provides that Member States shall ensure that subscribers are informed, free of charge and before they are included in the directory, about the purpose(s) of a printed or electronic directory of subscribers available to the public or obtainable through directory enquiry services, in which their personal data can be included and of any further usage possibilities based on search functions embedded in electronic versions of the directory.

Member States shall ensure that subscribers are given the opportunity to determine whether their personal data are included in a public directory, and if so, which, to the extent that such data are relevant for the purpose of the directory as determined by the provider of the directory, and to verify, correct or withdraw such data.[27] Not being included in a public subscriber directory, verifying, correcting or withdrawing personal data from it shall be free of charge.

Member States may require that for any purpose of a public directory other than the search of contact details of persons on the basis of their name and, where necessary, a minimum of other identifiers, additional consent be asked of the subscribers.[28]

Article 12(1) and (2) shall apply to subscribers who are natural persons. Member States shall also ensure, in the framework of Community law and applicable Member State legislation, that the legitimate interests of subscribers other than natural persons with regard to their entry in public directories are sufficiently protected.[29]

---

27. art 12(2) *ibid.*
28. art 12(3) *ibid.*
29. art 12(4) *ibid.*

ePrivacy Directive: Technical Features

ePrivacy Directive[30] Article 14 refers to technical features and standardisation. Article 14(1) provides that in implementing the provisions of the Directive, Member States shall ensure, subject to Article 14(2) and (3), that no mandatory requirements for specific technical features are imposed on terminal or other electronic communication equipment that could impede the placing of equipment on the market and the free circulation of such equipment in and between Member States.

Where provisions of the Directive can be implemented only by requiring specific technical features in electronic communications networks, Member States shall inform the Commission in accordance with the procedure provided for by Directive 98/34/EC of the European Parliament and of the Council of 22 June 1998 laying down a procedure for the provision of information in the field of technical standards and regulations and of rules on information society services.[31]

Article 14(3) provides that where required, measures may be adopted to ensure that terminal equipment is constructed in a way that is compatible with the right of users to protect and control the use of their personal data, in accordance with Directive 1999/5/EC and Council Decision 87/95/EEC of 22 December 1986 on standardisation in the field of information technology and communications.

ePrivacy Directive: Re DP Directive 95

Article 15 refers to the application of certain provisions of DP Directive 95. Article 15(1) provides that Member States may adopt legislative measures to restrict the scope of the rights and obligations provided for in Articles 5, 6, 8(1), 8(2), 8(3), 8(4) and 9 of the ePrivacy Directive when such restriction constitutes a necessary, appropriate and proportionate measure within a democratic society to safeguard national security (i.e. State security), defence, public security, and the prevention, investigation, detection and prosecution of criminal offences or of unauthorised use of the electronic communication system, as referred to in Article 13(1) of DP Directive 95. To this end, Member States may, *inter alia*, adopt legislative measures providing for the retention of data for a limited period justified on the grounds laid down in this paragraph. All the measures referred to in this paragraph shall be in accordance with the general principles of Community law, including those referred to in Article 6(1) and (2) of the Treaty on European Union.

Article 15(1) provides that the provisions of Chapter III on judicial remedies, liability and sanctions of DP Directive 95 shall apply with regard to Member State provisions adopted pursuant to the Directive and with regard to the individual rights derived from the Directive.

---

30. *ibid.*
31. art 14(2) *ibid.*

The WP29 shall also carry out the tasks laid down in Article 30 of that Directive with regard to matters covered by the ePrivacy Directive, namely the protection of fundamental rights and freedoms and of legitimate interests in the electronic communications sector.[32]

ePrivacy Directive Amended by Directive 2006/24/EC

The ePrivacy Directive was amended by Directive 2006/24/EC of 15 March 2006 on the retention of data generated or processed in connection with the provision of publicly available electronic communications services or of public communications networks and amending the ePrivacy Directive.[33]

Directive 2006/24/EC: Background

Recital 1 of Directive 2006/24/EC notes that DP Directive 95 requires Member States to protect the rights and freedoms of natural persons with regard to the processing of personal data, and in particular their right to privacy, and in order to ensure the freeflow of personal data in the Community.

Recital 2 notes that the ePrivacy Directive (and the previous 1997 Directive) translates the principles set out in DP Directive 95 into specific rules for the electronic communications sector (previously the telecommunications sector).

Articles 5, 6 and 9 of the ePrivacy Directive lay down the rules applicable to the processing by network and service providers of traffic and location data generated by using electronic communications services. Such data must be erased or made anonymous when no longer needed for the purpose of the transmission of a communication, except for the data necessary for billing or interconnection payments. Subject to consent, certain data may also be processed for marketing purposes and the provision of value-added services.[34]

Article 15(1) of the ePrivacy Directive sets out the conditions under which Member States may restrict the scope of the rights and obligations provided for in Articles 5, 6, 8(1), 8(2), 8(3), 8(4), and 9 of that Directive. Any such restrictions must be necessary, appropriate and proportionate within a democratic society for specific public order purposes, i.e. to safeguard national security, defence, public security or the prevention, investigation, detection and prosecution of criminal offences or of unauthorised use of the electronic communications systems.[35]

---

32. art 15(3) *ibid.*
33. *ibid.*
34. Recital 3 Directive 2006/24/EC.
35. Recital 4 Directive 2006/24/EC.

Several Member States have adopted legislation providing for the retention of data by service providers for the prevention, investigation, detection, and prosecution of criminal offences. Those Member State provisions vary considerably.[36] They are also controvercial and subject to litigation, e.g., Digital Rights Ireland.

The legal and technical differences between Member State provisions concerning the retention of data for the purpose of prevention, investigation, detection and prosecution of criminal offences present obstacles to the internal market for electronic communications, since service providers are faced with different requirements regarding the types of traffic and location data to be retained and the conditions and periods of retention.[37]

The Declaration on Combating Terrorism adopted by the European Council on 25 March 2004 instructed the Council to examine measures for establishing rules on the retention of communications traffic data by service providers.[38]

Given the importance of traffic and location data for the investigation, detection, and prosecution of criminal offences, as demonstrated by research and the practical experience of several Member States, there is a need to ensure at European level that data that are generated or processed, in the course of the supply of communications services, by providers of publicly available electronic communications services or of a public communications network are retained for a certain period, subject to the conditions provided for in the Directive.[39]

Recital 12 notes that Article 15(1) of the ePrivacy Directive continues to apply to data, including data relating to unsuccessful call attempts, the retention of which is not specifically required under the Directive and which therefore fall outside the scope thereof, and to retention for purposes, including judicial purposes, other than those covered by the Directive.

Recital 13 notes that the Directive relates only to data generated or processed as a consequence of a communication or a communication service and does not relate to data that are the content of the information communicated. Data should be retained in such a way as to avoid their being retained more than once. Data generated or processed when supplying the communications services concerned refers to data that are accessible. In particular, as regards the retention of data relating to internet email and internet telephony, the obligation to retain data may apply only in respect of data from the providers' or the network providers' own services.

Technologies relating to electronic communications are changing rapidly and the legitimate requirements of the competent authorities may evolve. In order to obtain

---

36.   Recital 5 *ibid.*
37.   Recital 6 *ibid.*
38.   Recital 8 *ibid.*
39.   Recital 11 *ibid.*

advice and encourage the sharing of experience of best practice in these matters, the Commission intends to establish a group composed of Member States' law enforcement authorities, associations of the electronic communications industry, representatives of the European Parliament and data protection authorities, including the European Data Protection Supervisor.[40]

Recital 15 notes that DP Directive 95 and ePrivacy Directive are fully applicable to the data retained in accordance with the Directive. Article 30(1)(c) of DP Directive 95 requires the consultation of the Article 29 Working Party established under Article 29 of that Directive.

The obligations incumbent on service providers concerning measures to ensure data quality, which derive from Article 6 of DP Directive 95, and their obligations concerning measures to ensure confidentiality and security of processing of data, which derive from Articles 16 and 17 of that Directive, apply in full to data being retained within the meaning of the Directive.[41]

It is essential that Member States adopt legislative measures to ensure that data retained under the Directive are provided to the competent national authorities only in accordance with Member State legislation in full respect of the fundamental rights of the persons concerned.[42]

Recital 18 notes that in this context Article 24 of DP Directive 95 imposes an obligation on Member States to lay down sanctions for infringements of the provisions adopted pursuant to that Directive. Article 15(2) of the ePrivacy Directive imposes the same requirement in relation to Member State provisions adopted pursuant to the ePrivacy Directive. Council Framework Decision 2005/222/JHA of 24 February 2005 on attacks against information systems provides that the intentional illegal access to information systems, including to data retained therein, is to be made punishable as a criminal offence.

The right of any person who has suffered damage as a result of an unlawful processing operation or of any act incompatible with Member State provisions adopted pursuant to DP Directive 95 to receive compensation, which derives from Article 23 of that Directive, applies also in relation to the unlawful processing of any personal data pursuant to the Directive.

Recital 20 notes that the 2001 Council of Europe Convention on Cybercrime and the 1981 Council of Europe Convention for the Protection of Individuals with Regard to Automatic Processing of Personal Data also cover data being retained within the meaning of the Directive.

---

40. Recital 14 *ibid.*
41. Recital 16 Directive 2006/24/EC.
42. Recital 17 *ibid.*

Recital 21 notes that since the objectives of the Directive, namely to harmonise the obligations on providers to retain certain data and to ensure that those data are available for the purpose of the investigation, detection and prosecution of serious crime, as defined by each Member State in its national law, cannot be sufficiently achieved by the Member States and can therefore, by reason of the scale and effects of the Directive, be better achieved at Community level. The Community may adopt measures in accordance with the principle of subsidiarity as set out in Article 5 of the Treaty. In accordance with the principle of proportionality, as set out in that Article, the Directive does not go beyond what is necessary in order to achieve those objectives.

Recital 22 notes that the Directive respects the fundamental rights and observes the principles recognised, in particular, by the Charter of Fundamental Rights of the European Union. In particular, the Directive, together with the ePrivacy Directive, seeks to ensure full compliance with citizens' fundamental rights to respect for private life and communications and to the protection of their personal data, as enshrined in Articles 7 and 8 of the Charter.

Given that the obligations on providers of electronic communications services should be proportionate, the Directive requires that they retain only such data as are generated or processed in the process of supplying their communications services.[43] To the extent that such data are not generated or processed by those providers, there is no obligation to retain them. The Directive is not intended to harmonise the technology for retaining data, the choice of which is a matter to be resolved at national level.

Recital 25 notes that the Directive is without prejudice to the power of Member States to adopt legislative measures concerning the right of access to, and use of, data by Member State authorities, as designated by them. Issues of access to data retained pursuant to the Directive by national authorities for such activities as are referred to in the first indent of Article 3(2) of DP Directive 95 fall outside the scope of Community law. However, they may be subject to Member State law or action pursuant to Title VI of the Treaty on European Union. Such laws or action must fully respect fundamental rights as they result from the common constitutional traditions of the Member States and as guaranteed by the ECHR. Under Article 8 of the ECHR, as interpreted by the European Court of Human Rights, interference by public authorities with privacy rights must meet the requirements of necessity and proportionality and must therefore serve specified, explicit and legitimate purposes and be exercised in a manner that is adequate, relevant and not excessive in relation to the purpose of the interference.

---

43.   Recital 23 Directive 2006/24/EC.

Directive 2006/24/EC: Scope

Article 1 refers to subject matter and scope. Article 1(1) provides that the Directive aims to harmonise Member States' provisions concerning the obligations of the providers of publicly available electronic communications services or of public communications networks with respect to the retention of certain data that are generated or processed by them, in order to ensure that the data are available for the purpose of the investigation, detection and prosecution of serious crime, as defined by each Member State in its national law.

Article 1(2) provides that the Directive shall apply to traffic and location data on both legal entities and natural persons and to the related data necessary to identify the subscriber or registered user. It shall not apply to the content of electronic communications, including information consulted using an electronic communications network.

Directive 2006/24/EC: Definitions

Article 2 of Directive 2006/24/EC refers to definitions. The definitions in DP Directive 95,[44] in the ePrivacy Directive shall apply.

Article 2(1) of Directive 2006/24/EC provides that for the purpose of this Directive:

"data"
means traffic data and location data and the related data necessary to identify the subscriber or user;

"user"
means any legal entity or natural person using a publicly available electronic communications service, for private or business purposes, without necessarily having subscribed to that service;

"telephone service"
means calls (including voice, voicemail and conference and data calls), supplementary services (including call forwarding and call transfer) and messaging and multi-media services (including short message services, enhanced media services and multi-media services);

"user ID"
means a unique identifier allocated to persons when they subscribe to or register with an internet access service or internet communications service;

"cell ID"
means the identity of the cell from which a mobile telephony call originated or in which it terminated;

---

44. *ibid.*

| "unsuccessful call attempt" | means a communication where a telephone call has been successfully connected but not answered or there has been a network management intervention. |

Directive 2006/24/EC: Obligation to Retain Data

Article 3 of Directive 2006/24/EC refers to an obligation to retain data. Article 3(1) provides that by way of derogation from Articles 5, 6 and 9 of the ePrivacy Directive, Member States shall adopt measures to ensure that the data specified in Article 5 of the Directive are retained in accordance with the provisions thereof, to the extent that those data are generated or processed by providers of publicly available electronic communications services or of a public communications network within their jurisdiction in the process of supplying the communications services concerned.

Article 3(2) provides that the obligation to retain data provided for in paragraph 1 shall include the retention of the data specified in Article 5 relating to unsuccessful call attempts where those data are generated or processed, and stored (as regards telephony data) or logged (as regards internet data) by providers of publicly available electronic communications services or of a public communications network within the jurisdiction of the Member State concerned in the process of supplying the communication services concerned. The Directive shall not require data relating to unconnected calls to be retained.

Directive 2006/24/EC: Access

Article 4 of Directive 2006/24/EC refers to access to data. It provides that Member States shall adopt measures to ensure that data retained in accordance with the Directive are provided only to the competent national authorities in specific cases and in accordance with Member State law. The procedures to be followed and the conditions to be fulfilled in order to gain access to retained data in accordance with necessity and proportionality requirements shall be defined by each Member State in its national law, subject to the relevant provisions of European Union law or public international law, and in particular the ECHR as interpreted by the European Court of Human Rights.

Directive 2006/24/EC: Data Categories

Article 5 of Directive 2006/24/EC refers to categories of data to be retained. Article 5(1) provides that Member States shall ensure that the following categories of data are retained under the Directive:

(a) data necessary to trace and identify the source of a communication;

     (1) concerning fixed network telephony and mobile telephony:

        (i) the calling telephone number;

        (ii) the name and address of the subscriber or registered user;

     (2) concerning internet access, email and internet telephony:

        (i) the user ID(s) allocated;

        (ii) the user ID and telephone number allocated to any communication entering the public telephone network;

        (iii) the name and address of the subscriber or registered user to whom an Internet Protocol (IP) address, user ID or telephone number was allocated at the time of the communication;

(b) data necessary to identify the destination of a communication;

     (1) concerning fixed network telephony and mobile telephony:

        (i) the number(s) dialled (the telephone number(s) called), and, in cases involving supplementary services such as call forwarding or call transfer, the number or numbers to which the call is routed;

        (ii) the name(s) and address(es) of the subscriber(s) or registered user(s);

     (2) concerning email and internet telephony:

        (i) the user ID or telephone number of the intended recipient(s) of an internet telephony call;

        (ii) the name(s) and address(es) of the subscriber(s) or registered user(s) and user ID of the intended recipient of the communication;

(c) data necessary to identify the date, time and duration of a communication:

     (1) concerning fixed network telephony and mobile telephony, the date and time of the start and end of the communication;

     (2) concerning internet access, email and internet telephony:

        (i) the date and time of the log-in and log-off of the internet access service, based on a certain time zone, together with the IP address, whether dynamic or static, allocated by the internet access service provider to a communication, and the user ID of the subscriber or registered user;

        (ii) the date and time of the log-in and log-off of the email service or internet telephony service, based on a certain time zone;

(d) data necessary to identify the type of communication:

(1) concerning fixed network telephony and mobile telephony: the telephone service used;

(2) concerning email and internet telephony: the internet service used;

(e) data necessary to identify users' communication equipment or what purports to be their equipment:

(1) concerning fixed network telephony, the calling and called telephone numbers;

(2) concerning mobile telephony:

(i) the calling and called telephone numbers;

(ii) the International Mobile Subscriber Identity (IMSI) of the calling party;

(iii) the International Mobile Equipment Identity (IMEI) of the calling party;

(iv) the IMSI of the called party;

(v) the IMEI of the called party;

(vi) in the case of prepaid anonymous services, the date and time of the initial activation of the service and the location label (Cell ID) from which the service was activated;

(3) concerning internet access, email and internet telephony:

(i) the calling telephone number for dial-up access;

(ii) the digital subscriber line (DSL) or other end point of the originator of the communication;

(f) data necessary to identify the location of mobile communication equipment:

(1) the location label (Cell ID) at the start of the communication;

(2) data identifying the geographic location of cells by reference to their location labels (Cell ID) during the period for which communications data are retained.

No data revealing the content of the communication may be retained pursuant to the Directive.

Directive 2006/24/EC: Periods of Retention

Article 6 of Directive 2006/24/EC refers to periods of retention. Member States shall ensure that the categories of data specified in Article 5 are retained for periods of not less than six months and not more than two years from the date of the communication.

Directive 2006/24/EC: Security

Article 7 of Directive 2006/24/EC refers to data protection and data security. It provides that without prejudice to the provisions adopted pursuant to DP95 and Directive 2002/58/EC, each Member State shall ensure that providers of publicly available electronic communications services or of a public communications network respect, as a minimum, the following data security principles with respect to data retained in accordance with the Directive:

- the retained data shall be of the same quality and subject to the same security and protection as those data on the network;
- the data shall be subject to appropriate technical and organisational measures to protect the data against accidental or unlawful destruction, accidental loss or alteration, or unauthorised or unlawful storage, processing, access or disclosure;
- the data shall be subject to appropriate technical and organisational measures to ensure that they can be accessed by specially authorised personnel only; and
- the data, except those that have been accessed and preserved, shall be destroyed at the end of the period of retention.

Directive 2006/24/EC: Storage Requirements for Retained Data

Article 8 of Directive 2006/24/EC refers to storage requirements for retained data. It provides that Member States shall ensure that the data specified in Article 5 are retained in accordance with the Directive in such a way that the data retained and any other necessary information relating to such data can be transmitted upon request to the competent authorities without undue delay.

Directive 2006/24/EC: Data Protection Commissioner

Article 9 of Directive 2006/24/EC refers to the supervisory authority. Each Member State shall designate one or more public authorities to be responsible for monitoring the application within its territory of the provisions adopted by the Member States pursuant to Article 7 regarding the security of the stored data. Those authorities may be the same authorities as those referred to in Article 28 of DP Directive 95. The authorities referred to in paragraph 1 shall act with complete independence in carrying out the monitoring referred to in that paragraph.

Directive 2006/24/EC: Statistics on Retention

Article 10 of Directive 2006/24/EC refers to statistics. Article 10(1) provides that Member States shall ensure that the Commission is provided on a yearly basis with statistics on the retention of data generated or processed in connection with the provision of publicly available electronic communications services or a public communications network. Such statistics shall include:

- the cases in which information was provided to the competent authorities in accordance with applicable Member State law;

- the time elapsed between the date on which the data were retained and the date on which the competent authority requested the transmission of the data; and

- the cases where requests for data could not be met.

Article 10(2) provides that such statistics shall not contain personal data.

Directive 2006/24/EC: ePrivacy Directive

Article 11 of Directive 2006/24/EC refers to amendment of the ePrivacy Directive. The following paragraph was inserted in Article 15 of the ePrivacy Directive:

> 1a. Paragraph 1 shall not apply to data specifically required by Directive 2006/24/EC of the European Parliament and of the Council of 15 March 2006 on the retention of data generated or processed in connection with the provision of publicly available electronic communications services or of public communications networks [] to be retained for the purposes referred to in Article 1(1) of that Directive.

Directive 2006/24/EC: Future Measures

Article 12 of Directive 2006/24/EC refers to future measures. Article 12(1) provides that a Member State facing particular circumstances that warrant an extension for a limited period of the maximum retention period referred to in Article 6 may take the necessary measures. That Member State shall immediately notify the Commission and inform the other Member States of the measures taken under this Article and shall state the grounds for introducing them.

Directive 2006/24/EC: Remedies, Liability and Penalties

Article 13 of Directive 2006/24/EC refers to remedies, liability and penalties. Article 13(1) provides that each Member State shall take the necessary measures to ensure that the Member State measures implementing Chapter III of DP Directive 95 providing for judicial remedies, liability and sanctions are fully implemented with respect to the processing of data under this Directive.

Article 13(2) of Directive 2006/24/EC provides that each Member State shall, in particular, take the necessary measures to ensure that any intentional access to, or transfer of, data retained in accordance with this Directive that is not permitted under Member State law adopted pursuant to this Directive is punishable by penalties, including administrative or criminal penalties, that are effective, proportionate and dissuasive.

Conclusion

Originally envisaged as relating to telecoms type data only, this secondary aspect of the data protection regime has expanded in substance, scope and detail. While much of it is still specific to telecoms companies and entities involved in the transfer of electronic communications, certain issues are more generally applicable. The ePrivacy Directive as amended applies to all organisations who wish to engage in direct marketing through a variety of means. Compliance is necessary and needs to be planned in advance. If not specifically exempted from the default rule it is difficult to envisage in permissible direct marketing (DM).

CHAPTER 23

Electronic Direct Marketing and Spam

Introduction

Direct marketing (DM) tends to be a growing contentious area of data protection practice, in addition to data breach/data loss and internet/social networking data protection issues.

Most organisations need to engage in direct marketing (DM) at some stage, some more heavily than others. Many organisations may even go so far as to say that direct marketing is an essential ingredient of continued commercial success.

However, direct marketing (DM) is sometimes viewed as Spam and unsolicited commercial communications, which are unwanted and also unlawful. The data protection regime (and e-commerce legal regime) refers to permissible direct marking (DM) and sets out various obligatory requirements while at the same time setting a default position of prohibiting non-exempted or non-permitted electronic direct marketing.

Direct marketing (DM)

If the organisation anticipates that personal data kept by it will be processed for the purposes of direct marketing, it must inform the persons to whom the data relates that they may object by means of a request in writing to the data controller and free of charge.[1]

Unsolicited Communications in the ePrivacy Directive

Article 13 of the ePrivacy Directive refers to unsolicited communications. Article 13(1) provides that the use of automated calling systems without human intervention

---

1. See, for example, Edwards, "Consumer Privacy Law 1: Online Direct Marketing", and Edwards and Hatcher, "Consumer Privacy Law: Data Collection, Profiling and Targeting", each in Edwards and Waelde (eds), *Law and the Internet* (Oxford: Hart, 2009), pp 489 *et seq* and pp 511 *et seq* respectively.

(automatic calling machines), facsimile machines (fax) or electronic mail for the purposes of direct marketing may only be allowed in respect of subscribers who have given their prior consent.

Article 13(2) provides that, notwithstanding Article 13(1), where a natural or legal person obtains from its customers their electronic contact details for electronic mail, in the context of the sale of a product or a service, in accordance with DP Directive 95, the same natural or legal person may use these electronic contact details for direct marketing of its own similar products or services provided that customers clearly and distinctly are given the opportunity to object, free of charge and in an easy manner, to such use of electronic contact details when they are collected and on the occasion of each message in case the customer has not initially refused such use.

Member States shall take appropriate measures to ensure that, free of charge, unsolicited communications for purposes of direct marketing, in cases other than those referred to in Article 13(1) and (2), are not allowed either without the consent of the subscribers concerned or in respect of subscribers who do not wish to receive these communications, the choice between these options to be determined by Member State legislation.[2]

In any event, the practice of sending electronic mail for purposes of direct marketing disguising or concealing the identity of the sender on whose behalf the communication is made, or without a valid address to which the recipient may send a request that such communications cease, shall be prohibited.[3]

Article 13(5) provides that Article 13(1) and (3) shall apply to subscribers who are natural persons. Member States shall also ensure, in the framework of Community law and applicable Member State legislation, that the legitimate interests of subscribers other than natural persons with regard to unsolicited communications are sufficiently protected.

Marketing Default Position

How should organisations go about data protection compliant direct marketing? When is DM permitted? All organisations should carefully assess compliance issues when considering any direct marketing activities. Getting it wrong can be costly and can have enforcement and investigation consequences.

Article 13 of the ePrivacy Directive provides a number of rules in relation to unsolicited communications. Article 13(1) provides that:

---

2.   art 13(3) Directive 2002/58/EC of the European Parliament and of the Council of 12 July 2002 concerning the processing of personal data and the protection of privacy in the electronic communications sector.

3.   art 13(4) *ibid.*

- automated calling systems without human intervention (automatic calling machines);
- facsimile machines (fax); or
- electronic mail,

for the purposes of direct marketing may *only* be allowed in respect of subscribers who have given their *prior consent*.

Therefore, there is a default rule prohibiting the forms of direct marketing (DM) referred to above *without* prior consent. Many marketing-orientated organisations may consider this a hindrance to what may have been considered legitimate marketing and business activities.

Limited Direct Marketing Permitted

Limited direct marketing is permitted, namely, of subscribers or customers who have given their prior consent. This implies consent in advance or simultaneous to the direct marketing.

However, in terms of direct marketing by email, this is further restricted.

Direct Marketing to Existing Customers' Email

In the context of existing customers, there is a possibility to direct market using emails. Article 13(2) of the ePrivacy Directive provides that where an organisation obtains from its customers their electronic contact details for electronic mail, in the context of the sale of a product or a service, in accordance with DP Directive 95, the organisation may use these electronic contact details for direct marketing (DM) of its own similar products or services provided that customers clearly and distinctly are given the opportunity to object, free of charge and in an easy manner, to such use of electronic contact details when they are collected and on the occasion of each message in case the customer has not initially refused such use.

Therefore, once the email details are obtained at the time of a product or service transaction, it will be possible to use that email for direct marketing purposes. Conditions or limitations apply, however. First, the organisation is only permitted to market and promote similar products or services. This, therefore, rules out unrelated, non-identical and non-similar products and services. Secondly, at the time of each subsequent act of direct marketing (DM), the customer must be given the opportunity in an easy and accessible manner to opt-out or cancel the direct marketing (DM). Effectively, they must be taken off of the organisation's DM list.

National Marketing Opt-out Registers

Article 13(3) of the ePrivacy Directive provides that Member States shall take appropriate measures to ensure that, free of charge, unsolicited communications for purposes of direct marketing, in cases other than those referred to in paragraphs 13(1) and 2, are not allowed either without the consent of the subscribers concerned or in respect of subscribers who do not wish to receive these communications, the choice between these options to be determined by Member State legislation. This means that each Member State must determine and provide a means for individuals to opt-out of receiving direct marketing (DM) in advance.[4]

Deceptive Emails: Marketing Emails Must Not Conceal Identity

Article 13(4) of the ePrivacy Directive provides that the practice of sending electronic mail for purposes of direct marketing (DM) disguising or concealing the identity of the sender on whose behalf the communication is made shall be prohibited. This means that organisations cannot conceal their identity if permitted to engage in direct marketing. If these are not complied with, what might otherwise be permissible direct marketing (DM) can be deemed to be impermissible. Complaints, investigations or enforcement proceedings can thus arise.

Marketing Emails Must Provide Opt-Out

In addition, Article 13(4) of ePrivacy Directive provides that the practice of sending electronic mail for purposes of direct marketing (DM) without a valid address to which the recipient may send a request that such communications cease shall be prohibited. This means that organisations must also include an easy contact address or other details at which the recipient can contact them if he wishes to object to receiving any further direct marketing (DM). If these are not complied with, what might otherwise be permissible direct marketing (DM) can be deemed to be impermissible. Complaints, investigations or enforcement proceedings can thus also arise.

Marketing Protection for Organisations

Article 13(5) of the ePrivacy Directive provides that paragraphs 1 and 3 shall apply to subscribers who are natural persons. Member States shall also ensure, in the framework of Community law and applicable Member State legislation, that the legitimate interests of subscribers other than natural persons with regard to unsolicited communications are sufficiently protected. This means that protection from unsolicited direct marketing (DM) can also be extended to organisations.

---

4.   See ICO website, available at http://www.ico.gov.uk/for_the_public/topic_specific_guides/
     marketing.aspx, last accessed 23 September 2012.

ePR/PECR

Detailed provisions governing direct marketing by electronic communications are set out in the ePR, implementing the ePrivacy Directive in Ireland.

It provides rules in relation to automated calling machines, fax, email, unsolicited calls by automated calling machine or fax, unsolicited telephone calls, disguising or concealing identity, contact addresses, opt-in/opt-out, and "soft opt-in".

The ePR is also interesting in that it applies to both legal and natural persons. Generally, rights are not recognised for organisations in the data protection regime.

The ePR refers to the implementation of the rules regarding electronic communications and direct marketing. Regulations 22 and 23 refer to email marketing.[5]

The Spam Problem

Spam is just one of a number of names taken to describe the problem of unsolicited electronic commercial marketing materials. The Spam name comes originally from a Monty Python comic sketch. However, electronic Spam is far from comic and costs industry hundreds of millions of euro each year in employees' lost time and resources, in lost bandwidth, in reduced capacity and network speed, as well as other problems.

Spam Internationally

The growing recognition of the problems caused by Spam has meant an increasing number of local and Member State laws specifically dedicated to preventing Spam.

In the US, for example, there are a large number of local state laws[6] and national federal laws dedicated to tackling Spam. These include both new specific laws and Spam specific amendments to pre-existing laws. The US federal Spam act, known as the CANSPAM Act, has been introduced.[7]

Related Issues

Certain related issues also arise that are beyond detailed analysis presently but may be used for specific organisations to consider further.

---

5. Privacy and Electronic Communications (EC Directive) Regulations 2003, available at http://www.legislation.gov.uk/uksi/2003/2426/contents/made, last accessed 23 September 2012.
6. See www.spamlaws.com, last accessed 4 September 2012.
7. See Reid, "Recent Developments in Private Enforcement of the Can-Spam Act" (2010)(4) *Akron Intellectual Property Journal* 281–307.

One example is the increasingly controversial area of profiling, advertising and direct marketing in relation to children.[8]

Online behavioural advertising (OBA) and the behavioural targeting of internet advertising is increasingly debated.[9]

Commentators, and media, often focus on the issue of threats to privacy, data protection and reputation rights caused by Web 2.0 activities such as social networking, search engine services, etc. The query arises as to whether revenue versus privacy is better respected by certain online services providers than others.[10]

Conclusion

Few organisations will not be interested in direct marketing and advertising. The key is to get it right. The consequences of sending unlawful electronic communications can include offences, prosecutions, official enforcement, investigations as well as being sued. This is one of the areas that is consistently an area of focus for investigation.

8. Munukutla-Parker, "Unsolicited Commercial Email, Privacy Concerns Related to Social Network Services, Online Protection of Children, and Cyberbullying" (2006)(2) *I/S: A Journal of Law and Policy* 628–650.
9. Deane-Johns, "Behavioural Targeting of Internet Advertising" (2009)(20) *Computers and Law* 22.
10. Edwards and Waelde (eds), *Law and the Internet* (Oxford: Hart, 2009), p 539.

CHAPTER 24

Case Studies

Data Protection Commissioner Employment Complaint Decisions

Set out below are some of the relevant case studies of complaints and decisions by the DPC.

Fair Obtaining

Case study 7 of 2009: Recruitment companies sharing CVs.

Case study 14 of 2009: Employer breaches Acts by covert surveillance using a private investigator.

Case study 1 of 2008: HSE West and a consultant ophthalmic surgeon breach the Data Protection Acts.

Case study 10 of 2008: An employer attempts to use CCTV for disciplinary purposes.

Case study 6 of 2007: Data controller breaches data protection law in regard to use of covert CCTV footage.

Case study 6 of 2006: News of the World: limits of the media exemption.

Case study 2 of 2003: PMI Limited mailing list rented in good faith by a bank resulted in minors being marketed for credit cards without proper consent.

Case study 1 of 2001: Bank and insurance company – cross-marketing of a third-party product – incompatible use and disclosure – fair obtaining and processing – small print and transparency.

Case study 4 of 2001: Credit card transaction – use of details from a previous transaction without consent – fair obtaining – transparency – retention period.

Case study 2 of 2000: Department of Education & Science – use of trade union membership subscription data to withhold pay – fair obtaining and processing – specified purpose – compatible use – purpose as described in register entry.

Right of Access

Case study 10 of 2011: Financial institutions deny right of access to credit assessments.

Case study 11 of 2011: Access request for old records.

Case study 12 of 2011: Access requests to solicitors for copies of files.

Case study 13 of 2011: Access to reports compiled by private investigators.

Case study 6 of 2008: Total Fitness Ireland and legal powers used to ensure compliance with an access request.

Case study 9 of 2008: An access request and a successful claim of legal privilege by a data controller.

Case study 21 of 2008: Access is wrongly denied in respect of an accident report.

Case study 2 of 2007: Data controller breaches several provisions by processing of sensitive personal data.

Case study 8 of 2007: Failure to finalise a complaint against Money Corp Limited.

Case study 13 of 2007: Dairygold – failure to comply in full with an access request.

Case study 9 of 2006: An Garda Síochána – failure to respond to an access request on time.

Case study 10 of 2006: Caredoc – failure to comply with an access request and appeal of an enforcement notice.

Case study 11 of 2006: Barcode/Westwood Club – failure to comply with an access request for CCTV footage.

Disclosure

Case study 6 of 2011: Customer data legitimately passed from car dealership to new buyer.

Case study 8 of 2011: Veterinary practice discloses dog owner's personal data.

Case study 1 of 2009: Disclosure of personal data due to inappropriate security measures.

Case study 3 of 2009: Disclosure of personal details by a local authority on its website.

Case study 12 of 2009: Paternity test result sent to wrong address.

Case study 13 of 2009: Use of postcards to communicate with customers regarding overdue account.

Case study 1 of 2008: HSE West and a consultant ophthalmic surgeon breach the Data Protection Acts.

Case study 2 of 2008: Disclosure of email addresses by a financial institution.

Case study 14 of 2008: Credit union commits several breaches by failing to update a member's address record.

Case study 15 of 2008: Tesco – resale of an apple iPod containing a customer's personal data.

Case study 19 of 2008: Personal data is disclosed in a letter.

Case study 2 of 2007: Data controller breaches several provisions in its processing of sensitive personal data.

Case study 7 of 2007: Aer Lingus – disclosure of employee information.

Case study 14 of 2006: School archiving project – disclosure of personal data.

Case study 4 of 2005: Complaint by a school manager about disclosure to parents of his personal data contained in a school inspection report.

Further Processing

Case study 9 of 2009: Further processing personal data without consent.

Case study 1 of 2008: HSE West and a consultant ophthalmic surgeon breach the Data Protection Acts.

Case study 10 of 2008: An employer attempts to use CCTV for disciplinary purposes.

Case study 2 of 2007: Data controller breaches several provisions in its processing of sensitive personal data.

Case study 3 of 2007: Inappropriate use of CCTV footage by West Wood Club.

Case study 4 of 2004: The Bar Council's in-house legal diary and Ashville Media.

Case study 5 of 2004: Political database and a charity request, spamming of constituents and non co-operation from a County Councillor.

Case study 1 of 2003: Drogheda Hospital – investigation into a consultant's practice- patients felt consent was necessary – balance to be struck with concerns for public health issues overall.

Accurate and Up-To-Date

Case study 10 of 2009: Mobile network operator fails to suppress customer marketing preferences.

Case study 14 of 2008: Credit union commits several breaches by failing to update a member's address record.

Case study 18 of 2008: A civil summons is served on the wrong person.

Case study 1 of 2007: Right of rectification of personal data held by a data controller.

Case study 1 of 2000: An Garda Síochána – subject access request – time limit for response – accuracy of personal data – excessive and irrelevant personal data – date of birth.

Case study 6 of 1999: Financial institution – inaccurate credit rating – rectification – notification of third parties to whom incorrect data had been released.

Case study 2 of 1997: Data about two people combined in one record kept by a credit referencing agency – issue of accuracy.

Case study 11 of 1997: Direct mail for previous householder – decline direct marketing – inaccurate data – repeated promises.

Case study 2 of 1996: A customer disputed his credit rating by a financial institution – issue of accuracy – the rating as understood by the institution.

Case study 8 of 1997: Credit record indicated that borrower had faced litigation and loan had been partly written off – issue of accuracy – previous concerns about fair obtaining revived.

Security of Data

Case study 12 of 2008: Credit unions transmitting personal data via unsecured emails.

Case study 16 of 2008: Failure to properly safeguard a staff member's medical certificate.

Case study 10 of 2007: Member of staff at Revenue accessing and using personal data of a taxpayer.

Case study 3 of 2003: Visa application details accidentally put on website of Department of Justice, Equality and Law Reform.

Case study 9 of 2002: Details of other bank account holders of the same name, supplied in response to access request-inadequate response to customer-security procedures – lack of awareness at branch level of data protection.

Case study 3 of 2001: Employee performance ratings disclosed to other staff – inadequate security.

Case study 6 of 2000: Financial institution – Laser card – printing of home address on receipts – incompatible disclosure – adequate security.

Case study 2 of 1999: Life insurance company – retention by ex-employee of customer data – unauthorised access – obligation to take appropriate security measures.

Case study 1 of 1998: Employee data – appropriate security measures – disclosure.

Direct Marketing – Email

Case study 5 of 2011: Unlawful obtaining and use of email addresses for marketing purposes by the zone extreme activity centre.

Case study 4 of 2010: Tesco prosecuted for email marketing.

Case study 6 of 2009: Email marketing error causes data protection breach.

Case study 8 of 2008: BuyAsYouFly and a failure to respect opt-outs from direct marketing by email.

Case study 17 of 2008: A web design company is requested to delete a marketing database.

Case study 14 of 2007: Ryanair – remedial action taken for customers to unsubscribe from marketing.

Case study 15 of 2007: Online shoppers receive unsolicited marketing from Tesco.

Case study 5 of 2004: Political database and a charity request, spamming of constituents and non co-operation from a County Councillor.

Direct Marketing – Postal

Case study 3 of 2008: A marketing campaign sets up personalised website addresses and breaches the Data Protection Acts.

Case study 3 of 2006: Dell – Persistent direct marketing.

Case study 4 of 2006: Sky Ireland – Direct marketing by email.

Case study 6 of 2005: Cross marketing of a credit card by a travel agent.

Case study 2 of 2003: PMI Limited – mailing list rented in good faith by a bank resulted in minors being marketed for credit cards without proper consent.

Case study 7 of 1998: Unsolicited direct mail from abroad – mutual assistance between parties to the 1981 Council of Europe Convention on Data Protection.

Direct Marketing – SMS

Case study 2 of 2011: Telecommunications companies prosecuted for marketing offences.

Case study 3: Prosecution of Regime Limited for the sending of unsolicited marketing text messages.

Case study 2 of 2009: Prosecution of Jackie Skelly Fitness for unsolicited marketing text messages.

Case study 5 of 2009: Harvesting of mobile numbers from a website for the sending of marketing text messages.

Case study 11 of 2009: Car dealership breaks the law by sending direct marketing text messages.

Case study 4 of 2008: Interactive Voice Technologies and unsolicited text messages.

Case study 5 of 2008: Unfounded complaint about unsolicited marketing text messages.

Case study 7 of 2008: Opt-in to subscription service text messages found following investigation.

Case study 5 of 2006: Opera Telecom – forced to delete database.

Case study 12 of 2005: Night club – collection of mobile numbers for marketing purposes.

Case study 5 of 2005: Realm Communications – unsolicited SMS texting and direct marketing.

Direct Marketing – Telephone

Case study 2 of 2011: Telecommunications companies prosecuted for marketing offences.

Case study 4: Marketing phone call made to a number on the National Directory Database (NDD) opt-out register.

Case study 11 of 2008: Marketing telephone calls to numbers on the NDD opt-out register.

Case study 4 of 2007: NewTel Communications Communications – ordered to suspend marketing.

Case study 9 of 2007: Marketing calls by Éircom – remedial action – amicable resolution.

Case study 1 of 2006: TalkTalk – unsolicited direct marketing calls.

Case study 2 of 2006: Gaelic Telecom/Global Windows – cold calling.

Case study 10 of 2005: Optic Communications – persistent unsolicited marketing phone calls.

Case study 11 of 2005: Prosecution of 4's A Fortune Limited – unsolicited marketing communications.

Case study 6 of 1997: Ex-directory phone number obtained by insurance broker – information notice used to establish circumstances.

Retention

Case study 11 of 2011: Access request for old records.

Case study 13 of 2008: Retention of personal data provided online.

Case study 11 of 2007: Croke Park – retention of personal data of nearby residents.

Case study 4 of 2001: Credit card transaction – use of details from a previous transaction without consent – fair obtaining – transparency – retention period.

Case study 7 of 1999: Debt collection service – acting on behalf of hospital – whether data had been "disclosed" for purposes of Data Protection Acts – whether debt-collecting agency is entitled to build a database of debtors.

Case study 2 of 1999: Life insurance company – retention by ex-employee of customer data – unauthorised access – obligation to take appropriate security measures.

Case study 13 of 1996: Criminal conviction struck out but details remain on Garda records – accuracy and retention of data – policy issues arising.

Right of Rectification/Deletion
Case study 1 of 2007: Right of rectification of personal data held by a data controller.

Case study 13 of 2006: Irish Insurance Federation – complaint about information on central registry.

Case study 8 of 2003: Catholic church baptismal records deletion request not upheld.

Case study 6 of 1999: Financial institution – inaccurate credit rating – rectification – notification of third parties to whom incorrect data had been released.

Case study 2 of 1996: A customer disputes his credit rating by a financial institution.

Excessive Information
Case study 1 of 2011: Leisure centre requests excessive personal data from patrons.

Case study 7: Allianz requests excessive personal information at quotation stage.

Case study 8 of 2009: Excessive data sought on penalty points.

Case study 5 of 2007: Excessive personal data on EU single-payment scheme application forms.

Case study 15 of 2006: Ulster Bank: excessive information sought from new customers.

Case study 7 of 2005: Complaint against AIB – excessive information sought regarding savings account.

Case study 1 of 2001: Motor insurance – excessive information – marital status not necessary.

Deletion of Database

As previously indicated, getting data protection wrong can be very costly. In a worse case scenario an entire database may have to be deleted – which can sometimes be one of an organisation's most valuable assets. One case study illustrates this.

Case study 17/2008 refers to a web design company required to delete a marketing database:

> I received a complaint from a data subject about the receipt of an unsolicited marketing email from Matrix Internet, a company advertising website design services. Disappointingly, this was the second time that this company had come to the attention of my Office concerning marketing emails sent to the same complainant. During a previous investigation, the company had given an undertaking that the complainant's email address would be removed from its marketing database.
>
> As a result of this complaint and given our previous encounter, my Office had serious concerns about the marketing activities of this company. We sought an immediate explanation as to how the complainant's details had remained on its marketing database. In response, the company apologised and it explained that an internal error had resulted in the email address of the complainant being listed twice on the marketing database. The company had removed only one of those entries and, as a result, the complainant had continued to receive marketing emails.
>
> I was encouraged by the company's swift response and co-operation with my Office's investigation. However, in light of what had happened to the complainant's personal data, it was clear that it was necessary to request the company to delete its entire marketing database. I considered that this was the only certain method of protecting other individuals on the company's marketing database from exposure to the receipt of unsolicited marketing emails. The company agreed to the request to delete its marketing database. In addition, the company undertook to cease marketing activity until such time as it had put in place a more appropriate system for carrying out marketing operations and managing "opt out" requests. After a period of three months, the company reported that it was in a position to recommence marketing activities as it had, in the intervening period, introduced a new system to ensure that its marketing systems were compliant with the requirements of data protection legislation. The complainant was satisfied with this outcome. Since then my Office has received no further complaints against this company.
>
> This complaint resulted in the deletion, at my request, of a data controller's marketing database. In terms of remedial action to protect the public from unsolicited marketing, a request for the deletion of a marketing database is not insignificant and it can result in a large loss of marketing targets for the data controller concerned.[1]

---

1.   See DPC, available at http://www.dataprotection.ie/ViewDoc.asp?fn=/documents/casestudies/CaseStudies_2008.htm&CatID=96&m=c#17, last accessed 11 January 2013.

PART 4

Updating the Data Protection Regime

CHAPTER 25

EU DP Review and Update

Introduction

The EU data protection regime is being fundamentally updated and expanded.[1] Many things have changed since the introduction of the DP Directive 95.[2] Data processing activities have changed as well as increased in scale and complexity. The EU undertook a review of the current effectiveness of the data protection regime. Partly on foot of the review, it was decided to propose a legal update to the DP Directive 95. This has culminated in the drafting and publication for a proposed new EU Data Protection Regulation. Indeed, the Council of Europe Convention on data protection,[3] which predates the DP Directive 95 and which was incorporated into the national law of many EU and other states (40 plus) prior to the DP Directive 95, is also being reviewed by the Council of Europe Convention to update its provisions in relation to data protection.[4]

The Article 29 Working Party in also referring to the need for future data protection measures in its opinion regarding *The Future of Privacy*.[5] There have also been calls for greater political activism in relation to particular data protection issues.[6]

---

1. Graham, "Prepare for European Data Protection Reform" (30 November 2011) SCL *Computer and Law*.
2. EU Data Protection Directive 1995 (Directive 95/46/EC of the European Parliament and of the Council of 24 October 1995 on the protection of individuals with regard to the processing of personal data and on the free movement of such data).
3. Convention for the Protection of Individuals with regard to Automatic Processing of Personal Data, Council of Europe (1982), available at http://conventions.coe.int/Treaty/en/Treaties/Html/108.htm, last accessed 11 January 2013.
4. See Kierkegaard *et al*, "30 Years On – The Review of the Council of Europe Data Protection Convention 108" (2011)(27) *Computer Law & Security Review* 223–231.
5. The Future of Privacy, WP29, referred to in Wong, "Data Protection: The Future of Privacy" (2011)(27) *Computer Law & Security Review* 53–57.
6. Ripoll Servent and MacKenzie, "Is the EP Still a Data Protection Champion? The Case of SWIFT" (2011)(12) *Perspectives on European Politics & Society* 390–406.

Others[7] have also highlighted new problematic developments in relation to such issues as location data and location-based services, which need to be dealt with.

Data Protection Commissioner Forecasts Changes

The Data Protection Commissioner's Annual Report for 2011 notes the following:

> the data protection landscape is changing. We are now seeing a definite shift in the nature and type of complaints received by the Office from the traditional complaint related to inappropriate or unfair use of personal data to a clearer technology focus with individuals concerned about the security of their personal data and the uses made of that data by software and technology applications. Last year for the first time the number of data breach notifications outstripped the number of complaints opened for investigation (by six). The need to deal with the reality of the potential impact on individual privacy and data protection rights which can be caused by poorly thought out technology is in many respects the back-drop to the European Commission's proposals for a new uniform Data Protection Regulation that will apply across all EU Member States.[8]

Formal Nature of Regulations and Directives

The DP Regulation[9] is still currently a draft. However, it is important to note that an EU Regulation differs from a Directive under formal EU law.[10] A Regulation is immediately directly effective in all EU Member States – without the need for Member State implementing laws. Once the Regulation is passed, it will apply in the EU. It will also change the data protection regime as well as Ireland. The reform will be "comprehensive".[11]

Review Policy

Rebecca Wong refers to some of the areas of concern the DP Regulation[12] addresses.[13]

---

7. Cuijpers and Pekarek, "The Regulation of Location-Based Services: Challenges to the European Union Data Protection Regime" (2011)(5) *Journal of Location Based Services* 223–241.
8. Annual Report, Data Protection Commissioner, 2011, p 6.
9. EU draft Data Protection Regulation (Proposal for a Regulation of the European Parliament and of the Council on the protection of individuals with regard to the processing of personal data and on the free movement of such data (General Data Protection Regulation) COM (2012) 11 final).
10. Generally see, for example, Biondi and Eeckhout (eds), *EU Law after Lisbon*, (2012); Foster, *Foster on EU Law* (2011); O'Neill, *EU Law for UK Lawyers* (2011); Steiner, *EU Law* (2011).
11. In Brief (2012)(17) *Communications Law* 3.
12. EU draft Data Protection Regulation.
13. Wong, "The Data Protection Directive 95/46/EC: Idealisms and Realisms" (2012)(26) *International Review of Law, Computers & Technology* 229–244.

These include:

- the data protection regime in the online age;
- social networking;
- Cloud computing;
- minimum/maximum standards; and
- the data protection principles.[14]

The Commission states[15] that the policy in reviewing the data protection regime is as follows:

- to modernise the EU legal system for the protection of personal data, in particular to meet the challenges resulting from globalisation and the use of new technologies;
- to strengthen individuals' rights, and at the same time reduce administrative formalities to ensure a freeflow of personal data within the EU and beyond; and
- to improve the clarity and coherence of the EU rules for personal data protection and achieve a consistent and effective implementation and application of the fundamental right to the protection of personal data in all areas of the EU's activities.[16]

It should also enhance consumer confidence in eCommerce.[17] In addition, it should also bring comprehensive savings to organisations as the obligations of complying with somewhat differing Member State data protection regimes will be reduced if not eliminated.[18]

The review process has been ongoing for some time.[19] It further summarises the need for new data protection rules as follows:

> The current EU data protection rules date from 1995. Back then, the internet was virtually unknown to most people. Today, 250 million people use the internet daily in Europe.

---

14. *ibid.*
15. Reform of Data Protection legal Framework, Commission, Justice directorate, available at http://ec.europa.eu/justice/data-protection/review/index_en.htm, last accessed 11 January 2013.
16. *ibid.*
17. In Brief (2012)(17) *Communications Law* 3.
18. *ibid.*
19. See details of some of the steps and consultations at http://ec.europa.eu/justice/data-protection/review/actions/index_en.htm, last accessed 11 January 2013.

Think how that has changed our personal data landscape through the explosion of ecommerce, social networks, online games and cloud computing.

The European Commission has therefore adopted proposals for updating data protection rules to meet the challenges of the digital age. In particular, the proposals will strengthen protection of your personal data online.

These proposals will now be debated by the Council and the European Parliament before they can become law.[20]

Commentators describe the draft proposed DP Regulation[21] as "a long (and ambitious) text".[22] In addition, the process by which this stage is also described as being a herculean effort.[23]

Some Key Changes

The key changes are referred to below. In some respects these could also be seen as advantages of the new DP Regulation data protection regime.

- administrative costs are to be reduced with a single EU wide set of rules and obligations;

- there may be less need to interact with the DPC as more responsibility and accountability is passed to the organisational level;

- the consent requirement has been clarified as to mean explicit consent (whereas previously there were references to different categories of consent);

- rights are improved with easier access to personal data, as well as its transferability;

- the enhanced right to be forgotten will improve the position of data subjects and the ability to delete it;

- the EU data protection regime will apply to non-EU entities operating with regard to EU personal data and EU citizens;

- the national authorities will be able to impose fines of €1,000,000 or up to 2 per cent of global turnover.[24]

---

20. See Commission, Why Do We Need New Data Protection Rules Now?, available at http://ec.europa.eu/justice/data-protection/minisite/index.html, last accessed 11 January 2013.
21. EU draft Data Protection Regulation.
22. De Hert and Papakonstantinou, "The Proposed Data Protection Regulation Replacing Directive 95/46/EC: A Sound System for the Protection of Individuals" (2012)(28) *Computer Law & Security Review* 130–142. Note also, Walden and Savage, "Data Protection and Privacy Laws: Should Organisations be Protected?" (1988)(37) *International and Comparativee Law Quarterly* 337–347.
23. *ibid.*
24. In Brief (2012)(17) *Communications Law* 3.

The ICO in the UK welcomes the DP Regulation stating that:

> In particular its strengthens the position of individuals, recognises important concepts such as privacy by design and privacy impact assessments and requires organisations to be able to demonstrate that they have measures in place to ensure personal information is properly protected.[25] •

New Definitions in DP Regulation

The DP Regulation introduces certain new definitions as follows.

Personal Data Breach

"Personal data breach" is defined to mean a breach of security leading to the accidental or unlawful destruction, loss, alteration, unauthorised disclosure of, or access to, personal data transmitted, stored or otherwise processed.

Genetic Data

"Genetic data" is defined to mean all data, of whatever type, concerning the characteristics of an individual that are inherited or acquired during early prenatal development.

Biometric Data

"Biometric data" is defined to mean any data relating to the physical, physiological or behavioural characteristics of an individual that allow their unique identification, such as facial images, or dactyloscopic data.

Data Concerning Health

"Data concerning health" is defined to mean any information that relates to the physical or mental health of an individual, or to the provision of health services to the individual.

Main Establishment

"Main establishment" is defined to mean as regards the data controller, the place of its establishment in the EU where the main decisions as to the purposes, conditions and means of the processing of personal data are taken; if no decisions as to the purposes, conditions and means of the processing of personal data are taken in the EU, the main establishment is the place where the main processing activities in the context of the activities of an establishment of a data controller in the EU take place.

---

25. Referred to in In Brief (2012)(17) *Communications Law* 3.

As regards the data processor, "main establishment" means the place of its central administration in the EU.

Representative

"Representative" is defined to mean any natural or legal person established in the EU who, explicitly designated by the data controller, acts and may be addressed by any supervisory authority and other bodies in the EU instead of the data controller, with regard to the obligations of the data controller under the Regulation.

Enterprise

"Enterprise" is defined to mean any entity engaged in an economic activity, irrespective of its legal form, thus including, in particular, natural and legal persons, partnerships or associations regularly engaged in an economic activity.

Group of Undertakings

"Group of undertakings" is defined to mean a controlling undertaking and its controlled undertakings.

Binding Corporate Rules

"Binding corporate rules" (BCR) is defined to mean personal data protection policies that are adhered to by a data controller or data processor established on the territory of a Member State of the EU for transfers or a set of transfers of personal data to a data controller or data processor in one or more third countries within a group of undertakings.

Child

"Child" is (originally) defined to mean any person below the age of 18 years.

Background to the DP Regulation

The Recitals to the proposed DP Regulation are also instructive and help to flesh out the background and context to the introduction of the DP Regulation. Some of these themes are referred to below.

Data Protection/Fundamental Right

The protection of natural persons in relation to the processing of personal data is a fundamental right. Article 8(1) of the Charter of Fundamental Rights of the European Union and Article 16(1) of the Treaty lay down that everyone has the right to the protection of personal data concerning them.[26]

---

26. Recital 1.

The processing of personal data is designed to serve man; the principles and rules on the protection of individuals with regard to the processing of their personal data should, whatever the nationality or residence of natural persons, respect their fundamental rights and freedoms, notably their right to the protection of personal data. It should contribute to the accomplishment of an area of freedom, security and justice and of an economic union, to economic and social progress, the strengthening and the convergence of the economies within the internal market, and the well-being of individuals.[27]

Processing Increase/Technology/Co-operation

The economic and social integration resulting from the functioning of the internal market has led to a substantial increase in cross-border flows. The exchange of data between economic and social, public and private actors across the EU has increased.[28] National authorities in the Member States are being called upon by EU law to co-operate and exchange personal data so as to be able to perform their duties or carry out tasks on behalf of an authority in another Member State.[29]

The rapid technological developments and globalisation have brought new challenges for the protection of personal data. The scale of data sharing and collecting has increased spectacularly. Technology allows both private companies and public authorities to make use of personal data on an unprecedented scale in order to pursue their activities.[30]

Individuals increasingly make personal information available publicly and globally. Technology has transformed both the economy and social life. It should facilitate the free flow of data within the EU, while ensuring a high level of protection of personal data.[31]

Need for Stronger Data Protection Regime Framework

These developments require building a strong and more coherent data protection framework in the EU, backed by solid enforcement, given the importance to create the trust that will allow the digital economy to develop across the EU internal market.[32]

Individuals should have control of their own personal data and legal and practical certainty for individuals; economic operators and public authorities should be reinforced.[33]

---

27. Recital 2.
28. Recital 4.
29. *ibid.*
30. Recital 5.
31. *ibid.*
32. Recital 6.
33. *ibid.*

The objectives and principles of DP Directive 95 remain sound, but it has not prevented fragmentation in the way data protection is implemented across the EU, legal uncertainty and a widespread public perception that there are significant risks for the protection of individuals associated notably with online activity.[34] Differences in the level of protection of the rights and freedoms of individuals, notably to the right to the protection of personal data, with regard to the processing of personal data afforded in the Member States may prevent the freeflow of personal data throughout the EU.[35]

These differences may therefore constitute an obstacle to the pursuit of economic activities at the level of the EU, distort competition and impede authorities in the discharge of their responsibilities under EU law. This difference in levels of protection is due to the existence of differences in the implementation and application of DP Directive 95.[36]

In order to ensure a consistent and high level of protection of individuals and to remove the obstacles to flows of personal data, the level of protection of the rights and freedoms of individuals with regard to the processing of such data should be equivalent in all Member States.[37] Consistent and homogenous application of the rules for the protection of the fundamental rights and freedoms of natural persons with regard to the processing of personal data should be ensured throughout the EU.[38]

It is stated that effective protection of personal data throughout the EU requires strengthening and detailing the rights of data subjects and the obligations of those who process and determine the processing of personal data, but also equivalent powers for monitoring and ensuring compliance with the rules for the protection of personal data and equivalent sanctions for offenders in the Member States.[39]

It also notes that Article 16(2) of the Treaty mandates the European Parliament and the Council to lay down the rules relating to the protection of individuals with regard to the processing of personal data and the rules relating to the free movement of personal data.[40]

In order to ensure a consistent level of protection for individuals throughout the EU and to prevent divergences hampering the free movement of data within the internal market, a Regulation is necessary to provide legal certainty and transparency for economic operators, including micro, small and medium-sized enterprises, and to provide individuals in all Member States with the same level of legally enforceable

---

34. Recital 7 EU draft Data Protection Regulation.
35. *ibid.*
36. *ibid.*
37. Recital 8 *ibid.*
38. *ibid.*
39. Recital 9 *ibid.*
40. Recital 10 *ibid.*

rights and obligations and responsibilities for data controllers and data processors, to ensure consistent monitoring of the processing of personal data, and equivalent sanctions in all Member States as well as effective co-operation by the supervisory authorities of different Member States.[41] To take account of the specific situation of micro, small and medium-sized enterprises, the Regulation includes a number of derogations. In addition, the EU institutions and bodies, Member States and their supervisory authorities are encouraged to take account of the specific needs of micro, small and medium-sized enterprises in the application of the Regulation. The notion of micro, small and medium-sized enterprises should draw upon Commission Recommendation 2003/361/EC of 6 May 2003 concerning the definition of micro, small and medium-sized enterprises (SMEs).[42]

The protection afforded by the Regulation concerns natural persons, whatever their nationality or place of residence, in relation to the processing of personal data.[43] With regard to the processing of data that concerns legal persons and in partic-ular undertakings established as legal persons, including the name and the form of the legal person and the contact details of the legal person, the protection of the Regulation should not be claimed by any person.[44] This should also apply where the name of the legal person contains the names of one or more natural persons.[45]

Technologically Neutral Protection

The protection of individuals should be technologically neutral and not depend on the techniques used; otherwise this would create a serious risk of circumven-tion.[46] The protection of individuals should apply to processing of personal data by automated means as well as to manual processing, if the data are contained or are intended to be contained in a filing system.[47] Files or sets of files as well as their cover pages, which are not structured according to specific criteria, should not fall within the scope of the Regulation.[48]

Exclusion

The Regulation does not address issues of protection of fundamental rights and free-doms or the freeflow of data related to activities that fall outside the scope of EU law, nor does it cover the processing of personal data by the EU institutions, bodies, offices and agencies, which are subject to Regulation (EC) No 45/200144, or the

---

41. Recital 11 *ibid.*
42. *ibid.*
43. Recital 12 *ibid.*
44. *ibid.*
45. *ibid.*
46. Recital 13 *ibid.*
47. *ibid.*
48. *ibid.*

processing of personal data by the Member States when carrying out activities in relation to the common foreign and security policy of the EU.[49]

Domestic

The Regulation should not apply to processing of personal data by a natural person, which are exclusively personal or domestic, such as correspondence and the holding of addresses, and without any gainful interest and thus without any connection with a professional or commercial activity.[50] The exemption should also not apply to data controllers or data processors that provide the means for processing personal data for such personal or domestic activities.[51]

Criminal Exemption

The protection of individuals with regard to the processing of personal data by competent authorities for the purposes of prevention, investigation, detection or prosecution of criminal offences or the execution of criminal penalties, and the free movement of such data, is subject to specific legal provisions at EU level.[52]

Therefore, the Regulation does not apply to the processing activities for those purposes. However, data processed by public authorities under the Regulation when used for the purposes of prevention, investigation, detection or prosecution of criminal offences or the execution of criminal penalties should be governed by the more specific legal instrument at EU level (a separate new Directive).[53]

ISPs

The Regulation should be without prejudice to the application of Directive 2000/31/EC, in particular of the three limited liability rules of intermediary service providers in Articles 12 to 15 of that Directive.[54]

Official Documents

The Regulation allows the principle of public access to official documents to be taken into account when applying the provisions set out in the Regulation.[55]

---

49. Recital 14 *ibid.*
50. Recital 15 *ibid.*
51. *ibid.*
52. Recital 16 *ibid.*
53. *ibid.*
54. Recital 17 *ibid.*
55. Recital 18 *ibid.*

Location/Jurisdiction/Processing

Any processing of personal data in the context of the activities of an establishment of a data controller or a data processor in the EU should be carried out in accordance with the Regulation, regardless of whether the processing itself takes place within the EU or not.[56] Establishment implies the effective and real exercise of activity through stable arrangements. The legal form of such arrangements, whether through a branch or a subsidiary with a legal personality, is not the determining factor in this respect.[57]

In order to ensure that individuals are not deprived of the protection to which they are entitled under the Regulation, the processing of personal data of data subjects residing in the EU by a data controller not established in the EU should be subject to the Regulation where the processing activities are related to the offering of goods or services to such data subjects, or to the monitoring of the behaviour of such data subjects.[58]

Monitoring

In order to determine whether or not a processing activity can be considered to "monitor the behaviour" of data subjects, it should be ascertained whether individuals are tracked on the internet with data processing techniques that consist of applying a "profile" to an individual, particularly in order to take decisions concerning him or for analysing or predicting his personal preferences, behaviours and attitudes.[59]

Public International Law

Where the national law of a Member State applies by virtue of public international law, the Regulation also applies to a data controller not established in the EU, such as in a Member State's diplomatic mission or consular post.[60]

Any Information

The principles of protection should apply to any information concerning an identified or identifiable person.[61] To determine whether or not a person is identifiable, account should be taken of all the means reasonably likely to be used either by the data controller or by any other person to identify the individual.[62] The principles of data protection should not apply to data rendered anonymous in such a way that the data subject is no longer identifiable.[63]

---

56. Recital 19 *ibid.*
57. *ibid.*
58. Recital 20 *ibid.*
59. Recital 21 *ibid.*
60. Recital 22 *ibid.*
61. Recital 23 *ibid.*
62. *ibid.*
63. *ibid.*

Internet

When using online services, individuals may be associated with online identifiers provided by their devices, applications, tools and protocols, such as Internet Protocol addresses or cookie identifiers.[64] This may leave traces which, combined with unique identifiers and other information received by the servers, may be used to create profiles of the individuals and identify them.[65] Identification numbers, location data, online identifiers or other specific factors as such may not necessarily be considered as personal data in all circumstances.[66]

Consent

The consent should be given explicitly by any appropriate method enabling a freely given specific and informed indication of the data subject's wishes, either by a statement or by a clear affirmative action by the data subject, ensuring that individuals are aware that they give their consent to the processing of personal data, including by ticking a box when visiting an internet website or by any other statement or conduct that clearly indicates in this context the data subject's acceptance of the proposed processing of their personal data.[67] Silence or inactivity should not, therefore, be sufficient to constitute consent.[68] Consent should cover all processing activities carried out for the same purpose or purposes.[69] One will recall that significantly different data collections and purposes may need to be registered seperately. If the data subject's consent is to be given following an electronic request, the request must be clear, concise and not unnecessarily disruptive to the use of the service for which it is provided.[70]

Health

Personal data relating to health includes in particular all data pertaining to the health status of a data subject; information about the registration of the individual for the provision of health services; information about payments or eligibility for healthcare with respect to the individual; a number, symbol or particular assigned to an individual to uniquely identify the individual for health purposes; any information about the individual collected in the course of the provision of health services to the individual; information derived from the testing or examination of a body part or bodily substance, including biological samples; identification of a person as provider of healthcare to the individual; or any information on, for example, a disease, disability, disease risk, medical history, clinical treatment, or the actual physiological or biomedical state of the data subject independent of its source, such as, for

---

64. Recital 24 *ibid.*
65. *ibid.*
66. *ibid.*
67. Recital 25 *ibid.*
68. *ibid.*
69. *ibid.*
70. *ibid.*

example, from a physician or other health professional, a hospital, a medical device, or an *in vitro* diagnostic test.[71]

Establishment

The main establishment of a data controller in the EU should be determined according to objective criteria and should imply the effective and real exercise of management activities determining the main decisions as to the purposes, conditions and means of processing through stable arrangements.[72] This criterion should not depend on whether or not the processing of personal data is actually carried out at that location; the presence and use of technical means and technologies for processing personal data or processing activities do not, in themselves, constitute such main establishment and are therefore no determining criteria for a main establishment. The main establishment of the data processor should be the place of its central administration in the EU.[73]

Group Companies

A group of undertakings includes a controlling undertaking and its controlled undertakings, whereby the controlling undertaking should be the undertaking that can exercise a dominant influence over the other undertakings by virtue, for example, of ownership, financial participation or the rules that govern it or the power to have personal data protection rules implemented.[74]

Lawful Processing

Any processing of personal data should be lawful, fair and transparent in relation to the individuals concerned. In particular, the specific purposes for which the data are processed should be explicit and legitimate and determined at the time of the collection of the data. The data should be adequate, relevant and limited to the minimum necessary for the purposes for which the data are processed; this requires in particular ensuring that the data collected are not excessive and that the period for which the data are stored is limited to a strict minimum. Personal data should only be processed if the purpose of the processing could not be fulfilled by other means. Every reasonable step should be taken to ensure that personal data that are inaccurate are rectified or deleted. In order to ensure that the data are not kept longer than necessary, time limits should be established by the data controller for erasure or for a periodic review.[75]

In order for processing to be lawful, personal data should be processed on the basis of the consent of the person concerned or some other legitimate basis, laid down by

---

71. Recital 26 *ibid.*
72. Recital 27 *ibid.*
73. *ibid.*
74. Recital 28 *ibid.*
75. Recital 30 *ibid.*

law, either in the Regulation or in other EU or Member State law as referred to in the Regulation.[76]

The processing should be lawful where it is necessary in the context of a contract or the intended entering into a contract.[77]

Where data processing is carried out in compliance with a legal obligation to which the data controller is subject or where processing is necessary for the performance of a task carried out in the public interest or in the exercise of an official authority, the processing should have a legal basis in EU law, or in a Member State law that meets the requirements of the Charter of Fundamental Rights of the European Union for any limitation of the rights and freedoms.[78] It is also for EU or Member State law to determine whether the data controller performing a task carried out in the public interest or in the exercise of official authority should be a public administration or another natural or legal person governed by public law, or by private law such as a professional association.[79]

The processing of personal data should equally be regarded as lawful where it is necessary to protect an interest that is essential for the data subject's life.[80]

The legitimate interests of a data controller may provide a legal basis for processing, provided that the interests or the fundamental rights and freedoms of the data subject are not overriding. This would need careful assessment in particular where the data subject is a child, given that children deserve specific protection. The data subject should have the right to object to the processing, on grounds relating to their particular situation and free of charge. To ensure transparency, the controller should be obliged to explicitly inform the data subject on the legitimate interests pursued and on the right to object, and also be obliged to document these legitimate interests. Given that it is for the legislator to provide by law the legal basis for public authorities to process data, this legal ground should not apply for the processing by public authorities in the performance of their tasks.[81]

The processing of data to the extent strictly necessary for the purposes of ensuring network and information security, i.e. the ability of a network or an information system to resist, at a given level of confidence, accidental events or unlawful or malicious actions that compromise the availability, authenticity, integrity and confidentiality of stored or transmitted data, and the security of the related services offered by, or accessible via, these networks and systems, by public authorities, Computer Emergency Response Teams (CERTs), Computer Security Incident Response Teams

---

76. Recital 31 *ibid.*
77. Recital 35 *ibid.*
78. Recital 36 *ibid.*
79. *ibid.*
80. Recital 37 *ibid.*
81. Recital 38 *ibid.*

(CSIRTs), providers of electronic communications networks and services and by providers of security technologies and services, constitutes a legitimate interest of the concerned data controller. This could, for example, include preventing unauthorised access to electronic communications networks and malicious code distribution and stopping "denial of service" attacks and damage to computer and electronic communication systems.[82]

The processing of personal data for other purposes should only be allowed where the processing is compatible with those purposes for which the data have been initially collected, in particular where the processing is necessary for historical, statistical or scientific research purposes.[83] Where the other purpose is not compatible with the initial one for which the data are collected, the data controller should obtain the consent of the data subject for this other purpose or should base the processing on another legitimate ground for lawful processing, in particular where provided by EU law or the law of the Member State to which the data controller is subject. In any case, the application of the principles set out by the Regulation and in particular the information of the data subject on those other purposes should be ensured.[84]

Consent

Where processing is based on the data subject's consent, the data controller should have the burden of proving that the data subject has given consent to the processing operation. In particular in the context of a written declaration on another matter, safeguards should ensure that the data subject is aware that and to what extent consent is given.[85]

In order to ensure free consent, it should be clarified that consent does not provide a valid legal ground where the individual has no genuine and free choice and is subsequently not able to refuse or withdraw consent without detriment.[86]

The consent should not provide a valid legal ground for the processing of personal data, where there is a clear imbalance between the data subject and the data controller.[87] This is especially the case where the data subject is in a situation of dependence on the data controller, among others, where personal data are processed by the employer of employees' personal data in the employment context.[88] Where the data controller is a public authority, there would be an imbalance only in the specific data processing operations where the public authority can impose an obligation by virtue of its relevant public powers and the consent cannot be deemed as freely given, taking into account the interest of the data subject.

---

82. Recital 39 *ibid.*
83. Recital 40 *ibid.*
84. *ibid.*
85. Recital 32 *ibid.*
86. Recital 33 *ibid.*
87. Recital 34 *ibid.*
88. *ibid.*

Sensitive Personal Data

The personal data that are, by their nature, particularly sensitive and vulnerable in relation to fundamental rights or privacy, deserve specific protection. Such data should not be processed, unless the data subject gives his or her explicit consent.[89] However, derogations from this prohibition should be explicitly provided for in respect of specific needs, in particular where the processing is carried out in the course of legitimate activities by certain associations or foundations the purpose of which is to permit the exercise of fundamental freedoms.[90]

The derogating from the prohibition on processing sensitive categories of data should also be allowed if under a law, and subject to suitable safeguards, so as to protect personal data and other fundamental rights, where grounds of public interest so justify and in particular for health purposes, including public health and social protection and the management of health-care services, especially in order to ensure the quality and cost-effectiveness of the procedures used for settling claims for benefits and services in the health insurance system, or for historical, statistical and scientific research purposes.[91]

Official Processing

The processing of personal data by official authorities for achieving aims, laid down in constitutional law or international public law, of officially recognised religious associations is carried out on grounds of public interest.[92]

Elections

Where in the course of electoral activities, the operation of the democratic system in a Member State requires that political parties compile data on people's political opinions, the processing of such data may be permitted for reasons of public interest, provided that appropriate safeguards are established.[93]

Access

If the data processed by a data controller do not permit the controller to identify a natural person, the data controller should not be obliged to acquire additional information in order to identify the data subject for the sole purpose of complying with any provision of the Regulation.[94] In case of a request for access, the data controller should be entitled to ask the data subject for further information to enable the data controller to locate the personal data that person seeks.[95]

---

89.   Recital 41 *ibid*.
90.   *ibid*.
91.   Recital 42 *ibid*.
92.   Recital 43 *ibid*.
93.   Recital 44 *ibid*.
94.   Recital 45 *ibid*.
95.   *ibid*.

Transparency/Children

The transparency principle requires that any information addressed to the public or to the data subject should be easily accessible and easy to understand, and that clear and plain language is used. This is in particular relevant in situations, such as online advertising, where the proliferation of actors and the technological complexity of practice makes it difficult for the data subject to know and understand if personal data relating to them are being collected, by whom and for what purpose. Given that children deserve specific protection, any information and communication, where processing is addressed specifically to a child, should be in such a clear and plain language that the child can easily understand.[96]

Exercising Rights

The modalities should be provided for facilitating the data subject's exercise of their rights provided by the Regulation, including mechanisms to request, free of charge, in particular access to data, rectification, erasure and to exercise the right to object.[97] The data controller should be obliged to respond to requests of the data subject within a fixed deadline and give reasons, in case he does not comply with the data subject's request.[98] The principles of fair and transparent processing require that the data subject should be informed in particular of the existence of the processing operation and its purposes, how long the data will be stored, on the existence of the right of access, rectification or erasure and on the right to lodge a complaint.[99] Where the data are collected from the data subject, the data subject should also be informed whether or not he is obliged to provide the data and of the consequences if he does not provide such data.[100]

Any person should have the right of access to data that has been collected concerning them, and to exercise this right easily, in order to be aware and verify the lawfulness of the processing. Every data subject should therefore have the right to know and obtain communication in particular for what purposes the data are processed, for what period, which recipients receive the data, what is the logic of the data that are undergoing the processing and what might be, at least when based on profiling, the consequences of such processing. This right should not adversely affect the rights and freedoms of others, including trade secrets or intellectual property and in particular the copyright protecting the software. However, the result of these considerations should not be that all information is refused to the data subject.[101]

The data controller should use all reasonable measures to verify the identity of a data subject that requests access, in particular in the context of online services and online

---

96. Recital 46 *ibid.*
97. Recital 47 *ibid.*
98. *ibid.*
99. Recital 48 *ibid.*
100. *ibid.*
101. Recital 51 *ibid.*

identifiers.[102] A data controller should not retain personal data for the unique purpose of being able to react to potential requests.[103]

Prior Information

The information in relation to the processing of personal data relating to the data subject should be given to them at the time of collection, or, where the data are not collected from the data subject, within a reasonable period, depending on the circumstances of the case.[104] Where data can be legitimately disclosed to another recipient, the data subject should be informed when the data are first disclosed to the recipient.[105]

However, it is not necessary to impose this obligation where the data subject already disposes of this information, or where the recording or disclosure of the data is expressly laid down by law, or where the provision of information to the data subject proves impossible or would involve disproportionate efforts.[106] The latter could particularly be the case where processing is for historical, statistical or scientific research purposes; in this regard, the number of data subjects, the age of the data, and any compensatory measures adopted may be taken into consideration.[107]

Rectification

Any person should have the right to have personal data concerning them rectified and a "right to be forgotten" where the retention of such data is not in compliance with the Regulation. In particular, data subjects should have the right that their personal data are erased and no longer processed, where the data are no longer necessary in relation to the purposes for which the data are collected or otherwise processed, where data subjects have withdrawn their consent for processing or where they object to the processing of personal data concerning them or where the processing of their personal data otherwise does not comply with the Regulation. This right is particularly relevant when the data subject has given his or her consent as a child, when not being fully aware of the risks involved by the processing, and later wants to remove such personal data, especially on the internet. However, the further retention of the data should be allowed where it is necessary for historical, statistical and scientific research purposes, for reasons of public interest in the area of public health, for exercising the right of freedom of expression, when required by law or where there is a reason to restrict the processing of the data instead of erasing them.[108]

---

102. Recital 52 *ibid.*
103. *ibid.*
104. Recital 49 *ibid.*
105. *ibid.*
106. Recital 50 *ibid.*
107. *ibid.*
108. Recital 53 *ibid.*

Enhancing Right to Be Forgotten

In order to strengthen the "right to be forgotten" in the online environment, the right to erasure should also be extended in such a way that a data controller who has made the personal data public should be obliged to inform third parties who are processing such data that a data subject requests them to erase any links to, or copies or replications of that personal data. To ensure this information, the data controller should take all reasonable steps, including technical measures, in relation to data for the publication of which the data controller is responsible. In relation to a third-party publication of personal data, the data controller should be considered responsible for the publication where the data controller has authorised the publication by the third party.[109]

Electronic Access

To further strengthen the control over their own data and their right of access, data subjects should have the right, where personal data are processed by electronic means and in a structured and commonly used format, to obtain a copy of the data concerning them also in commonly used electronic format. The data subject should also be allowed to transmit those data, which they have provided, from one automated application, such as a social network, into another one. This should apply where the data subject provides the data to the automated processing system, based on his consent or in the performance of a contract.[110]

Right to Object

In cases where personal data might lawfully be processed to protect the vital interests of the data subject, or on grounds of public interest, official authority or the legitimate interests of a data controller, any data subject should nevertheless be entitled to object to the processing of any data relating to him or her.[111] The burden of proof should be on the data controller to demonstrate that their legitimate interests may override the interests or the fundamental rights and freedoms of the data subject.[112]

Direct Marketing

Where personal data are processed for the purposes of direct marketing, the data subject should have the right to object to such processing free of charge and in a manner that can be easily and effectively invoked.[113]

---

109. Recital 54 *ibid.*
110. Recital 55 *ibid.*
111. Recital 56 *ibid.*
112. *ibid.*
113. Recital 57 *ibid.*

Automated Processing/Children

Every natural person should have the right not to be subject to a measure that is based on profiling by means of automated processing. However, such a measure should be allowed when expressly authorised by law, carried out in the course of entering or performance of a contract, or when the data subject has given his consent. In any case, such processing should be subject to suitable safeguards, including specific information of the data subject and the right to obtain human intervention, and such a measure should not concern a child.[114]

The restrictions on specific principles and on the rights of information, access, rectification and erasure or on the right to data portability, the right to object, measures based on profiling, as well as on the communication of a personal data breach to a data subject and on certain related obligations of the data controllers may be imposed by EU or Member State law, as far as necessary and proportionate in a democratic society to safeguard public security, including the protection of human life, especially in response to natural or manmade disasters; the prevention, investigation and prosecution of criminal offences or of breaches of ethics for regulated professions; other public interests of the EU or of a Member State, in particular an important economic or financial interest of the EU or of a Member State; or the protection of the data subject or the rights and freedoms of others. Those restrictions should be in compliance with requirements set out by the Charter of Fundamental Rights of the European Union and by the European Convention for the Protection of Human Rights and Fundamental Freedoms.[115]

Liability

The comprehensive responsibility and liability of the data controller for any processing of personal data carried out by the data controller or on the data controller's behalf should be established.[116] In particular, the data controller should ensure and be obliged to demonstrate the compliance of each processing operation with the Regulation.[117]

Policies and Measures

The protection of the rights and freedoms of data subjects with regard to the processing of personal data require that appropriate technical and organisational measures are taken, both at the time of the design of the processing and at the time of the processing itself, to ensure that the requirements of the Regulation are met. In order to ensure and demonstrate compliance with the Regulation, the data controller should adopt internal policies and implement appropriate measures, which meet in particular the principles of data protection by design and data protection by default.[118]

---

114. Recital 58 *ibid.*
115. Recital 59 *ibid.*
116. Recital 60 *ibid.*
117. *ibid.*
118. Recital 61 *ibid.*

The protection of the rights and freedoms of data subjects as well as the responsibility and liability of data controllers and data processors, and also the monitoring by and measures of supervisory authorities, requires a clear attribution of the responsibilities under the Regulation, including where a data controller determines the purposes, conditions and means of the processing jointly with other data controllers or where a processing operation is carried out on behalf of a data controller.[119]

In order to demonstrate compliance with the Regulation, the data controller or data processor should document each processing operation.[120] Each data controller and data processor should be obliged to co-operate with the supervisory authority and make this documentation, on request, available to it, so that it might serve for monitoring those processing operations.[121]

Third Counties

Where a data controller not established in the EU is processing personal data of data subjects residing in the EU whose processing activities are related to the offering of goods or services to such data subjects, or to the monitoring their behaviour, the data controller should designate a representative, unless the data controller is established in a third country ensuring an adequate level of protection, or the data controller is a small or medium-sized enterprise or a public authority or body or where the data controller is only occasionally offering goods or services to such data subjects. The representative should act on behalf of the data controller and may be addressed by any supervisory authority.[122]

In order to determine whether a data controller is only occasionally offering goods and services to data subjects residing in the EU, it should be ascertained whether or not it is apparent from the data controller's overall activities that the offering of goods and services to such data subjects is ancillary to those main activities.[123]

Security

In order to maintain security and to prevent processing in breach of the Regulation, the data controller or data processor should evaluate the risks inherent to the processing and implement measures to mitigate those risks. These measures should ensure an appropriate level of security, taking into account the state of the art and the costs of their implementation in relation to the risks and the nature of the personal data to be protected. When establishing technical standards and organisational measures to ensure security of processing, the Commission should promote technological

---

119. Recital 62 *ibid.*
120. Recital 65 *ibid.*
121. *ibid.*
122. Recital 63 *ibid.*
123. Recital 64 *ibid.*

neutrality, interoperability and innovation and, where appropriate, co-operate with third countries.[124]

Data Breach

A personal data breach may, if not addressed in an adequate and timely manner, result in substantial economic loss and social harm, including identity fraud, to the individual concerned. Therefore, as soon as the data controller becomes aware that such a breach has occurred, the data controller should notify the breach to the supervisory authority without undue delay and, where feasible, within 24 hours. Where this cannot be achieved within 24 hours, an explanation of the reasons for the delay should accompany the notification. The individuals whose personal data could be adversely affected by the breach should be notified without undue delay in order to allow them to take the necessary precautions. A breach should be considered as adversely affecting the personal data or privacy of a data subject where it could result in, for example, identity theft or fraud, physical harm, significant humiliation or damage to reputation. The notification should describe the nature of the personal data breach as well as recommendations for the individual concerned to mitigate potential adverse effects. Notifications to data subjects should be made as soon as reasonably feasible, and in close co-operation with the supervisory authority and respecting guidance provided by it or other relevant authorities (e.g. law enforcement authorities). For example, the chance for data subjects to mitigate an immediate risk of harm would call for a prompt notification of data subjects, whereas the need to implement appropriate measures against continuing or similar data breaches may justify a longer delay.[125]

In order to determine whether or not a personal data breach is notified to the supervisory authority and to the data subject without undue delay, it should be ascertained whether or not the data controller has implemented and applied appropriate technological protection and organisational measures to establish immediately that a personal data breach has taken place and to inform promptly the supervisory authority and the data subject, before damage to personal and economic interests occurs, taking into account in particular the nature and gravity of the personal data breach and its consequences and adverse effects for the data subject.[126]

In setting detailed rules concerning the format and procedures applicable to the notification of personal data breaches, due consideration should be given to the circumstances of the breach, including whether or not personal data had been protected by appropriate technical protection measures, effectively limiting the likelihood of identity fraud or other forms of misuse. Moreover, such rules and procedures should take into account the legitimate interests of law enforcement authorities in cases where

---

124. Recital 66 *ibid.*
125. Recital 67 *ibid.*
126. Recital 68 *ibid.*

early disclosure could unnecessarily hamper the investigation of the circumstances of a breach.[127]

Registration/Notification

DP Directive 95 provided for a general obligation to notify processing of personal data to the supervisory authorities. While this obligation produces administrative and financial burdens, it did not in all cases contribute to improving the protection of personal data. Therefore, such indiscriminate general notification obligations should be abolished, and replaced by effective procedures and mechanisms that focus instead on those processing operations that are likely to present specific risks to the rights and freedoms of data subjects by virtue of their nature, their scope or their purposes. In such cases, a data protection impact assessment should be carried out by the data controller or data processor prior to the processing, which should include in particular the envisaged measures, safeguards and mechanisms for ensuring the protection of personal data and for demonstrating the compliance with the Regulation.[128]

This should in particular apply to newly established large-scale filing systems, which aim at processing a considerable amount of personal data at regional, national or supranational levels and which could affect a large number of data subjects.[129]

Impact Assessments

There are circumstances under which it may be sensible and economic that the subject of a data protection impact assessment should be broader than a single project, for example, where public authorities or bodies intend to establish a common application or processing platform or where several data controllers plan to introduce a common application or processing environment across an industry sector or segment or for a widely used horizontal activity.[130]

The data protection impact assessments should be carried out by a public authority or public body if such an assessment has not already been made in the context of the adoption of the Member State law on which the performance of the tasks of the public authority or public body is based and which regulates the specific processing operation or set of operations in question.[131]

Where a data protection impact assessment indicates that processing operations involve a high degree of specific risks to the rights and freedoms of data subjects, such as excluding individuals from their right, or by the use of specific new technologies, the supervisory authority should be consulted prior to the start of operations on

---

127. Recital 69 *ibid.*
128. Recital 70 *ibid.*
129. Recital 71 *ibid.*
130. Recital 72 *ibid.*
131. Recital 73 *ibid.*

a risky processing that might not be in compliance with the Regulation, and allowed to make proposals to remedy such situation.[132] Such consultation should equally take place in the course of the preparation either of a measure by the Member State parliament or of a measure based on such legislative measure as defines the nature of the processing and lays down appropriate safeguards.[133]

Public Sector

Where the processing is carried out in the public sector or where, in the private sector, processing is carried out by a large enterprise, or where its core activities, regardless of the size of the enterprise, involve processing operations that require regular and systematic monitoring, a person should assist the data controller or data processor to monitor internal compliance with the Regulation.[134] Such data protection officers, whether or not employees of the data controller, should be in a position to perform their duties and tasks independently.[135]

Industry Codes

The associations or other bodies representing categories of data controllers should be encouraged to draw up codes of conduct, within the limits of the Regulation, so as to facilitate the effective application of the Regulation, taking account of the specific characteristics of the processing carried out in certain sectors.[136]

Certification

In order to enhance transparency and compliance with the Regulation, the establishment of certification mechanisms, data protection seals and marks should be encouraged, allowing data subjects to quickly assess the level of data protection of relevant products and services.[137]

Cross-border flows of personal data are necessary for the expansion of international trade and international co-operation. The increase in these flows has raised new challenges and concerns with respect to the protection of personal data.[138] However, when personal data are transferred from the EU to third countries or to international organisations, the level of protection of individuals guaranteed in the EU by the Regulation should not be undermined.[139] In any event, transfers to third countries may only be carried out in full compliance with the Regulation.[140]

---

132. Recital 74 *ibid.*
133. *ibid.*
134. Recital 75 *ibid.*
135. *ibid.*
136. Recital 76 *ibid.*
137. Recital 77 *ibid.*
138. Recital 78 *ibid.*
139. *ibid.*
140. *ibid.*

Global Data Protection

The Regulation is without prejudice to international agreements concluded between the EU and third countries regulating the transfer of personal data, including appropriate safeguards for the data subjects.[141]

The Commission may decide with effect for the entire EU that certain third countries, or a territory or a processing sector within a third country, or an international organisation, offer an adequate level of data protection, thus providing legal certainty and uniformity throughout the EU as regards the third countries or international organisations that are considered to provide such level of protection. In these cases, transfers of personal data to these countries may take place without needing to obtain any further authorisation.[142]

In line with the fundamental values on which the EU is founded, in particular the protection of human rights, the Commission should, in its assessment of the third country, take into account how a given third country respects the rule of law, access to justice as well as international human rights norms and standards.[143]

TBDFs, White List, etc.

The Commission may equally recognise that a third country, or a territory or a processing sector within a third country, or an international organisation, does not offer an adequate level of data protection.[144] Consequently the transfer of personal data to that third country should be prohibited. In that case, provision should be made for consultations between the Commission and such third countries or international organisations.[145]

In the absence of an adequacy decision, the data controller or data processor should take measures to compensate for the lack of data protection in a third country by way of appropriate safeguards for the data subject.[146] Such appropriate safeguards may consist of making use of binding corporate rules, standard data protection clauses adopted by the Commission, standard data protection clauses adopted by a supervisory authority or contractual clauses authorised by a supervisory authority, or other suitable and proportionate measures justified in the light of all the circumstances surrounding a data transfer operation or set of data transfer operations and where authorised by a supervisory authority.[147]

---

141. Recital 79 *ibid.*
142. Recital 80 *ibid.*
143. Recital 81 *ibid.*
144. Recital 82 *ibid.*
145. *ibid.*
146. Recital 83 *ibid.*
147. *ibid.*

The possibility for the data controller or data processor to use standard data protection clauses adopted by the Commission or by a supervisory authority should neither prevent the possibility for data controllers or data processors to include the standard data protection clauses in a wider contract nor to add other clauses as long as they do not contradict, directly or indirectly, the standard contractual clauses adopted by the Commission or by a supervisory authority or prejudice the fundamental rights or freedoms of the data subjects.[148]

A corporate group should be able to make use of approved binding corporate rules for its international transfers from the EU to organisations within the same corporate group of undertakings, as long as such corporate rules include essential principles and enforceable rights to ensure appropriate safeguards for transfers or categories of transfers of personal data.[149]

The Regulation states that provisions should be made for the possibility for transfers in certain circumstances where the data subject has given his consent, where the transfer is necessary in relation to a contract or a legal claim, where important grounds of public interest laid down by EU or Member State law so require or where the transfer is made from a register established by law and intended for consultation by the public or persons having a legitimate interest.[150] In this latter case such a transfer should not involve the entirety of the data or entire categories of the data contained in the register and, when the register is intended for consultation by persons having a legitimate interest, the transfer should be made only at the request of those persons or if they are to be the recipients.[151]

These derogations should in particular apply to data transfers required and necessary for the protection of important grounds of public interest, for example in cases of international data transfers between competition authorities, tax or customs administrations, financial supervisory authorities, between services competent for social security matters, or to competent authorities for the prevention, investigation, detection and prosecution of criminal offences.[152]

Transfers that cannot be qualified as frequent or massive could also be possible for the purposes of the legitimate interests pursued by the data controller or the data processor, when they have assessed all the circumstances surrounding the data transfer.[153] For the purposes of processing for historical, statistical and scientific research purposes, the legitimate expectations of society for an increase of knowledge should be taken into consideration.[154]

---

148. Recital 84 *ibid.*
149. Recital 85 *ibid.*
150. Recital 86 *ibid.*
151. *ibid.*
152. Recital 87 *ibid.*
153. Recital 88 *ibid.*
154. *ibid.*

Where the Commission has taken no decision on the adequate level of data protection in a third country, the data controller or data processor should make use of solutions that provide data subjects with a guarantee that they will continue to benefit from the fundamental rights and safeguards as regards processing of their data in the EU once this data has been transferred.[155]

Some third countries enact laws, regulations and other legislative instruments that purport to directly regulate data processing activities of natural and legal persons under the jurisdiction of the Member States. The extraterritorial application of these laws, regulations and other legislative instruments may be in breach of international law and may impede the attainment of the protection of individuals guaranteed in the EU by the Regulation. Transfers should only be allowed where the conditions of the Regulation for a transfer to third countries are met. This may *inter alia* be the case where the disclosure is necessary for an important ground of public interest recognised in EU law or in a Member State law to which the data controller is subject. The conditions under which an important ground of public interest exists should be further specified by the Commission in a delegated act.[156]

When personal data moves across borders it may put at increased risk the ability of individuals to exercise data protection rights in particular to protect themselves from the unlawful use or disclosure of that information. At the same time, supervisory authorities may find that they are unable to pursue complaints or conduct investigations relating to the activities outside their borders. Their efforts to work together in the cross-border context may also be hampered by insufficient preventative or remedial powers, inconsistent legal regimes, and practical obstacles like resource constraints. Therefore, there is a need to promote closer co-operation among data protection supervisory authorities to help them exchange information and carry out investigations with their international counterparts.[157]

Data Protection Commissioner/Supervisory Authorities

The establishment of supervisory authorities in Member States, exercising their functions with complete independence, is an essential component of the protection of individuals with regard to the processing of their personal data.[158] Member States may establish more than one supervisory authority, to reflect their constitutional, organisational and administrative structure.[159]

Where a Member State establishes several supervisory authorities, it should establish by law mechanisms for ensuring the effective participation of those supervisory

---

155. Recital 89 *ibid.*
156. Recital 90 *ibid.*
157. Recital 91 *ibid.*
158. Recital 92 *ibid.*
159. *ibid.*

authorities in the consistency mechanism.[160] That Member State should in particular designate the supervisory authority that functions as a single contact point for
the effective participation of those authorities in the mechanism, to ensure swift
and smooth co-operation with other supervisory authorities, the European Data
Protection Board and the Commission.[161]

Each supervisory authority should be provided with the adequate financial and
human resources, premises and infrastructure, that are necessary for the effective
performance of their tasks, including for the tasks related to mutual assistance and
co-operation with other supervisory authorities throughout the EU.[162]

The general conditions for the members of the supervisory authority should be laid
down by law in each Member State and should in particular provide that those
members should be either appointed by the parliament or the government of the
Member State, and include rules on the personal qualification of the members and
the position of those members.[163]

The supervisory authorities should monitor the application of the provisions pursuant
to the Regulation and contribute to its consistent application throughout the EU, in
order to protect natural persons in relation to the processing of their personal data and
to facilitate the free flow of personal data within the internal market.[164] For that purpose,
the supervisory authorities should co-operate with each other and the Commission.[165]

Processing in More than One Member State
Where the processing of personal data in the context of the activities of an establishment of a data controller or a data processor in the EU takes place in more than one
Member State, one single supervisory authority should be competent for monitoring
the activities of the data controller or data processor throughout the EU and taking the
related decisions, in order to increase the consistent application, provide legal certainty
and reduce administrative burden for such data controllers and data processors.[166]

One Stop Shop
The competent authority, providing such one-stop shop, should be the supervisory
authority of the Member State in which the data controller or data processor has its
main establishment.[167]

---

160. Recital 93 *ibid.*
161. *ibid.*
162. Recital 94 *ibid.*
163. Recital 95 *ibid.*
164. Recital 96 *ibid.*
165. *ibid.*
166. Recital 97 *ibid.*
167. Recital 98 *ibid.*

While the Regulation applies also to the activities of Member State courts, the competence of the supervisory authorities should not cover the processing of personal data
when courts are acting in their judicial capacity, in order to safeguard the independence of judges in the performance of their judicial tasks.[168] However, this exemption
should be strictly limited to genuine judicial activities in court cases and not apply to
other activities judges might be involved in, in accordance with Member State law.[169]

In order to ensure consistent monitoring and enforcement of the Regulation
throughout the EU, the supervisory authorities should have in each Member State
the same duties and effective powers, including powers of investigation, legally
binding intervention, decisions and sanctions, particularly in cases of complaints
from individuals, and to engage in legal proceedings. Investigative powers of supervisory authorities as regards access to premises should be exercised in conformity with
EU law and Member State law. This concerns in particular the requirement to obtain
a prior judicial authorisation.[170]

Each supervisory authority should hear complaints lodged by any data subject and
should investigate the matter. The investigation following a complaint should be
carried out, subject to judicial review, to the extent that is appropriate in the specific
case. The supervisory authority should inform the data subject of the progress and
the outcome of the complaint within a reasonable period. If the case requires further
investigation or coordination with another supervisory authority, intermediate information should be given to the data subject.[171]

Data Protection Awareness
Awareness-raising activities by supervisory authorities addressed to the public should
include specific measures directed at data controllers and data processors, including
micro, small and medium-sized enterprises, as well as data subjects.[172]

The supervisory authorities should assist each other in performing their duties and
provide mutual assistance, so as to ensure the consistent application and enforcement
of the Regulation in the internal market.[173]

Each supervisory authority should have the right to participate in joint operations
between supervisory authorities.[174] The requested supervisory authority should be
obliged to respond to the request in a defined time period.[175]

---

168. Recital 99 *ibid.*
169. *ibid.*
170. Recital 100 *ibid.*
171. Recital 101 *ibid.*
172. Recital 102 *ibid.*
173. Recital 103 *ibid.*
174. Recital 104 *ibid.*
175. *ibid.*

In order to ensure the consistent application of the Regulation throughout the EU, a consistency mechanism for co-operation between the supervisory authorities themselves and the Commission should be established. This mechanism should in particular apply where a supervisory authority intends to take a measure as regards processing operations that are related to the offering of goods or services to data subjects in several Member States, or to the monitoring such data subjects, or that might substantially affect the freeflow of personal data. It should also apply where any supervisory authority or the Commission requests that the matter should be dealt with in the consistency mechanism. This mechanism should be without prejudice to any measures that the Commission may take in the exercise of its powers under the Treaties.[176]

In application of the consistency mechanism, the European Data Protection Board should, within a determined period of time, issue an opinion, if a simple majority of its members so decides or if so requested by any supervisory authority or the Commission.[177]

In order to ensure compliance with the Regulation, the Commission may adopt an opinion on this matter, or a decision, requiring the supervisory authority to suspend its draft measure.[178]

Enforcement

There may be an urgent need to act in order to protect the interests of data subjects, in particular when the danger exists that the enforcement of a right of a data subject could be considerably impeded.[179] Therefore, a supervisory authority should be able to adopt provisional measures with a specified period of validity when applying the consistency mechanism.[180]

The application of this mechanism should be a condition for the legal validity and enforcement of the respective decision by a supervisory authority.[181] In other cases of cross-border relevance, mutual assistance and joint investigations might be carried out between the concerned supervisory authorities on a bilateral or multilateral basis without triggering the consistency mechanism.[182]

At EU level, a European Data Protection Board is to be set up. It should replace the Working Party on the Protection of Individuals with Regard to the Processing of Personal Data established by DP Directive 95. It should consist of a head of a

---

176. Recital 105 *ibid.*
177. Recital 106 *ibid.*
178. Recital 107 *ibid.*
179. Recital 108 *ibid.*
180. *ibid.*
181. Recital 109 *ibid.*
182. Recital 109 *ibid.*

supervisory authority of each Member State and of the European Data Protection Supervisor. The Commission should participate in its activities. The European Data Protection Board should contribute to the consistent application of the Regulation throughout the EU, including by advising the Commission and promoting co-operation of the supervisory authorities throughout the EU. The European Data Protection Board should act independently when exercising its tasks.[183]

Complaints to Data Protection Commissioner

Every data subject has the right to lodge a complaint with a supervisory authority in any Member State and the right to a judicial remedy if he considers that his rights under the Regulation are infringed upon or where the supervisory authority does not react on a complaint or does not act where such action is necessary to protect the rights of the data subject.[184]

Any body, organisation or association that aims to protect the rights and interests of data subjects in relation to the protection of their data and is constituted according to the law of a Member State should have the right to lodge a complaint with a supervisory authority or exercise the right to a judicial remedy on behalf of data subjects, or to lodge, independently of a data subject's complaint, a complaint of its own where it considers that a personal data breach has occurred.[185]

Court Remedies

Each natural or legal person has the right to a judicial remedy against decisions of a supervisory authority concerning him.[186] Proceedings against a supervisory authority should be brought before the courts of the Member State, where the supervisory authority is established.[187]

In order to strengthen the judicial protection of the data subject in situations where the competent supervisory authority is established in a different Member State than the one where the data subject is residing, the data subject may request any body, organisation or association aiming to protect the rights and interests of data subjects in relation to the protection of their data to bring on the data subject's behalf proceedings against that supervisory authority to the competent court in the other Member State.[188]

In situations where the competent supervisory authority established in another Member State does not act or has taken insufficient measures in relation to a

---

183. Recital 110 *ibid.*
184. Recital 111 *ibid.*
185. Recital 112 *ibid.*
186. Recital 113 *ibid.*
187. *ibid.*
188. Recital 114 *ibid.*

complaint, the data subject may request the supervisory authority in the Member State of his habitual residence to bring proceedings against that supervisory authority to the competent court in the other Member State.[189] The requested supervisory authority may decide, subject to judicial review, whether it is appropriate to follow the request or not.[190]

For proceedings against a data controller or data processor, the plaintiff should have the choice to bring the action before the courts of the Member States where the data controller or data processor has an establishment or where the data subject resides, unless the data controller is a public authority acting in the exercise of its public powers.[191]

Where there are indications that parallel proceedings are pending before the courts in different Member States, the courts should be obliged to contact each other. The courts should have the possibility to suspend a case where a parallel case is pending in another Member State. Member States should ensure that court actions, in order to be effective, should allow the rapid adoption of measures to remedy or prevent an infringement of the Regulation.[192]

Compensation

Any damage a person may suffer as a result of unlawful processing should be compensated by the data controllers or data processors, who may be exempted from liability if they prove that they are not responsible for the damage, in particular where they establish fault on the part of the data subject or in case of *force majeure*.[193]

Penalties

Penalties should be imposed to any person, whether governed by private or public law, who fails to comply with the Regulation.[194] Member States should ensure that the penalties should be effective, proportionate and dissuasive and should take all measures to implement the penalties.[195]

Sanctions

In order to strengthen and harmonise administrative sanctions against infringements of the Regulation, each supervisory authority should have the power to sanction administrative offences. The Regulation should indicate these offences and the upper

---

189. Recital 115 *ibid.*
190. *ibid.*
191. Recital 116 *ibid.*
192. Recital 117 *ibid.*
193. Recital 118 *ibid.*
194. Recital 119 *ibid.*
195. *ibid.*

limit for the related administrative fines, which should be fixed in each individual case proportionate to the specific situation, with due regard in particular to the nature, gravity and duration of the breach. The consistency mechanism may also be used to cover divergences in the application of administrative sanctions.[196]

Journalism

The processing of personal data solely for journalistic purposes, or for the purposes of artistic or literary expression, should qualify for exemption from the requirements of certain provisions of the Regulation in order to reconcile the right to the protection of personal data with the right to freedom of expression, and notably the right to receive and impart information, as guaranteed in particular by Article 11 of the Charter of Fundamental Rights of the European Union. This should apply in particular to the processing of personal data in the audiovisual field and in news archives and press libraries. Therefore, Member States should adopt legislative measures, which should lay down exemptions and derogations that are necessary for the purpose of balancing these fundamental rights. Such exemptions and derogations should be adopted by the Member States on general principles, on the rights of the data subject, on data controller and data processor, on the transfer of data to third countries or international organisations, on the independent supervisory authorities and on co-operation and consistency. This should not, however, lead Member States to lay down exemptions from the other provisions of the Regulation. In order to take account of the importance of the right to freedom of expression in every democratic society, it is necessary to interpret notions relating to that freedom, such as journalism, broadly.[197]

Therefore, Member States should classify activities as "journalistic" for the purpose of the exemptions and derogations to be laid down under the Regulation if the object of these activities is the disclosure to the public of information, opinions or ideas, irrespective of the medium used to transmit them. They should not be limited to media undertakings and may be undertaken for profit-making or for non-profit-making purposes.[198]

Health

The processing of personal data concerning health, as a special category of data that deserves higher protection, may often be justified by a number of legitimate reasons for the benefit of individuals and society as a whole, in particular in the context of ensuring continuity of cross-border health care. Therefore, the Regulation should provide for harmonised conditions for the processing of personal data concerning health, subject to specific and suitable safeguards so as to protect the fundamental rights and the personal data of individuals. This includes the right for individuals to have access to their personal data concerning their health, for example the data in

196. Recital 120 *ibid.*
197. Recital 121 *ibid.*
198. *ibid.*

their medical records containing such information as diagnosis, examination results, assessments by treating physicians and any treatment or interventions provided.[199]

Processing of personal data concerning health may be necessary for reasons of public interest in the areas of public health, without consent of the data subject. In that context, "public health" should be interpreted as defined in Regulation (EC) No 1338/2008 of the European Parliament and of the Council of 16 December 2008 on Community statistics on public health and health and safety at work, meaning all elements related to health, namely health status, including morbidity and disability, the determinants having an effect on that health status, health care needs, resources allocated to health care, the provision of, and universal access to, health care as well as health care expenditure and financing, and the causes of mortality. Such processing of personal data concerning health for reasons of public interest should not result in personal data being processed for other purposes by third parties such as employers, insurance and banking companies.[200]

Employment
The general principles on the protection of individuals with regard to the processing of personal data should also be applicable to the employment context.[201] Therefore, in order to regulate the processing of employees' personal data in the employment context, Member States should be able, within the limits of the Regulation, to adopt by law specific rules for the processing of personal data in the employment sector.[202]

Research
The processing of personal data for the purposes of historical, statistical or scientific research should, in order to be lawful, also respect other relevant legislation such as on clinical trials.[203]

The scientific research for the purposes of the Regulation should include fundamental research, applied research, and privately funded research, and in addition should take into account the EU's objective under Article 179(1) of the Treaty on the Functioning of the European Union of achieving a European Research Area.[204]

As regards the powers of the supervisory authorities to obtain from the data controller or data processor access to personal data and access to its premises, Member States may adopt by law, within the limits of the Regulation, specific rules in order to safeguard the professional or other equivalent secrecy obligations, insofar as necessary to

---

199. Recital 122 *ibid.*
200. Recital 123 *ibid.*
201. Recital 124 *ibid.*
202. *ibid.*
203. Recital 125 *ibid.*
204. Recital 126 *ibid.*

reconcile the right to the protection of personal data with an obligation of professional secrecy.[205]

Religious Not Effected

The Regulation respects and does not prejudice the status under national law of
churches and religious associations or communities in the Member States, as recognised in Article 17 of the Treaty on the Functioning of the EU. As a consequence,
where a church in a Member State applies, at the time of entry into force of the
Regulation, comprehensive rules relating to the protection of individuals with regard
to the processing of personal data, these existing rules should continue to apply if
they are brought in line with the Regulation. Such churches and religious associations should be required to provide for the establishment of a completely independent supervisory authority.[206]

Data Protection Rights and Laws

In order to fulfil the objectives of the Regulation, namely to protect the fundamental
rights and freedoms of natural persons, and in particular their right to the protection of personal data, and to ensure the free movement of personal data within the
EU, the power to adopt acts in accordance with Article 290 of the Treaty on the
Functioning of the European Union should be delegated to the Commission. In
particular, delegated acts should be adopted in respect of lawfulness of processing;
specifying the criteria and conditions in relation to the consent of a child; processing
of special categories of data; specifying the criteria and conditions for manifestly
excessive requests and fees for exercising the rights of the data subject; the right of
access; the right to be forgotten and to erasure; measures based on profiling; criteria
and requirements in relation to the responsibility of the data controller and to data
protection by design and by default; a data processor; criteria and requirements for
the documentation and the security of processing; criteria and requirements for establishing a personal data breach and for its notification to the supervisory authority,
and on the circumstances where a personal data breach is likely to adversely affect the
data subject; the criteria and conditions for processing operations requiring a data
protection impact assessment; the criteria and requirements for determining a high
degree of specific risks that require prior consultation; designation and tasks of the
data protection officer; codes of conduct; criteria and requirements for certification
mechanisms; criteria and requirements for transfers by way of binding corporate
rules; transfer derogations; administrative sanctions; processing for health purposes;
processing in the employment context and processing for historical, statistical and
scientific research purposes. It is of particular importance that the Commission carry
out appropriate consultations during its preparatory work, including at expert level.
The Commission, when preparing and drawing-up delegated acts, should ensure

---

205. Recital 127 *ibid.*
206. Recital 128 *ibid.*

a simultaneous, timely and appropriate transmission of relevant documents to the European Parliament and Council.[207]

In order to ensure uniform conditions for the implementation of the Regulation, implementing powers should be conferred on the Commission for: specifying standard forms in relation to the processing of personal data of a child; standard procedures and forms for exercising the rights of data subjects; standard forms for the information to the data subject; standard forms and procedures in relation to the right of access; the right to data portability; standard forms in relation to the responsibility of the data controller to data protection by design and by default and to the documentation; specific requirements for the security of processing; the standard format and the procedures for the notification of a personal data breach to the supervisory authority and the communication of a personal data breach to the data subject; standards and procedures for a data protection impact assessment; forms and procedures for prior authorisation and prior consultation; technical standards and mechanisms for certification; the adequate level of protection afforded by a third country or a territory or a processing sector within that third country or an international organisation; disclosures not authorised by EU law; mutual assistance; joint operations; decisions under the consistency mechanism. Those powers should be exercised in accordance with Regulation (EU) No 182/2011 of the European Parliament and of the Council of 16 February 2011 laying down the rules and general principles concerning mechanisms for control by the Member States of the Commission's exercise of implementing powers.[208]

Standards

The examination procedure should be used for the adoption of specifying standard forms in relation to the consent of a child; standard procedures and forms for exercising the rights of data subjects; standard forms for the information to the data subject; standard forms and procedures in relation to the right of access; the right to data portability; standard forms in relation to the responsibility of the data controller to data protection by design and by default and to the documentation; specific requirements for the security of processing; the standard format and the procedures for the notification of a personal data breach to the supervisory authority and the communication of a personal data breach to the data subject; standards and procedures for a data protection impact assessment; forms and procedures for prior authorisation and prior consultation; technical standards and mechanisms for certification; the adequate level of protection afforded by a third country or a territory or a processing sector within that third country or an international organisation; disclosures not authorised by EU law; mutual assistance; joint operations; and decisions under the consistency mechanism, given that those acts are of general scope.[209]

---

207. Recital 129 *ibid.*
208. Recital 130 *ibid.*
209. Recital 131 *ibid.*

Third Countries

The Commission will adopt measures, in justified cases relating to a third country or a territory or a processing sector within that third country or an international organisation that does not ensure an adequate level of protection and relating to matters communicated by supervisory authorities under the consistency mechanism, imperative grounds of urgency so require.[210]

Recital 133 states that since the objectives of the Regulation, namely to ensure an equivalent level of protection of individuals and the freeflow of data throughout the EU, cannot be sufficiently achieved by the Member States and can therefore, by reason of the scale or effects of the action, be better achieved at EU level, the EU may adopt measures, in accordance with the principle of subsidiarity as set out in Article 5 of the Treaty on European Union.[211] In accordance with the principle of proportionality as set out in that Article, the Regulation does not go beyond what is necessary in order to achieve that objective.[212]

DP Directive 95 Repeal

DP Directive 95 will be repealed by the Regulation.[213] However, Commission decisions adopted and authorisations by supervisory authorities based on DP Directive 95 should remain in force.[214]

ePrivacy Directive Amended

The Regulation should apply to all matters concerning the protection of fundamental rights and freedom *vis-à-vis* the processing of personal data that are not subject to specific obligations with the same objective set out in Directive 2002/58/EC, including the obligations on the data controller and the rights of individuals. In order to clarify the relationship between the Regulation and Directive 2002/58/EC, the latter Directive will be amended accordingly.[215]

Schengen

As regards Iceland and Norway, the Regulation constitutes a development of provisions of the Schengen acquis to the extent that it applies to the processing of personal data by authorities involved in the implementation of that acquis, as provided for by the Agreement concluded by the Council of the European Union and the Republic of Iceland and the Kingdom of Norway concerning the association of those two states with the implementation, application and development of the Schengen acquis.[216]

---

210. Recital 132 *ibid.*
211. Recital 133 *ibid.*
212. *ibid.*
213. Recital 134 EU draft Data Protection Regulation.
214. *ibid.*
215. Recital 135 *ibid.*
216. Recital 136 *ibid.*

As regards Switzerland, the Regulation constitutes a development of provisions of the Schengen acquis to the extent that it applies to the processing of personal data by authorities involved in the implementation of that acquis, as provided for by the Agreement between the European Union, the European Community and the Swiss Confederation concerning the association of the Swiss Confederation with the implementation, application and development of the Schengen acquis.[217]

As regards Liechtenstein, the Regulation constitutes a development of provisions of the Schengen acquis to the extent that it applies to the processing of personal data by authorities involved in the implementation of that acquis, as provided for by the Protocol between the European Union, the European Community, the Swiss Confederation and the Principality of Liechtenstein on the accession of the Principality of Liechtenstein to the Agreement between the European Union, the European Community and the Swiss Confederation on the Swiss Confederation's association with the implementation, application and development of the Schengen acquis.[218]

Proportionality

In view of the fact that, as underlined by the Court of Justice of the European Union, the right to the protection of personal data is not an absolute right, but must be considered in relation to its function in society and be balanced with other fundamental rights, in accordance with the principle of proportionality, the Regulation respects all fundamental rights and observes the principles recognised in the Charter of Fundamental Rights of the European Union as enshrined in the Treaties, notably the right to respect for private and family life, home and communications, the right to the protection of personal data, the freedom of thought, conscience and religion, the freedom of expression and information, the freedom to conduct a business, the right to an effective remedy and to a fair trial as well as cultural, religious and linguistic diversity.[219]

DP Regulation: Children

The issue of children in the data protection regime have been steadily rising. The increased use of social networking and Web 2.0 services enhance the exposures and risks for children and the uninitiated.[220]

This has included childrens' groups, regulators and also the Article 29 Working Party. Article 29 Working Party has issued Opinion 2/2009 on the Protection of Children's Personal Data (General Guidelines and the Special Case of Schools) in 2009 and also

---

217. Recital 137 *ibid.*
218. Recital 138 *ibid.*
219. Recital 139 *ibid.*
220. See, for example, Gourlay and Gallagher, "Collecting and Using Children's Information Online: the UK/US Dichotomy" (12 December 2011) SCL *Computers and Law.*

Working Document 1/2008 on the Protection of Children's Personal Data (General Guidelines and the Special Case of Schools) in 2008. Schools are being encouraged to be proactive and to have appropriate codes and policies for childrens' social networking and internet usage.[221]

There is now going to be an explicit acknowledgement of childrens' interest in the EU data protection regime, unlike with the DP Directive 95, which contained no explicit reference.

Children deserve specific protection of their personal data, as they may be less aware of risks, consequences, safeguards and their rights in relation to the processing of personal data. To determine when an individual is a child, the Regulation should take over the definition laid down by the UN Convention on the Rights of the Child.[222]

The DP Regulation defines a "child" mean any person below the age of 18 years. This is significant in relation consent, contracting, etc. It is significant for social networks who have significant numbers of children. Up until now it was common for certain social networks to purport to accept users only over the age of 13. Now that a child is defined as up to 18 (subject to amendment), it may require careful assessment in relation to social networking contracts, terms, processes, registrations, sign ups, etc.

Article 8 of the DP Regulation contains provisions in relation to the processing of personal data of a child. Article 8(1) provides that for the purposes of the Regulation, in relation to the offering of information society services directly to a child, the processing of personal data of a child below the age of 13 years shall only be lawful if and to the extent that consent is given or authorised by the child's parent or custodian. The data controller shall make reasonable efforts to obtain verifiable consent, taking into consideration available technology.

Article 8(2) provides that Article 8(1) shall not affect the general contract law of Member States such as the rules on the validity, formation or effect of a contract in relation to a child.

Under Article 8(3) the Commission shall be empowered to adopt delegated acts for the purpose of further specifying the criteria and requirements for the methods to obtain verifiable consent referred to in paragraph 1. In doing so, the Commission shall consider specific measures for micro, small and medium-sized enterprises.

---

221. Note generally, for example, Groppe, "A Child's Playground or a Predator's Hunting Ground? – How to Protect Children on Internet Social Networking Sites" (2007)(16) *CommLaw Conspectus* 215–245; Steadman, "MySpace, But Who's Responsibility? Liability of Social Networking Websites When Offline Sexual Assault of Minors Follows Online Interaction" (2007)(14) *Villanova Sports and Entertainment Law Journal* 363–397; Beckstrom, "Who's Looking at Your Facebook Profile? The Use of Student Conduct Codes to Censor College Students' Online Speech" (2008) *Willamette Law Review* 261–312.
222. Recital 29 EU draft Data Protection Regulation.

In addition, the Commission under may lay down standard forms for specific methods to obtain verifiable consent referred to in paragraph 1. Those implementing acts shall be adopted in accordance with the examination procedure referred to in Article 87(2).

DP Regulation: Processing Not Allowing Identification

Article 10 refers to processing not allowing identification, and provides that if the data processed by a data controller do not permit the data controller to identify a natural person, the data controller shall not be obliged to acquire additional information in order to identify the data subject for the sole purpose of complying with any provision of the Regulation.

DP Directive 95: Processing, Journalism, Freedom of Expression

Article 9 of the DP Directive 95 refers to the processing of personal data and freedom of expression, and provides that Member States shall provide for exemptions or derogations from the provisions of this Chapter, Chapter IV and Chapter VI for the processing of personal data carried out solely for journalistic purposes or the purpose of artistic or literary expression only if they are necessary to reconcile the right to privacy with the rules governing freedom of expression.

DP Regulation: Processing and Freedom of Expression

Chapter IX of the DP Regulation also makes provisions relating to specific data processing situations. Under Article 80 the heading is processing of personal data and freedom of expression.

Article 80(1) Member States shall provide for exemptions or derogations from the provisions on the general principles in Chapter II, the rights of the data subject in Chapter III, on data controller and data processor in Chapter IV, on the transfer of personal data to third countries and international organisations in Chapter V, the independent supervisory authorities in Chapter VI, and on co-operation and consistency in Chapter VII, for the processing of personal data carried out solely for journalistic purposes or the purpose of artistic or literary expression in order to reconcile the right to the protection of personal data with the rules governing freedom of expression.

In accordance with Article 80(2) each Member State shall notify the Commission of the law that it has adopted pursuant to Article 80(1), and of any subsequent amendment affecting it.

DP Regulation: Health Data

Chapter IX of the DP Regulation makes provisions relating to specific data processing situations. Article 81 refers to processing of personal data concerning health.

Article 81(1) provides that within the limits of DP Regulation and in accordance with Article 9(2)(h), processing of personal data concerning health must be on the basis of EU law or Member State law that shall provide for suitable and specific measures to safeguard the data subject's legitimate interests, and be necessary for:

- the purposes of preventive or occupational medicine, medical diagnosis, the provision of care or treatment or the management of health-care services, and where those data are processed by a health professional subject to the obligation of professional secrecy or another person also subject to an equivalent obligation of confidentiality under Member State law or rules established by national competent bodies; or

- reasons of public interest in the area of public health, such as protecting against serious cross-border threats to health or ensuring high standards of quality and safety, inter alia for medicinal products or medical devices; or

- other reasons of public interest in areas such as social protection, especially in order to ensure the quality and cost-effectiveness of the procedures used for settling claims for benefits and services in the health insurance system.

Under Article 81(2), it is provided that processing of personal data concerning health that is necessary for historical, statistical or scientific research purposes, such as patient registries set up for improving diagnoses and differentiating between similar types of diseases and preparing studies for therapies, is subject to the conditions and safeguards referred to in Article 83.

Article 81(3) empowers the Commission to adopt delegated acts for the purpose of further specifying other reasons of public interest in the area of public health as referred to Article 81(1)(b), as well as criteria and requirements for the safeguards for the processing of personal data for the purposes referred to in Article 81(1).

DP Regulation: Employment Data

The DP Regulation[223] refers to provisions relating to specific data processing situations. Article 82 refers to processing in the employment context. Article 82(1) provides that, within the limits of the DP Regulation, Member States may adopt by law specific rules regulating the processing of employees' personal data in the employment context, in particular for the purposes of the recruitment, the performance of the contract of employment, including discharge of obligations laid down

---

223. Chapter IX, EU draft Data Protection Regulation.

by law or by collective agreements, management, planning and organisation of work, health and safety at work, and for the purposes of the exercise and enjoyment, on an individual or collective basis, of rights and benefits related to employment, and for the purpose of the termination of the employment relationship.

Article 82(2) states that each Member State shall notify to the Commission those provisions of its law that it adopts pursuant to paragraph 1, by the date specified in Article 91(2) at the latest and, without delay, any subsequent amendment affecting them.

In addition, Article 82(3) provides that the Commission shall be empowered to adopt delegated acts for the purpose of further specifying the criteria and requirements for the safeguards for the processing of personal data for the purposes referred to in Article 82(1).

DP Regulation: Employment Data

Chapter IX of the DP Regulation refers to provisions relating to specific data processing situations. Article 83 refers to processing for historical, statistical and scientific research purposes.

Under Article 83(1) it is provided that within the limits of the DP Regulation, personal data may be processed for historical, statistical or scientific research purposes only if:

- these purposes cannot be otherwise fulfilled by processing data that does not permit or does not any longer permit the identification of the data subject; or

- data enabling the attribution of information to an identified or identifiable data subject is kept separately from the other information as long as these purposes can be fulfilled in this manner.

Under Article 83(2), bodies conducting historical, statistical or scientific research may publish or otherwise publicly disclose personal data only if:

- the data subject has given consent, subject to the conditions laid down in Article 7;

- the publication of personal data is necessary to present research findings or to facilitate research insofar as the interests or the fundamental rights or freedoms of the data subject do not override these interests; or

- the data subject has made the data public.

Article 83(3) provides that the Commission is empowered to adopt delegated acts for the purpose of further specifying the criteria and requirements for the processing of personal data for the purposes referred to in Article 83(1) and (2) as well as any necessary limitations on the rights of information to and access by the data subject and detailing the conditions and safeguards for the rights of the data subject under these circumstances.

DP Regulation: Rights of Data Subjects

Recital 1 states that the protection of natural persons in relation to the processing of personal data is a fundamental right. Article 8(1) of the Charter of Fundamental Rights of the European Union and Article 16(1) of the Treaty lay down that everyone has the right to the protection of personal data concerning him.

Recital 2 indicates that the processing of personal data is designed to serve man; the principles and rules on the protection of individuals with regard to the processing of their personal data should, whatever the nationality or residence of natural persons, respect their fundamental rights and freedoms, notably their right to the protection of personal data. It should contribute to the accomplishment of an area of freedom, security and justice and of an economic union, to economic and social progress, the strengthening and the convergence of the economies within the internal market, and the well-being of individuals.

Recital 19 states that any processing of personal data in the context of the activities of an establishment of a data controller or a data processor in the EU should be carried out in accordance with the Regulation, regardless of whether the processing itself takes place within the EU or not. Establishment implies the effective and real exercise of activity through stable arrangements. The legal form of such arrangements, whether through a branch or a subsidiary with a legal personality, is not the determining factor in this respect.

Recital 20 states that in order to ensure that individuals are not deprived of the protection to which they are entitled under the Regulation, the processing of personal data of data subjects residing in the EU by a data controller not established in the EU should be subject to the Regulation where the processing activities are related to the offering of goods or services to such data subjects, or to the monitoring of the behaviour of such data subjects.

Recital 21 states that in order to determine whether a processing activity can be considered to "monitor the behaviour" of data subjects, it should be ascertained whether individuals are tracked on the internet with data processing techniques that consist of applying a "profile" to an individual, particularly in order to take decisions concerning him or for analysing or predicting his personal preferences, behaviours and attitudes.

Recital 22 states that where the national law of a Member State applies by virtue of public international law, the Regulation should also apply to a data controller not established in the EU, such as in a Member State's diplomatic mission or consular post.

Recital 23 states that the principles of protection should apply to any information concerning an identified or identifiable person. To determine whether a person is identifiable or not, account should be taken of all the means likely reasonably to be used either by the data controller or by any other person to identify the individual. The principles of data protection should not apply to data rendered anonymous in such a way that the data subject is no longer identifiable.

Chapter III of the DP Regulation refers to rights of the data subject. Section 1 refers specifically to transparency and modalities.

Article 11 is headed "Transparent Information and Communication". Under Article 11(1) the data controller shall have transparent and easily accessible policies with regard to the processing of personal data and for the exercise of data subjects' rights.

Under Article 11(2) the data controller shall provide any information and any communication relating to the processing of personal data to the data subject in an intelligible form, using clear and plain language, adapted to the data subject, in particular for any information addressed specifically to a child.

Article 12 refers to procedures and mechanisms for exercising the rights of the data subject. Article 12(1) provides that the data controller shall establish procedures for providing the information referred to in Article 14 and for the exercise of the rights of data subjects referred to in Article 13 and Articles 15 to 19. The data controller shall provide in particular mechanisms for facilitating the request for the actions referred to in Article 13 and Articles 15 to 19. Where personal data are processed by automated means, the data controller shall also provide means for requests to be made electronically.

Article 12(2) provides that the data controller shall inform the data subject without delay and, at the latest within one month of receipt of the request, whether or not any action has been taken pursuant to Article 13 and Articles 15 to 19 and shall provide the requested information. This period may be prolonged for a further month, if several data subjects exercise their rights and their co-operation is necessary to a reasonable extent to prevent an unnecessary and disproportionate effort on the part of the data controller. The information shall be given in writing. Where the data subject makes the request in electronic form, the information shall be provided in electronic form, unless otherwise requested by the data subject.

Under Article 12(3), it is provided that if the data controller refuses to take action on the request of the data subject, the data controller shall inform the data subject of the reasons for the refusal and on the possibilities of lodging a complaint to the supervisory authority and seeking a judicial remedy.

Under Article 12(4) the information and the actions taken on requests referred to in paragraph 1 shall be free of charge. Where requests are manifestly excessive, in particular because of their repetitive character, the data controller may charge a fee for providing the information or taking the action requested, or the data controller may not take the action requested. In that case, the data controller shall bear the burden of proving the manifestly excessive character of the request.

The Commission is empowered, under Article 12(5), to adopt delegated acts for the purpose of further specifying the criteria and conditions for the manifestly excessive requests and the fees referred to in Article 12(4). In addition, Article 12(6) provides that the Commission may lay down standard forms and specify standard procedures for the communication referred to in Article 12(2), including the electronic format. In doing so, the Commission shall take the appropriate measures for micro, small and medium-sized enterprises. Those implementing acts shall be adopted in accordance with the examination procedure referred to in Article 87(2).

Article 13 refers to rights in relation to recipients. It provides that the data controller shall communicate any rectification or erasure carried out in accordance with Articles 16 and 17 to each recipient to whom the data have been disclosed, unless this proves impossible or involves a disproportionate effort.

"Personal data breach" is defined to mean a breach of security leading to the accidental or unlawful destruction, loss, alteration, unauthorised disclosure of, or access to, personal data transmitted, stored or otherwise processed.

DP Regulation: Secrecy

The DP Regulation[224] refers to provisions relating to specific data processing situations. Article 84 is headed "Obligations of Secrecy". Under Article 84(1) it is provided that, within the limits of the DP Regulation, Member States may adopt specific rules to set out the investigative powers by the supervisory authorities laid down in Article 53(2) in relation to data controllers or data processors that are subjects under national law or rules established by national competent bodies to an obligation of professional secrecy or other equivalent obligations of secrecy, where this is necessary and proportionate to reconcile the right of the protection of personal data with the obligation of secrecy. These rules shall only apply with regard to personal data the data controller or data processor has received from or has obtained in an activity covered by this obligation of secrecy.

Also, each Member State must notify the Commission of the rules it has adopted under Article 84(1), and any subsequent amendment.[225]

---

224. Chapter IX, *ibid.*
225. art 84(2) *ibid.*

DP Regulation: Religion

The DP Regulation[226] refers to provisions relating to specific data processing situations. Article 85 refers to existing data protection rules of churches and religious associations. Under Article 85(1), where in a Member State, churches and religious associations or communities apply, at the time of entry into force of the Regulation, comprehensive rules relating to the protection of individuals with regard to the processing of personal data, such rules may continue to apply, provided that they are brought in line with the provisions of the Regulation. Churches and religious associations that apply comprehensive rules in accordance with Article 85(1) shall provide for the establishment of an independent supervisory authority in accordance with Chapter VI of the Regulation.[227]

DP Regulation: Impact Assessment

Section 3 of the DP Regulation refers to data protection impact assessment and prior authorisation. Article 33 is headed data protection impact assessment. Article 33(1) states that where processing operations present specific risks to the rights and freedoms of data subjects by virtue of their nature, their scope or their purposes, the data controller or the data processor acting on the data controller's behalf shall carry out an assessment of the impact of the envisaged processing operations on the protection of personal data.

Under Article 33(2) the following processing operations in particular present specific risks referred to in paragraph 1:

- a systematic and extensive evaluation of personal aspects relating to a natural person or for analysing or predicting in particular the natural person's economic situation, location, health, personal preferences, reliability or behaviour, which is based on automated processing and upon which decisions are made that produce or result in legal effects concerning the individual or significantly affect the individual;

- information on sex life, health, race and ethnic origin or for the provision of health care, epidemiological researches, or surveys of mental or infectious diseases, where the data are processed for taking measures or decisions regarding specific individuals on a large scale;

- monitoring publicly accessible areas, especially when using optic-electronic devices (video surveillance) on a large scale;

- personal data in large-scale filing systems on children, genetic data or biometric data;

---

226. Chapter IX, EU draft Data Protection Regulation.
227. art 85(2) *ibid.*

- other processing operations for which the consultation of the supervisory authority is required pursuant to Article 34(2)(b).

In accordance with Article 33(3) the assessment shall contain at least a general description of the envisaged processing operations, an assessment of the risks to the rights and freedoms of data subjects, the measures envisaged to address the risks, safeguards, security measures and mechanisms to ensure the protection of personal data and to demonstrate compliance with the DP Regulation,[228] taking into account the rights and legitimate interests of data subjects and other persons concerned.

Under Article 33(4) the data controller shall seek the views of data subjects or their representatives on the intended processing, without prejudice to the protection of commercial or public interests or the security of the processing operations.

If the data controller is a public authority or body and where the processing results from a legal obligation pursuant to Article 6(1)(c) providing for rules and procedures pertaining to the processing operations and regulated by EU law, Article 34(1) to (4) shall not apply, unless Member States deem it necessary to carry out such assessment prior to the processing activities.[229]

Also, under Article 33(6), the Commission shall be empowered to adopt delegated acts for the purpose of further specifying the criteria and conditions for the processing operations likely to present specific risks referred to in Article 33(1) and (2) and the requirements for the assessment referred to in Article 33(3), including conditions for scalability, verification and auditability. In doing so, the Commission shall consider specific measures for micro, small and medium-sized enterprises.[230]

Under Article 33(7), the Commission may specify standards and procedures for carrying out and verifying and auditing the assessment referred to in Article 33(3). Those implementing acts shall be adopted in accordance with the examination procedure referred to in Article 87(2).[231]

DP Regulation: Data Protection Officer

The DP Regulation[232] refers to the data protection officer. Article 35 is headed "The Designation of the Data Protection Officer". Article 35(1) states that the data controller and the data processor shall designate a data protection officer in any case where:

- the processing is carried out by a public authority or body; or

---

228. *ibid.*
229. art 33(5) *ibid.*
230. art 33(6) *ibid.*
231. art 33(7) *ibid.*
232. s 4, EU draft Data Protection Regulation *ibid.*

- the processing is carried out by an enterprise employing 250 persons or more; or

- the core activities of the data controller or the data processor consist of processing operations that, by virtue of their nature, their scope and/or their purposes, require regular and systematic monitoring of data subjects.

In a case where the processing is carried out by an enterprise employing 250 persons or more a group of undertakings may appoint a single data protection officer.[233]

Where the data controller or the data processor is a public authority or body, the data protection officer may be designated for several of its entities, taking account of the organisational structure of the public authority or body.[234]

In cases other than those referred to in Article 35(1), the data controller or data processor or associations and other bodies representing categories of data controllers or data processors may designate a data protection officer.

Under Article 35(5) the data controller or data processor shall designate the data protection officer on the basis of professional qualities and, in particular, expert knowledge of data protection law and practices and ability to fulfil the tasks referred to in Article 37. The necessary level of expert knowledge shall be determined, in particular, according to the data processing carried out and the protection required for the personal data processed by the data controller or the data processor.

The data controller or the data processor shall ensure, in accordance with Article 35(6), that any other professional duties of the data protection officer are compatible with the person's tasks and duties as data protection officer and do not result in a conflict of interests.

Article 35(7) provides that the data controller or the data processor shall designate a data protection officer for a period of at least two years. The data protection officer may be reappointed for further terms. During their term of office, the data protection officer may only be dismissed if the data protection officer no longer fulfils the conditions required for the performance of his duties.

The data protection officer may be employed by the data controller or data processor, or fulfil his tasks on the basis of a service contract.[235]

The data controller or the data processor shall communicate the name and contact details of the data protection officer to the supervisory authority and to the public.[236]

---

233. art 35(1) *ibid.*
234. art 35(3) *ibid.*
235. art 35(8) *ibid.*
236. art 35(9) *ibid.*

Article 35(10) provides that data subjects shall have the right to contact the data protection officer on all issues related to the processing of the data subject's data and to request the exercise of their rights under the DP Regulation.

Also, under Article 35(11) the Commission shall be empowered to adopt delegated acts for the purpose of further specifying the criteria and requirements for the core activities of the data controller or the data processor referred to in Article 35(1)(c) and the criteria for the professional qualities of the data protection officer referred to in Article 35(5).

Article 36 refers to the position of the data protection officer. Article 36(1) provides that the data controller or the data processor shall ensure that the data protection officer is properly and in a timely manner involved in all issues that relate to the protection of personal data.

Article 36(2) provides that the data controller or data processor shall ensure that the data protection officer performs the duties and tasks independently and does not receive any instructions as regards the exercise of the function. The data protection officer shall directly report to the management of the data controller or the data processor.[237] The data controller or the data processor shall support the data protection officer in performing the tasks and shall provide staff, premises, equipment and any other resources necessary to carry out the duties and tasks referred to in Article 37.[238]

Article 37 refers to the tasks of the data protection officer. Under Article 37(1) the data controller or the data processor shall entrust the data protection officer at least with the following tasks:

- to inform and advise the data controller or the data processor of his obligations pursuant to the DP Regulation and to document this activity and the responses received;

- to monitor the implementation and application of the policies of the data controller or data processor in relation to the protection of personal data, including the assignment of responsibilities, the training of staff involved in the processing operations, and the related audits;

- to monitor the implementation and application of the DP Regulation, in particular as to the requirements related to data protection by design, data protection by default and data security and to the information of data subjects and their requests in exercising their rights under the DP Regulation;

- to ensure that the documentation referred to in Article 28 is maintained;

- to monitor the documentation, notification and communication of personal data breaches pursuant to Articles 31 and 32;

237. *ibid.*
238. art 36(3) *ibid.*

- to monitor the performance of the data protection impact assessment by the data controller or data processor and the application for prior authorisation or prior consultation, if required pursuant Articles 33 and 34;

- to monitor the response to requests from the supervisory authority and, within the sphere of the data protection officer's competence, to co-operate with the supervisory authority at the latter's request or on the data protection officer's own initiative;

- to act as the contact point for the supervisory authority on issues related to the processing and consult with the supervisory authority, if appropriate, on his own initiative.

The Commission shall be empowered to adopt delegated acts for the purpose of further specifying the criteria and requirements for tasks, certification, status, powers and resources of the data protection officer referred to in Article 37(1).[239]

DP Regulation: General Obligations Data Controllers and Data Processors

Chapter IV refers to data controllers and data processors, or data controllers and data processors. Section 1 sets out general obligations. Article 22 refers to the responsibility of the data controller. The data controller shall adopt policies and implement appropriate measures to ensure and be able to demonstrate that the processing of personal data is performed in compliance with the DP Regulation.[240]

The measures provided for in Article 22(1) are set out in Article 22(2) and include:

- keeping the documentation pursuant to Article 28;

- implementing the data security requirements laid down in Article 30;

- performing a data protection impact assessment pursuant to Article 33;

- complying with the requirements for prior authorisation or prior consultation of the supervisory authority pursuant to Article 34(1) and (2); and

- designating a data protection officer pursuant to Article 35(1).

The data controller shall implement mechanisms to ensure the verification of the effectiveness of the measures referred to in Article 22(1) and (2). If proportionate, this verification shall be carried out by independent internal or external auditors.[241]

---

239. art 37(2) *ibid.*
240. art 22(1), *ibid.*
241. art 22(3) *ibid.*

The Commission shall be empowered to adopt delegated acts for the purpose of specifying any further criteria and requirements for appropriate measures referred to in Article 22(1) other than those already referred to in Article 22(2), the conditions for the verification and auditing mechanisms referred to in Article 22(3) and as regards the criteria for proportionality under Article 22(3), and considering specific measures for micro, small and medium-sized enterprises (SMEs).[242]

DP Regulation: Data Protection By Design (DPbD)(PbD)

Article 23 of the DP Regulation refers to data protection by design and by default. It is also referred to as privacy by design (PbD). This is an increasingly important area in data protection.

Article 23(1) introduces this topic by saying that having regard to the state of the art and the cost of implementation, the data controller shall, both at the time of the determination of the means for processing and at the time of the processing itself, implement appropriate technical and organisational measures and procedures in such a way that the processing will meet the requirements of the DP Regulation and ensure the protection of the rights of the data subject.

The data controller shall implement mechanisms for ensuring that, by default, only those personal data are processed that are necessary for each specific purpose of the processing and are especially not collected or retained beyond the minimum necessary for those purposes, both in terms of the amount of the data and the time of their storage. In particular, those mechanisms shall ensure that by default personal data are not made accessible to an indefinite number of individuals.[243]

In addition, the Commission is empowered to adopt delegated acts for the purpose of specifying any further criteria and requirements for appropriate measures and mechanisms referred to in Article 23(1) and (2), in particular for data protection by design requirements applicable across sectors, products and services.[244]

Furthermore, the Commission may also lay down technical standards for the requirements laid down in Article 23(1) and (2). Those implementing acts shall be adopted in accordance with the examination procedure referred to in Article 87(2).[245]

DP Regulation: Joint Data Controllers

Article 24 refers to the new concept of joint data controllers or joint data controllers. It provides that where a data controller determines the purposes, conditions and

---

242. art 22(4) *ibid.*
243. art 23(2) *ibid.*
244. art 23(3) *ibid.*
245. art 23(4) *ibid.*

means of the processing of personal data jointly with others, the joint data controllers shall determine their respective responsibilities for compliance with the obligations under the DP Regulation, in particular as regards the procedures and mechanisms for exercising the rights of the data subject, by means of an arrangement between them.

DP Regulation: Non-EU Data Controllers

The DP Regulation[246] refers to representatives of data controllers not established in the EU. Article 25(1) provides that "[i]n the situation referred to in Article 3(2), the [data] controller shall designate a representative in the [EU]".

Article 25(2) explains that this obligation shall not apply to:

- a data controller established in a third country where the Commission has decided that the third country ensures an adequate level of protection in accordance with Article 41; or
- an enterprise employing fewer than 250 persons; or
- a public authority or body; or
- a data controller only occasionally offering goods or services to data subjects residing in the EU.

The representative shall be established in one of those Member States where the data subjects whose personal data are processed in relation to the offering of goods or services to them, or whose behaviour is monitored, reside.[247]

The designation of a representative by the data controller shall be without prejudice to legal actions that could be initiated against the data controller itself.[248]

DP Regulation: Data Processors

Article 26 of the DP Regulation refers to data processors. Where a processing operation is to be carried out on behalf of a data controller, the data controller shall choose a data processor providing sufficient guarantees to implement appropriate technical and organisational measures and procedures in such a way that the processing will meet the requirements of the DP Regulation[249] and ensure the protection of the rights of the data subject, in particular in respect of the technical security measures and organisational measures governing the processing to be carried out and shall ensure compliance with those measures.

246. art 25, *ibid.*
247. art 25(3) *ibid.*
248. art 25(4) *ibid.*
249. art 26(1), *ibid.*

The carrying out of processing by a data processor shall be governed by a contract or other legal act binding the data processor to the data controller and stipulating in particular that the data processor shall:

- act only on instructions from the data controller, in particular, where the transfer of the personal data used is prohibited;

- employ only staff who have committed themselves to confidentiality or are under a statutory obligation of confidentiality;

- take all required measures pursuant to Article 30;

- enlist another data processor only with the prior permission of the data controller;

- insofar as this is possible given the nature of the processing, create in agreement with the data controller the necessary technical and organisational requirements for the fulfilment of the data controller's obligation to respond to requests for exercising the data subject's rights laid down in Chapter III;

- assist the data controller in ensuring compliance with the obligations pursuant to Articles 30 to 34;

- hand over all results to the data controller after the end of the processing and not process the personal data otherwise;

- make available to the data controller and the supervisory authority all information necessary to control compliance with the obligations laid down in the Article.[250]

Article 26(3) also sets out obligations whereby the data controller and the data processor shall document in writing the data controller's instructions and the data processor's obligations referred to in Article 26(2).

If a data processor processes personal data other than as instructed by the data controller, the data processor shall be considered to be a data controller in respect of that processing and shall be subject to the rules on joint data controllers laid down in Article 24.

The Commission shall be empowered under Article 26(5) to adopt delegated acts (in accordance with Article 86) for the purpose of further specifying the criteria and requirements for the responsibilities, duties and tasks in relation to a data processor in line with Article 26(1), and conditions that allow facilitating the processing of personal data within a group of undertakings, in particular for the purposes of control and reporting.

---

250. art 26(2) *ibid.*

DP Regulation: Processing Under Authority

Article 27 refers to processing under the authority of the data controller and data processor and provides that the data processor and any person acting under the authority of the data controller or of the data processor who has access to personal data shall not process them except on instructions from the data controller, unless required to do so by EU or Member State law.

DP Regulation: Documentation

Each data controller and data processor and, if any, the data controller's representative, shall maintain documentation of all processing operations under its responsibility.[251]

The documentation shall contain at least the following information:

- the name and contact details of the data controller, or any joint data controller or data processor, and of the representative, if any;

- the name and contact details of the data protection officer, if any;

- the purposes of the processing, including the legitimate interests pursued by the controller where the processing is based on Article 6(1)(f);

- a description of categories of data subjects and of the categories of personal data relating to them;

- the recipients or categories of recipients of the personal data, including the controllers to whom personal data are disclosed for the legitimate interest pursued by them;

- where applicable, transfers of data to a third country or an international organisation, including the identification of that third country or international organisation and, in case of transfers referred to Article 44(1)(h), the documentation of appropriate safeguards;

- a general indication of the time limits for erasure of the different categories of data;

- the description of the mechanisms referred to in Article 22(3).[252]

The data controller and the data processor and, if any, the data controller's representative, shall make the documentation available, on request, to the supervisory authority.[253]

---

251. art 28(1) *ibid.*
252. art 28(2) *ibid.*
253. art 28(3) *ibid.*

However, under Article 28(4) the obligations referred to in Article 28(1) and (2) shall not apply to the following data controllers and data processors:

- a natural person processing personal data without a commercial interest; or

- an enterprise or an organisation employing fewer than 250 persons that is processing personal data only as an activity ancillary to its main activities.

The Commission shall be empowered to adopt delegated acts for the purpose of further specifying the criteria and requirements for the documentation referred to in Article 28(1), to take account of in particular the responsibilities of the data controller and the data processor and, if any, the data controller's representative.[254]

In addition, the Commission may, per Article 28(6), lay down standard forms for the documentation referred to in Article 28(1). Those implementing acts shall be adopted in accordance with the examination procedure referred to in Article 87(2).

DP Directive 95: Codes and Certification

The DP Directive 95[255] refers to codes of conduct. The Member States and the Commission shall encourage the drawing-up of codes of conduct intended to contribute to the proper implementation of the national provisions adopted by the Member States pursuant to the Directive, taking account of the specific features of the various sectors.[256]

Member States shall make provision for trade associations and other bodies representing other categories of data controllers that have drawn up draft national codes or that have the intention of amending or extending existing national codes to be able to submit them to the opinion of the national authority. Member States shall make provision for this authority to ascertain, among other things, whether the drafts submitted to it are in accordance with the Member State provisions adopted pursuant to the Directive or not. If it sees fit, the authority shall seek the views of data subjects or their representatives.[257]

Under Article 27(3) draft Community codes, and amendments or extensions to existing Community codes, may be submitted to the Article 29 Working Party. The Article 29 Working Party shall determine, among other things, whether the drafts submitted to it are in accordance with the Member State provisions adopted pursuant to the DP Directive 95. If it sees fit, the authority shall seek the views of data subjects or their representatives. The Commission may ensure appropriate publicity for the codes that have been approved by the Article 29 Working Party.

---

254. art 28(5) *ibid.*
255. Chapter V, EU Data Protection Directive 1995 *ibid.*
256. art 27(1) *ibid.*
257. art 27(2) *ibid.*

DP Regulation: Codes

Section 5 refers to and is headed Codes of Conduct and Certification. Article 38 refers to codes of conduct and Article 38(1) provides that Member States, the supervisory authorities and the Commission shall encourage the drawing-up of codes of conduct intended to contribute to the proper application of the Regulation, taking account of the specific features of the various data processing sectors, in particular in relation to:

- fair and transparent data processing;

- the collection of data;

- the information of the public and of data subjects;

- requests of data subjects in exercise of their rights;

- information and protection of children;

- transfer of data to third countries or international organisations;

- mechanisms for monitoring and ensuring compliance with the code by the controllers adherent to it;

- out-of-court proceedings and other dispute-resolution procedures for resolving disputes between data controllers and data subjects with respect to the processing of personal data, without prejudice to the rights of the data subjects pursuant to Articles 73 and 75.

Associations and other bodies representing categories of data controllers or data processors in one Member State that intend to draw up codes of conduct or to amend or extend existing codes of conduct may submit them to an opinion of the supervisory authority in that Member State. The supervisory authority may give an opinion on whether the draft code of conduct or the amendment is in compliance with the DP Regulation or not.[258] The supervisory authority shall seek the views of data subjects or their representatives on these drafts.

Associations and other bodies representing categories of data controllers in several Member States may submit draft codes of conduct and amendments or extensions to existing codes of conduct to the Commission.[259]

The Commission may adopt implementing acts for deciding that the codes of conduct and amendments or extensions to existing codes of conduct submitted to it pursuant to Article 38(3) have general validity within the EU. Those implementing acts shall be adopted in accordance with the examination procedure set out in Article 87(2).[260]

---

258. art 38(2), EU draft Data Protection Regulation.

259. art 38(3) *ibid*.

260. art 38(4) *ibid*.

The Commission shall also ensure appropriate publicity for the codes that have been decided as having general validity in accordance with Article 38(4).[261]

DP Regulation: Certification

Member States and the Commission shall encourage, in particular at European level, the establishment of data protection certification mechanisms and of data protection seals and marks, allowing data subjects to quickly assess the level of data protection provided by data controllers and data processors.[262] The data protection certifications mechanisms shall contribute to the proper application of the Regulation, taking account of the specific features of the various sectors and different processing operations.

The Commission shall be empowered to adopt delegated acts in accordance with Article 86 for the purpose of further specifying the criteria and requirements for the data protection certification mechanisms referred to in Article 39(1), including conditions for granting and withdrawal, and requirements for recognition within the EU and in third countries.[263]

The Commission is also empowered by Article 39(3) to lay down technical standards for certification mechanisms and data protection seals and marks and mechanisms to promote and recognise certification mechanisms and data protection seals and marks. Those implementing acts shall be adopted in accordance with the examination procedure set out in Article 87(2).

DP Directive 95: National Supervisory Authorities and Agencies

Chapter VI is headed "Supervisory Authority and Working Party on the Protection of Individuals with regard to the Processing of Personal Data". Article 28 refers to the supervisory authority. Article 28(1) provides that each Member State shall provide that one or more public authorities are responsible for monitoring the application within its territory of the provisions adopted by the Member States pursuant to the Directive. These authorities shall act with complete independence in exercising the functions entrusted to them.

Each Member State shall provide that the supervisory authorities are consulted when drawing up administrative measures or regulations relating to the protection of individuals' rights and freedoms with regard to the processing of personal data.[264]

---

261. art 38(5) *ibid.*
262. art 39(1) *ibid.*
263. art 39(2) *ibid.*
264. art 28(2) *ibid.*

In accordance with Article 28(3) each authority shall in particular be endowed with:

- investigative powers, such as powers of access to data forming the subject-matter of processing operations and powers to collect all the information necessary for the performance of its supervisory duties;

- effective powers of intervention, such as, for example, that of delivering opinions before processing operations are carried out, in accordance with Article 20, and ensuring appropriate publication of such opinions, of ordering the blocking, erasure or destruction of data, of imposing a temporary or definitive ban on processing, of warning or admonishing the data controller, or that of referring the matter to Member State parliaments or other political institutions; and

- the power to engage in legal proceedings where the Member State provisions adopted pursuant to the Directive have been violated or to bring these violations to the attention of the judicial authorities.

Decisions by the supervisory authority that give rise to complaints may be appealed through the courts.[265]

Each supervisory authority shall hear claims lodged by any person, or by an association representing that person, concerning the protection of his rights and freedoms in regard to the processing of personal data. The person concerned shall be informed of the outcome of the claim.[266] He shall also hear claims for checks on the lawfulness of data processing lodged by any person when the Member State provisions adopted pursuant to Article 13 of the Directive apply. The person shall at any rate be informed that a check has taken place.[267]

Each supervisory authority shall draw up a report on its activities at regular intervals, which shall be made public.[268]

Article 28(6) provides that each supervisory authority is competent, whatever the Member State law applicable to the processing in question, to exercise, on the territory of its own Member State, the powers conferred on it in accordance with Article 28(3). Each authority may be requested to exercise its powers by an authority of another Member State. The supervisory authorities shall co-operate with one another to the extent necessary for the performance of their duties, in particular by exchanging all useful information.[269]

---

265. art 28(3) *ibid.*
266. art 28(4) *ibid.*
267. *ibid.*
268. art 28(5) *ibid.*
269. art 28(6) *ibid.*

Member States shall provide that the members and staff of the supervisory authority, even after their employment has ended, are to be subject to a duty of professional secrecy with regard to confidential information to which they have access.

DP Regulation: National Supervisory Authorities and Agencies

Chapter VI of the DP Regulation refers to the national independent supervisory authorities as well as their independent status.

Article 46 of the DP Regulation provides that each Member State shall provide that one or more public authorities are responsible for monitoring the application of the Regulation and for contributing to its consistent application throughout the EU, in order to protect the fundamental rights and freedoms of natural persons in relation to the processing of their personal data and to facilitate the freeflow of personal data within the EU. For these purposes, the supervisory authorities shall co-operate with each other and the Commission.[270]

Where a Member State has more than one supervisory authority, it shall designate one supervisory authority for participation in the European Data Protection Board.[271] Each Member State shall notify to the Commission those provisions of its law that it adopts and any subsequent amendment affecting them.[272]

Article 47 refers to the independence of the supervisory authorities. The supervisory authority shall act with complete independence in exercising the duties and powers entrusted to it.[273] Furthermore, the members of the supervisory authority shall, in the performance of their duties, neither seek nor take instructions from anybody.[274] Also, the members of the supervisory authority shall refrain from any action incompatible with their duties and shall not, during their term of office, engage in any incompatible organisational communications usage policies, whether gainful or not, in accordance with Article 47(3). There are also obligations after leaving office. The members of the supervisory authority shall behave, after their term of office, with integrity and discretion as regards the acceptance of appointments and benefits.[275]

Each Member State is obliged to ensure that the supervisory authority is provided with the adequate human, technical and financial resources, premises and infrastructure necessary for the effective performance of its duties and powers, including those to be carried out in the context of mutual assistance, co-operation and participation in the European Data Protection Board. Each Member State shall ensure, in

---

270. art 46(1) *ibid.*
271. art 46(2) *ibid.*
272. art 46(3) *ibid.*
273. art 47(1) *ibid.*
274. art 47(2) *ibid.*
275. art 4(4) *ibid.*

accordance with Article 47(6), that the supervisory authority has its own staff, which shall be appointed by and be subject to the direction of the head of the supervisory authority. Importantly perhaps, Article 47(7) provides that Member States shall ensure that the supervisory authority is subject to financial control, which shall not affect its independence. Member States shall ensure that the supervisory authority has separate annual budgets. The budgets shall be made public. One could speculate whether or not this includes sufficient resources to be able to properly undertake and fulfil its obligations. Many national supervisory authorities are experiencing additional workload above what was originally envisaged. There is an issue, therefore, in terms of whether they are entitled to be adequately resourced or not.

Article 48 is headed "General Conditions for the Members of the Supervisory Authority". Member States shall provide that the members of the supervisory authority must be appointed either by the parliament or the government of the Member State concerned, and must be independent, skilled and experienced.[276]

Article 49 sets out provisions regarding the rules on the establishment of the supervisory authority. Each Member State shall provide by law, within the limits of the Regulation:

- the establishment and status of the supervisory authority;

- the qualifications, experience and skills required to perform the duties of the members of the supervisory authority;

- the rules and procedures for the appointment of the members of the supervisory authority, as well the rules on actions or organisational communications usage policies incompatible with the duties of the office;

- the duration of the term of the members of the supervisory authority, which shall be no less than four years, except for the first appointment after entry into force of the DP Regulation, part of which may take place for a shorter period where this is necessary to protect the independence of the supervisory authority by means of a staggered appointment procedure;

- whether the members of the supervisory authority shall be eligible for reappointment or not;

- the regulations and common conditions governing the duties of the members and staff of the supervisory authority;

- the rules and procedures on the termination of the duties of the members of the supervisory authority, including in the case that they no longer fulfil the conditions required for the performance of their duties or if they are guilty of serious misconduct.

---

276. art 48(2) *ibid.*

Article 50 refers to professional secrecy. The members and the staff of the supervisory authority shall be subject, both during and after their term of office, to a duty of professional secrecy with regard to any confidential information that has come to their knowledge in the course of the performance of their official duties.

Section 2 refers to duties and powers. Article 51 refers to competence and provides that each supervisory authority shall exercise, on the territory of its own Member State, the powers conferred on it in accordance with the Regulation.[277]

Article 51(2) provides that where the processing of personal data takes place in the context of the activities of an establishment of a data controller or a data processor in the EU, and the data controller or data processor is established in more than one Member State, the supervisory authority of the main establishment of the data controller or data processor shall be competent for the supervision of the processing activities of the data controller or the data processor in all Member States. This is without prejudice to the provisions of Chapter VII of the DP Regulation.

The supervisory authority shall not be competent to supervise processing operations of courts acting in their judicial capacity.[278]

Article 52 refers to duties. It is provided that the supervisory authority shall:

- monitor and ensure the application of the DP Regulation;
- hear complaints lodged by any data subject, or by an association representing that data subject in accordance with Article 73, and to investigate, to the extent appropriate, the matter and inform the data subject or the association of the progress and the outcome of the complaint within a reasonable period, in particular if further investigation or co-ordination with another supervisory authority is necessary;
- share information with and provide mutual assistance to other supervisory authorities and ensure the consistency of application and enforcement of the DP Regulation;
- conduct investigations either on its own initiative or on the basis of a complaint or on request of another supervisory authority, and inform the data subject concerned, if the data subject has addressed a complaint to this supervisory authority, of the outcome of the investigations within a reasonable period;
- monitor relevant developments, insofar as they have an impact on the protection of personal data, in particular the development of information and communication technologies and commercial practices;

---

277. art 51(1) *ibid.*
278. art 51(3) *ibid.*

- be consulted by Member State institutions and bodies on legislative and administrative measures relating to the protection of individuals' rights and freedoms with regard to the processing of personal data;

- authorise and be consulted on the processing operations referred to in Article 34;

- issue an opinion on the draft codes of conduct pursuant to Article 38(2);

- approve binding corporate rules pursuant to Article 43;

- participate in the activities of the European Data Protection Board.

Each supervisory authority shall promote the awareness of the public on risks, rules, safeguards and rights in relation to the processing of personal data.[279]

Article 52(2) also provides that activities addressed to children shall receive specific attention. This was not explicitly mentioned before in the DP Directive 95.

National supervisory authorities shall, upon request, advise any data subject in exercising the rights under the DP Regulation and, if appropriate, co-operate with the supervisory authorities in other Member States to this end.[280]

For complaints referred to in Article 52(1)(b), the supervisory authority shall provide a complaint submission form, which can be completed electronically, without excluding other means of communication.[281] Previously, certain authorities did not require a specific form.

Importantly for individuals, Article 52(5) provides that the performance of the duties of the supervisory authority shall be free of charge for the data subject.

However, Article 52(6) provides that where requests are manifestly excessive, in particular due to their repetitive character, the supervisory authority may charge a fee or not take the action requested by the data subject. The supervisory authority shall bear the burden of proving the manifestly excessive character of the request.[282]

Article 53(1) provides that each supervisory authority shall have the power:

- to notify the data controller or the data processor of an alleged breach of the provisions governing the processing of personal data, and, where appropriate, order the data controller or the data processor to remedy that breach, in a specific manner, in order to improve the protection of the data subject;

---

279. art 52(2) *ibid.*
280. art 52(3) *ibid.*
281. art 52(4) *ibid.*
282. art 52(6) *ibid.*

- to order the data controller or the data processor to comply with the data subject's requests to exercise the rights provided by the DP Regulation;

- to order the data controller and the data processor and, where applicable, the representative to provide any information relevant for the performance of its duties;

- to ensure the compliance with prior authorisations and prior consultations referred to in Article 34;

- to warn or admonish the data controller or the data processor;

- to order the rectification, erasure or destruction of all data when they have been processed in breach of the provisions of the DP Regulation and the notification of such actions to third parties to whom the data have been disclosed;

- to impose a temporary or definitive ban on processing;

- to suspend data flows to a recipient in a third country or to an international organisation;

- to issue opinions on any issue related to the protection of personal data;

- to inform the Member State parliament, the government or other political institutions as well as the public on any issue related to the protection of personal data.

Each supervisory authority shall have the investigative power to obtain from the data controller or the data processor: access to all personal data and to all information necessary for the performance of its duties (Article 53(2)(a)); access to any of its premises, including to any data processing equipment and means, where there are reasonable grounds for presuming that an activity in violation of the Regulation is being carried out there (Article 53(2)(b)). The investigatory powers must be exercised in conformity with EU law and Member State law.

Article 53(3) provides that each supervisory authority shall have the power to bring violations of the Regulation to the attention of the judicial authorities (i.e. the courts) and to engage in legal proceedings, in particular pursuant to Article 74(4) and Article 75(2).

In addition, Article 53(4) provides that each supervisory authority shall have the power to sanction administrative offences, in particular those referred to in Article 79(4), (5) and (6).

Article 54 provides for an activity report. Each supervisory authority must draw up an annual report on its activities. The report shall be presented to the Member State parliament and shall be made be available to the public, the Commission and the European Data Protection Board.

Chapter VII refers to co-operation and consistency. Article 55 makes provision as regards what is called "mutual assistance".

Supervisory authorities shall provide each other relevant information and mutual assistance in order to implement and apply the DP Regulation[283] in a consistent manner, and shall put in place measures for effective co-operation with one another. Mutual assistance shall cover, in particular, information requests and supervisory measures, such as requests to carry out prior authorisations and consultations, inspections and prompt information on the opening of cases and ensuing developments where data subjects in several Member States are likely to be affected by processing operations.[284]

Each supervisory authority shall take all appropriate measures required to reply to the request of another supervisory authority without delay and no later than one month after having received the request. Such measures may include, in particular, the transmission of relevant information on the course of an investigation or enforcement measures to bring about the cessation or prohibition of processing operations contrary to the DP Regulation.[285]

Article 55(3) provides that the request for assistance shall contain all the necessary information, including the purpose of the request and reasons for the request. Information exchanged shall be used only in respect of the matter for which it was requested.[286]

Requests must be complied with. Article 55(4) provides that a supervisory authority to which a request for assistance is addressed may not refuse to comply with it unless: (a) it is not competent for the request; or (b) compliance with the request would be incompatible with the provisions of the DP Regulation.

The requested supervisory authority shall inform the requesting supervisory authority of the results or, as the case may be, of the progress or the measures taken in order to meet the request by the requesting supervisory authority.[287] The information is to be supplied by electronic means and within the shortest possible period of time, using a standardised format.[288]

There is no fee charged for any action taken following a request for mutual assistance.[289]

Article 55(8) provides that:

> Where a supervisory authority does not act within one month on request of another supervisory authority, the requesting supervisory authorities shall be competent to

---

283. *ibid.*
284. art 55(1) *ibid.*
285. art 55(2), EU draft Data Protection Regulation *ibid.*
286. art 55(3) *ibid.*
287. art 55(5) *ibid.*
288. art 55(6) *ibid.*
289. art 55(7) *ibid.*

take a provisional measure on the territory of its Member State in accordance with Article 51(1) and shall submit the matter to the European Data Protection Board in accordance with the procedure referred to in Article 57.

The supervisory authority shall specify the period of validity, not to exceed three months, of such provisional measure and shall without delay communicate those measures, with full reasons, to the European Data Protection Board and to the Commission.[290] The Commission may specify the format and procedures for mutual assistance referred to in the Article and the arrangements for the exchange of information by electronic means between supervisory authorities, and between supervisory authorities and the European Data Protection Board, in particular the standardised format.[291]

Article 56 provides for joint operations of supervisory authorities. In order to step up co-operation and mutual assistance, the supervisory authorities shall carry out joint investigative tasks, joint enforcement measures and other joint operations, in which designated members or staff from other Member States' supervisory authorities are involved.[292]

Article 56(2) continues that in cases where data subjects in several Member States are likely to be affected by processing operations, a supervisory authority of each of those Member States shall have the right to participate in the joint investigative tasks or joint operations, as appropriate. The competent supervisory authority shall invite the supervisory authority of each of those Member States to take part in the respective joint investigative tasks or joint operations and respond to the request of a supervisory authority to participate in the operations without delay.

In addition, Article 56(3) states that each supervisory authority may, as a host supervisory authority, in compliance with its own Member State law, and with the seconding supervisory authority's authorisation, confer executive powers, including investigative tasks, on the seconding supervisory authority's members or staff involved in joint operations or, insofar as the host supervisory authority's law permits, allow the seconding supervisory authority's members or staff to exercise their executive powers in accordance with the seconding supervisory authority's law. Such executive powers may be exercised only under the guidance and, as a rule, in the presence of members or staff from the host supervisory authority. The seconding supervisory authority's members or staff shall be subject to the host supervisory authority's national law. The host supervisory authority shall assume responsibility for their actions.

The supervisory authorities are obliged to set out down the practical aspects of specific co-operation actions.[293]

---

290. art 55(9) *ibid.*
291. art 55(10) *ibid.*
292. art 56(1) *ibid.*
293. art 56(4) *ibid.*

If a supervisory authority does not comply within one month with the obligation, the other supervisory authorities shall be competent to take a provisional measure on the territory of its Member State in accordance with Article 51(1).[294]

The supervisory authority shall specify the period of validity, not to exceed three months, of a provisional measure referred to in Article 56(5), and shall, without delay, communicate those measures, with full reasons, to the European Data Protection Board and to the Commission and shall submit the matter in the mechanism referred to in Article 57.[295]

Section 2 refers to consistency. Article 57 is headed consistency mechanism. It states that for the purposes set out in Article 46(1), the supervisory authorities shall co-operate with each other and the Commission through the consistency mechanism as set out in this section.

European Data Protection Board

Article 58 is headed "Opinion by the European Data Protection Board". Article 58(1) provides that before a supervisory authority adopts a measure referred to in Article 58(2), this supervisory authority shall communicate the draft measure to the European Data Protection Board and the Commission.

The obligation set out in Article 58(1) shall apply to a measure intended to produce legal effects and that:

- relates to processing activities that are related to the offering of goods or services to data subjects in several Member States, or to the monitoring of their behaviour; or

- may substantially affect the free movement of personal data within the EU; or

- aims at adopting a list of the processing operations subject to prior consultation pursuant to Article 34(5); or

- aims to determine standard data protection clauses referred to in Article 42(2)(c); or

- aims to authorise contractual clauses referred to in Article 42(2)(d); or

- aims to approve binding corporate rules within the meaning of Article 43.[296]

Article 58(3) provides that any supervisory authority or the European Data Protection Board may request that any matter shall be dealt with in the consistency mechanism,

---

294. art 56(5) *ibid.*
295. art 56(6) *ibid.*
296. art 58(2) *ibid.*

in particular where a supervisory authority does not submit a draft measure referred to in Article 58(2) or does not comply with the obligations for mutual assistance in accordance with Article 55 or for joint operations in accordance with Article 56.

To ensure correct and consistent application of this Regulation, the Commission may request that any matter shall be dealt with in the consistency mechanism.[297] Both supervisory authorities and the Commission shall electronically communicate any relevant information, including as the case may be a summary of the facts, the draft measure, and the grounds that make the enactment of such measure necessary, using a standardised format.[298]

Under Article 58(6) the European Data Protection Board chair shall immediately electronically inform the members of the European Data Protection Board and the Commission of any relevant information that has been communicated to it, using a standardised format. The chair of the European Data Protection Board shall provide translations of relevant information, where necessary.

Article 58(7) provides that the European Data Protection Board shall issue an opinion on the matter, if the European Data Protection Board so decides by simple majority of its members, or any supervisory authority or the Commission so requests within one week after the relevant information has been provided according to Article 58(5). The opinion shall be adopted within one month by simple majority of the members of the European Data Protection Board. The chair of the European Data Protection Board shall inform, without undue delay, the supervisory authority referred to, as the case may be, in Article 58(1) and (3), the Commission and the supervisory authority competent under Article 51 of the opinion and make it public.

Finally, Article 58(8) provides that the supervisory authority referred to in Article 58(1) and the supervisory authority competent under Article 51 shall take account of the opinion of the European Data Protection Board and shall within two weeks after the information on the opinion by the chair of the European Data Protection Board, electronically communicate to the chair of the European Data Protection Board and to the Commission whether it maintains or amends its draft measure and, if any, the amended draft measure, using a standardised format.

Article 59 refers to the opinion by the Commission. Within ten weeks after a matter has been raised under Article 58, or at the latest within six weeks in the case of Article 61, the Commission may adopt, in order to ensure correct and consistent application of this Regulation, an opinion in relation to matters raised pursuant to Articles 58 or 61.[299] If the Commission has adopted an opinion in accordance with Article 59(1), the supervisory authority concerned shall take utmost account of the Commission's opinion and inform the Commission and the European Data Protection Board

---

297. art 58(4) *ibid.*
298. art 58(5) *ibid.*
299. art 59(1) *ibid.*

whether it intends to maintain or amend its draft measure.[300] Where the supervisory authority concerned intends not to follow the opinion of the Commission, it shall inform the Commission and the European Data Protection Board and provide a justification.[301] In this case the draft measure shall not be adopted for one further month.

Article 60 refers to the suspension of a draft measure. Under Article 60(1) it is provided that within one month after the communication referred to in Article 59(4), and where the Commission has serious doubts as to whether or not the draft measure would ensure the correct application of the Regulation or would otherwise result in its inconsistent application, the Commission may adopt a reasoned decision requiring the supervisory authority to suspend the adoption of the draft measure, taking into account the opinion issued by the European Data Protection Board pursuant to Article 58(7) or Article 61(2), where it appears necessary in order to: (a) reconcile the diverging positions of the supervisory authority and the European Data Protection Board, if this still appears to be possible; or (b) adopt a measure pursuant to Article 62(1)(a). The Commission shall specify the duration of the suspension, which shall not exceed 12 months.[302] During the period of the suspension, the supervisory authority may not adopt the draft measure.[303]

Article 61 refers to an urgency procedure. Article 61(1) provides that in exceptional circumstances, where a supervisory authority considers that there is an urgent need to act in order to protect the interests of data subjects, in particular when the danger exists that the enforcement of a right of a data subject could be considerably impeded by means of an alteration of the existing state or for averting major disadvantages or for other reasons, by way of derogation from the procedure referred to in Article 58, it may immediately adopt provisional measures with a specified period of validity. The supervisory authority shall, without delay, communicate those measures, with full reasons, to the European Data Protection Board and to the Commission.

Enforcement

Article 63 refers to enforcement. Article 63(1) provides that an enforceable measure of the supervisory authority of one Member State shall be enforced in all Member States concerned. In addition, Article 63(2) provides that where a supervisory authority does not submit a draft measure to the consistency mechanism in breach of Article 58(1) to (5), the measure of the supervisory authority shall not be legally valid and enforceable.

---

300. art 59(2) *ibid.*
301. art 59(4) *ibid.*
302. art 60(2) *ibid.*
303. art 60(3) *ibid.*

DP Regulation: Co-operation with National Supervisory Authorities and Agencies

Article 29 of the DP Regulation makes provision in relation to co-operation with the supervisory authority. Article 29(1) provides that the data controller and the data processor and, if any, the representative of the data controller, shall co-operate, on request, with the supervisory authority in the performance of its duties, in particular by providing the information referred to in Article 53(2)(a) and by granting access as provided in Article 53(2)(b).

In response to the supervisory authority's exercise of its powers under Article 53(2), the data controller and the data processor shall reply to the supervisory authority within a reasonable period to be specified by the supervisory authority. The reply shall include a description of the measures taken and the results achieved, in response to the remarks of the supervisory authority.[304]

DP Directive 95: WP29

Article 29 of the DP Directive 95 provides for the influential working group on data protection, which advises, interprets and undertakes research of EU data protection issues, and which is comprised of members of the respective national data protection authorities throughout the EU. Given that it is comprised of national authority members and is an EU working group, the decisions and recommendations are very persuasive to say the least at national level.

The official title of WP29 is the Working Party on the Protection of Individuals with regard to the Processing of Personal Data.

Article 29(1) provides that a Working Party on the Protection of Individuals with regard to the Processing of Personal Data ("the Working Party") be established. It shall have advisory status and act independently.

The WP29 shall be composed of a representative of the supervisory authority or authorities designated by each Member State and of a representative of the authority or authorities established for the Community institutions and bodies, and of a representative of the Commission.[305] Each member of the WP29 shall be designated by the institution, authority or authorities that he represents. Where a Member State has designated more than one supervisory authority, they shall nominate a joint representative. The same shall apply to the authorities established for Community institutions and bodies.

---

304. art 29(2) *ibid.*
305. art 29(2) *ibid.*

The WP29 shall take decisions by a simple majority of the representatives of the supervisory authorities.[306] A chairman shall be elected, for a renewable period of two years.[307] The WP29's secretariat shall be provided by the Commission under Article 29(5).

The WP29 shall adopt its own rules of procedure (Article 29(6)) and shall consider items placed on its agenda by its chairman, either on his own initiative or at the request of a representative of the supervisory authorities or at the Commission's request.[308]

The WP29 shall, in accordance with Article 30(1):

- examine any question covering the application of the national measures adopted under the DP Directive 95 in order to contribute to the uniform application of such measures;
- give the Commission an opinion on the level of protection in the Community and in third countries;
- advise the Commission on any proposed amendment of the DP Directive 95, on any additional or specific measures to safeguard the rights and freedoms of natural persons with regard to the processing of personal data and on any other proposed Community measures affecting such rights and freedoms;
- give an opinion on codes of conduct drawn up at Community level.

If the WP29 finds that divergences likely to affect the equivalence of protection for persons with regard to the processing of personal data in the Community are arising between the laws or practices of Member States, it shall inform the Commission accordingly.[309]

In addition, the WP29 may, on its own initiative, make recommendations on all matters relating to the protection of persons with regard to the processing of personal data in the Community.[310]

The WP29's opinions and recommendations shall be forwarded to the Commission and to the committee referred to in Article 31.[311]

The WP29 shall draw up an annual report on the situation regarding the protection of natural persons with regard to the processing of personal data in the Community and in third countries, which it shall transmit to the Commission, the European Parliament and the Council. The report shall be made public.[312]

---

306. art 29(3) *ibid.*
307. art 29(4) *ibid.*
308. art 20(7) *ibid.*
309. art 30(2) *ibid.*
310. art 30(3) *ibid.*
311. art 30(4) *ibid.*
312. art 30(6) *ibid.*

DP Regulation: The EU Data Protection Board

Section 3 of the DP Regulation related to the establishment of the new European Data Protection Board. This will be an EU-wide data protection advisory and research board. It will take over from the previous influential WP29 established under the DP Directive 95.

Article 64 of the DP Regulation refers to the European Data Protection Board. Article 64(1) states that "A European Data Protection Board is hereby set up". Under Article 62(2) the European Data Protection Board shall be composed of the head of one supervisory authority of each Member State and of the European Data Protection Supervisor. If a Member State has more than one supervisory authority which is responsible for monitoring the application of the provisions pursuant to the DP Regulation,[313] they shall nominate the head of one of those supervisory authorities as joint representative.[314] Under Article 64(4) the Commission shall have the right to participate in the activities and meetings of the European Data Protection Board and shall designate a representative to do so. The chair of the European Data Protection Board shall also, "without delay", inform the Commission on all activities of the European Data Protection Board.

Article 65 of the DP Regulation provides for the independence of the European Data Protection Board. Article 65(1) states that the European Data Protection Board shall act independently when exercising its tasks pursuant to Articles 66 and 67 of the DP Regulation.[315]

Article 62(2) states that:

> [w]ithout prejudice to requests by the Commission referred to in point (b) of paragraph 1 and in paragraph 2 of Article 66, the European Data Protection Board shall, in the performance of its tasks, neither seek nor take instructions from anybody.

The various activities or tasks of the European Data Protection Board are provided for in Article 66. Article 66(1), headed "Tasks of the European Data Protection Board", states that the European Data Protection Board shall ensure the "consistent application" of the DP Regulation. To this effect, the European Data Protection Board shall, "on its own initiative or at the request of the Commission":

- advise the Commission on any issue related to the protection of personal data in the EU, including on any proposed amendment of the DP Regulation;

- examine, on its own initiative or on request of one of its members or on request of the Commission, any question covering the application of the

---

313. *ibid.*
314. art 64(3) *ibid.*
315. *ibid.*

DP Regulation[316] and issue guidelines, recommendations and best practices addressed to the supervisory authorities in order to encourage consistent application of the DP Regulation;

- review the practical application of the guidelines, recommendations and best practices referred to in the above paragraph and report regularly to the Commission on these;

- issue opinions on draft decisions of supervisory authorities pursuant to the consistency mechanism referred to in Article 57;

- promote the co-operation and the effective bilateral and multilateral exchange of information and practices between the supervisory authorities;

- promote common training programmes and facilitate personnel exchanges between the supervisory authorities, as well as, where appropriate, with the supervisory authorities of third countries or of international organisations;

- promote the exchange of knowledge and documentation on data protection legislation and practice with data protection supervisory authorities worldwide.

Article 66(2) provides that where the Commission requests advice from the European Data Protection Board, it may lay out a time limit within which the European Data Protection Board shall provide such advice, taking into account the urgency of the matter.

Under Article 66(3) the European Data Protection Board shall forward its opinions, guidelines, recommendations, and best practices to the Commission and to the committee referred to in Article 87 and make them public.

The Commission, under Article 66(4), shall inform the European Data Protection Board of the action it has taken following the opinions, guidelines, recommendations and best practices issued by the European Data Protection Board.

Article 67 refers to reports. Article 67(1) provides that the European Data Protection Board shall regularly and timely inform the Commission about the outcome of its activities. It shall draw up an annual report on the situation regarding the protection of natural persons (data subjects) with regard to the processing of personal data in the EU and in third countries. The report shall include the review of the practical application of the guidelines, recommendations and best practices referred to in Article 66(1)(c). Per Article 67(2) the report shall be made public and transmitted to the European Parliament, the Council and the Commission.

Article 68 refers to procedures. Under Article 68(1) the European Data Protection Board shall take decisions by a simple majority of its members. Article 68(2) provides that the European Data Protection Board shall adopt its own rules of procedure

---

316. *ibid.*

and organise its own operational arrangements. In particular, it shall provide for the continuation of exercising duties when a member's term of office expires or a member resigns, for the establishment of subgroups for specific issues or sectors and for its procedures in relation to the consistency mechanism referred to in Article 57.

Article 69 states that the European Data Protection Board shall elect a chair and two deputy chairpersons from amongst its members. One deputy chairperson shall be the European Data Protection Supervisor, unless he has been elected chair.[317]

The term of office of the chair and of the deputy chairpersons shall be five years but can be renewable.

Article 70 refers to the tasks of the chair. Under Article 70(1) the chair shall have the following tasks:

- to convene the meetings of the European Data Protection Board and prepare its agenda; and

- to ensure the timely fulfilment of the tasks of the European Data Protection Board, in particular in relation to the consistency mechanism referred to in Article 57.

Article 70(2) provides that the European Data Protection Board shall lay down the attribution of tasks between the chair and the deputy chairpersons in its rules of procedure.

Article 71 provides for the secretariat of the European Data Protection Board and the secretariat of the European Data Protection Supervisor.

Article 72 makes provisions in relation to confidentiality. Under Article 72(1) the discussions of the European Data Protection Board shall be confidential. In addition Article 72(2) provides that documents submitted to members of the European Data Protection Board, experts and representatives of third parties shall be confidential. That is unless access is granted to those documents in accordance with Regulation (EC) No 1049/2001 or the European Data Protection Board otherwise makes them public.

In addition, Article 72(3) provides that the members of the European Data Protection Board, as well as experts and representatives of third parties, shall be required to respect the confidentiality obligations set out in this Article. The chair shall ensure that experts and representatives of third parties are made aware of the confidentiality requirements imposed upon them.

---

317. art 69(1) *ibid.*

DP Regulation: Regarding DP Directive 95 and ePrivacy Directive

Article 88(1) of the DP Regulation proposes the repeal of DP Directive 95. Under Article 88(2), it states that references to the repealed DP Directive 95 shall be construed as references to this new Regulation, the DP Regulation once enacted). It also provides that references to the WP29 established by Article 29 of DP Directive 95 shall be construed as references to the European Data Protection Board established by the Regulation. WP29 shall become the European Data Protection Board.

The DP Regulation also refers to the ePrivacy Directive.[318] Article 89 refers to the relationship to and amendment of the ePrivacy Directive. It states that the DP Regulation shall not impose additional obligations on natural or legal persons in relation to the processing of personal data in connection with the provision of publicly available electronic communications services in public communication networks in the EU in relation to matters for which they are subject to specific obligations with the same objective set out in the ePrivacy Directive. Article 89(2) states that Article 1(2) of the ePrivacy Directive shall be deleted.

Costa and Poullet indicate that once the DP Regulation "comes into force, the document will be the new general legal framework of data protection, repealing [DP Directive 95] more than twenty-seven years after its adoption".[319] The DP Regulation as well as Article 8(1) of the EU Charter of fundamental rights of 2000 and Article 16(1) and reassert the importance of privacy and data protection "as a fundamental right".[320] "[E]ffective and more coherent protection" is required.[321]

In terms of policy as between modernising via a directive or via a regulation "in order to ensure a full consistent and high level of protection equivalent in all the EU member states, a Regulation was judged as the adequate solution to ensure full harmonisation"[322] throughout the EU. The Commission may also oversee and monitor the national data protection authorities (Data Protection Acts).[323]

"Individuals are rarely aware of how their data are collected and processed while they are surfing on the internet at home, using their cellphones, walking down a video-surveyed street or with a TFID tag embedded in their clothes and so on."[324] There is a

---

318. Directive 2002/58/EC of the European Parliament and of the Council of 12 July 2002 concerning the processing of personal data and the protection of privacy in the electronic communications sector (Directive on privacy and electronic communications)(as amended by Directives 2006/24/EC and 2009/136/EC).
319. Costa and Poullet, "Privacy and the Regulation of 2012" (2012)(28) *Computer Law & Security Review* 254–262 at 254.
320. *ibid* at 254.
321. *ibid.*
322. *ibid* at 255.
323. *ibid.*
324. *ibid* at 256.

need for greater transparency. As regards data processing, "transparency translates the widening of the knowledge about information systems ... coupled with fairness".[325]

Transparency

Article 5 of the DP Regulation provides that personal data shall be "processed lawfully, fairly and in a transparent manner in relation to the data subject". Transparency "requires greater awareness among citizens about the processing going on: its existence, its content and the flows generated in and out by using terminals".[326]

Transparency also relates to security of data and risk management.[327]

Some commentators have suggested the DP Regulation could go further. It is suggested that "the greater the flow of information systems, the more opaque it becomes in modern information systems and with new ICT applications. In that case the right to transparency must increase alongside these new processes."[328]

Reaction to New Regulation

Commentators have indicated that parts of the DP Regulation contain particular "legislative innovation".[329] Some examples of this innovation are indicated to be the:

- data protection principles;
- data subjects' rights;
- data controllers' and data processors' obligations; and
- regulation issues regarding technologies.[330]

It has been noted that while the DP Directive 95 emphasises protection for the fundamental rights and freedoms of individuals "and in particular their right to privacy", the DP Regulation in Articles 1 and 2 stresses the need to protect the fundamental rights and freedoms of individuals "and in particular their right to the protection of personal data".[331] Further references also emphasise data protection as a stand-alone concept from privacy, such as data protection assessments and data protection by design (DPbD) (also PbD).

---

325. *ibid.*
326. *ibid.*
327. *ibid*, at 256.
328. Costa and Poullet, *art. cit.*, at 256.
329. Costa and Poullet, *art. cit.*
330. *ibid.*
331. *ibid* at 255.

There is a new consistency mechanism whereby the national data protection authorities are obliged to co-operate with each other and with the Commission.[332] Two examples given include data protection assessments and also obligation in terms of notifying data subjects in relation to data breaches.[333]

The obligations in terms of insufficient security and data breaches are more detailed in the DP Regulation than previously.[334] The obligations are now more detailed than the obligation in relation to telcos and ISPs in the ePrivacy Directive.[335] Data breaches are referred to in Articles 4 and 9 of the DP Regulation. In the event of a data breach the data controller must notify the ICO.[336] In addition the data controller must also communicate to the data subjects if there is a risk of harm to their privacy or personal data.[337]

Data portability is a newly expressed right. It

> implies the right of data subjects to obtain from the [data] controller a copy of their personal data in a structured and commonly used format (Article 18.1) … data portability is a kind of right to backup and use personal information under the management of the data controller. Second, data portability grants the right to transmit personal data and other information provided by the data subject from one automated processing system to another one (Article 18.2) … therefore the right to take personal data and leave.[338]

The DP Directive 95 requires that the data controller must not process personal data excessively. However, this is now more limited. The DP Regulation states that data collection and processing must be limited to the minimum.

Broader parameters are contained in the DP Regulation in relation to consent. The definition and conditions are broader than previously. The inclusion of the words freely given, informed and explicit in Article 4(5) is more specific than the previous "unambiguously" consented.

The DP Directive 95 Article 15 protection in relation to automated individual decisions "is considerably enlarged"[339] regarding profiling in DP Regulation Article 20. The use of, *inter alia*, the word "measure" in the DP Regulation as opposed to "decision" in the DP Directive 95 makes the category of activity encompassed within the

---

332. Chapter VII, section 10. Costa and Poullet, *art. cit.*, at 255.

333. *ibid.*

334. Costa and Poullet, *art. cit.*, at 256.

335. *ibid.*

336. art 31 *ibid.*

337. art 32 *ibid.*

338. *ibid* at 15.

339. Costa and Poullet, *art. cit.*, at 258. Also see Council of Europe Recommendation regarding profiling, 25 November 2010.

obligation now much wider.[340] There is greater data subject protection. While there were previously two exemptions, in terms of contract and also a specific law, the DP Regulation adds a third in terms of consent from the data subject. However, data controllers will need to ensure a stand-alone consent for profiling separate from any consent for data collection and processing per se.[341]

The DP Regulation also moves significantly further than the DP Directive 95 in terms of creating obligations, responsibility and liability on data controllers.[342] Appropriate policies must be implemented by data controllers, as well as compliaint data processing, secure data processing, the undertaking of data protection impact assessments, liability as between joint data controllers, appointing representatives within the EU where the data controllers is located elsewhere and provisions regarding data processors.[343]

While the DP Directive 95 imposed compensation obligations on data controllers in the case harm to data subjects, the DP Regulation extends liability to data processors. In addition, where harm is suffered by data subjects, any joint data controller and or data processors shall be "jointly and severally liable for the entire amount of the damage".[344]

The concepts of data protection by design (DP Directive 95), data protection by default and impact assessments all emphasise the ability of the data protection regime to become involved in standards setting and the regulation of particular technologies and technical solutions.[345] The Ontario Data Protection Commissioner, Anne Cavoukian, refers to data protection and privacy by design.[346] The DP Regulation describes it as follows in DP Regulation Article 23(1), by indicating that:

> [h]aving regard to the state of the art and the cost of implementation, the data controller shall, both at the time of the determination of the means for processing and at the time of the processing itself, implement appropriate technical and organisational measures and procedures in such a way that the processing will meet the requirements of the DP Regulation and ensure the protection of the rights of the data subject

Data protection by default is referred to and defined in Article 23(2) as follows:

---

340. *ibid* at 258–259.
341. *ibid* at 259.
342. *ibid*.
343. *ibid*.
344. *ibid*.
345. *ibid*.
346. For example, Anne Cavoukian (DPC Ontario, Privacy Guidelines for RFID Information Systems, at www.ipc.on.ca), says the privacy and security must be built into the solution from the outset, at the design stage. Referred to *ibid*.

The data controller shall implement mechanisms for ensuring that, by default, only those personal data are processed which are necessary for each specific purpose of the processing and are especially not collected or retained beyond the minimum necessary for those purposes, both in terms of the amount of the data and the time of their storage. In particular, those mechanisms shall ensure that by default personal data are not made accessible to an indefinite number of individual

These accord with the general principle of data minimisation, whereby non-personal data should be processed first and where the collection and processing of personal data is required, it must be the minimum data as opposed to the maximum data that is so processed. This is referred to in Article 5(c).

Data subjects have more control over their personal data. In the context of social networks, individual profiles should be kept private from others by default.[347]

The concept of PbD and data protection by default as provided in the DP Regulation are predicted to soon impact upon organisational contracts and contracting practices relating to data processing activities.[348]

As mentioned above, one of the new areas is the obligation to engage in data protection impact assessments. Article 33(1) provides that:

> [w]here processing operations present specific risks to the rights and freedoms of data subjects by virtue of their nature, their scope or their purposes, the data controller or the data processor acting on the data controller's behalf shall carry out an assessment of the impact of the envisaged processing operations on the protection of personal data.

This is particularly so where the envisaged processing could give rise to specific risks.

One further addition is the possibility of mass group claims or claims through representative organisations. This is referred to as "collective redress" and allows data protection and privacy NGOs to complain to both the ICO and to the courts (see Articles 73(2), 74, 75 and 76(1)).[349] "Civil procedure rules"[350] may also need to be introduced.

The regime as regards trans-border data flows or TBDFs will be "significantly altered".[351] These are included in Articles 40 and 41.

---

347. *ibid* at 260, and referring to European Data Protection Supervisor on the Communications from Commission to the European Parliament, the Council, the Economic and Social Committee and the Committee of the Regions, "A Comprehensive Approach on Personal Data Protection in the European Union" at 23.

348. *ibid* at 260.

349. See also Commission on a common framework for collective redress, http://ec.europa.eu/consumers/redress_cons/collective_redress_en.htm, last accessed 11 January 2013.

350. Costa and Poullet, *art. cit.*, at 261.

351. *ibid.*

Enhanced Provisions

One of the more important extensions and enhancements relates to the right to be forgotten: the "right to be forgotten and to erasure, which consists of securing from the [data] controller the erasure of personal data as well prevention of any further dissemination of his data".[352] (It is also said to interface with the new right to data portability.[353])

The right to be forgotten is even more enhanced in instances where the personal data was originally disclosed when the data subject was a child. Some commentators refer to the option of an entire "clean slate".[354]

Costa states:

> The use of data from social networks in employment contexts is a representative example. Personal data such as photos taken in private contexts have been used to refuse job positions and fire people. But forgetfulness is larger. It is one dimension of how people deal with their own history, being related not only to leaving the past behind but also to living in the present without the threat of a kind of 'Miranda' warning, where whatever you say can be used against you in the future. In this sense the right to be forgotten is closely related to entitlements of dignity and self-development. Once again, privacy appears as the pre-requisite of our liberties, assuring the possibility to freely express ourselves and move freely on the street …[355]

The right to be forgotten is most clearly associated and related to the following in particular:

- where the personal data is no longer necessary in relation to the purposes for which they were originally collected and processed (and the associated finality principle);
- where the data subject has withdrawn their consent for processing;
- where data subjects object to the processing of the personal data concerning them;
- where the processing of the personal data does not comply with the DP Regulation.[356]

The DP Regulation and the right to be forgotten "amplifies the effectiveness of *data protection principles* and rules".[357]

---

352. Costa and Poullet, *art. cit.*, at 256.
353. *ibid.*
354. Costa and Poullet, *art. cit.*, at 257.
355. *ibid.*
356. *ibid.*
357. *ibid.*

Data subjects can have their data erased under the right to be forgotten when there is no compliance as well as where they simply withdraw their consent.[358] User control and data subject control are, therefore, enhanced.

The DP Regulation and right to be forgotten create the following compliance obligations, namely:

- erasing personal data and not processing it further;
- informing third parties that the data subject has requested the deletion of the personal data; and
- taking responsibility for publication by third parties under the data controller's authority.[359]

The DP Regulation also enhances and expands the various powers of the national authorities, such as the ICO.[360]

Children

The explicit reference to children is new, and some would argue overdue. Increasingly, the activities of children on the internet and on social networking poses risks and concerns.[361] Risks obviously arise from their activities online (e.g. inappropriate content, online abuse, cyber bullying), but also from the collection and use of their personal data online and collected online, sometimes without their knowledge or consent. Their personal data and privacy is more vulnerable than that of older people.

It is important for organisations to note the definition of "child" in the DP Regulation. A child is defined (originally) to mean any person below the age of 18 years. This will have implications in how organisations:

- consider the interaction with children and what personal data may be collected and processed;
- ensure that there is appropriate compliance for such collection and processing for children as distinct from adults.

---

358. *ibid.*
359. *ibid* arts 17, 2 and 8.
360. Costa and Poullet, *art. cit.*, at 260.
361. See, for example, McDermott, "Legal Issues Associated with Minors and Their Use of Social Networking Sites" (2012)(17) *Communications Law* 19–24.

Cloud

The popularity of Cloud computing and virtualisation services with users, enterprise and official organisations is ever-increasing. However, there are real concerns in relation to privacy, data protection, data security,[362] continuity, discovery, liability, record keeping, etc.[363] One commentator refers to cloud computing as the privacy storm on the horizon.[364] Any organisation considering cloud services needs to carefully consider the advantages, disadvantages, assessments and contract assurances that will be required. Such organisations, as well as the service operators, also need to assure themselves as to how they ensure data protection compliance.

What is New in the New Regulation?

The proposed DP Regulation will overhaul and modernise the data protection regime throughout the EU and elsewhere. Irish organisations will be affected and will have to prepare for the upcoming regime. What will the new DP regime bring under the forthcoming DP Regulation?

The whole area of transfers of personal data outside of the EEA (TBDFs) is regularly changing, for example as new countries are added to a white list of permitted export countries after having been examined on behalf of the EU Commission. There are also other changes such as contractual clauses and binding corporate rules. If an organisation needs to consider the possibility of data transfer exports to non-EEA countries, the most up-to-date transfer rules should be assessed, as well as appropriate professional advice sought. It may be necessary to have specific legal contracts in place. These rules may also be sector-specific for certain industries, e.g. airlines flying to the US from Europe.

Further topical issues are regularly being analysed by WP29. These issues may be consulted at:
http://ec.europa.eu/justice/policies/privacy/workinggroup/index_en.htm.

---

362. See, for example, Soghoian, "Caught in the Cloud: Privacy, Encryption, and Government Back Doors in the Web 2.0 Era" (2010)(8) *Journal of Telecommunications & High Technology Law* 359–424.

363. ICO, *Guidance on the Use of Cloud Computing*, available at http://www.ico.gov.uk/for_organisations/data_protection/topic_guides/online/cloud_computing.aspx, last accessed 11 January 2013; Article 29 Working Party, *Opinion 05/2012 on Cloud Computing*, WP 196, 1 July 2012; Lanois, "Caught in the Clouds: The Web 2.0, Cloud Computing, and Privacy?" (2010)(9) *Northwestern Journal of Technology and Intellectual Property* 29–49; Pinguelo and Muller, "Avoid the Rainy Day: Survey of US Cloud Computing Caselaw" (2011) *Boston College Intellectual Property & Technology Forum* 1–7; Kattan, "Cloudy Privacy Protections: Why the Stored Communications Act Fails to Protect the Privacy of Communications Stored in the Cloud" (2010–2011)(3) *Vandenburg Journal of Entertainment and Technology Law* 617–656.

364. DeVere, "Cloud Computing: Privacy Storm on the Horizon?" (2010)(20) *Albany Law Journal* 365–373.

Investigation and Evidence

The issue of electronic evidence is critical, whether for the organisation or the data subject wishing to use such evidence. It is recommended that organisations consider these issues proactively in advance rather than hoping to be able to deal with them adequately in a reactive manner.

Conclusion

Data protection compliance is never a one size fits all or a single one time policy document. The nature of what amounts to personal data and the activities to which such data can be processed for are ever changing. Those within an organisation, therefore, need to be constantly alert to compliance issues and changes. Organisations also need to be constantly alert to new issues and dangers.

All organisations need to become very familiar with the DP Regulation. While not yet enacted, it is getting closer. It reflects the shape of the new and expanded EU data protection regime. While in some instances the current compliance mechanisms are continued, there are many new requirements to compliance. Organisations need to start now in terms of ensuring compliance. Indeed, the most prudent organisations are continually adopting best practice, and data protection compliance is an area where best practice has positive benefits above and beyond mere compliance.

The new proposals are also enhanced with the announcement in February 2013 that the EU Commission is also proposing a new Directive specifically to deal with security issues and notifications of security breach incidents.

CHAPTER 26

Leveson, the Press and Data Protection

Introduction

The UK Leveson Report deals with (certain) data protection issues in detail. It made recommendations relating to data protection and journalism. The evidence and issues are more fully described in Part H, 5 of the actual Report.

Section 32 UK DPA

The current s 32 of the UK DPA 1998 refers to journalism activities. It provides,

(1) Personal data which are processed only for the special purposes are exempt from any provision to which this subsection relates if—

  (a) the processing is undertaken with a view to the publication by any person of any journalistic, literary or artistic material,

  (b) the data controller reasonably believes that, having regard in particular to the special importance of the public interest in freedom of expression, publication would be in the public interest, and

  (c) the data controller reasonably believes that, in all the circumstances, compliance with that provision is incompatible with the special purposes.

(2) Subsection (1) relates to the provisions of—

  (a) the data protection principles except the seventh data protection principle,

  (b) section 7,

  (c) section 10,

  (d) section 12, and

  (e) section 14(1) to (3).

(3) In considering for the purposes of subsection (1)(b) whether the belief of a data controller that publication would be in the public interest was or is a reasonable one, regard may be had to his compliance with any code of practice which—

    (a)   is relevant to the publication in question, and

    (b)   is designated by the [Secretary of State] by order for the purposes of this subsection.

(4)   Where at any time ('the relevant time') in any proceedings against a data controller under section 7(9), 10(4), 12(8) or 14 or by virtue of section 13 the data controller claims, or it appears to the court, that any personal data to which the proceedings relate are being processed—

    (a)   only for the special purposes, and

    (b)   with a view to the publication by any person of any journalistic, literary or artistic material which, at the time twenty-four hours immediately before the relevant time, had not previously been published by the data controller,

    the court shall stay the proceedings until either of the conditions in subsection (5) is met.

(5)   Those conditions are—

    (a)   that a determination of the Commissioner under section 45 with respect to the data in question takes effect, or

    (b)   in a case where the proceedings were stayed on the making of a claim, that the claim is withdrawn.

(6)   For the purposes of this Act 'publish', in relation to journalistic, literary or artistic material, means make available to the public or any section of the public.

The equivalent Irish provision reads:

(1)   Personal data that are processed only for journalistic, artistic or literary purposes shall be exempt from compliance with any provision of this Act specified in subsection (2) of this section if—

    (a)   the processing is undertaken solely with a view to the publication of any journalistic, literary or artistic material,

    (b)   the data controller reasonably believes that, having regard in particular to the special importance of the public interest in freedom of expression, such publication would be in the public interest, and

    (c)   the data controller reasonably believes that, in all the circumstances, compliance with that provision would be incompatible with journalistic, artistic or literary purposes.

(2)   The provisions referred to in subsection (1) of this section are—

    (a)   section 2 (as amended by the Act of 2003), other than subsection (1)(d),

(b)   sections 2A, 2B and 2D (which sections were inserted by the Act of 2003),

(c)   section 3,

(d)   sections 4 and 6 (which sections were amended by the Act of 2003), and

(e)   sections 6A and 6B (which sections were inserted by the Act of 2003).

(3)   In considering for the purposes of subsection (1)(b) of this section whether publication of the material concerned would be in the public interest, regard may be had to any code of practice approved under subsections (1) or (2) of section 13 (as amended by the Act of 2003) of this Act.

(4)   In this section 'publication', in relation to journalistic, artistic or literary material, means the act of making the material available to the public or any section of the public in any form or by any means.

Lord Lester of Herne Hill is referred to in the Report (p 1067) as having "warned at length that, as drafted and because of cl 31, the DPA failed to implement the Directive and authorised interference by the press with the right to privacy in breach of Art 8 of the ECHR".

At page 1068 of the Leveson Report, it refers to:

> Mr Coppel's arguments … would be that on the current state of the UK authorities, s32 fails to implement the Directive from which it derives, and is inconsistent with the relevant parts of the ECHR to which it is intended to give effect, because the relationship between privacy and expression rights has got out of balance. A proper balance is a fundamental obligation. The UK is therefore positively *required* to change the law to restore the balance. That is indeed Mr Coppel's own contention: that UK data protection law currently fails to implement our obligations, and that Lord Lester's concerns had proved to be prescient.

The Report itself then states:

> 2.11   Without going so far as that, even if the current balance were within the spectrum permitted by our international obligations, the argument could be expressed in terms that it is at an extreme end of that spectrum, and the UK can as a matter of law, and should as a matter of policy, restore a more even-handed approach, not least given the asymmetry of risks and harms as between the individual and the press.

> 2.12   Put at its very lowest, the point could be made that the effect of the development of the case law has been to push personal privacy law in media cases out of the data protection regime and into the more open seas of the Human Rights Act. This has happened for no better reason than the slowness of the legal profession to assimilate data protection law and, in the case of the judiciary, its greater

familiarity with (and, he suggests, perhaps a preference for) the latitude afforded by the human rights regime over the specificity of data protection. But this, the argument goes, is undesirable because the data protection regime is much more predictable, detailed and sophisticated in the way it protects and balances rights, and significantly reduces the risks, uncertainties and expense of litigation concomitant on more open-textured law dependent on a court's discretion. Where the law has provided specific answers, the fine-nibbed pen should be grasped and not the broad brush. The balancing of competing rights in a free democracy is a highly sophisticated exercise; appropriate tools have been provided for the job and should be used.

Leveson Recommendations to the Ministry of Justice

The Leveson Report makes the following recommendations, namely:

> 48. The exemption in section 32 of the Data Protection Act 1998 should be amended so as to make it available only where:49 (a) the processing of data is necessary for publication, rather than simply being in fact undertaken with a view to publication; (b) the data controller reasonably believes that the relevant publication would be or is in the public interest, with no special weighting of the balance between the public interest in freedom of expression and in privacy; and (c) objectively, that the likely interference with privacy resulting from the processing of the data is outweighed by the public interest in publication.

> 49. The exemption in section 32 of the Data Protection Act 1998 should be narrowed in scope, so that it no longer allows, by itself, for exemption from:50 (a) the requirement of the first data protection principle to process personal data fairly (except in relation to the provision of information to the data subject under paragraph 2(1) (a) of Part II Schedule 1 to the 1998 Act) and in accordance with statute law; (b) the second data protection principle (personal data to be obtained only for specific purposes and not processed incompatibly with those purposes); (c) the fourth data protection principle (personal data to be accurate and kept up to date); (d) the sixth data protection principle (personal data to be processed in accordance with the rights of individuals under the Act); (e) the eighth data protection principle (restrictions on exporting personal data); and (f) the right of subject access. The recommendation on the removal of the right of subject access from the scope of section 32 is subject to any necessary clarification that the law relating to the protection of journalists' sources is not affected by the Act.

> 50. It should be made clear that the right to compensation for distress conferred by section 13 of the Data Protection Act 1998 is not restricted to cases of pecuniary loss, but should include compensation for pure distress.

51. The procedural provisions of the Data Protection Act 1998 with special application to journalism in: (a) section 32(4) and (5) (b) sections 44 to 46 inclusive should be repealed.52

51. In conjunction with the repeal of those procedural provisions, consideration should be given to the desirability of including in the Data Protection Act 1998 a provision to the effect that, in considering the exercise of any powers in relation to the media or other publishers, the Information Commissioner's Office should have special regard to the obligation in law to balance the public interest in freedom of expression alongside the public interest in upholding the data protection regime.

53. Specific provision should be made to the effect that, in considering the exercise of any of its powers in relation to the media or other publishers, the Information Commissioner's Office must have regard to the application to a data controller of any relevant system of regulation or standards enforcement which is contained in or recognised by statute.

54. The necessary steps should be taken to bring into force the amendments made to section 55 of the Data Protection Act 1998 by section 77 of the Criminal Justice and Immigration Act 2008 (increase of sentence maxima) to the extent of the maximum specified period; and by section 78 of the 2008 Act (enhanced defence for public interest journalism).

55. The prosecution powers of the Information Commissioner should be extended to include any offence which also constitutes a breach of the data protection principles.

56. A new duty should be introduced (whether formal or informal) for the Information Commissioner's Office to consult with the Crown Prosecution Service in relation to the exercise of its powers to undertake criminal proceedings.

57. The opportunity should be taken to consider amending the Data Protection Act 1998 formally to reconstitute the Information Commissioner's Office as an Information Commission, led by a Board of Commissioners with suitable expertise drawn from the worlds of regulation, public administration, law and business, and active consideration should be given in that context to the desirability of including on the Board a Commissioner from the media sector.

Recommendations to the Information Commissioner

The Leveson Report also makes recommendation to the ICO. These are:

58. The Information Commissioner's Office should take immediate steps to prepare, adopt and publish a policy on the exercise of its formal regulatory functions in order to ensure that the press complies with the legal requirements of the data protection regime.

59. In discharge of its functions and duties to promote good practice in areas of public concern, the Information Commissioner's Office should take immediate steps, in consultation with the industry, to prepare and issue comprehensive good practice guidelines and advice on appropriate principles and standards to be observed by the press in the processing of personal data. This should be prepared and implemented within six months from the date of this Report.

60. The Information Commissioner's Office should take steps to prepare and issue guidance to the public on their individual rights in relation to the obtaining and use by the press of their personal data, and how to exercise those rights.

61. In particular, the Information Commissioner's Office should take immediate steps to publish advice aimed at individuals (data subjects) concerned that their data have or may have been processed by the press unlawfully or otherwise than in accordance with good practice.

62. The Information Commissioner's Office, in the Annual Report to Parliament which it is required to make by virtue of section 52(1) of the Act, should include regular updates on the effectiveness of the foregoing measures, and on the culture, practices and ethics of the press in relation to the processing of personal data.

63. The Information Commissioner's Office should immediately adopt the Guidelines for Prosecutors on assessing the public interest in cases affecting the media, issued by the Director of Public Prosecutions in September 2012.

64. The Information Commissioner's Office should take immediate steps to engage with the Metropolitan Police on the preparation of a long-term strategy in relation to alleged media crime with a view to ensuring that the Office is well placed to fulfil any necessary role in this respect in the future, and in particular in the aftermath of Operations Weeting, Tuleta and Elveden.

65. The Information Commissioner's Office should take the opportunity to review the availability to it of specialist legal and practical knowledge of the application of the data protection regime to the press, and to any extent necessary address it.

66. The Information Commissioner's Office should take the opportunity to review its organisation and decision-making processes to ensure that large-scale issues, with both strategic and operational dimensions (including the relationship between the culture, practices and ethics of the press in relation to personal information on the one hand, and the application of the data protection regime to the press on the other) can be satisfactorily considered and addressed in the round.

Increased Sentencing for Data Breach

The Leveson Report also makes other law recommendations. These are:

> 67. On the basis that the provisions of s77-78 of the Criminal Justice and Immigration
> Act 2008 are brought into effect, so that increased sentencing powers are available for
> breaches of s55 of the Data Protection Act 1998,68 the Secretary of State for Justice
> should use the power vested in him by s124(1)(a)(i) of the Coroners and Justice Act
> 2009 to invite the Sentencing Council of England and Wales to prepare guidelines in
> relation to data protection offences (including computer misuse).

Comparison

A comparison of the UK and Irish provisions, as well as the Leveson comments, as
set out on pages 500–501.

Conclusion

The recommendations of the Leveson Report appear to have been accepted at a political level in the UK. The exact manner of the amendments to be introduced remain
to be finalised at the time of writing. However, any change in the UK cannot but
draw attention to the nature of the equivalent provision in Ireland. It remains to be
seen what effect this will have.

Ireland (s 22A)	UK (s 32)	Leveson
(1) Personal data that are processed only for journalistic, artistic or literary purposes shall be exempt from compliance with any provision of this Act specified in subsection (2) of this section if— (a) the processing is undertaken solely with a view to the publication of any journalistic, literary or artistic material, (b) the data controller reasonably believes that, having regard in particular to the special importance of the public interest in freedom of expression, such publication would be in the public interest, and (c) the data controller reasonably believes that, in all the circumstances, compliance with that provision would be incompatible with journalistic, artistic or literary purposes. (2) The provisions referred to in subsection (1) of this section are— (a) section 2 (as amended by the Act of 2003), other than subsection (1)(d), (b) sections 2A, 2B and 2D (which sections were inserted by the Act of 2003), (c) section 3, (d) sections 4 and 6 (which sections were amended by the Act of 2003), and (e) sections 6A and 6B (which sections were inserted by the Act of 2003). (3) In considering for the purposes of subsection (1)(b) of this section whether publication of the material concerned would be in the public interest, regard may be had to any code of practice approved under subsections (1) or (2) of section 13 (as amended by the Act of 2003) of this Act.	(1) Personal data which are processed only for the special purposes are exempt from any provision to which this subsection relates if— (a) the processing is undertaken with a view to the publication by any person of any journalistic, literary or artistic material, (b) the data controller reasonably believes that, having regard in particular to the special importance of the public interest in freedom of expression, publication would be in the public interest, and (c) the data controller reasonably believes that, in all the circumstances, compliance with that provision is incompatible with the special purposes. (2) Subsection (1) relates to the provisions of— (a) the data protection principles except the seventh data protection principle, (b) section 7, (c) section 10, (d) section 12, and (e) section 14(1) to (3). (3) In considering for the purposes of subsection (1) (b) whether the belief of a data controller that publication would be in the public interest was or is a reasonable one, regard may be had to his compliance with any code of practice which— (a) is relevant to the publication in question, and (b) is designated by the [Secretary of State] by order for the purposes of this subsection. (4) Where at any time ('the relevant time') in any proceedings against a data controller under section 7(9), 10(4), 12(8) or 14 or by virtue of section 13 the data controller claims, or it appears to the court, that any	48. The exemption in section 32 of the Data Protection Act 1998 should be amended so as to make it available only where:49 (a) the processing of data is necessary for publication, rather than simply being in fact undertaken with a view to publication; (b) the data controller reasonably believes that the relevant publication would be or is in the public interest, with no special weighting of the balance between the public interest in freedom of expression and in privacy; and (c) objectively, that the likely interference with privacy resulting from the processing of the data is outweighed by the public interest in publication. 49. The exemption in section 32 of the Data Protection Act 1998 should be narrowed in scope, so that it no longer allows, by itself, for exemption from:50 (a) the requirement of the first data protection principle to process personal data fairly (except in relation to the provision of information to the data subject under paragraph 2(1) (a) of Part II Schedule 1 to the 1998 Act) and in accordance with statute law; (b) the second data protection principle (personal data to be obtained only for specific purposes and not processed incompatibly with those purposes); (c) the fourth data protection principle (personal data to be accurate and kept up to date); (d) the sixth data protection principle (personal data to be processed in accordance with the rights of individuals under the Act); (e) the eighth data protection principle (restrictions on exporting personal data); and (f) the right of subject access. The

Ireland (s 22A)	UK (s 32)	Leveson
(4) In this section 'publication', in relation to journalistic, artistic or literary material, means the act of making the material available to the public or any section of the public in any form or by any means.	personal data to which the proceedings relate are being processed— (a) only for the special purposes, and (b) with a view to the publication by any person of any journalistic, literary or artistic material which, at the time twenty-four hours immediately before the relevant time, had not previously been published by the data controller, the court shall stay the proceedings until either of the conditions in subsection (5) is met. (5) Those conditions are— (a) that a determination of the Commissioner under section 45 with respect to the data in question takes effect, or (b) in a case where the proceedings were stayed on the making of a claim, that the claim is withdrawn. (6) For the purposes of this Act 'publish', in relation to journalistic, literary or artistic material, means make available to the public or any section of the public.	recommendation on the removal of the right of subject access from the scope of section 32 is subject to any necessary clarification that the law relating to the protection of journalists' sources is not affected by the Act. 50. It should be made clear that the right to compensation for distress conferred by section 13 of the Data Protection Act 1998 is not restricted to cases of pecuniary loss, but should include compensation for pure distress. 51. The procedural provisions of the Data Protection Act 1998 with special application to journalism in: (a) section 32(4) and (5) (b) sections 44 to 46 inclusive should be repealed.52 51. In conjunction with the repeal of those procedural provisions, consideration should be given to the desirability of including in the Data Protection Act 1998 a provision to the effect that, in considering the exercise of any powers in relation to the media or other publishers, the Information Commissioner's Office should have special regard to the obligation in law to balance the public interest in freedom of expression alongside the public interest in upholding the data protection regime. 53. Specific provision should be made to the effect that, in considering the exercise of any of its powers in relation to the media or other publishers, the Information Commissioner's Office must have regard to the application to a data controller of any relevant system of regulation or standards enforcement which is contained in or recognised by statute.

Appendix

Reference Links
Data Protection Commissioner's Office:
www.dataprotection.ie

Article 29 Working Party:
http://ec.europa.eu/justice/policies/privacy/workinggroup/index_en.htm

Irish Computer Society:
www.ics.ie

Annual Data Protection Conference:
www.ics.ie

Association of Data Protection Officers:
www.dpo.ie

Irish Internet Association:
www.iia.ie

Society of Computers and Law:
www.scl.org

Legislation Links
Data Protection Act 1988:
http://www.irishstatutebook.ie/1988/en/act/pub/0025/index.html

Data Protection (Amendment) Act 2003:
http://www.irishstatutebook.ie/2003/en/act/pub/0006/index.html

Data Protection Directive 1995:
http://eur-lex.europa.eu/LexUriServ/LexUriServ.do?uri=CELEX:31995L0046:en:HTML

Proposed Data Protection Regulation:
http://ec.europa.eu/justice/data-protection/document/review2012/com_2012_11_en.pdf

Proposed Data Protection Directive:
http://ec.europa.eu/home-affairs/doc_centre/police/docs/com_2012_10_en.pdf

Appendix

Proposed Data Protection Network and Information Security Directive:
http://ec.europa.eu/dgs/home-affairs/what-is-new/news/news/2013/docs/1_directive_20130207_en.pdf

Index